Micro Database Management
Practical Techniques for Application Development

This is a volume in
COMPUTER SCIENCE AND APPLIED MATHEMATICS
A Series of Monographs and Textbooks
Editor: WERNER RHEINBOLDT
A complete list of titles in this series appears at the end of this volume.

Micro Database Management

Practical Techniques for Application Development

ROBERT H. BONCZEK

CLYDE W. HOLSAPPLE

ANDREW B. WHINSTON
Management Information Research Center
Krannert Graduate School of Management
Purdue University
West Lafayette, Indiana

1984

ACADEMIC PRESS, INC.
Harcourt Brace Jovanovich, Publishers
Orlando   San Diego   New York
Austin   London   Montreal   Sydney
Tokyo   Toronto

ACADEMIC PRESS, INC.
Orlando, Florida 32887

United Kingdom Edition published by
ACADEMIC PRESS, INC. (LONDON) LTD.
24/28 Oval Road, London NW1 7DX

Library of Congress Cataloging in Publication Data

Bonczek, Robert H.
   Micro database management.

   (Computer science and applied mathematics)
   1. Data base management. 2. Microcomputers--
Programming. I. Holsapple, C. W. II. Whinston,
Andrew B. III. Title. IV. Series.
QA76.9.D3B66 1984   001.64   83-15670
ISBN 0-12-113060-6

PRINTED IN THE UNITED STATES OF AMERICA

85 86 87 88   9 8 7 6 5 4 3 2

CONTENTS

Chapter 3 Evolution of Database Management

Chapter 4 Fundamentals of Logical Structuring

Chapter 5 Schema Design

Chapter 6   Database Processing: Basic Retrieval Commands

Chapter 7   Database Processing: Storage and Update Commands

Chapter 8   Programming Considerations

Chapter 9   Semi-Structured Data Manipulation Tools

Chapter 10   Advanced Logical Structuring

Chapter 11   Physical Considerations and Performance Control

Chapter 12 Advanced Processing Commands

Chapter 13 A Case Study

Chapter 14 Other Development Issues

Chapter 15   Multi-User Processing

Appendices

Index

PREFACE

As the title suggests, the central purpose of this book is to help readers understand the possibilities and practicalities of building application systems with database management software. The microcomputer world presents nearly limitless opportunities for creators of application systems. Though not yet widely exploited by microcomputer users, database management is an extremely valuable aid in the design, construction, and maintenance of integrated application systems that are nontrivial and "bullet-proof." Despite our focus on utilizing database management in the micro world, the presentation is generally applicable to mini- and mainframe worlds as well. Descriptions of leading mainframe database management systems (DBMSs) are included to allow us to put micro database management capabilities into proper perspective.

We assume that the reader has a knowledge of the basic principles of programming. Preferably, this should be based on the first-hand experience of having written programs in either a traditional programming language (such as BASIC, COBOL, FORTRAN, Pascal, C, or PL/1) or the programming facilities offered in high-end integrated systems (such as KnowledgeMan). The book itself is not specifically oriented toward any one of these languages. It is helpful, though not mandatory, to have some familiarity with file management. An appendix reviewing file management highlights is provided as a refresher or introduction to the topic. There are no further prerequisites.

The book has been designed to fill several gaps in the existing collection of database management books. As the others, this book enables the reader to acquire a reading knowledge of database management. However, it also enables the reader to gain first-hand working knowledge of database management. The presentation is organized so that it can be used in conjunction with a fully functional micro database management system. Such hands-on experience in actually using a DBMS to build application systems is an invaluable ingredient in developing a full and true appreciation of database management.

While the conceptual underpinnings and theoretical aspects of database management are not ignored here, there is a much greater emphasis on applied aspects of database management than is normally encountered in DBMS books. Extensive examples are included for illustrative purposes. In our view, the applied emphasis makes this book a useful introductory complement to strictly theoretical DBMS texts.

Another departure from existing DBMS texts is the extensive treatment given to a comparatively new postrelational approach to database management. Perhaps due to its name *(extended-network),* some observers mistakenly categorize it with the CODASYL-network model. There are both subtle (yet important) and quite striking differences between the two. We examine the traits and significance of this new approach. Due to its great flexibility in representing relationships and its high- and low-level manipulation languages, we find that an understanding of this approach makes it very easy to quickly reach an understanding of the older approaches. These older data models (inverted list, relational, hierarchical, shallow-network, CODASYL-network) are treated in sufficient depth to convey a practical appreciation of what is involved in using a DBMS based on any of them.

For the most part, existing DBMS texts ignore the micro world. We have chosen to emphasize the micro world because of its explosive growth and because it allows hands-on DBMS instruction very inexpensively relative to costs of mini- and mainframe DBMS usage. A few short books aimed specifically at the issue of data management on microcomputers have recently begun to appear. These typically consist of useful feature comparisons among popular micro file handling systems. In some cases, they also include descriptions of DBMSs. In keeping with the prevalent trend in the micro world, these books typically use the term "database management" very loosely. As a result, the multitude of micro file handlers (which store data in flat files and which sometimes allow the merging of files based on their redundant data), and in some cases even programming languages and operating systems, are frequently called "database management systems."

This is not a book about file management. We believe that it is very important for application developers to understand the distinction between database management and file management. Without this understanding, they are likely to remain unaware of the tremendous opportunities that exist for building extensive, integrated application systems for micros. Throughout this presentation, we use the term "database management" in a manner consistent with its customary, well-established meaning in the mainframe world.

The decision to support learn-by-doing experiences with this book necessitated the selection of a particular micro DBMS for use in discussion, examples, exercises, and projects. This selection was based on a variety of criteria, the most important of which were as follows:

(1)   availability of a comprehensive collection of database management abilities comparable to what is normally expected of a mainframe DBMS (e.g., logical structuring, physical structuring, query, multi-user, security, host language interface, recovery mechanisms);

(2)   a proven track record in the micro world, having been successfully used by professional application developers to build systems that handle extensive and/or complex applications in diverse application areas;

(3)   availability in a variety of the popular micro hardware/operating system environments (including Z80, 8086/8088, and 68000 hardware; CP/M, PCDOS/MSDOS, and UNIX operating systems);

(4)   ability to be used with a variety of host languages, so that a reader need not learn a new programming language to make full use of the DBMS.

The product MDBS (Version 3 created by Micro Data Base Systems, Inc.) satisfies these criteria.

Because it provides so many of the abilities of a fully functional mainframe DBMS, MDBS is a useful vehicle for illustrating a wide range of database management facilities. Professional application developers have used it to build diverse application systems, some of which handle very complex application problems involving tens of megabytes of data. This DBMS is supported in a variety of popular micro (and mini) environments including: PCDOS (on the IBM PC and XT), MSDOS (on various 8086-based machines), CP/M (on Z80, 8080 and 8086 based computers), UNIX (on the AT&T 3B2-3B5 series, PDP-11 series, and various 68000-based machines), XENIX (on the Intel 80286-based model 286/310 and Altos 8086-based machines), and ULTRIX (on the Vax 11/780). MDBS has interfaces to numerous host programming languages and to the integrated KnowledgeMan system. Furthermore, a special inexpensive version of MDBS for use in educational settings is available from Micro Data Base Systems, Inc.

The book has been written with several audiences in mind:

(1)   students in introductory database management courses of undergraduate computer science, management, and technology curricula or an MBA curriculum; the material has been organized also to be suitable for a two-semester sequence (with a recommended break at Chapter 9) that gives application development an in-depth treatment;

(2)   application developers (analysts, designers, programmers) and consultants catering to the microcomputer software market;

(3)   developers of decentralized systems on small computers within large organizations;

(4)   small business proprietors and professionals with an interest in developing their own customized application systems;

(5)   research scientists in large and small organizations who are already accustomed to small computers and who have an interest in more sophisticated ways of handling their data;

(6)   microcomputer enthusiasts, in general, and those interested in database management, in particular.

In closing, we express our thanks to the many university students and application developers whose participation in coursework and in professional training seminars has played an important role in the evolution and refinement of the lecture notes on which this book is based. The general atmosphere of the Management Information Research Center (MIRC) in Purdue University's Krannert Graduate School of Management was particularly conducive to the development of insights and perspectives presented in this book. MIRC has received generous corporate support from IBM and General Electric. Mr. Frank G. Rodgers, Vice President of Marketing, and Mr. Charles Bowen, Director of Plans and Program Administration, both at IBM, have supported our MIS program in many ways, and we wish to thank them. We are also grateful to Dr. Gary Koehler and Dr. Mike Gagle (and their respective technical staffs) of Micro Data Base Systems, Inc. for providing the MDBS software that was used to verify the accuracy of examples shown in this book.

Chapter 1

THE SIGNIFICANCE OF DATABASE MANAGEMENT FOR MICROCOMPUTERS

The pervasive impact of microcomputers on business and society is universally recognized. However, the significance of database management for microcomputers is not yet widely realized. Although most persons working with microcomputers would agree that a database management system is valuable, very few of them have a full appreciation of what database management really is. This is largely a result of repeated misuse of terminology in much of the micro trade press and marketing literature.

It is commonplace to see file management systems erroneously called database management systems. Sometimes even programming languages and operating systems are loosely referred to as database management systems. The unfortunate result is that there are many who believe that they know about database management and that they are in fact using database management systems. As long as they labor under this misconception, microcomputer users remain oblivious to the startling capabilities and benefits of real database management.

A different kind of misconception is common among persons working with mainframe computers. Database management systems have a long history on mainframes, and their significance is appreciated by mainframe users. However, there is a tendency to regard micros as *toys* that are incapable of effectively supporting the storage and processing of large volumes of interrelated data. While this is a fair assessment for low-end micros, there are 8- and 16-bit micros

1

that support database management software comparable in every respect to the most advanced mainframe database management systems. Indeed, an integrated micro database can be spread across numerous multi-megabyte hard disks.

Over time, the significance of database management for microcomputers will become more widely appreciated. It is an important key for unleashing the entire potential of high-end micros and is essential for taking micros beyond games, word processing, file management, spreadsheet analysis, and mediocre applications systems based solely on programming languages. With micro database management tools, micro application software of superlative quality becomes economically and technically possible. Chapter 2 provides an in-depth examination of the critical ingredients for building high-quality application software. Chapter 3 traces the origin and evolution of database management. The remaining chapters focus on practical techniques for using micro database management in the design and implementation of application software.

In this introductory chapter, we concentrate on organizational contexts within which microcomputers can appear. The implications of micro database management are examined in each of these contexts. In particular, we explore its potential contribution to decision support systems, its facilitation of information decentralization in large organizations, and its importance for small organizations.

1.1 DECISION SUPPORT SYSTEMS

Nobel laureate Herbert Simon has stated that we are experiencing the initial stages of the third information revolution, the first two such revolutions corresponding to the development of written language and the printed book respectively. According to Simon, the current revolution is motivated by the major technological improvements in computing and the dramatic increase in the complexity of our social, business, and governmental organizations. The latter phenomenon results in the increasing difficulty of analyzing problems that face organizations and a resulting demand for technological support of decision-making processes. The former phenomenon, which manifests itself as a continual fall in the hardware cost of processing information, has a great potential for assisting in the complex decision-making processes that are required for organizational survival.

Both human and computer systems can be effective information processors. Humans have problem-solving abilities based on training, experience, and intuition. These abilities cannot be used effectively unless the human decision maker has information relevant to the problem at hand. Computer systems can be effective providers of relevant information through data retrieval and/or computations. The nature of the support that a computer system can provide to organizational decision making depends on the nature of the decision.

To classify decisions, it is convenient to distinguish between structured and unstructured decision processes. Often the frequency and regularity of a problem are recognized, allowing the needed information and calculations to be organized in advance. This is a structured problem in that there is a known, finite sequence of actions that leads to the solution of the problem and consequent achievement of some goal. A typical example of a structured task in a company is the periodic preparation of the payroll. Highly structured and repetitive information process-ing tasks were the first to be implemented on a computer. The actions involved in such information processing are so structured and well understood that they require little, if any, human decision making.

The second category, unstructured (or semi-structured) decision processes, is a very broad one. In general, it includes decision problems for which no entirely well-defined analytical solution processes are known. Such solution processes may be unknown because the problems are not analytically solvable, or because they arise unexpectedly or so infrequently that the effort of discovering an entirely structured solution process would not be cost-effective. Heuristic, ex-ploratory information processing is used to arrive at a solution.

For problems in the structured category, we can substitute computerized pro-cessing of an algorithm for human information processing. However, this is not feasible in the unstructured category. Nevertheless, we can make use of comput-er systems in unstructured decision situations if the systems are designed with the capability of performing various kinds of unanticipated, exploratory information processing. This involves the integration of the two types of information pro-cessors, human and computer, so that the human is able to guide and evaluate the sequence of exploratory information processing.

The newly emerging field of decision support systems (DSSs) focuses on the development of integrated, interactive human–computer information processing systems. An organization is a decision-making (problem-solving) system. A DSS is an organizational subsystem which processes information in support of a spectrum of decision-making processes. A DSS can be a computer system or a human system (individual or group). Here we shall concentrate on computerized decision support systems that aid human decision makers.

As explained in ''The Foundations of Decision Support Systems,''† a comput-er-based DSS has three interrelated components: a language system, a knowl-edge system, and a problem-processing system. Their interrelationships are illus-trated in Fig. 1.1. A DSS user uses the language system to request information needed to support a decision-making process. A request is interpreted by the

---

†R. H. Bonczek, C. W. Holsapple, and A. B. Whinston (1981). Academic Press, New York.

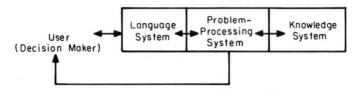

Fig. 1.1   Generic structure of a decision support system (DSS).

problem-processing system, which consults the knowledge system to determine how to fulfill the information request. Satisfying the request may cause the problem-processing system to perform such tasks as selective information retrieval, model selection or formulation, model execution, and report formatting. By responding to an unanticipated series of requests, a DSS can provide valuable support during the course of an unstructured decision-making process.

A central theme of "The Foundations of Decision Support Systems" is the critical importance of database management in the construction of DSSs. Micro database management can make a significant contribution to the emerging DSS field by making possible the development of very extensive DSSs on microcomputers, with capabilities well beyond those of micro spreadsheet packages. The result is personal, yet very powerful DSSs, which are free from dependence on centralized, mainframe computing resources.

In the chapters that follow we shall show how a micro database management system (DBMS) can be used effectively as a tool for facilitating the construction of DSSs, as well as other more structured kinds of application systems. The knowledge system for a DSS can be designed, implemented, and maintained using a micro database management system. The data-manipulation language of the micro DBMS is well suited to the implementation of customized DSS problem-processing systems. A DSS language system can utilize elements of a micro DBMS query language and/or customized screens for interactive, menu-driven processing. In the case of a query language, the associated micro query system software serves as a generalized, preconstructed portion of the problem-processing system software. Thus the micro DBMS can serve as a valuable tool in the design and construction of each of three major DSS components.

1.2   COMPUTERS IN ORGANIZATIONS

The role of computers in organizations has changed drastically over the past 30 years. The first computers, developed in the 1940s and early 1950s, were used to solve complex scientific problems. In the 1950s they were first used to handle structured business problems such as payroll, inventory control, and general accounting. Because of the high fixed cost of early computer systems, the users of these computers were typically the corporate staffs of large companies and major government agencies.

Because of software and hardware limitations, batch processing was the rule, and there was little or no opportunity for exploratory ("what if?") information processing. The impact of the computer on the organization was that of carrying out a structured series of tasks (previously done manually) in a more rapid, accurate, and cost-effective manner. Access to the computer was limited to the data processing staff, and all requests for modifications and extensions of software had to be approved by that group. In summary, the first commercial usage of computers was for highly centralized tasks performed in a batch processing mode within large organizations.

In the 1960s and 1970s several trends emerged which altered the role of computers in organizations. On-line access to a central computer by diverse organizational units became feasible, with the introduction of operating systems software. Database management software appeared, facilitating centralized and more or less integrated management of an organization's data resources. Various organizational units were able to access the same pool of data.

Smaller and cheaper computers (i.e., minicomputers) evolved so that smaller organizations, financially unable to justify a mainframe, could afford this type of machine. Eventually minicomputers developed to the point where they could perform most of the same functions as a mainframe, although on smaller volumes of data. Minicomputers have also come to play a significant role in large organizations. For instance, they serve the needs of divisional staff and of various functional groups such as marketing or engineering units. In the 1970s large organizations experienced a proliferation of diverse computers generally incompatible with one another and a shift from the sole reliance on strictly centralized computing resources.

This trend accelerated in the early 1980s with the flood of microcomputers appearing in large organizations. Typically, these micros have been acquired by small and diverse organizational units without the direction or coordination of a centralized data processing group. Because these small groups (or individuals) usually do not have expertise in data processing, most of the micros are used with software that does not necessitate technical skill: word processing, spreadsheet analysis, and rudimentary file management. Thus we have a situation in which large volumes of data are processed on mainframes operated by a skilled central data processing group, moderate volumes are processed on minicomputers operated by skilled divisional staffs, and a multitude of micros are operated by people relatively unskilled at data processing to handle some of their own immediate information-processing needs. This situation is the result of a combination of technical and economic factors. A key issue confronting organizations is how to take advantage of the micro proliferation while avoiding the potential dangers that it presents.

1.3 ECONOMICS OF COMPUTING

As in most technologically oriented aspects of our society, economic circumstances combine with the basic technology to produce products or services in forms that reflect these two forces. Since the initial installation of computer systems on a commercial basis, economic considerations have had an impact on computer technology. Specific software innovations were motivated by the need to make the technology as cost-effective as possible. Furthermore, economic influences have played a major role in the dramatic, positive acceptance of microcomputers since their introduction in the late 1970s.

Computer processors (i.e., central processing units, or CPUs) were very expensive in the early 1960s. To increase the usage of a processor (to approach saturation level) and lower the cost per user to a reasonable level, time-sharing software was developed. Time-sharing provided a means for distributing the costs of computations over many users. To encourage economical usage, various pricing schemes were devised which charged each user, to cover the costs of CPU time and storage requirements. Each individual user's interaction with the processor is slow compared to the speed of the computer; therefore, while one user is thinking, his program is replaced by an active user's program. As a result, each user has the feeling of exercising almost complete control over a large and expensive machine.

The impetus for time-sharing as a way of resource sharing was the high cost of the computer processor. This cost fell dramatically in the late 1960s. User charges for CPU time fell accordingly. However, a new factor arose. Users maintained and processed increasingly large volumes of data, but memory costs remained high. As memory demands became pronounced, the critical problem in resource sharing shifted from sharing a processor to sharing data.

The cost of data goes beyond the cost of memory. It includes the costs of capturing, organizing, and maintaining data. The economic impetus for sharing data costs led to the appearance of database management software. The objectives of this software were to permit many users to share the same data, thereby avoiding fragmentation of data into various redundant and inconsistent files, and to reduce the human effort (i.e., cost and time) expended in data organization and maintenance.

In the 1970s all hardware costs, including memory, fell to the point where an individual could economically have direct control over a computer. A microcomputer dedicated to a single user's needs in a highly interactive environment provided an enhancement of productivity beyond what was possible under time-sharing. In a modest microcomputer environment, a terminal linked to a micro-processor has a transmission speed of 2000 characters/sec, whereas a typical time-sharing line transmits at 1000 characters/sec. In a time-sharing environment, delays of 0.5 to 5 seconds are common because of the resource sharing, with even longer delays when the system is heavily loaded. Even more dramatic differences exist when the user communication link is limited to 120 characters/sec (high-speed phone link) or to 30 characters/sec (low-speed phone link). In these cases user productivity falls to a relatively low level. Furthermore, there may be substantial ongoing charges for communication.

With continuing decreases in the costs of all facets of computing hardware, including both processor and memory, the emphasis is now no longer on econo-mizing in hardware costs, but on increasing user productivity. This depends on timely access to information which may be local to the organizational subunit in which the user directly participates or which may be maintained in other parts of the organization. In other cases information external to the organization is needed, such as industry marketing data or national income statistics. As mentioned earlier, there is no end in sight for the increasing volume and complexity of information with which viable organizations must deal. The cost to an organi-zation of building, maintaining, and recalling information and of developing or acquiring the software to facilitate these processes has already begun to dwarf hardware costs. The crucial emerging question is how to design future informa-tion systems to exploit the decline in hardware costs and how to manage the significant software and information management costs.

1.4 THE FUTURE ROLE OF THE MICROCOMPUTER IN LARGE ORGANIZATIONS

In the early 1980s the growth rate of microcomputers in large organizations has exceeded 100%/yr. In some cases there has been centralized micro purchas-ing. However, the predominant trend has been decentralized micro acquisition. Thus, within a typical large organization today, we can observe micros from a wide diversity of manufacturers.

By far the dominant usage of these machines has been for running spreadsheet packages, using micros as convenient *electronic scratch pads*. The second most common usage has been for executing word processing software. Unlike spreadsheet analysis, word processing has relatively little value from a decision support standpoint. However, it does allow a micro to be used as a powerful *electronic typewriter* which is much less expensive than mini-based word processing systems. Using micros to run file management packages is the third most common form of micro usages. These packages enable records to be stored in and retrieved from a disk file; the microcomputer functions as an "electronic file cabinet."

A fourth important microcomputer usage is the execution of application packages. These are software packages that handle information processing tasks for a specific application area (e.g., inventory management or sales lead tracing) and which are easy for nontechnical persons to operate. Half of the applications packages are purchased from sources outside of the organization, 30% are developed by the functional unit of the organization which purchased the micro, and the remainder is developed by the organization's central data processing group. Through the early 1980s the great majority of micro application packages was developed using programming languages such as BASIC or Pascal; these packages, therefore, relied on file management techniques and consequently had only modest capabilities. The characteristics of application packages are more fully discussed in the next chapter.

Although these current uses of microcomputers are valuable, we should expect micros to play even more important roles in large organizations. With the continuing technological advances in micro computing power (faster CPU and data-transfer speeds, greater memory capacity) accompanied by falling hardware costs, organizations are asking how to take greater advantage of their microcomputers. That is, how can the microcomputer become much more than an electronic scratch pad, typewriter, or file cabinet? The answer hinges on two important developments: communications linkages for microcomputers and database management for microcomputers.

With the appearance of communications linkages between a micro and a mainframe (or mini), it is possible to transmit a file of data from a mainframe to a micro or from a micro to a mainframe. Transmission of a file of data to a micro means that the micro can be used to process data that has been extracted from an organization's central data base or from public data banks external to the organization. This processing might consist of spreadsheet analysis, report generation, graphical presentation, and certain kinds of limited application packages oriented toward decision support.

Transmission of a data file in the reverse directions means that the micro can be used as a data entry station. Data-collection software executing on a micro accepts data from an operator and batches it into a file for transmission to the mainframe, where it is input to a program that uses it to modify a centralized mainframe database. The micro data-collection software performs necessary prompting, editing, and data validity checking.

Mainframe–micro communications linkages enable micros to be used as intelligent terminals. Another emerging type of communications linkage is data transmission among microcomputers. Various types of configurations are possible for these microcommunication networks. In one kind of configuration, multiple micro CPUs share a common pool of data resources. This situation is explored in considerable detail in Chapter 15. Another kind of configuration permits each micro to control its own data resources and to acquire data (subject to security restrictions) from other micros. That is, data are distributed in terms of physical location and in terms of who controls the data's integrity. Nevertheless, the data are accessible to multiple micros.

Aside from communications linkages, a second development is crucial for catapulting micros beyond the roles of electronic scratch pads, typewriters, and file cabinets and also beyond their role as intelligent terminals. This is the development of database management software that is operable within the constraints of a microcomputer. Such software is well suited for handling large volumes of intricately related data in such a way that the ongoing validity and consistency of the data is assured. In other words, it is the key to outfitting micros with applications packages that are every bit as powerful and of as high quality as those expected in the mainframe world. Thus, information processing that was previously restricted to mainframes and minicomputers becomes feasible on micros.

This development has an interesting implication for information processing in an organization. It enables a greater decentralization of information processing, which can be advantageous in several respects. To appreciate the advantages, consider the following premises:

(a)   The more control and responsibility an organizational unit has over its own local data, the more effort it will exert to ensure that the data are accurate and timely.

(b)   The level in the organization is highly correlated to the degree of detail in the data needed for decision making.

(c)   The more functionally oriented an organizational unit is, the more detailed the data needed.

The first premise has a behavioral foundation: to the extent that a group controls a resource, the group will manage the resources more effectively. The second and third premises are based on cognitive limitations and the resulting nature of decision making in organizations. Groups that are high in the organizational structure have a responsibility to take a broad view of issues. To manage the complexity at that level in the organization, highly aggregated data are used in the decision process. Lower-level groups have more specialized orientations and need to deal with less aggregated, more detailed data.

Organizational structure can be measured along a spectrum ranging from total centralization to total decentralization. In the centralized case, all information flows to a central group which develops operating plans that are communicated to the rest of the organization for execution. For instance, an accounting control system provides information on the performance of the organization and allows the central group to make decisions regarding corrective action, when appropriate. In a decentralized organization, on the other hand, subgoals are assigned to different operating units. Each unit is responsible for making decisions and taking actions to achieve its assigned goals.

In view of the previously noted premises, it is reasonable to contend that the design of a corporate-wide information system should depend on the organizational structure. A highly centralized organization, in which lower-level groups are primarily gathering information to be funneled to a central decision-making unit and carrying out tasks specified by the central unit, would have relatively little need for extensive local applications systems. On the other hand, decentralization suggests that extensive local applications systems are reasonable and valuable. This implies that the organization's overall data resources are distributed, with some data maintained locally by lower level groups while other (more aggregate) data may be maintained centrally.

Many organizations have built their information systems in a centralized fashion even though the organizations themselves have a certain degree of decentralization. Why should an information system be centralized when an organization is decentralized? Attempting to maintain a centralized information system weakens the ability of the decentralized units to effectively carry out their assigned tasks. They are dependent for satisfaction of their information needs on a centralized system over which they have little control. A more subtle effect is that, in the effort to support the needs of all decentralized groups, the central computer system will be less able to support the information needs of the central group. It is not desirable to clog the central computer with the masses of detailed data and data processing requests not pertinent to the central group. Furthermore, to the extent that the data needs of this high-level group depend on information provided by decentralized functional groups, quality and timeliness may suffer (recall the premises mentioned earlier). In a decentralized organization, a distributed system may very well enhance the quality and timeliness of information for both low-level and high-level groups.

Thus, there are three major types of forces at work behind the emerging trend of decentralized information systems: economic, technological, and behavioral. The initial manifestations of this trend can already be seen in the rapidly accelerating acquisition of micros by low-level, decentralized groups for use as electronic scratch pads and filing cabinets. If existing centralized information systems were able to handle these needs adequately and in a cost-effective manner, this phenomenon would not exist. With the appearance of ever more powerful and relatively inexpensive micro hardware and with the advent of mainframe-quality DBMS software on these micros, it is probable that very extensive application systems will become commonplace in micros within decentralized organizational units.

The existing central data processing staff can make an important contribution in the transition to a distributed information system. Although it is true that much of a low-level group's information processing is not related to the information processing of other groups, a sizable portion of it is. This suggests the importance of a coordinating agent that provides some standards for assuring that the impact of one group's application system on other group's information needs is not ignored. An obvious choice for such an agent is the existing central data processing staff. This coordinating agent would specify requirements to be met by the various decentralized application systems. For instance, if the central group needs aggregate information from a lower-level group, this should be factored into the micro application system design. Uncoordinated attempts by various operating groups to locally meet their information processing needs can be suboptimal from the global organizational perspective.

A central data processing staff can provide another essential service. Low-level groups will very often lack the expertise to use a DBMS effectively in building customized application systems. In such cases, the group can pay to have the system designed, implemented, and maintained by an external consultant. Alternatively, the group may draw on the expertise of the data processing staff, which typically has extensive DBMS experience. This function goes hand-in-hand with the staff's role as a coordinating agency and can help various groups with similar applications to avoid "reinvention of the wheel." Ideally, the DBMS selected runs on a wide variety of micro hardware (as well as mini or mainframe hardware), so that the staff does not have to work with many different DBMSs. That is, the same DBMS is used regardless of the target hardware–operating system environment.

Yet another role that may possibly be played by the central data processing staff involves the economic evaluation of proposed application systems. An application system that can be financially justified by the proposing group is generally assumed to be beneficial in the company-wide sense. In other cases a proposed application system may be too costly for a single group. However, because there may be other groups in an organization that can benefit from the proposed project, its cost may be justifed on a corporate-wide basis. The task of the central data processing staff is to determine corporate-wide benefits and to assess the appropriate influence of each contributor on the design of the system. Of course, one expects that the financial contributions of different groups to the project will be related to the degrees of their influence on system design.

1.5   AN EXAMPLE OF A DECENTRALIZED ORGANIZATION

In this section we illustrate a typical organization in which a decentralized information system is plausible. Universal Drugs is a major drug manufacturer offering a wide range of drugs that are sold through distributors to pharmacy chains under its own label or with private labels. To promote the marketing of Universal's products, the marketing department has organized regional sales offices that are responsible for sales to local drug chains, promotion at local hospitals, and regional advertising. Although the corporate computer staff in Chicago has (over the years) developed a marketing database, it is limited to data aggregated by region and by product group. Total sales data on major drug chains has been accumulated for several years. However, the primary source of this data has been financial reports of these companies, received at the Chicago headquarters.

The sales staff at the Los Angeles marketing office has decided that, to increase and monitor their effectiveness, they need a regional marketing information system. Such a system will help schedule their time to achieve maximal results and keep a detailed measure of product sales by distribution channel. Specifically, each salesman wants to schedule his or her activity to maximize results, taking into account the potential of the client and the time it takes to travel between calls. The promotion group, in its desire to provide support, wants to coordinate advertising and visits to hospitals with the sales activities. Note that these local information needs are largely irrelevant to the central group in Chicago.

To develop the application, including the construction of a strategic marketing database and the scheduling of salesmen, the regional marketing office has acquired a microcomputer, with the intention of having a local software consulting firm aid in the development of the software. However, the central corporate computer staff has adopted a policy whereby all software developed anywhere in the company must meet certain professional standards that will satisfy the following requirements.

(a)   Appropriate software tools should be used to ensure that documentation standards are met and the most cost-effective method of implementation is used.

(b)   Portability should be assured so that a specific application developed at one site can be used at the other regional marketing centers, perhaps on different computers.

(c)   Accessibility by the central computing facility should be assured so that aggregated data appropriate for analysis by the corporate headquarters group are available.

A decision has been made to build the application using database management tools. Besides the core database management system, it was felt important to have a query system to generate ad hoc reports for exploratory decision support. Recovery mechanisms to guarantee integrity in the event of a system crash were deemed essential. Another requirement was a screen management facility to provide for the rapid development and alteration of user-oriented screens. Furthermore, since central corporate computer applications are built with database tools, the compatibility between the new software system and current corporate systems was enhanced.

The development process proceeded in the following phases:

(a)   preliminary design,
(b)   consultancy evaluation,
(c)   central group evaluation,
(d)   implementation and documentation,
(e)   prototype testing,
(f)   introduction at primary site,
(g)   dissemination to other sites,
(h)   integration with other computer facilities.

In the first phase emphasis was placed on determining the reports needed by the sales people and other individuals who would rely on the computer system to guide or support their decision making. It was understood that, in addition to the specified reports, ad hoc or unanticipated reports would be required and that they would be generated using the query language. Based on the standard reports and general characteristics of the possible queries, a preliminary database schema was designed using methods similar to those described in Chapter 4 and subsequent chapters.

The central consulting group then reviewed the work of the local group in constructing a database schema to support the desired reports. Although the local group followed well-accepted schema construction techniques, there were subtle issues involving efficiency and physical organization of the database that had to be taken into account. Many of these issues are addressed in Chapters 10 and 11.

The consulting group then examined the interest of the rest of the organization in this application system. Reporting needs were discussed and a concensus was obtained regarding a modified database structure suitable for both the local group and the rest of the organization. The cost of implementing and operating the system solely for the Los Angeles office was estimated to be greater than the benefits that office could derive. However, the central group realized that by making some minimal alterations in the design, the system could provide significant benefits to other marketing offices. Although each marketing office would cover the costs of operating and maintaining the system, the initial development cost would be shared between several marketing sites. Based on the expanded set of calculations, the central group, in consultation with the various marketing sites, concluded that the application system would be cost-effective.

With the fixing of the structure, attention turned to completing development of the information system. Given the database structure, report forms, and menu structure, programmers were engaged to complete the implementation of a prototype system. In Chapter 6 and subsequent chapters the various techniques and tools that were used are presented. Preliminary documentation was completed at both the systems level and the end-user level.

The documentation task commenced almost at the inception of the project and continued until the final corporate-wide installation and acceptance. The initial emphasis was on system documentation, including the database schema and the meaning and structure of various programs to load and retrieve data. In a similar manner, the menu structure and associated programs were documented. As the information system progressed toward the implementation phase, end–user-oriented documentation was prepared. Samples of all marketing management reports were included with a commentary on the basis for their preparation and potential uses. The nature and importance of input data were also documented.

Prototype testing, which took place at the Los Angeles site, involved several sales people. Their performance was carefully monitored to determine whether there was a significant alteration in sales results. Were appropriate data inputs available on a timely and accurate basis, or were data availability questions dealt with in an unrealistic manner? Were reports organized in such a way that sales people could make effective use of them? Were ad hoc query facilities used to advantage? Behavioral questions were dealt with in prototype testing with the same care given to more traditional questions of program code corrections. As a result of the test phase, it became apparent that several alterations were needed in the underlying data structure. Chapter 14 explains the methods used in carrying out this restructuring task.

As a result of intensive prototype testing, introduction of the application at the primary site for operational use by all sales people went smoothly. Because there was an intensive collaboration by other marketing centers in the initial design, the dissemination phase was also fairly smooth.

1.6 MICRO DATABASE MANAGEMENT
IN SMALL ORGANIZATIONS

The fact that an organization is small does not mean that its information processing needs are trivial. Indeed, the inability to adequately handle anything beyond minimal processing tasks is a deterrent to organizational growth, productivity, and perhaps even survival. Yet mainframes and minis, together with their DBMS software, are far beyond the means of small organizations.

In many cases even time-sharing or service bureaus are not affordable or are unsuitable for addressing the individual peculiarities of a particular small organization. All of this has changed with the appearance of extremely powerful micros for about $\frac{1}{50}$ to $\frac{1}{100}$ the price of mainframes (i.e., \$5000–17,000) and extraordinarily powerful micro database management software for about $\frac{1}{50}$ to $\frac{1}{100}$ the price of a mainframe DBMS (i.e., \$2000–7000).

There is, however, a bottleneck that is delaying the widespread advent of high-quality application systems. This is the shortage of application system builders with sufficient expertise to take advantage of a highly sophisticated database management system. This is perfectly natural in light of the relative youth of the micro field. There is a growing number of novice developers able to use programming languages or file management to build modest application systems. However, professional application builders who fully appreciate what is possible with the more powerful and flexible micro database management tools are still comparatively rare in the early 1980s. This situation will be remedied as the demand for extensive micro application systems grows.

Since most small organizations do not have the in-house expertise needed to build professional-quality, customized application systems, we can expect the growth of an important new industry. Builders of micro application systems who are well versed in classical database management and in serving small organizations may well become commonplace businesses in both small and large communities. Just as local construction companies exist to build, repair, and remodel customized structures within a community, local system builders will handle customized application system construction and maintenance, using powerful tools such as database management systems. It will not be surprising if this type of service becomes as widespread or indispensible as are accounting services. Indeed, the two may very well be integrated in some cases.

1.7 SUMMARY

This introductory chapter has briefly examined why database management is important in the micro world. Its significance can only be fully appreciated when one understands what database management is (and what it is not) and how to use it effectively. The central objective of the remaining chapters is to contribute to this understanding and to demonstrate that it is possible to build micro application software that is every bit as high in quality as that available for mainframes.

Micro database management is the key for elevating micros above the level of electronic scratch pads, typewriters and file cabinets, intelligent terminals, and pedestrian application systems. It has an important role to play in the construction of sophisticated micro decision support systems. In large organizations micro database management greatly facilitates the decentralization of the information system, with benefits to the entire organization. For small organizations it greatly lowers the threshold cost for the acquisition of extensive application systems, putting the small organization more on a par with larger organizations in terms of computer-based support of operations and decision making.

RELATED READINGS

R. H. Bonczek, C. W. Holsapple, and A. B. Whinston, "Foundations of Decision Support Systems," Academic Press, New York, 1981.

R. H. Bonczek, C. W. Holsapple, and A. B. Whinston, Developments in decision support systems, *in* "Advances in Computers" (M. Yovits, ed.), Vol. 23, Academic Press, New York, 1984.

P. Keen and M. S. Scott Morton, "Decision Support Systems: An Organizational Perspective," Addison-Wesley, Reading, Massachusetts, 1978.

M. S. Scott Morton, "State of the Art in Research in Management Support Systems," Harvard Business School, Division of Research, 1983.

EXERCISES

1. What are the harmful effects of using the term "database management" to refer to file management?
2. Cite the differences between structured and unstructured decision processes. Give examples of each.
3. What are the three major components of a decision support system, and how are they interrelated?
4. Explain how a DBMS can be useful in constructing a DSS.
5. Describe the major driving forces behind today's information revolution. Compare the information revolution with the industrial revolution.
6. Discuss the various roles that an organization's data processing staff can play in the recommendation, selection, and usage of microcomputer software.
7. What are the major short- and long-term dangers to an organization that allows uncontrolled micro acquisition? Comment on the validity of data generated by "application systems" devised by first-time computer users (e.g., a manager who uses a newly acquired electronic file cabinet or programming language to try to devise a micro system for managing data). What happens when such persons leave an organization?
8. Suggest ways for rapidly increasing DBMS literacy.
9. Discuss the importance of micro database management for small organizations.

PROJECT

An important ingredient for achieving a practical understanding of database management is first-hand experience in using database management in an ongoing project that culminates in an application system developed with database management software. Suggested stages in such a project are described at the conclusions of subsequent chapters.

As an initial step, identify an application area of interest. A number of examples are suggested below:

Payroll	Inventory management
Personnel administration	Purchasing
Accounting	Warehouse control
Order processing	Vehicle scheduling
Project tracking	Pollution control
Customer billing	Reservation systems
Police records	Patient history and billing
Traffic analysis	Media analysis
Alumni record keeping	Sales lead tracking
Vehicle maintenance	Crop management
Horse breeding	Personal tax record-keeping

Chapter 2

APPLICATION SOFTWARE DEVELOPMENT

Perhaps the greatest challenge presently facing the computer industry is the development of high-quality application software. Chapter 1 outlined the tremendous advances being made in hardware technology. These advances are rapidly making very powerful microcomputer hardware affordable to the general public. This, in turn, fuels a nearly insatiable demand for application software. Regardless of its processing power and capacity, microcomputer hardware is of no value unless application software exists to exploit it.

Just as mainframe application software is developed by data processing professionals, high-quality application software for microcomputers also requires skilled developers. We should not expect application development to require less effort or skill just because it is targeted for a microcomputer rather than a mainframe. Demand for application software, coupled with present and predicted shortages of skilled data processing personnel, makes it clear why application software development presents both a challenge and an opportunity.

It is highly unrealistic to expect the technically naive end user to be able to build a passable application system, much less one of high quality. In large measure, the solution lies in training new developers and in improving the productivity of existing developers. Although training is useful in the long run, productivity gains can be realized today. This can be accomplished by providing the developer with the finest generalized software development tools that exist for microcomputers. To the extent that such tools are portable across a variety of microcomputer environments, there is the added benefit that the necessity of learning different tools is avoided.

This chapter examines the types of tools that are valuable for application development. It also explores the traits that are important for application development tools to possess. An understanding of these traits provides a basis for evaluating alternative tools.

2.1 END USERS AND APPLICATION SYSTEMS

An important distinction, which all too often goes unrecognized, exists between application systems and application development tools. An application system is a consumer product. It is intended for end users (consumers). It is built with the aid of application development tools (analogous to the machine tools used in the production of other consumer products) by application developers who are skilled in the use of such tools.

Equally important is the difference between end users and application developers. A typical end user, just like any other consumer, is not technically skilled. End users generally have little knowledge of programming, data structuring, and data handling. Nevertheless, they need to be able to store, modify, and retrieve data pertinent to their application areas. An end user can accomplish this by using application system software that has been designed to handle automatically all technical details of the data storage, modification, and retrieval required by the application. Of course, an end user is knowledgeable about the nature of the application for which data is processed by the application software.

Types of Applications

The list of application areas is practically endless, including inventory control, order entry, accounts payable, accounts receivable, medical record-keeping, hotel management, conference scheduling, pollution control, personnel administration, and project management. Regardless of which application area is addressed, it is vital that an application system be user-friendly. That is, it must be readily usable by a person knowledgeable in the application area, without the necessity of extensive training. Aside from competently handling all necessary processing activities, such systems are usually interactive. This means that the application system guides the end user through the necessary and proper actions.

An application system can be tailor-made for a particular consumer's (end user's) needs. Alternatively, it can be a "generic" consumer product that more or less fits the needs of a class of customers and is distributed as a ready-made, off-the-shelf package. In either case, the end user is not concerned about the tools used to build the application system. Like any consumer, the end user is concerned with how well the product (the application system) meets his needs and how much it costs. If existing off-the-shelf application packages do not suit an end user's needs, then their prices are irrelevant and the cost of a tailor-made application system becomes significant.

End-User Needs

It is instructive to examine end-user needs, because they impact heavily on the needs of an application developer. An end user requires an application system that

(a) allows the end user to store, modify, and acquire data without concern about data structures, data handling, screen handling, or programming;

(b) automatically provides data integrity, data security, and media security;

(c) fits the hardware and software (operating system) that are already in place;

(d) is portable, if there is a possibility of changing to or adding new hardware and operating systems;

(e) provides high performance or efficiency from the standpoints of storage and processing;

(f) is extendable, if there is a possibility that new reports (either unanticipated or repetitive) may later be required or that new types of data may later need to be stored, modified, and retrieved.

Finally, the end user desires an application system which meets the above criteria as inexpensively as possible.

2.2 STRUCTURE OF AN INTERACTIVE APPLICATION SYSTEM

The tasks performed by interactive application software fall into three broad categories: data handling, screen handling, and control–computation. These three activities should be performed in such a way that the end-user requirements identified in the prior section are satisfied. In performing these tasks, an application system serves as an interface between an end user and a repository of data in auxiliary memory. This is illustrated in Fig. 2.1.

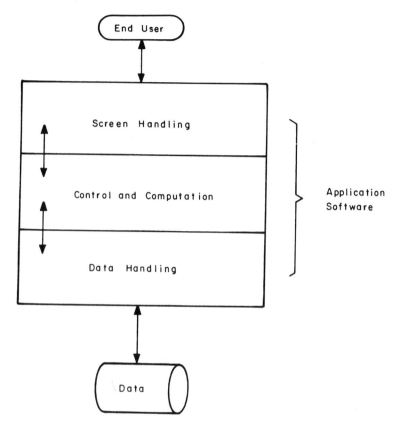

Fig. 2.1   Generic structure of an interactive application system.

Screen Handling

The screen-handling aspect of an application system involves the acquisition of information from, and display of information to, an end user.

As depicted in Fig. 2.2, there are two distinct kinds of information that can be input to an application system by the end user. One consists of data values; the other is control information, which indicates what step an end user desires to do next. When data values are input, the application system either deposits them in the data repository, uses them to modify previously stored data, or uses them (e.g., a customer's name) to find logically related data (e.g., the customer's address) that already exists in the data repository. An end user typically provides control information in response to a menu which presents the processing options that are available.

Four main kinds of information can be displayed to the end user of an applica-

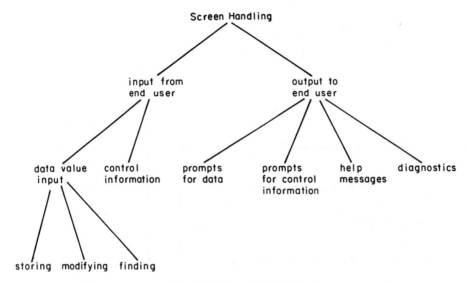

Fig. 2.2   Screen-handling tasks.

tion system. One consists of prompts to the end user for data value inputs. Figure 2.3 illustrates prompts for three pieces of information: name, address, and identification number. Similarly, screen handling also involves the presentation of menus to end users. A sample menu offering five different options is depicted in Fig. 2.4.

User-friendly application systems are able to provide end users with help messages, which give detailed information that is helpful to the end user in deciding the next step. Figure 2.5 depicts an example of a help message. A final type of screen-handling output involves the display of diagnostic messages when the end user has made an error in interacting with the application system. For instance, if the end user types an alphabetic character when inputing a social security number, a diagnostic message should be displayed indicating the nature of the error.

Data Handling

The diagram of Fig. 2.1 correctly suggests that the interplay between the data-handling component of an application system and the data repository is analogous to the interplay between the screen-handling component and the end user. The data-handling aspect of an application system involves the extraction of data values from the data repository and the output of data values into the data

```
┌─────────────────────────────────────────────────────────┐
│                 EMPLOYEE INFORMATION FORM                │
│                                                          │
│                                                          │
│   Name:                                                  │
│   Address:                                               │
│                                                          │
│                                                          │
│                                                          │
│                                                          │
│             ID:                                          │
│                                                          │
└─────────────────────────────────────────────────────────┘
```

Fig. 2.3   Sample prompts for data.

repository. When a data value is output to the data repository, it is used either to modify an existing value or to serve as a new stored data value. Typically, data extraction is conditional. That is, only a certain subset of the stored data—those values satisfying some particular group of conditions—is extracted at any one time (e.g., only the names of employees who work in Department 3).

Control–Computation

The third aspect of an interactive application system involves controlling and coordinating the system's screen-handling and data-handling behavior. The control structure of an application system determines how it responds to each end-user input. The possible responses include output to the screen, computation,

```
┌─────────────────────────────────────────────────────────┐
│               PERSONNEL INFORMATION SYSTEM               │
│                                                          │
│   Please select one of the following options:           │
│                                                          │
│      (1)  Display employee information                   │
│      (2)  Modify employee information                    │
│      (3)  Enter a new employee                           │
│      (4)  Delete an existing employee                    │
│      (5)  Quit                                           │
│                                                          │
└─────────────────────────────────────────────────────────┘
```

Fig. 2.4   Sample menu.

HELP FOR THE EMPLOYEE INFORMATION FORM

The name you enter can consist of up to 30 characters. Nonalphabetic characters are not accepted by the system. The system automatically converts the name you enter to uppercase.

An address of up to 4 lines of 32 characters each can be entered.

The identification number must be a social security number. The system automatically positions dashes in the proper positions.

To abort data entry for an employee, press CTRL-X. Press the ENTER key when you finish entering a name, address line, or identification number.

- •
- •
- •

Fig. 2.5   Sample help message.

extraction of data from the data repository, and/or output of data to the data repository.

2.3   APPLICATION DEVELOPMENT

The needs and desires of an end user inevitably affect the needs of an application developer, who is successful to the extent that he satisfies the end user on a profitable basis. In the case of an in-house application developer, success is likely to be measured in terms of the number of quality application systems that can be developed per unit cost within some time frame. Independent developers can be involved in building either off-the-shelf or tailor-made application systems. In-house developers typically construct tailor-made application systems, though some of the systems developed for large organizations can be used at many sites.

A developer of off-the-shelf application systems is interested in producing, as inexpensively as possible, an unchanging product that will appeal to a large class of end users. Since the development cost can be spread over many sales of the application system, the system's price can typically be lower than a roughly comparable application system that has been tailor-made for a single end user.

A tailor-made application developer is interested in producing, as inexpensively as possible, a product that will appeal to one end user. It is quite likely that this end user will expect the developer to make alterations to the package over time.

Like any producer of consumer products, an application developer makes use of tools to aid in production. For example, a database management system

(DBMS) is a tool that can be used to implement an application system's data-handling abilities. Just as automobiles are created through the use of machine tools, application systems are built with the aid of application development tools such as DBMSs. The user of an automobile is not involved with the machine tools that produced it; similarly, an end user is *not* directly involved with a DBMS that is used to build application software.

The tools used by a developer should help him meet end-user needs, and should do so in a developer-friendly manner. A tool is developer-friendly to the extent that it increases the developer's productivity. The three classes of tasks shown in Fig. 2.1 imply three classes of tools: data-handling tools, screen-handling tools, and control tools. The value of any of these application development tools can be gauged by the extent to which it satisfies the needs of an application developer while minimizing the developer's effort and costs.

Given the end-user needs noted in Section 2.1, the corresponding needs of an application developer can be identified. Each of these is examined with respect to its impact on each of the three types of tasks illustrated in Fig. 2.1: data handling, screen handling, and control.

2.4 NECESSARY FEATURES OF DATA-HANDLING TOOLS

The *first* stated requirement for a successful application system means that an end user need not possess any special training about how data are stored, modified, and retrieved by computers. Thus, to satisfy the end user's need, an application developer needs a mechanism for organizing and manipulating stored data. This data-handling tool should be entirely invisible to end users.

The data handler should furnish a powerful and flexible data description language for specifying data organization. A tool is *powerful* to the extent that it allows an application developer to represent clearly the nature of all of the kinds of data that are to be stored and the nature of their interrelationships, while minimizing concern about the physical layout of data and the physical implementation of data interrelationships. *Flexibility* is the richness or variety of data-structuring features offered by the data handler. In working with an inflexible tool, a developer is typically forced to contrive artificial, unwieldly data structures for representing data and their interrelationships (e.g., structures with considerable redundancy or artificial constructs). Such is the situation when a data-handling tool is unable to model closely the data and data interrelationships that exist in the real world.

With respect to data manipulation, the data handler should furnish a language or languages for storing, modifying, deleting, and extracting data from a data repository. At least one of these languages should be *integrable* (i.e., compatible) with the control–computation tool used by the developer for building interactive application software (recall Fig. 2.1). Such languages should also be *complete* in the sense that they should allow an application developer to extract any and all information held in a data repository.

It is also desirable for a data-handling language to be devised in such a way that it frees the developer from concern about low-level tasks such as input–output of data to and from disk, pointer and index manipulation, file manipulation (e.g., merging two files), management of free (i.e., unused) space in the data repository, etc. If the data handler automatically performs such tasks for a developer, greater developer productivity results. The languages supported by a data-handling tool should permit both routine, repetitive data extraction (e.g., standard reports) and ad hoc, spur-of-the-moment data extraction.

Finally, it is desirable for the data handler to provide the developer with a way of defining tabular end-user views. That is, the developer can present an end user with a variety of tabular forms, and as far as the end user is concerned these tabular forms reflect the way in which data is actually structured in the data repository. (Of course, it could be highly inefficient to actually organize data in such a manner.)

Beyond the tabular views defined by the developer, it is desirable that an end-user language be provided for extracting any data from any tabular view. In this way, the end user is provided with another kind of interface to the data repository, aside from application-specific interactive software built by the application developer. This additional interface is illustrated in Fig. 2.6 and is discussed more fully in Chapter 14. Clearly, this end-user–language interface to tabular views of data must be devoid of any requirement for programming skill on the part of an end user.

There are many specific details of data organization and manipulation that are desirable in a data-handling tool. These are extensively examined in Chapters 4–10 and 12–15.

The *second* end-user need calls for data security and data integrity. As far as is possible, it should be unnecessary for an end user to worry about guaranteeing data security and integrity. For the most part, data security and integrity should be provided by the application software. This implies that the application developer needs a tool that can assist in providing both security and integrity.

It is important to clarify the similarities and differences between integrity and security. *Data integrity* is the validity or correctness of the data and data relationships which exist in the data repository. Guaranteeing data integrity consists of three activities: defense, detection, and recovery. Defense involves guarding against invalid creation, deletion, or modification of data and data relationships. Changes in a data repository that leave it in an incorrect or inconsistent state are invalid. Defense guards against both intentional and accidental invalid changes.

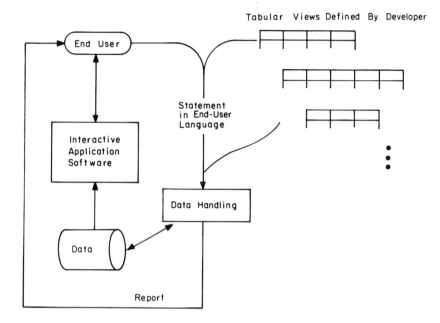

Fig. 2.6 An end-user–language interface.

Detection involves the discovery of invalid data or data relationships in the data repository. When a compromise of data integrity has been detected, it is important that the system be able to recover. Recovery involves restoration of the data repository to a valid, consistent. and correct state. It is vital that loss of data during the recovery activity be minimized.

Data security is the protection of data from unauthorized access. This includes both read and write access. With respect to read access, a piece of data is secure if only authorized persons are allowed to view it. A piece of data is secure from a write access standpoint if it can be modified or deleted only by authorized persons. Security also involves protecting data relationships from unauthorized access. Read access for a relationship involves using that relationship to find related pieces of data. Write access is the creation, modification, or removal of relationships between pieces of data. Data security is concerned with both intentional and unintentional assaults on security.

As depicted in Fig. 2.7, the common element of data integrity and data security is protection against unauthorized (or invalid) changes to the data repository. Related to both data security and data integrity is the notion of media (or physical) security. The data repository physically resides on some medium (e.g., a floppy disk). *Media security* is the protection of this medium from theft

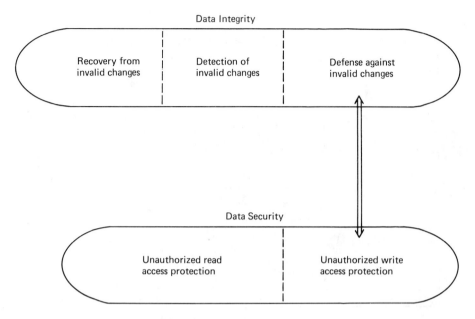

Data Integrity

Recovery from invalid changes

Detection of invalid changes

Defense against invalid changes

Data Security

Unauthorized read access protection

Unauthorized write access protection

Fig. 2.7   Data integrity and data security.

and physical hazards such as fire. Of course, recovery is crucial in the event of a failure in media security.

Application developers need a data-handling tool that provides facilities for automatic security and integrity checking. As the structure of data held in the data repository is specified, it should also be possible to specify security and integrity constraints. These constraints can then be enforced automatically during all data manipulation. For instance, when specifying the existence of salary data it is desirable to state the range of valid salary values (e.g., $13,000–69,000) and to have the data handler automatically thwart any attempt to put into the data repository a value outside of this range. In the interests of security, it would be useful to be able to assign access restrictions to salary data and access privileges to users when the data structure is being defined. A data-handling tool should automatically verify whether the access privilege of a particular user attempting to access salary data supercedes the salary access restriction.

The many specific features of security and integrity that are desirable in a data-handling tool are examined more fully in Chapters 4, 10, 11, and 14.

The *third* and *fourth* end-user requirements imply that a data-handling tool must be portable across hardware and operating system environments. When this portability is lacking, the application developer is forced to use different tools in different environments. This prevents the uniform, standardized approach to creating applications that is possible when a single data-handling tool can be made to serve in many environments. The results of a lack of portability are higher training costs, longer development times, and more difficult (i.e., costly) maintenance as personnel change. A standardized approach to the data-handling aspect of application development is a significant aid in keeping down the developer's costs and shortening development time.

The *fifth* end-user requirement is high performance. This suggests that the application developer needs a data-handling tool that gives extensive control over the degree of data redundancy, the physical placement of data in auxiliary memory, and the specification of access methods. These impact on both processing and storage efficiency. For improved processing efficiency, the tool should also provide a relatively procedural approach to data manipulation.

Just as an algorithm can be implemented more efficiently in assembly language (relatively procedural) than in COBOL (relatively nonprocedural), a data-handling task can often be implemented more efficiently through procedural data manipulation than through nonprocedural data manipulation. Of course, procedural data manipulation should not involve the complexity of an assembly language, and as previously noted, it should not be concerned with pointers, indices, disk input–output, etc.

Specific features of performance control that are useful in data-handling tools are explored in Chapters 5, 10, and 11.

The *sixth* end-user requirement is extensibility. This is primarily of concern to the developer of tailor-made applications, who often must alter an application system after its installation. To enable the developer to respond rapidly to requests for new types of reports, an application development tool should furnish nonprocedural data-manipulation facilities.

Procedural data manipulation is used for developing interactive software that an end user employs repeatedly, thus allowing high-performance processing for carrying out frequently needed tasks. Nonprocedural data manipulation is the best choice for rapidly generating ad hoc reports. Rather than devising a program to generate the newly desired report, the report is generated with a single nonprocedural statement. Although processing performance may not be as high as with procedural data manipulation, much less effort is required of the developer to produce a report. Moreover, processing performance tends to be less important if the processing occurs only once or rarely. Chapters 9 and 14 provide a detailed examination of a versatile, easy-to-use, nonprocedural data-handling language that drastically increases developer productivity.

The developer of tailor-made applications must sometimes respond to an end user's demand for new kinds of data. This implies that the data-handling tool should permit revisions in the original data structure after the application system has been in operation for some time. The important point here is the extent to which structural changes force the application software to change. Ideally, the data-handling tool should allow application programs to be written in such a way as to be insulated from structural changes. This is known as the principle of *logical data independence.*

If a data handler provides a high degree of logical data independence, then the developer has relatively few changes to make to application software when an end user's data needs expand beyond what the initial data structure will support. Although no data handler provides complete logical data independence, data-handling tools do vary in the degree of logical data independence they provide.

Physical data independence is the insulation of an application system's software and data structure from changes in hardware and physical data organization. For instance, if an end user acquires an additional disk drive or a new type of drive (e.g., a hard disk to replace a floppy disk), are changes in software or data structure necessitated? If data in the data repository are reorganized so that it physically changes position, are changes in software or data structure necessitated? Data-handling tools differ with respect to the extent of physical data independence provided. From the application developer's standpoint, it is desirable for a tool to furnish a high degree of physical data independence.

2.5 NECESSARY FEATURES OF SCREEN-HANDLING TOOLS

The *first* end-user requirement implies that an application developer needs a mechanism for defining and manipulating screens to elicit data and control information from and present data to an end user. The screen handler should allow this to be accomplished in an end–user-friendly manner. Although the screen handler itself should be invisible to end users, it should be developer-friendly, allowing the application developer to perform screen-definition and screen-manipulation tasks with relative ease and rapidity.

The screen handler should furnish a powerful and flexible screen-description language for specifying screen layouts (positions of elements within screens) and characteristics (foreground–background colors, bells, blinking, underlining, etc.). The tool is powerful to the extent that it enables the application developer to define screens for accomplishing all of the tasks of Fig. 2.2 in a relatively high-level (i.e., nonprocedural) manner. This means that the developer specifies the structural characteristics of screens without specifying the dynamics of *how* screen layouts and characteristics are to be generated for presentation to end users. *Flexibility* is the richness or variety of screen characteristics offered by the screen handler. A wide variety of desirable screen-definition characteristics is detailed in Chapter 14.

The screen handler should also furnish a language for displaying and clearing screens (and portions of screens), capturing the user response to a menu, and transferring data to and from screens. The screen manipulation language should be integrable (i.e., compatible) with the control–computation tool (recall Fig. 2.1). For instance, an end user's menu selection must be readily available to the control tool for it to govern the system's execution flow. From a productivity standpoint, it is desirable for the screen-manipulation language to support relatively high-level commands. As an example, a single command (rather than several) may be used for presenting an entire form of data values to an end user.

A developer-friendly screen handler should allow the developer to specify the text of a help message for any screen and should be able to present that message automatically to an end user during the processing of that screen. The application programs devised by the developer should be entirely unconcerned with presenting help text, remembering the screen status while help text is displayed, and restoring the screen to its former status when the user is finished with the help message. In the interest of developer productivity, all of these tasks should be performed by the screen handler.

Recall that the *second* end-user need is for an application system to automatically ensure data security and integrity. A screen handler should be capable of automatically editing data and checking its validity as it is entered by an end user. It is extremely important for an interactive application system to detect data-entry errors immediately and notify the end user about the nature of the mistake before the erroneous data reaches the data handler. Especially powerful screen-handling tools can deal with data-entry errors before they are passed along to the control–computation element of an application system. Such a tool allows the developer to specify the characteristics of valid data entries with a screen-description language.

For instance, the developer might specify that the third symbol entered for a particular kind of data must be digit and that the fourth symbol must be edited to be uppercase (regardless of whether an end user enters the symbol as uppercase or lowercase). Once the screen integrity–edit characteristics for a particular kind of data have been defined, the developer is never again concerned with them. They are automatically enforced by the screen handler, which immediately notifies the end user of errors and refuses to accept any invalid data. The many important integrity–edit features that a screen handler should support to maximize developer productivity are enumerated in Chapter 14.

The *third* and *fourth* end-user requirements suggest the extra value of a screen-handling tool that is portable across hardware and operating system environments. Where this portability is lacking, the developer must use different tools in different environments. This prevents the uniform, standardized approach to creating applications that is possible when a single screen-handling tool can be made to serve in many environments. The results are similar to those we have seen in the case of data-handling tools: higher training costs, longer development times, and more difficult (i.e., costly) maintenance as personnel change. A standardized approach to the screen-handling aspect of application development is a significant aid in holding down the developer's costs and shortening development time.

Perhaps even more significant than portability across CPUs and operating systems is portability of the screen handler with respect to the multitude of terminal types that exist. That is, a screen-handling tool should not be oriented toward a particular terminal or small group of terminals. Ideally, a screen handler should furnish a high degree of *terminal independence* by allowing the developer to build application systems that are independent of the types of terminals employed by end users. With terminal independence the developer need make no change whatsoever in an application system when an end user switches from a light–dark to an 8-color terminal, acquires a dual-intensity terminal, changes to a terminal that supports blinking and 16 colors, etc. Terminal independence is a very developer-friendly trait.

The *fifth* end-user requirement is high performance. Although application development time and costs are both highly sensitive to the data-handling and screen-handling tools, screen-handling tools have a relatively minor influence on the performance efficiency of an application system. From the standpoint of storage efficiency, it is typical for the volume of data stored to dwarf the stored information on screen layouts and characteristics. In terms of processing, the overriding priorities are to find data held in auxiliary memory and to transfer data between central and auxiliary memory. These are not screen-handling functions. If a screen handler retains information about screen layouts and characteristics in auxiliary memory, such information should quickly become accessible when it is needed by the screen handler (e.g., using virtual memory techniques).

The *sixth* end-user requirement is extensibility. Suppose that an end user needs a new screen, wants an existing screen layout to change (e.g., different positionings or prompt messages), or desires that an existing screen characteristic be modified (e.g., different background colors or intensity, and that this need was unanticipated. It is highly desirable for the application developer to have a screen-handling tool which can accommodate such end-user needs without necessitating changes in the original application software. This is known as the principle of *screen independence*.

If a screen handler supports a high degree of screen independence, then the developer can alter screen layouts and characteristics without needing to recompile the application system's program(s). It should be clear that such a trait is important for increasing developer productivity during the development of both off-the-shelf and tailor-made application systems, as well as in the ongoing maintenance of tailor-made application systems. Finally, note that the principle of screen independence is analogous to that of logical data independence, and that terminal independence is highly analogous to physical data independence.

2.6   NECESSARY FEATURES OF CONTROL–COMPUTATION TOOLS

The *first* end-user need suggests that a control–computation tool must be compatible with both the screen handler and data handler. On the basis of end-user desires (as detected by the screen handler), the control logic built by the developer determines what happens next: some data are retrieved or stored by the data handler, a computation is performed, a prompt or menu is presented to the end user, etc. In the event of data transference (or attempted data transference), the control logic determines what happens if data is successfully or unsuccessfully transferred. In the latter case, various actions are taken, depending on the reason the transfer was unsuccessful (e.g., owing to integrity violation, inadequate security clearance, nonexistent data, or media corruption).

Aside from the compatibility factor, the tool (i.e., the language) for specifying control logic should be developer-friendly. It should allow a developer to specify easily the important types of control structures, including IF–THEN–ELSE–ENDIF, WHILE–DO–ENDDO, PERFORM module, TEST-CASE, etc. From the standpoint of supporting computations, the tool should allow a developer to specify all of the usual kinds of arithmetic operations on a wide variety of data types (e.g., integer, unsigned, floating point, fixed decimal). A tool is even more valuable if it offers an extensive set of functions, such as square root, log, random number generation, etc. Concatenation of data values is another useful feature.

The *second* end-user need of security and integrity can be largely solved by the use of sophisticated screen- and data-handling tools. However, if relatively primitive data and/or screen handlers are used, then security and integrity checks must be built into the control logic by the application developer. This is another reason why a tool should support extensive, flexible control structure mechanisms. Even if sophisticated screen- and data-handling tools are employed, it may nevertheless be necessary for a developer to specify certain special (i.e., complex or nonstandard) integrity and/or security checks within the application system's control structure.

The *third* and *fourth* end-user needs suggest that the tool used in specifying control logic and computations should be portable to help maximize developer productivity. If a control–computation language can be used without alteration for a wide variety of operating systems and CPUs, then standardization of development and maintenance is achievable.

The *fifth* end-user need, high performance, implies that the control language should be compilable. For the sake of performance, the compiler should produce object code that is small in size and executes rapidly. Minimizing object code size has the effect of maximizing the amount of central memory that can be used by the data handler and screen handler, resulting in faster data handling and screen handling. Another factor related to compilation is the speed of the compiler in generating object code. Slow compilers can have a significant detrimental effect on developer productivity during the construction and debugging of an application system.

The *sixth* end-user need is modification of an application system over time. In other words, it may be necessary for a developer to alter an application system's control logic over time. This implies that the language for specifying control logic should naturally support modularization and structured control logic; this will facilitate maintenance. Another important factor is documentation (or self-documentation) of the control logic.

2.7 TOOL SELECTION

The developer's needs, as identified in the three preceding sections, form a useful set of criteria for evaluating and selecting application development tools. These criteria are very important to serious, professional application developers. Of course, they are of lesser importance to amateurs and hobbyists, whose applications require managing only a few files of data.

As shown in Fig. 2.8, several tool configurations are possible. The oldest type of configuration uses only one tool to accomplish all three types of tasks: screen handling, control–computation, and data handling. This single tool is a programming language. Although all common programming languages support screen handling, control–computation, and data handling, their screen- and data-handling facilities tend to be meager relative to the needs cited in Sections 2.4 and 2.5. This is especially true of their data-handling capabilities, which do not go beyond file management (i.e., creating files, adding records to files, merging files together).

At the opposite end of the spectrum is a very powerful configuration in which data handling is performed by a database management system and screen handling is performed by a screen management system. These two tools are compatible with a programming language which is used to specify computations and control logic. The programming language's data-handling features are replaced by the much more powerful and flexible database management system. Similarly, the built-in screen-handling features are ignored in favor of the more powerful and flexible screen management system.

With respect to the three data-handling alternatives shown in Fig. 2.8, data handling with a programming language (Fig. 2.8a) is not stressed in this book. Likewise, data handling through a file management system compatible with a programming language (Fig. 2.8b,c) is of little interest here. Data handling through a database management system that is compatible with a programming language (Fig. 2.8d,e) is of primary concern. Because this book focuses on the

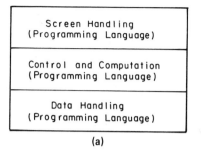

(a)

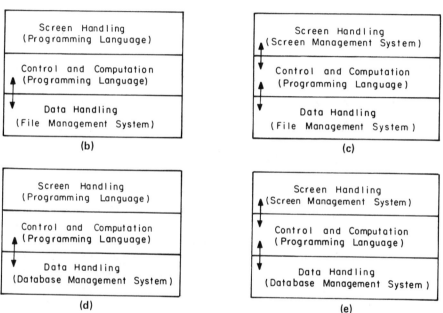

Fig. 2.8 Alternative tool configurations: (a) programming language; (b) programming language and file management system; (c) programming language, file management system, and screen management system; (d) programming language and database management system; (e) programming language, database management system, and screen management system.

role of database management tools in micro application development, the details of screen handling (whether furnished by a programming language or a screen management system) are not discussed in subsequent chapters. The one exception is Chapter 14, which briefly describes a comprehensive screen management system for use with microcomputers.

In addition to comparing alternative tools on the basis of how well they meet a developer's needs, there are several other significant considerations. The organization, clarity, thoroughness, and overall quality of a tool's documentation should be carefully examined. Poor documentation can make even a good tool difficult to grasp and use. Another necessity is good support for the tool being considered. The availability and competence of a professional staff that can answer technical questions about the tool should be assessed. A related issue is the ongoing viability of the tool, its vendor, and author.

Is the organization that authored (i.e., designed and implemented) the tool a well-established research and development organization? Does it have an experienced, innovative staff devoted to enhancing the tool as well as producing new tools? How responsive is the company to correcting problems? Is the tool's vendor committed to seeing users succeed in developing and marketing superior application software? Is the vendor aware of the needs of application developers? Can the vendor cite an example of a truly outstanding or unique application system built with its tool? Does the vendor furnish intensive, practical, training in the utilization of its tool? It is important to ask questions such as these when considering a tool.

2.8   THE PRICE OF A TOOL

A final application developer need, which is derived from the end user's desire for a low cost, is that a development tool have a "reasonable" cost. Just as a factory of machine tools costs much more than the automobile it produces, one would expect an application development tool to cost more than the list price of an application system built with it. The developer who is a vendor or consultant should quickly recoup the investment in a tool through the sale of many copies of the application system or, in the tailor-made case, selling many application systems created with the same tool. An in-house developer may use the tool to create numerous applications for internal use. For reasons of versatility, the one-time cost of the tool (together with developer staff costs) may be attractive, relative to the alternative of purchasing off-the-shelf application software from a vendor or consultant.

There is a common view, at least among micro users, that software should not have a higher price than the hardware on which it executes. Such a view has *no* rational basis. A piece of software, if it is to have a long life in the marketplace, must be priced so that it enables its vendor to recover marketing and support costs as well as allowing its author to recoup the costs of design, implementation, documentation, and maintenance. The author's costs depend very little on the target hardware. Consider the authors of database management systems. One author may have created a database management system for a mainframe computer. For another author to create a database management system having the same features and functions for a microcomputer will not cost less merely because the target machine is a micro. The research and development problems are not diminished or eased in any way. Indeed, the problems may very well be more challenging (i.e., costly), because the author must deal with a much more constrained environment (e.g., slower hardware speeds, smaller memory capacity, more primitive operating system).

Typical prices for mainframe database management systems range from $100,000 to $250,000. Clearly, such prices could not be charged for comparable database management systems that operate on microcomputers. Nevertheless, the micro author must be able to recover costs at the same level as those of mainframe authors. To recoup costs while charging a price much lower than mainframe levels, an author must sell many more units of a micro database management system. The price that must be charged is inversely proportional to the market size (the larger the market, the lower the price can be). Thus, a second significant determinant of price, aside from cost to the author, is market size.

For a sophisticated tool such as a full-scale database management system, the market is much smaller than for a more primitive tool, such as a programming language or an off-the-shelf application system (e.g., an integrated accounting package). Thus, there are two factors which prevent the price of a database management system from falling to the level of a programming language, operating system, or spreadsheet package: the relatively high cost of authoring very sophisticated, powerful software and the relatively small potential market of skilled, professional application developers. This second factor may change over time as the micro market matures, vendors invest more in educating the micro market, and data processing professionals using mainframe computers become aware that micros are not "toys" and that high-quality micro software tools actually do exist.

When an application developer assesses whether the price of a tool is *reasonable* for his situation, a comparison of the tool price with the target hardware's price is irrelevant. What *is* relevant is a comparison of the price of the tool with the costs incurred by not having that tool. Does the productivity gain that results from using the tool rapidly offset the price of the tool? This is the relevant question. Suppose that a micro applications developer anticipates employing four programmers, at an annual cost of $30,000 apiece to implement application software using file-handling tools (i.e., a programming language or file management system). Suppose that the target hardware costs $5000. Also suppose that the developer has the opportunity to purchase a database management system for $10,000. It is commonly reported that high-quality database management systems can increase developer productivity by 50 to 80%. This implies that the $10,000 price is a bargain. Assuming only a 50% gain in productivity, the result is a $50,000 savings the first year (only half the anticipated number of programmers being needed) and a $60,000 savings each year thereafter. Of course, this analysis ignores the many qualitative advantages of the database management approach to data handling that allow the production of better (e.g., higher performance, higher integrity) application systems than are generally possible with the other data-handling approaches.

Now suppose that a developer has identified two alternative tools, each having a reasonable price with respect to productivity gains it can support. Which one should be selected? This can be answered only by a thorough comparison of the alternatives with respect to the pertinent criteria described in Sections 2.4–2.7.

In situations where some tool other than a programming language is used, there is one final economic factor that deserves mention. In such situations, it may be necessary to sell a copy of a portion of the application development tool with the application software. This is certainly true in the case of a database management system, because the application software is useless without a copy of the data manipulation routines on which it is based. The problem is that an application developer does not own rights to copy and resell portions of the development tool. One *solution* which is not particularly workable is to require the end user to purchase not only the application software but also the tool on which that software is based. This is an expensive proposition for the end user. Alternatively, the application developer might purchase, for a flat fee, the unlimited right to sell copies of the development tool. This is hardly attractive to the author of the development tool, unless the author does not value the tool very highly or unless the flat fee is extraordinarily high.

A compromise between these two alternatives may be reached if it is required that the application developer pay a royalty to the author of the development tool for the right to copy certain portions of the tool for inclusion with the application software sold to an end user. The royalty schedule may be based on a percentage of the application software's list price to an end user and on volume discounts. The in-house developer is unconcerned with these copying issues, provided the tool is used solely on the particular CPU for which it is licensed.

The development of application software is therefore a collaborative venture. The development tool's author, although generally very knowledgeable in the art of constructing a versatile and generalized high-performance tool, is not necessarily equipped to carry out the tool's potential in terms of constructing application software. Conversely, the application developer, although knowledgeable in the use of the tool and the functionality of the application area, typically does not have the resources, skill, and relative advantage necessary to build the development tool. Clearly, a collaborative arrangement recognizing this division of labor is most beneficial for the development tool's author, the application developer, and the end user.

2.9 SUMMARY

In this chapter we have discussed the important distinction between application developers and end users. Developers are technically skilled persons who build application systems that can be used by technically unskilled end users. This presentation has been oriented toward professional application developers and the tools which they can use in constructing interactive application systems. There are three main types of tasks performed by interactive application software: screen handling, data handling, and control–computation. Various tools are available to aid a developer in building application software to accomplish these tasks.

Desirable characteristics of tools from the standpoint of increasing developer productivity have been described at considerable length. These characteristics are implicit in an understanding of end-user needs. The description has been segmented into three parts: one each for screen-handling tools, data-handling tools, and tools for specification of control logic. The desirable characteristics that have been identified furnish a set of criteria for evaluating and selecting application development tools. Those tools with high ratings on the various criteria can be considered as developer-friendly tools for building user-friendly application systems. Beyond developer-friendliness, other important factors in tool selection include documentation quality, tool support, and tool price.

RELATED READINGS

C. W. Holsapple, Choosing the right data base management systems, *Hardcopy* **12,** No. 24 (1983).

C. W. Holsapple and A. B. Whinston, Guidelines for DBMS evaluation, *in* "Data Base Management: Theory and Applications" (C. W. Holsapple and A. B. Whinston, eds.), Reidel: Dordrecht, Holland, 1983.

D. Hussain and K. M. Hussain, "Information Processing for Management," Irwin, Homewood, Illinois, 1981.

J. A. Senn, "Analysis and Design of Information Systems," McGraw-Hill, New York, 1984.

H. J. Watson and A. B. Carroll, "Computers for Business," Business Publications Inc., Dallas, 1980.

EXERCISES

1. List and describe the general needs of an end user.
2. List and describe the general needs of a software developer.
3. Contrast the needs of an end user with those of a software developer.
4. Describe three capabilities that are desirable in an interactive application software system.
5. Briefly describe how each of the three capabilities must relate to the needs of the end user.
6. Describe the important factors in determining a royalty structure for incorporation of a development tool within application software.
7. You are the manager of an application software development firm and have recently come to know about a very powerful database management tool from ABC Software Tools. Before you decide to buy the tool, you want to perform a cost–benefit analysis to make sure that your investment will yield the desired rates of return. You have gathered the following data.

   (a) You have P_1 programmers working for you at $\$Q$ annual salary per programmer.
   (b) The cumulative production rate is N_1 software packages per year with the help of your current development tools.
   (c) The selling price per package is $\$S_1$ and all packages produced are sold.

   You have determined (with a high degree of confidence) that if you decide to purchase the ABC database management tool, it will have the following impacts.

   (d) You will be able to reduce the number of programmers to P_2. The salary of $\$Q$ will remain the same.
   (e) Owing to higher productivity resulting from the tool, the cumulative production rate will increase to N_2 packages per year.
   (f) Because of the user-friendly nature and other powerful features of your software package, you'll be able to market it at $\$S_2$ per package ($\$S_2 > \$S_1$).

   The cost of the ABC database tool is quoted at $\$C$. You are also aware that you'll have to pay $\$R$ per package in royalty for every software package you sell with the ABC database tool.
   With this information at hand, determine the following.

   (g) What is the rate of return on this investment over a 3-year period?
   (h) If the cost of money to you is 20%, what is the payback period for this investment?

8. The product manager of ABC's database management tool wants to set a reasonable market price for a new version of the tool that has been devel-

oped for microcomputers. The following data are available from market research and other sources.

(a) Demand for the ABC microcomputer tool is N_{MC} units this year and will increase at an exponential rate of $N_{MC}(1 + e^T)$, where T is the number of years that have elapsed since the introduction of the product ($T = 1, 2, 3, 4,$ and 5).

(b) The cost of development is C_{MC} per tool.

(c) Mainframe computer database tools are sold at $\$S_{MF}$ per tool.

(d) The demand for mainframe database tools is N_{MF} units this year and will increase at a linear rate of $N_{MF}(1 + T)$, where T is the number of years ($T = 1, 2, 3, 4, 5$).

(e) The cost of development of the mainframe database tool is $\$C_{MF}$ per tool.

If the product manager of ABC wants to achieve the same rate of return from the sale of database tools for microcomputers as is available for mainframe database management tools, what should the market price (in dollars per tool) for the new ABC micro database management tool?

9. Describe the different kinds of information that can be displayed on a screen for an end user.

10. Why are data security and integrity important for application software?

11. As an application development tool, how does a programming language differ from database management and screen management systems?

12. What features should a database management system have if it is to be used on microcomputers? How should it differ from a mainframe database system?

13. Suppose two or more users can access a database concurrently. What potential problems can result?

PROJECT

Prepare a narrative description that demonstrates a clear understanding of the information processing application selected in the Project of Chapter 1 in terms of

(a) the organizational setting in which the information processing occurs,
(b) the kinds of reports to be produced,
(c) the kinds of data necessary to produce the reports,
(d) the kinds of processing required for updating data and producing reports.

The application should be substantial enough to require the generation of at least three different kinds of reports. Describe in detail the appearance and content of each report. Indicate how often and under what circumstances each report is generated. Explain the purpose for which each report is used.

Compile a list of all the kinds of data to be held in the application system's database. Give a descriptive name to each of these data items and elaborate on the precise meaning or role of each. Explain where the values of the various data items come from and how often they arrive.

Describe how each report is produced by identifying the data items used for that report, stating the nature of any data that is given at the time the report is generated (e.g., by the person desiring the report), and citing any computations that are used. Also describe the basic processing needed to update data held in the database by explaining the nature of the application's transactions.

Chapter 3

EVOLUTION OF DATABASE MANAGEMENT

The main impetus behind the origin of database management was the recognition of inadequacies and problems inherent in file management. Each of the major file management approaches (sequential, indexed sequential, and hashing) has particular strengths and weaknesses relative to the others. However, they all share a common set of problems because each is limited to file-oriented data organization and processing. Database management arose in an effort to overcome these limitations.

Database approaches to data management are fundamentally different from file management approaches. The reader should be careful to avoid the common mistake of confusing the terms "database management" and "data management." "Data management" is a very broad term, referring to both computerized and noncomputerized methods of managing data. As Fig. 3.1 indicates, file management and database management are two types of computerized data management. "Database management" is a much more specific term than "data management" and refers to methods for managing data that have been organized into a database. Major types of database management approaches that have emerged since the late 1960s are *hierarchical, shallow network, relational, CODASYL network,* and *extended network.*

In this chapter we examine the limitations of using file management for application development. A newly emerging category of micro software, all-in-one systems, is briefly described. The characteristics of DBMSs are presented and

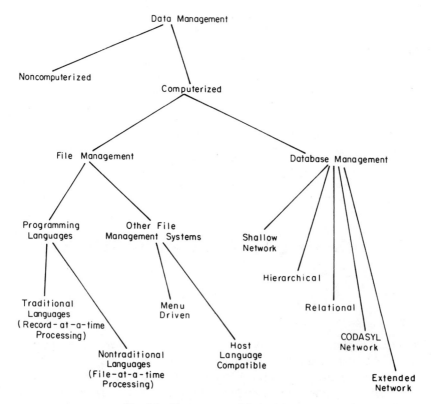

Fig. 3.1 The spectrum of data management.

basic terminology is introduced. Major developments in the history of database management are cited and put into perspective. The chapter closes with some reflections on the unfortunate effects of ''diluted'' terminology.

3.1 DATABASE MANAGEMENT:
WHAT IT IS NOT

We shall assume that the reader clearly grasps the distinction between file organization and file processing and is familiar with common file access methods such as *indexed sequential, address calculation,* and *secondary key indexing* (i.e., inverted files). Appendix A provides a brief refresher on these basics. All of these are workable techniques for managing a file. They have relative advantages and disadvantages which depend on the kind of processing that is necessary for a file. However, the fundamental weakness of each file management approach is that it is oriented toward processing a single file. For nontrivial applications it quickly becomes impractical to attempt to organize all data into a single flat file. Therefore, application systems based on file management typically involve a data repository consisting of many files.

An example is shown in Fig. 3.2. Here, Files A and B are used by Application Program 1 to produce a report. File B is also used by Application Program 3, along with Files F and G, to yield another report. File F is itself an output of Program 2. This program uses File D to produce an updated version of File C. Data from Files C, D, and E are used to generate a report and file F. File E is also used in conjunction with File H by Program 4. Finally, Application Program 5 uses transactions in File I to update File J.

Note that this simplified example ignores the issue of consistently updating data values that exist redundantly across several files. Suppose that Files C, I, and G have a field in common (e.g., employee name). When any value of that field changes, the change must be reflected in Files C, I, and G (as well as any secondary key indices based on that field). This integrity processing might be incorporated into Program 2, which would require it to access Files I and G in addition to those shown in Fig. 3.2. Alternatively, there could be yet another program that accesses all files involved to ensure data integrity. The application

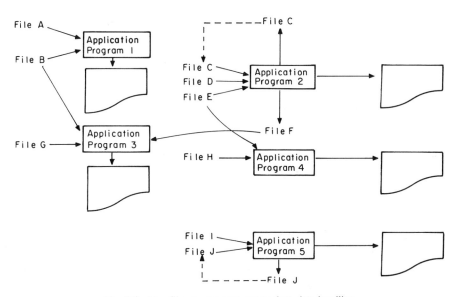

Fig. 3.2   The file management approach to data handling.

developer must ensure that consistency is preserved for *all* fields across all files used in an application system.

File management is not particularly well suited to representation of logical relationships between data in one file and data in another. The commonly used method of representation is to repeat a unique field of one file as a field in the related file. Two records (one in each file) are considered to be logically related if they have the same value for the redundant field. For instance, Files A and B have a redundant field which enables Program 1 to determine which records in B are related to a record in A. This method of specifying a relationship between records in two different files results in several very undesirable effects.

First, there is the redundancy of data across files, which can lead to a rather significant consumption of storage. Second, there is the redundancy of data within any given file, which can also have a negative impact on storage. Third, and perhaps most important, there is the difficulty of maintaining the integrity of data and data relationships in the face of redundancy. The application developer must guarantee this integrity by ensuring that any application program which alters a data value in one file also simultaneously alters repetitions of that data value in the same and different files. This is particularly troublesome for cases in which many users are attempting to access data concurrently. Fourth, unless secondary key indices are used, access (on any of a variety of criteria) to desired records in a given file is relatively slow. Fifth, access to records in one file that are related to records in another file, which in turn are related to a record in yet another file, etc., is extremely slow (though secondary key indices can alleviate this somewhat). Sixth, the representation of relationships by redundant fields is not particularly intuitive or natural (conveying nothing about the nature or semantics of the relationship) and is in practice a clumsy and cumbersome method with which to work. Seventh, there is the proliferation of files, which leads to the common situation in which developers and end users are forced to keep track of large numbers of files.

The undesirability of such effects cannot be overstressed. They account for the relatively low developer productivity that characterizes attempts to build and maintain nontrivial application systems using file management. Aside from low productivity, there are also the crucial issues of system efficiency, integrity, and feasibility.

Can the functions that must be performed by a proposed application system be accomplished through file management in such a way that the resultant system is user-friendly, efficient, and guaranteed to have its integrity and security preserved? The answer is affirmative for simple applications that demand nothing more than the management of a few files (e.g., keeping track of the coins in a coin collection). However, as soon as an application begins to involve many types of data with many interrelationships (as in a realistic business application), file management becomes quite cumbersome with respect to the criteria identified in Chapter 2.

File management systems for microcomputers are available in several forms. The most common file managers are programming languages. Nearly all programming languages have facilities for writing records into and retrieving records from a file. As noted in the preceding chapter, programming languages also have facilities for specifying control logic and for screen handling. Of the traditional programming languages, it is fair to say that COBOL supports the most extensive file management features (e.g., both indexed–sequential and hashed files).

However, there is another class of languages aside from the traditional FORTRAN, BASIC, Pascal, PL/l, COBOL, and C. This class has been designed with the goal of making file handling easier than it is in the traditional languages. The more widely known of these nontraditional languages include dBASE and Condor. Like traditional programming languages, they support various control logic specifications and some input–output operations. However, they are typically interpretive languages (relatively large and slow) rather than compiled languages. The dBASE program control structures permit DO–WHILE iteration and IF–THEN–ELSE branching; Condor is relatively limited, allowing IF–ENDIF program structures.

With respect to data handling, these kinds of file managers typically allow definition of files, addition of records to files, retrieval of desired records from a file, the merging of two files based on redundant data values to produce a new file, deletion of records from files, addition of new fields to a file (by making a new copy of the file), deletion of fields from a file (by making a new copy of the file), creation of secondary key indices for a file, etc. Although there is nothing new or remarkable about these file-handling tasks, they are supported with higher level commands than traditional languages provide. The prices of these file-handling–programming languages are roughly comparable to those of traditional programming language compilers and interpreters.

A second kind of file manager supports the usual file-handling tasks mentioned previously along with various screen-handling facilities. The user of this kind of file manager generally interacts with it in menu fashion. A common example of such a file manager is FMS-80. Some file managers in this category support user interaction by way of a command language rather than menus. A third kind of file management system is one in which file-handling commands can be invoked from traditional programming languages. This has the effect of giving the traditional language a higher level file-handling capacity. It allows a developer to continue using a favorite traditional language while employing higher level or more extensive file-handling facilities.

The higher-level file management commands furnished by some file managers in no way overcome the previously mentioned difficulties and shortcomings inherent in file management. In no way do they prevent the situation shown in Fig. 3.2. On the other hand, database management offers a very different approach to application development, overcoming many of the difficulties of file management. Before exploring this approach in detail, there is one other type of micro system that deserves mention: all-in-one systems.

3.2   ALL-IN-ONE SYSTEMS

An all-in-one system is a single software package which performs more than one kind of information processing. For instance, it may function as both an electronic spreadsheet and an electronic file cabinet in such a way that the same data can be processed in both spreadsheet and file cabinet modes. Such a package offers a substitute to the alternative of purchasing and using two packages (spreadsheet and file cabinet) which may or may not be able to operate on the same data. All-in-one systems for micros began to appear in 1982.

Two of the earliest such systems were MBA and 1-2-3. Each of these is basically a spreadsheet package to which additional types of information processing abilities have been added. For instance, 1-2-3 goes beyond traditional spreadsheet packages by supporting additional commands which allow some filelike processing of blocks of spreadsheet cells and which can make spreadsheet data available to a graphics presentation module. The MBA system allows similar pseudo-file processing of spreadsheet cells and supports graphical display of spreadsheet data. In addition, it has a modest word processing facility that can be used within a spreadsheet. Although the data management aspects of such systems are certainly an advance over first-generation spreadsheet packages, they are quite rudimentary by comparison with the file managers cited in the previous section.

A very different kind of all-in-one system is a package called the Knowledge Manager (KnowledgeMan). Unlike the MBA and 1-2-3 packages, KnowledgeMan does not restrict its users to a spreadsheet view of the world. Its rather extensive data management capabilities can be used independently of (or in conjunction with) its spreadsheet capabilities.

KnowledgeMan is composed of a variety of integrated components, which are particularly useful in building customized decision support systems. The components include data management, screen input–output management, ad hoc inquiry, printed forms management, spreadsheet analysis, business graphics, statistical analysis, and a structured programming language. Each component can be used independently of the others. A user can perform ad hoc inquiry without knowing about data management, manage data without knowing about programming, perform spreadsheet analysis without knowing about screen management, etc. However, the components can also be used in conjunction with each other. For instance, a spreadsheet cell can be defined by an entire structured program, a program can perform ad hoc inquiry, a spreadsheet cell can be output to a desired location on a preprinted report form, the results of statistical analyses on data maintained by the data management component can be deposited in spreadsheet cells, or a program can invoke commands of any of the other six components within its control structures.

The data management and ad hoc inquiry features of KnowledgeMan go well beyond those of the micro file managers discussed in Section 3.1. The KnowledgeMan data-handling features are largely consistent in syntax and operation with IBM's SQL/DS, the *de facto* standard for relational database management (see Appendix C). For instance, only a single command is necessary to generate a desired report using data from more than one table (i.e., a "relation"). Because of their SQL/DS-like appearance, the data management–inquiry components of KnowledgeMan can be regarded as a relational database management system. Among its more unusual features are support of virtual fields, virtual tabular views, inquiry based on wildcard matches, data encryption, and data security via access code combinations.

The KnowledgeMan spreadsheet features are comparable to those of the most widely used spreadsheet packages. Included are variable column widths; edit–entry–prompt lines; cell, row, and/or column formats; border control; relative and absolute replication; and functions. Unlike other spreadsheet packages, it also has extensive security features and conditionally activated special effects. Another notable difference between KnowledgeMan and spreadsheet packages is the integration with other KnowledgeMan capabilities, that enables any cell to be defined by an entire program which may involve other cells, data retrieved from tables, and/or statistics generated from that data. Statistics (e.g., mean or standard deviation) can be generated for any stored data, virtual data, or arithmetic expressions involving data. Conditional statistics and statistics at control breaks are supported.

KnowledgeMan's screen management component allows input and output forms to be defined for display on a console. The user has control over the layout of prompts and other elements in a screen form. Special effects such as color, blinking, and reverse video can be declared for elements in a screen form. Each screen management command processes an entire form at a time, either accepting input through the form or displaying output data. KnowledgeMan performs automatic editing and character-by-character integrity checks as data are entered. Printed forms management is similar, except that it involves routing output to customized or preprinted forms produced on a printer.

All of the foregoing components can be used without any knowledge of programming. However, advanced users of KnowledgeMan can invoke commands of any of the other six components from within a KnowledgeMan program. A variety of control statements are supported, including do–while, if–then–else, and test–case. Subprograms can be invoked with up to 26 parameters. All of these control structures can be nested to arbitrary depths.

Because it does not require programming expertise, a system like KnowledgeMan is appropriate for first-time computer users. As a result of its decision support orientation, it is of interest for personal decision support processing of data that have been extracted from large databases (e.g., data downloaded from a mainframe). Because of its flexibility and versatility, it is also valuable to developers of modest micro application systems. In spite of all of its capabilities, KnowledgeMan does have limits with respect to application development. These limits are largely due to KnowledgeMan's approach to data management. Because KnowledgeMan uses only a file-oriented relational approach, it is not the best choice for large-scale application development, application systems with numerous or intricate data relationships, or situations in which the best possible performance and integrity guarantees are desired. The focus of this book is on more powerful database management tools.

3.3   DATABASE MANAGEMENT: WHAT IT IS

A *database* is a collection of records of many different types, organized according to a single, integrated, logical structure that allows redundancy to be eliminated (or at least controlled to a significant degree). A *database management system* (DBMS) is software that enables a developer

(a)   to define a database by specifying its logical (and perhaps physical) structure and

(b)   to create, modify, delete, and retrieve data held in the database, subject to automatic security and integrity checks performed by the DBMS.

The database management counterpart to Fig. 3.2 is shown in Fig. 3.3. Note that the idea of separating all records of one type into one file is completely absent. There is no multitude of separate files. Instead, all data are held *nonredundantly* in a single database. As we shall see in chapter 5, the degree of nonredundancy that can be achieved varies among different kinds of database management systems. Physically, a database resides in one or more operating system files. However, the application programmer is unconcerned with physical considerations, all of which are handled by the DBMS.

As Fig. 3.3 suggests, the developer of application programs in a database environment never needs to think in terms of files. There is no concern whatsoever with opening or closing files, file input–output, merging files that have redundant fields, indices, pointers, management of space made available by record deletion, etc. The application programmer issues commands to the DBMS software, which in turn handles all of the physical details involved in creating, modifying, deleting, or retrieving data. As we shall see in Chapters 6–8, 12, and

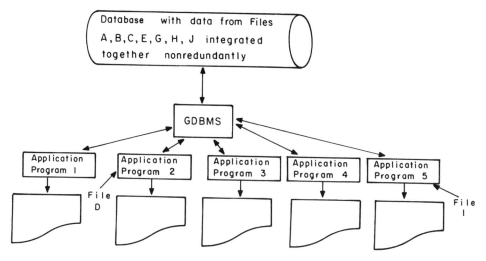

Fig. 3.3   The database approach.

13, the notion of a file does not arise when manipulating the data held in a database.

Collectively, the commands that can be issued to a DBMS are referred to as its *data manipulation language* (DML). DML commands can be invoked from within the control logic of an application program. A programming language whose programs can contain DML commands is called a *host language.* For instance, COBOL is said to be a host language for a DBMS if a COBOL program can be written which includes calls to the DBMSs data manipulation commands. A DML has the effect of drastically extending the host language's data-handling power so that the programmer is no longer limited to file management. A DML allows programs written in the host language to interact with a database.

In Chapters 6–8 which describe the nature and use of DML commands, we shall show that the notion of a file never appears and that a DML programmer is unconcerned with the physical aspects of a database. All DML commands are stated in terms of a database's logical structure. This logical structure can be regarded as a blueprint of the database that indicates the kinds of data held in the database and the kinds of relationships that exist among different types of data. A database's logical structure is designed by the application developer prior to and apart from any data manipulation. The design should be based on careful system analysis.

A *data description language* (DDL) is furnished by a DBMS to allow the developer to specify a logical structure formally. The DDL is strictly a representational language. It is not executed in any way. It is, however, analyzed by a DBMS software component, which we shall refer to as the *DDL Analyzer.* A

DDL Analyzer examines the formal specification of a logical structure, checking it for syntactic correctness and consistency. If no errors are detected, the analyzer uses the specification to create a *data dictionary*.

A DBMSs internal data dictionary contains all information about the types of data and data interrelationships that can exist in a database. Thus, information is held in an internal form which is of no concern to the developer. Included are the names of fields, the names of data relationships, the characteristics of fields (e.g., type and size), the characteristics of relationships, integrity conditions, security constraints, and various performance control specifications. Figure 3.4 shows the relationship between a database's logical structure, the DDL specification of that structure, and the data dictionary.

When a DML command is invoked, a portion of DBMS software called the

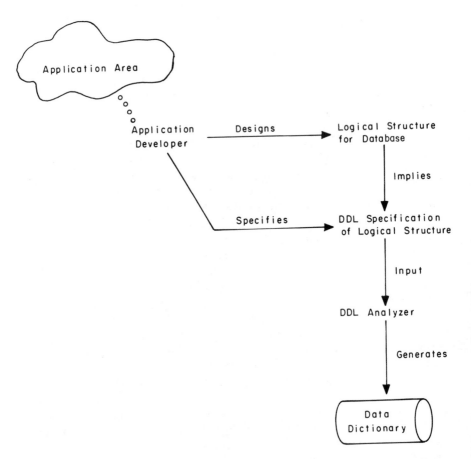

Fig. 3.4 Data dictionary generation.

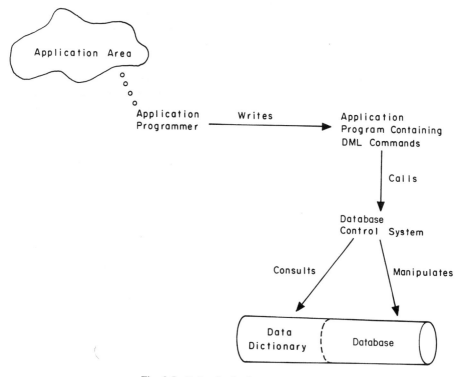

Fig. 3.5   Role of a database control system.

database control system (DBCS) executes the command. In the course of execution, the DBCS consults the data dictionary to obtain information pertinent to performing the data-manipulation task. That is, the actual execution of a DML command is both controlled by and driven by information held in the data dictionary. These tasks include the creation, deletion, and modification of data and relationships. It is the DBCS which performs all memory management, disk input–output, manipulation of pointers or indices, security and integrity enforcements, etc. The role of a DBCS is illustrated in Fig. 3.5. As shown, many database management systems store the data dictionary within the database itself.

Typically, DBMS software includes several utilities in addition to the mandatory DDL Analyzer and DBCS. One of the most important of these from the standpoint of developer productivity is a *query system*. Associated with a query system is a *query language*. In response to a query language statement, the query system generates a desired report. Thus, a query system is an important aid to developer productivity, enabling a nonprogrammer to obtain reports without programming.

Database management systems in use today vary widely in the nature of the logical structures they support and in the nature of their DMLs. There are also very substantial differences in the power, flexibility, and ease of use of their query systems. For the most part, DBMSs fall into one of five categories: hierarchical, shallow network, relational, CODASYL network, and extended network. Although the differences are dealt with extensively beginning in chapter 5, it is worthwhile here to trace the major developments in the database management field.

3.4 MAJOR DATABASE MANAGEMENT DEVELOPMENTS

File management was widely used for application development in the 1960s and is still widely used today. In the late 1960s, database management emerged as an alternative to file management. The impetus behind the rise of database management was the recognized need to overcome the limitations inherent in file management. Within the database management field there have occasionally been major new developments. The impetus behind evolution within the database management field has been the need to improve upon existing database management approaches. This has led to the appearance of DBMS tools that are increasingly developer-friendly.

Major milestones in the evolution of database management are summarized in Fig. 3.6. Database management systems based on the hierarchical approach were among the earliest to appear. The preeminent hierarchical DBMSs are IBM's Data Language/1 (DL/1) and Information Management System (IMS). The former may be regarded as a subset of the latter (see Appendix D). Another fairly widely used hierarchical system is Intel's System 2000. Still other hierarchical systems include Mathematica's Ramis and Information Builder's FOCUS. Hierarchical DBMSs generally date from the late 1960s and early 1970s. Few hierarchical DBMSs have appeared in the last decade.

The late 1960s also witnessed the introduction of the shallow-network approach. The prime example of this approach is Cincom's TOTAL (see Appendix D). One of the unusual aspects of TOTAL is that it is operable in an extremely wide variety of environments. It runs on nearly every major mainframe and on approximately 20 manufacturers' minicomputers. Most DBMSs are designed to run on only one (or a few) types of machines. The only other notable shallow-network DBMS is Hewlett-Packard's IMAGE, which runs only on certain HP machines.

In 1970 E. F. Codd of the IBM Research Laboratories proposed the relational approach to database management. After many years of development, IBM

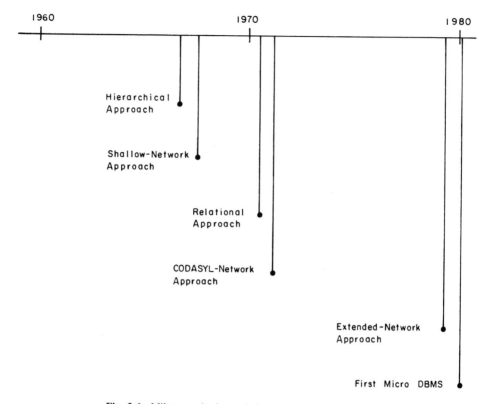

Fig. 3.6   Milestones in the evolution of database management.

released a relational DBMS in 1982. Called SQL/DS, this system should probably be considered as having set the standard for implementations of the relational approach (see Appendix C). To date there are no implementations of the relational approach with widespread usage comparable to IMS–DL/1 or TOTAL.

Just as the relational proposal was based on work initiated in the late 1960s, the CODASYL-network proposal stemmed from an effort that began in the 1960s. However, the CODASYL-network proposal was the result of a group effort, the Data Base Task Group (DBTG). This group included government representatives, computer manufacturers, and computer users. The result of their work was the ''1971 CODASYL DBTG Report,'' which defined the CODASYL-network approach to database management and specified a particular DDL and DML.

The CODASYL-network approach borrowed substantially from the ideas of Charles Bachman, as embodied in Honeywell's Integrated Data Store (IDS). Throughout the 1970s many DBMSs were successfully implemented according to CODASYL's DBTG proposals. With minor variations, these CODASYL-compliant systems support CODASYL's DDL and DML (see Appendix B). Most CODASYL-compliant systems are targeted for a particular manufacturer's hardware. Some of the more prominent CODASYL-compliant DBMSs include: Cullinet's IDMS (for IBM mainframes), Honeywell's IDS II (for Honeywell mainframes), Univac's DMS 1100 (for Univac mainframes), Data General's DBMS (for Data General minis), and Prime's DBMS (for Prime minis).

Ever since they were introduced more than a decade ago, the relational and CODASYL-network approaches have been the subject of an ongoing debate. Both sides quickly dismiss the older hierarchical and shallow-network approaches. As in most debates, each side has certain relative strengths and weaknesses. Relational advocates point to the power of a high-level manipulation language such as SQL. CODASYL-network proponents point to the widespread successes of CODASYL-compliant systems in developing high-quality application systems.

An unfortunate consequence of this debate is a tendency to ignore the possibility of new approaches that supersede the old relational and CODASYL-network approaches. Some observers have implicitly adopted the rather curious premise that all of the major DBMS approaches were invented by 1971 and that only marginal refinements to these old approaches remain possible.

In 1979 a new approach to database management appeared, a departure from relational–CODASYL-network confines. This has come to be known as the *postrelational,* or extended-network, approach. We shall see beginning in Chapter 5 that it not only incorporates the respective strengths of the CODASYL-network and relational approaches but also overcomes many of the limitations and inconveniences inherent in the two older approaches.

By far the most widely installed extended-network database management system is MDBS. This system also is the first viable DBMS to be available for 8- and 16-bit microcomputers. In fact, MDBS is presently operable on many different mini and micro hardware systems ranging from Kaypro and Tandy machines to Cromemco, Dynabyte, and Altos micros, to the IBM Personal Computer and Pixel 68000 micro and through the entire range of PDP-11 models. This unusual portability coupled with the novel extended-network features explains why the MDBS system has in a very short time become one of the most widely installed professional DBMSs.

A final observation on the database management field: there are some DBMSs that do not fit neatly into the five major categories. With respect to a global view of the field, such systems have had a very minor impact, at most. There are also a number of inverted file systems which some authors classify as DBMSs. It is fair to characterize inverted file systems as bridging the gap between file management and database management. With one exception such systems are not dealt with here, since we assume that the reader already has some familiarity with file handling (including inverted files). The exception is Software AG's ADABAS, which dates from the early 1970s. ADABAS is based on inverted file techniques but goes a step further by permitting the explicit coupling of related records in different files (see Appendix D).

3.5 THE PRICE OF A DATABASE MANAGEMENT SYSTEM

In general DBMSs are more expensive than file management systems. This is to be expected because considerably more effort is required to implement a DBMS. Nevertheless, the ongoing productivity gains that are possible using a DBMS can justify the additional one-time expenditure. For most DBMSs, a developer can purchase a perpetual (or monthly) license to use the DBMS on a particular machine. Discounts are usually available for situations in which a developer desires to use the DBMS on more than one machine (e.g., at multiple-computer sites).

For mainframes the minimum DBMS software components (the DDL Analyzer and the DBCS) are commonly priced in the $50,000–100,000 range. If one adds various DBMS utilities (e.g., a query system), the entire DBMS package price can be $250,000 or higher. For minicomputers the minimum components usually fall in the $15,000–50,000 range. With an entire array of software utilities, a mini DBMS is typically priced from $30,000 to $65,000. For micro-computers minimum DBMS components are priced in the neighborhood of $2000 to $6000. With add-on utilities this range becomes $3000–12,000. The annual fee for support and maintenance in each of the three environments is usually about 10–15% of the license price.

3.6 THE MISUSE OF TERMINOLOGY

The vast majority of persons involved with microcomputers have no schooling or experience with the classical database tradition as it evolved in the late 1960s and 1970s, nor do they have a working knowledge or familiarity with major mainframe (or mini) DBMSs. Nevertheless, database management is widely considered to be good and valuable. This combination of factors is largely responsible for frequent misuse of the terms *database* and *database management* among microcomputer users.

Though there are some who ''call a file a file,'' large segments of the micro trade press and numerous micro software vendors replace the term *file* with the term *database*. This abuse of the term *database* is quite understandable when there is little appreciation for the vast differences between the two terms and when there is a desire to be identified with fashionable terminology. Of course, merely referring to files as databases and to file management as database management does nothing to overcome the inherent limitations of file-handling software. A file is a file.

Although no useful purpose is served by calling a file a database, some might argue that it does no harm. This is perhaps true if we consider only the hobbyist subgroup of micro users. Hobbyists are rarely interested in real database management. For instance, it probably makes no difference to the hobbyist if his programming language or other file management system is called a *relational database management system* even though it bears no resemblance to SQL/DS. More generally, however, there are several negative consequences to the loose, flippant use of the term *database*.

When the term is debased to mean (or include) file management, it becomes a nearly meaningless buzzword and a source of considerable confusion. The traditional term *data management* is entirely adequate for broadly referring to the two major categories of data management methods: file management and database management (recall Fig. 3.1). There is no compelling reason why, among micro users, "data management" should be renamed *database management*. Similarly, the traditional term *file management* suffices quite nicely for broadly referring to various methods of managing files (Fig. 3.1). There is no justification for attempting to glorify the long-established notion of file management by calling it *database management*.

The confusion caused by indiscriminant use of the term *database management* hinders the maturation of micro utilization. The user of a file management system may very well have the incorrect perception that he knows a great deal about database management. As long as this perception prevails, the file management user remains unaware of what he is missing. He is oblivious to the power, flexibility, and productivity gains that are possible with real database management. In the short run he unknowingly forgoes the possibility of a substantial competitive advantage over application developers who still practice file management. In the long run, as the sophistication of micro application developers grows (with more developers turning to database management), the file-oriented developer will find it increasingly difficult to remain competitive.

Although mainframe data processing (DP) professionals may find the pretenses of micro file management systems mildly amusing, there is the danger that they may overlook the fact that real DBMSs actually do exist for microcomputers. After briefly examining a few of the micro software packages that purport to be database management systems, a DP manager or professional (e.g., in a Fortune 1000 corporation) can be forgiven for not taking microcomputers seriously. The result is that such professionals are deterred from seeking microcomputer-based solutions to nontrivial application problems. If, however, they were aware of the existence of a micro DBMS with classical mainframe DBMS features, they would be more inclined to investigate the relatively inexpensive micro hardware and software solutions to a variety of nontrivial application problems.

Regardless of whether one prefers loose or precise terminology, selection of an application development tool should be based on the extent to which it satisfies the criteria identified in Chapter 2. In general, database management systems do better on these criteria than file management systems. This fact will be more fully appreciated after studying the chapters that follow. These chapters provide a comprehensive description of what is possible with micro database management.

3.7 SUMMARY

In this chapter we introduced the field of database management, which arose in response to inconveniences and shortcomings inherent in file management systems. The newly emerging all-in-one systems were also described. We viewed a database as a collection of records of many different types, integrated according to a single logical structure that allows redundancy to be eliminated (or at least substantially controlled).

A database is not merely a file or collection of files, each containing occurrences of only one record type. A DBMS consists of the software that allows the definition of database structure and the manipulation of data organized according to a logical structure. A DBMS supports a data description language (DDL) and a data manipulation language (DML). A DDL is used to specify the logical structure of a database. A DML consists of commands that can be invoked from within the confines of a host language, thereby extending the data-handling capabilities of the host language beyond file management. Most DBMSs also have some kind of query language interface.

A brief account of the evolution of the database management field was provided. DBMSs progressed from the hierarchical and shallow-network approaches of the late 1960s to the relational and CODASYL-network approaches of the early 1970s. The most recent innovation was the extended-network approach, which retains the strengths of the older approaches and overcomes many of their weaknesses. The major differences among these five approaches will be examined in detail beginning in Chapter 5.

In this chapter we took considerable care to stress the quantum gap between file management and database management. There is a fairly widespread tendency among micro users to employ garbled terminology when referring to data-handling tools. To prevent misinterpretation, confusion, and a loss of credibility, the use of technically accurate terminology is recommended (and is adopted throughout this book).

It is fairly easy to detect when *database management* is being used in a loose sense to describe a file management system. First, a DBMS is not a programming language. Second, during data manipulation, do we have to think in primitive terms of adding records to a file, retrieving records from a file, merging two files based on redundant data values, etc.? If so, we are manipulating files rather than a database. Third, does the system documentation use the terms *file* and *database* interchangeably? Can we substitute the word *file* where the documentation uses the term *database*? If so, then we simply have a renaming of file management. Fourth, do we need to know about various kinds of files, such as files to hold data values, files for indices, files for record formats? This is typical of many file management systems.

These are a few of the tell-tale signs of a file management system. There are many subtler yet important distinctions which will become apparent throughout this book, as we take a much more detailed look at just what should be expected of a DBMS. Since this book focuses on how to use classical database management, file management systems are dismissed from any further consideration. These first three chapters have sketched the background against which one can understand the role, the significance, and the utilization of micro database management.

RELATED READINGS

R. N. Aarons, Wising up with KnowledgeMan, *PC* **3,** No. 4 (1984).

M. M. Astrahan *et al.,* System R. relational approach to data base management, *ACM Trans. Database Systems* **1,** No. 2 (1976).

R. H. Bonczek, C. W. Holsapple, and A. B. Whinston, "Foundations of Decision Support Systems," Academic Press, New York, 1981.

J. Bradley, "File and Data Base Techniques," Holt, Rinehart, and Winston, New York, 1982.

A. F. Cardenas, "Data Base Management Systems," Allyn & Bacon, Boston, 1979.

D. D. Chamberlin *et al.,* "SEQUEL 2: A unified approach to data definition, manipulation, and control," *IBM J. Res. Devel.* **20,** No. 6 (1976).

Cincom Systems, Inc., "TOTAL/8 Reference Manual," Cincinnati, Ohio, 1982.

CODASYL, "Data Base Task Group Report," Assoc. Comput. Mach., New York, 1971.

CODASYL DDLC, "DDL Journal of Development," Canadian Federal Government, Hull, Quebec, 1978.

E. F. Codd, A relational model of data for large shared data banks, *Comm. ACM* **14,** No. 3 (1970).

E. F. Codd *et al.,* The data base debate, *Computerworld* **16,** No. 37 (1982).

Cullinet Corporation, "IDMS Systems Overview," Wellesley, Massachusetts, 1979.

D. Gradwell (ed.), "Database—The 2nd Generation: State of the Art Report," Pergamon, Oxford, 1982.

C. W. Holsapple, SQL on the IBM PC, *PC Tech J.* **1,** No. 3 (1983).

C. W. Holsapple, From dBASE II to the Knowledge Manager, *Data Based Advisor* **2,** No. 2–3 (1984).

C. W. Holsapple and A. B. Whinston, Software tools for knowledge fusion, *Computerworld* **17,** No. 15 (1983).

C. W. Holsapple and A. B. Whinston, Aspects of integrated software, *in* "Proceedings of the National Computer Conference, Las Vegas," 1984.

IBM Corporation, "IMS/VS General Information Manual," IBM Document GH20-1260-4, 1977.

IBM Corporation, "SQL/Data System General Information Manual," IBM Document GH24-5012-0, 1981.

B. Machrone, MDBS: A database management system, *Microsystems* **3,** No. 3 (1982).

J. Martin, "Computer Data-Base Organization," Prentice-Hall, Englewood Cliffs, New Jersey, 1975.

T. W. Olle, "The CODASYL Approach to Data Base Management," Wiley, New York, 1978.

I. Palmer, "Data Base Systems: A Practical Reference," QED Information Sciences, Wellesley, Massachusetts, 1975.

J. W. Walker, KnowledgeMan, *Byte* **9,** No. 2 (1984).

EXERCISES

1. Discuss and compare file management and database management systems.
2. List five DBMS approaches and discuss representative examples of each.
3. Develop a model for a new DBMS approach and compare with existing DBMS methods.
4. Describe the inadequacies and limitations of file management systems.
5. What are DMLs and DDLs? Explain their role with respect to DBMSs.
6. Explain how each of the KnowledgeMan components is important for build-

ing a DSS. For each component, describe its relationship to a DSSs knowledge system, problem-processing system, and language system.
7.   Elaborate on the role of KnowledgeMan for a microcomputer that serves as an intelligent terminal.

PROJECT

As a result of the previous stage in the project, you now have a rough specification of what your application system must do. Operationalization of the proposed system is discussed in Chapters 4–12. Consider your application system in terms of the end-user needs presented in Chapter 2. Which of the needs pertaining to data handling are most important for your application system and which are of lesser importance? Are there other significant end-user needs that are peculiar to your application?

Chapter 4

FUNDAMENTALS OF LOGICAL STRUCTURING

It is important to appreciate the distinction between data and the logical structure according to which data are organized. The objectives of this chapter are to make that distinction clear and to give a basic understanding of logical data structures. All manipulation of data within a database depends on a knowledge of the logical structure of the database. All commands to store, modify, extract, delete, or otherwise manipulate data are stated in terms of that logical structure. They do not depend on a knowledge of the physical structure of data, such as where a data value is physically located or how one data value is physically related to another. We shall therefore avoid the issue of physical structuring until Chapter 11, after a presentation of some fundamental data manipulation commands.

The logical structure of a database is called a *schema*. A schema shows the kinds of data that can exist in a database and how those kinds of data are logically (i.e., conceptually) related to each other. For instance, the schema for an order-entry application system might show that the database contains data about customers, products, and orders. Furthermore, it would show that customer data are logically related to data about orders (e.g., placing orders). Similarly, the fact that orders refer to particular products would be represented also as a relationship in the schema. A schema can be regarded as a blueprint that portrays both the kinds of data used in building a database and the logical relationships that exist among the various kinds of data.

The major approaches to logical data structuring (relational, hierarchical, shal-low-network, CODASYL-network, extended-network) differ primarily in terms of the facilities they make available for representing data relationships. On the other hand, they are very similar in the facilities they offer for representing the kinds of data involved in an application.

4.1   DATA ITEMS

The fundamental schema building block for each of the five approaches is the *data item*. A data item identifies a kind of data that is not decomposed into more elementary types of data. A schema can contain many data items each of which is given a name when the schema is designed.

In the database schema for an order-entry application, one data item might be named ORDERNO (to represent order numbers). An order number will not consist of more elementary kinds of data. Another data item in the schema might be CUSTNAME (to represent customer names). Defining a single data item for customer name data implies that we are not interested in decomposing customer names into first and last names. If we are sometimes interested in dealing with last name data separately from first name data, we could define two data items (say, LNAME and FNAME) rather than CUSTNAME.

For each data item existing in a database schema, the database itself can contain many occurrences of that data item. For instance, a database might contain many order numbers, and many customer names. An occurrence of a data item is called a data item occurrence or, simply, a *data value*. Data items exist in a database schema, while their data values exist in the database. As an example, five occurrences of ORDERNO might be 101, 103, 104, 107, and 109.

In some database management systems (DBMSs) a data item is called a field and in others it is called an attribute. When a data item is defined for a schema, the schema designer gives it a name, specifies the type of its occurrences (e.g., integer, character, or real), and specifies the size of its occurrences. For instance, ORDERNO might be declared to be of the type integer with a size of 2 bytes. This means that each occurrence of ORDERNO is an integer value stored in 2 bytes.

While all DBMSs identify a data item with a name, type, and size, the more sophisticated DBMSs allow a schema designer to specify still other charac-teristics. These include read and write access restrictions for a data item, syn-onyms for a data item, whether the occurrences of the data item are to be stored in encrypted form, and a range of feasible values for those occurrences. These and other advanced characteristics are fully described in Chapter 10.

Fig. 4.1 CUSTOMER record type.

4.2 RECORD TYPES

It is important in a schema to indicate which data items are related to each other. One method for depicting data item relationships, which is common to all five approaches to logical data structuring, is a *record type*. A record type is a named group of data items. As an example, the CUSTNAME, CUSTADDR (customer address), and CUSTPHN (telephone) data items might be grouped into a record type named CUSTOMER.

For each record type defined in a schema, the database itself can contain many occurrences of that record type. A *record occurrence* (or record) consists of one data item occurrence for each of the data items of a record type. Thus each occurrence of the CUSTOMER record type would consist of a customer name, a customer address, and a customer telephone number. A record type, consisting of data items, exists in a schema. A record occurrence, consisting of data values, exists in a database. In some DBMSs a record type is called a segment type; in others, a relation or table *structure*. Alternative terms for record occurrences are records, segments, and tuples.

For reasons of convenience, schemas are frequently depicted pictorially. As shown in Fig. 4.1, a record type is represented by a rectangle enclosing the names of its data items. It is also useful to depict record occurrences pictorially. Figure 4.2 shows three occurrences of CUSTOMER, with the data values of each being enclosed in an ellipse. These record occurrences are *not* part of a schema. Diagrams showing record occurrences will be referred to as occurrence structures. They are a conceptual representation of database contents and imply nothing about the physical organization or placement of record occurrences.

| Bob Smith
Fifth Ave,New York
212-755-4880 | Frank Zieman
Tibbs St, Indianapolis
317-291-3907 | Steve Moore
Rosemont Dr,Chicago
312-292-4738 | CUSTOMER |

Fig. 4.2 CUSTOMER record occurrences.

Fig. 4.3 Relationship by redundancy (CUSTNO).

4.3 RELATIONSHIPS BETWEEN RECORD TYPES

The primary difference among the five approaches to logical data structuring is their various methods for representing a relationship between two record types. The method used allows us to clearly distinguish among the five major approaches to database management. Consider the case of customers and orders. If we define a CUSTOMER record type and an ORDER record type, then how can we represent (in the schema) the fact that customers place orders?

One solution, which is permissible with most DBMSs, involves the redundant definition of the same data item in the two record types. As shown in Fig. 4.3, we can define the CUSTNO (customer identification number) data item to be in both the CUSTOMER and ORDER record types. Thus the customer number will be stored with the order information in each occurrence of ORDER. An occurrence structure is shown in Fig. 4.4. Suppose we are interested in a particular order, say, order number 103. Then we can find the order 103 occurrence, and extract the customer number (2093338). Next we use this data value to locate the CUSTOMER occurrence with a CUSTNO data value of 2093338. Finally, we can determine the customer's name and address.

This is a symmetric kind of processing. That is, given a customer name, we can find all orders placed by that customer through the use of the common CUSTNO data values. Thus, through the processing outlined, redundant data items provide a method of relating occurrences of different record types.

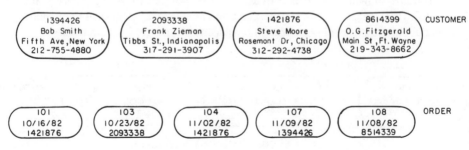

Fig. 4.4 Occurrence structure for Fig. 4.3.

Fig. 4.5   The named relationship PLACES.

As an alternative to representing a relationship with redundant data items, some DBMSs allow the schema designer to merely declare that a relationship exists between two record types. Each such relationship is given a name that describes the nature of the relationship. No redundancy of data items is needed. For example, to represent the relationship between CUSTOMER and ORDER, the schema designer could declare a relationship called PLACES. In a schema diagram, the PLACES relationship is represented by an arrow as shown in Fig. 4.5. It is immediately clear that the database for this schema contains customer and order data and that it keeps track of which customers place which orders. The schema contains no redundant data items.

The foregoing example is an illustration of what is called a *one-to-many* named relationship. One customer can place many orders, but a given order is not placed by more than one customer. This kind of relationship is extremely common in practice. When a one-to-many relationship between two record types is specified in a schema, one record type is called the *owner* and the other record type is called the *member*. The named relationship itself is called a 1:N *set*. An occurrence of the owner record type of a 1:N set can be associated with many (N ≥ 0) occurrences of the member record type. An occurrence of the member record type of a 1:N set can be associated with no more than one (0 or 1) occurrence of the owner record type.

In a schema diagram, the arrow is used to indicate a 1:N set. The arrow always points toward the member record type. In Fig. 4.5, the member record type for PLACES is ORDER and the owner record type is CUSTOMER. It would be incorrect for the arrow to point from ORDER to CUSTOMER, because this would imply that an order is associated with many customers and a customer is associated with at most one order.

An example occurrence structure based on the schema of Fig. 4.5 appears in Fig. 4.6. This shows that T. Ferguson has placed three orders (102, 105, 106) and that D. Lehr has placed two orders (112, 123). Notice that no member record occurrence is related to more than one owner occurrence. This is not allowed, since it would violate the definition of a 1:N set.

The lines between record occurrences represent occurrence relationships, which are consistent with the 1:N set PLACES that exists in the schema. They

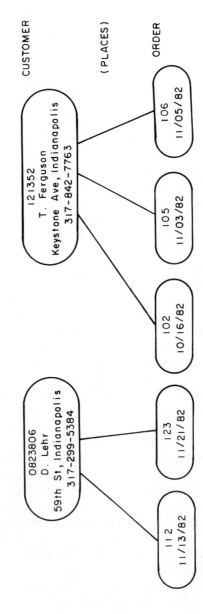

Fig. 4.6 Occurrence structure for Fig. 4.5.

imply nothing about how relationships between record occurrences are physically implemented. Knowledge of physical implementation is not necessary for data manipulation.

As presented in Chapters 6 and 7, there are data manipulation commands that allow us to find any member record that is associated with a given owner record or to find the owner record that is associated with a given member record. For instance, it is a simple matter to find that order 112 was placed by D. Lehr or that T. Ferguson placed order 102.

4.4   VARIETIES OF LOGICAL DATA STRUCTURING

We have seen how a 1:N set can be used to represent a one-to-many relationship between two record types. Depending on the nature of the application being developed, a schema will typically have anywhere from a few record types (for simple applications) to fifty or more (for extensive applications). The five main approaches to logical data structuring can be differentiated on the basis of the restrictions they place on using 1:N sets to represent numerous record type interrelationships.

The Relational Approach

This approach to logical structuring entirely prohibits the use of 1:N sets. The only means available for representing a relationship between two record types is with data item redundancy (recall Figs. 4.3 and 4.4). This limitation presents several problems for an application developer. Cross referencing by redundancy does not preserve the integrity of one-to-many relationships, even though such relationships are extremely common in practice. It is clear from Fig. 4.3 that there is no structural mechanism to prevent a given order from being associated with more than one customer.

Whenever an inter-record type relationship is represented by data item redundancy, we are structurally allowing a *many-to-many* relationship to exist between the two record types. This means that an occurrence of one record type can be associated with many occurrences of the other record type, and vice versa. The field redundancy approach to representing relationships does not allow us to easily distinguish between one-to-many relationships and many-to-many relationships.

The schema in Fig. 4.3 shows that CUSTOMER and ORDER are related, but gives no clue that this relationship is anything other than a many-to-many relationship. Of course, the application developer must somehow maintain a one-to-many relationship among occurrences of CUSTOMER and ORDER in the database. In attempting to overcome the problems of a lack of structural integrity and a lack of structural descriptive power, researchers have devised a complex theory of normal forms (see Appendix D). If a relational schema is designed to conform to the third (or higher) normal form, then it will generally portray one-to-many and many-to-many relationships in distinctly different ways. Because relational implementations often do not require adherence to third normal form designs, the issue of guaranteeing structural integrity is often the responsibility of the developer.

Another difficulty with representing relationships through redundancy is that it forces an application developer to view the database as if it were a collection of files. This is not a significant drawback for trivial applications involving only a few record types. Perhaps this is why most database textbooks illustrate the relational approach with schemas of only three to five record types. However, for realistic applications involving more than a few record types and relationships, redundancy quickly becomes cumbersome.

Redundancy also gives no clue as to the semantics of each relationship. For instance, Fig. 4.3 shows that a relationship between CUSTOMER and ORDER exists, but it does not tell us the meaning of the relationship. Does it refer to customers placing orders, inquiring about orders, or cancelling orders? The schema does not, by itself, answer this question.

Finally, note that any data manipulation involving record occurrences of more than one record type requires the specification of a series of one or more matching clauses (e.g., matching CUSTNO in CUSTOMER with CUSTNO in ORDER) rather than concisely naming the set(s) involved (e.g., PLACES). Redundancy forces an application developer to use a relatively simplistic means for representing real world relationships that are not at all simple.

The Hierarchical Approach

Hierarchical data structures allow a schema designer to use 1:N sets if he or she so wishes. However, there is a very severe restriction on the way in which they can be used. No record type can be the member of more than one 1:N set. A record type is allowed to be the owner of many 1:N sets. Figure 4.7 depicts a hierarchical structure composed of three record types and two 1:N sets. A customer can place many orders and an order can consist of many order lines. A given order line exists in no more than one order and a given order is placed by no more than one customer. The integrity of the two one-to-many relationships is automatically enforced by the structural specification of two 1:N sets.

What data items should be placed in the ORDLINE record type? From Fig. 4.8

CUSTOMER
ORDER
ORDLINE
(PLACES)
(CONTAINS)

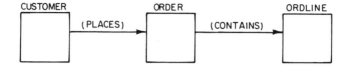

Fig. 4.7 Schema with two sets.

we see that an order line consists of a quantity, the product number, its description, and unit price. What kind of conceptual relationship exists between a product and an order line? An order line references only one product, however, a given product could be referenced on many different order lines in many different orders. Thus there is conceptually a one-to-many relationship between product and order line. This is represented by the 1:N set called REF in Fig. 4.9. Combining the schema fragments from Figs. 4.7 and 4.9, we obtain the schema of Fig. 4.10.

Of course, this schema is *not* supported under the hierarchical approach, since it contains a record type (ORDLINE) that is the member of two 1:N sets.

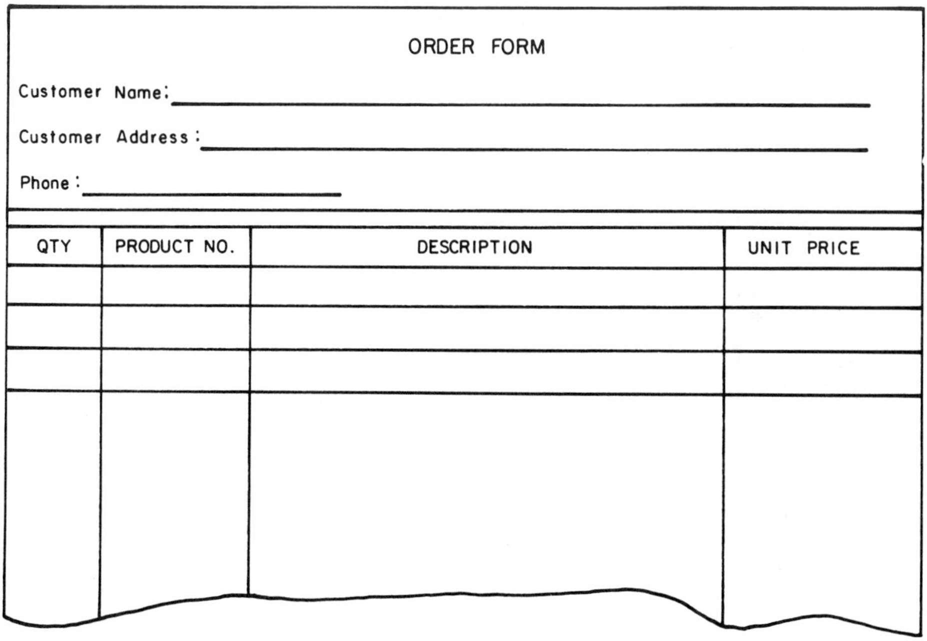

ORDER FORM
Customer Name:
Customer Address:
Phone:
QTY
PRODUCT NO.
DESCRIPTION
UNIT PRICE

Fig. 4.8 Sample order form.

Fig. 4.9 Representing the product–order line relationship.

One way around this limitation of the hierarchical approach is to define a schema that includes redundant data in the database. This has been accomplished in the hierarchical structure of Fig. 4.11. What is conceptually a one-to-many relationship in Fig. 4.9 collapses here into a single record type (ORDLINE1). Since there is one occurrence of ORDLINE1 for each order line, the same product data will be repeated over and over again in ORDLINE1 record occurrences. If there are 56 order lines that reference a particular product, then the database will contain 56 ORDLINE1 occurrences that have identical data values for PRODCODE, PDESC, and UNTPRICE. Aside from the storage cost of such redundancy, it also makes the task of maintaining data consistency more difficult. If the identifying number of that product changes, 56 occurrences of ORDLINE1 must be modified.

A second method for circumventing the hierarchical limitation is to revert to redundant data items, as shown in Fig. 4.12. We create two hierarchies, one consisting of a single record type without any 1:N sets. The two hierarchies are considered to constitute the schema for a single database, just as multiple disjoint record types form the relational schema for a single database. This solution has

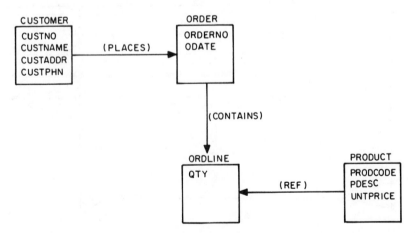

Fig. 4.10 Combination of schemas from Figs. 4.7 and 4.9.

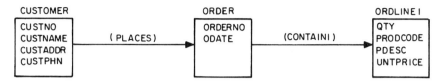

Fig. 4.11 Schema that forces redundant product data.

an advantage over Fig. 4.11, in that it restricts data value redundancy to occurrences of PRODCODE. The product code of our product will exist in 57 record occurrences in the database (in 56 occurrences of ORDLINE2 and in one occurrence of PROD). The unit price and product description data values for product exists only once in the entire database (in an occurrence of PROD). Repetition of the PRODCODE data item in two record types has the effect of representing the fact of a relationship between PROD and ORDLINE2.

Data item redundancy is employed as a substitute for the inability of the hierarchical approach to use a 1:N set for representing the needed relationship. The problems with using data item redundancy for representing relationships that were discussed earlier apply here as well.

The term "1:N set" is usually not used in hierarchical systems when referring to the schematic representation of a one-to-many relationship. It is more commonly referred to as a parent–child relationship. Parent is synonomous with owner and child with member. Each parent–child relationship is typically unnamed. The semantics of the relationship are left to the imagination or documented separately from the hierarchical schema. Nontrivial applications that can naturally be represented with hierarchical schemas (i.e., without forced redundancy) are very rare in practice.

The Shallow-Network Approach

This approach to logical data structuring allows a schema designer to use 1:N sets if desired. However, there is again a severe restriction on the way in which

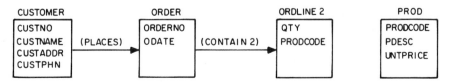

Fig. 4.12 Redundant data item to represent a relationship.

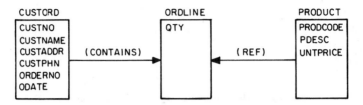

Fig. 4.13   Schema that forces redundant order data.

they can be used. In a shallow-network schema, no record type that is the owner of a 1:N set can be the member record type of another 1:N set. Furthermore, it is not permissive to have two 1:N sets between the same two record types.

The schema of Fig. 4.7 is not allowed in the shallow-network approach. The ORDER record type is the member of one 1:N set and the owner of another. The schemas of Figs. 4.10–4.12 are also not supported with the shallow-network approach. How then can this situation be represented in a shallow-network schema?

One method is to collapse two record types together, as shown in Fig. 4.13. This forces considerable redundancy into the record occurrences of the database. If a customer has placed fifty orders, then the database contains fifty CUSTORD record occurrences with the same customer data.

Another method is depicted in Fig. 4.14, where an artificial or dummy record type (called DUM) has replaced the PLACES set. This record type is called a dummy because it contains no data items that are not already in another record

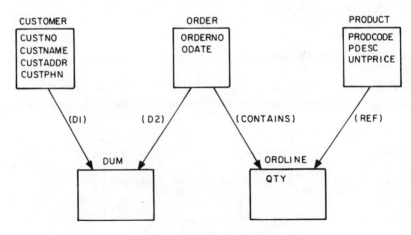

Fig. 4.14   Shallow-network schema.

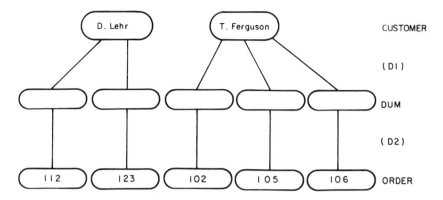

Fig. 4.15   Occurrence structure for a schema with an artificial record type.

type. Two new 1:N sets have been added, each one with DUM as its member. The resultant schema qualifies as a shallow-network schema and it still allows us to determine which customer has placed which order. From the occurrence structure in Fig. 4.15 note that D. Lehr is related to orders 112 and 123 through two DUM record occurrences; T. Ferguson is associated with orders 102, 105, and 106 by means of three data-less DUM record occurrences.

Observe that this usage of an artificial record type, which is forced on us by the shallow-network limitation, destroys the integrity of the one-to-many relationship between CUSTOMER and ORDER. Since D1 is a 1:N set, each occurrence of CUSTOMER can be related to many occurrences of DUM, each of which can be related (via D2) to a different occurrence of ORDER. Structurally, this means that we are properly able to associate many occurrences of ORDER with a CUSTOMER occurrence.

However, D2 is a 1:N set, so each occurrence of ORDER can be associated with many occurrences of DUM, and each of those can be related (via D1) to a different occurrence of CUSTOMER. Structurally, there is nothing to prevent us from indirectly associating many occurrences of CUSTOMER with an ORDER occurrence. Thus the integrity of a one-to-many relationship between customers and orders is not guaranteed by the shallow-network structure. There is also a substantial loss of efficiency and structural simplicity when artificial record types are used to represent one-to-many relationships.

In most shallow-network systems the term *linkage path* is used instead of 1:N sets, the owner record type is called a master record type, and the member record type, a detail record type. Applications that can naturally (i.e., without artificial record types or forced redundancy) be represented with shallow-network schemas are not particularly common in practice.

The CODASYL-Network Approach

Nearly all restrictions on the way in which 1:N sets can be used in a schema are removed under this approach. Any record type can be the member of numerous 1:N sets; it can simultaneously be the owner of many 1:N sets. Also, many 1:N sets can exist between any pair of record types. The schema of Fig. 4.10 is valid for CODASYL DBMSs. In fact, every schema shown so far in this chapter is allowable as a CODASYL-network schema. However, they are not all advisable. Why should we incur the disadvantages inherent in the schemas of Figs. 4.3, 4.11–4.14, when they are alleviated by the schema of Fig. 4.10?

There is still one restriction on the use of 1:N sets in a CODASYL-network schema. Cyclic structures such as the two shown in Fig. 4.16 are *not* permitted in CODASYL-network schemas; nor for that matter are they allowed in relational, hierarchical, or shallow-network schemas. Although the CODASYL-network approach offers great flexibility in using 1:N sets, it does have a significant shortcoming beyond the absence of cyclic structures: its inability to represent many-to-many relationships directly.

Consider the schema of Fig. 4.10. Note that the two 1:N sets CONTAINS and REF automatically capture the fact that there is conceptually a many-to-many relationship between products and orders (an order can contain many products and a product can be referenced in many orders). Because it is a 1:N set, CONTAINS allows a given ORDER occurrence to be associated with many ORDLINE occurrences, each of which can be related to a particular PRODUCT occurrence (via the REF 1:N set). Conversely, REF allows a given product occurrence to be associated with many ORDLINE occurrences and therefore (via CONTAINS) with many ORDER occurrences.

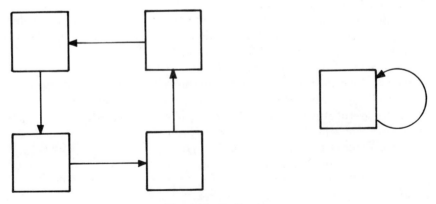

Fig. 4.16 Cyclic schemas.

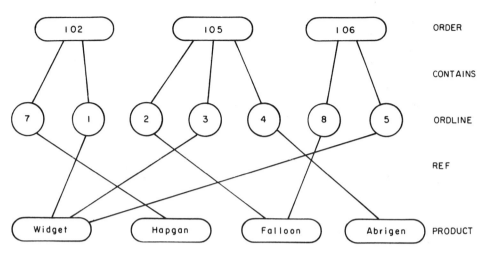

Fig. 4.17   Occurrence structure of a many-to-many relationship.

Thus the REF and CONTAINS 1:N sets, together with the intervening ORDLINE record type, represent not only the one-to-many relationships between orders and order lines and between products and order lines, but also the many-to-many relationship that exists between orders and products. The occurrence structure of Fig. 4.17 clearly shows which products are associated with any order and which orders are associated with any product (e.g., Widget is associated with all three orders, while at the same time order 102 is associated with Widget and Hapgan).

Now suppose that we also need to know which suppliers can supply which products. A SUPPLIER record type, containing data items pertaining to supplier name and location, is added to the schema. A supplier can supply many products, and a product can be supplied by many suppliers. This is a many-to-many relationship and therefore cannot be represented with a 1:N set. The CODASYL-network approach for representing this relationship makes use of an artificial record type and two 1:N sets as shown in Fig. 4.18, where ARTIF is an artificial record type having no data items. Occurrences of ARTIF physically exist in the database, but they contain no data values. The example occurrence structure shown in Fig. 4.19 illustrates that there can be many SUPPLIER occurrences (indirectly) associated with a particular PRODUCT occurrence and many PRODUCT occurrences (indirectly) associated with a particular SUPPLIER occurrence.

An alternative, though inadvisable, method for representing this many-to-many relationship is to rely on data item redundancy rather than the two 1:N sets, CAN and SUPPLY. As depicted in Fig. 4.20, SUPNAME is repeated in both

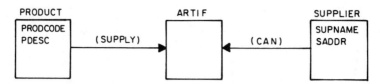

Fig. 4.18   Using an artificial record type to represent a many-to-many relationship.

ARTIF1 and SUPPLIER; PRODCODE is repeated in both ARTIF1 and PROD-
UCT. Of course, adopting this method incurs all of the previously mentioned
problems that are inherent in using redundant data items to represent relationships.

Although this method is not recommended for users of the CODASYL-network approach, it is the method that is generally recommended for users of the
relational approach. If the schema of Fig. 4.20 is viewed as being a relational
schema (rather than CODASYL-network), it adheres to the relational *third normal form* (3NF) mentioned earlier. A digression into the definitions of various
relational normal forms is not called for here (see Appendix D). It suffices to say
that relational theorists generally regard 3NF as one of the "best" forms for a
relational schema design.

The Extended-Network Approach

The most recent innovation in database structuring is the extended-network
approach. Every type of schema allowed with the older structuring approaches is

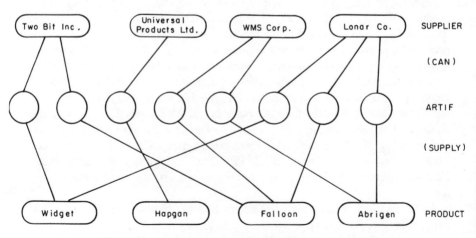

Fig. 4.19   Occurrence structure for the artificial record type.

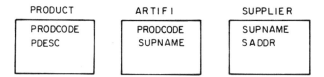

Fig. 4.20 Using redundant data items to represent a many-to-many relationship.

also permitted by the extended-network approach. Beyond these, the extended-network approach supports cyclic structures and other kinds of sets (i.e., named relationships), aside from 1:N sets. One of these different types of sets allows the design of extended-network schemas without ever being forced to resort to artificial record types or data item redundancy. A discussion of these and other extended-network features is deferred until Chapter 10, where advanced data structuring features are described.

4.5 SET ORDER

Because any owner record occurrence can be related to many member record occurrences, we can specify an access order for these members. For instance, when we access T. Ferguson's orders we may want to obtain them based on the order number (102 first, then 105, and then 106). If so, we would declare the *member order* for the set PLACES to be SORTED on the basis of the ORDER-NO data item. This declaration is made when the schema is formally defined with the data description language (DDL). All orders for a given customer can then be easily accessed from the lowest order number to the highest. When the member order of a set is declared to be sorted, we must specify a *sort key* that consists of one or more data items in the member record type. In the above example, the sort key consisted of a single data item: ORDERNO.

Alternative member orders (other than sorted) can be specified for a 1:N set. These include FIFO, LIFO, and IMMATERIAL. FIFO (first-in-first-out) means that the first member record occurrence to be accessed is the chronologically first occurrence connected to the given owner occurrence, the second occurrence to be accessed is the chronologically next occurrence connected, and so forth. For example, suppose PLACES is declared to be FIFO, rather than SORTED. Assume that 105 was the number of the first order connected to T. Ferguson, 102 was second, and 106 was third. Then for purposes of access, 105 would be the first member of T. Ferguson, 102 the second, and 106 the last.

LIFO (last-in-first-out) member ordering is the reverse of FIFO. The chronologically last member connected becomes the first member to be accessed. The

Fig. 4.21   Two different relationships between the same pair of record types.

chronologically first member record connected to a given owner record becomes the last member to be accessed. FIFO ordering is similar to the function of a queue, whereas LIFO ordering is similar to the function of a stack.

If the member order of a set is declared to be IMMATERIAL, then the access order for member record occurrences associated with a given owner record is arbitrary. Two other kinds of member ordering are NEXT and PRIOR. These are discussed in Chapter 8.

It must be emphasized that only one member order can be declared for a given 1:N set. Suppose that for our application we need to be able to sometimes access any customer's orders on a LIFO basis. On other occasions we need to be able to access them SORTED by ascending ORDERNO. This processing is supported by declaring *two* 1:N sets between CUSTOMER and ORDER. As shown in Fig. 4.21 each has CUSTOMER as its owner and ORDER as its member. The LPLACES set is declared to have a LIFO member order, while the SPLACES set is declared to have a member order that is SORTED on ORDERNO. For a given customer (i.e., owner occurrence), the first member occurrence of LPLACES will always be the ORDER occurrence most recently added to the database for that customer, while the first member occurrence of SPLACES will always be that customer's ORDER occurrence having the lowest value for ORDERNO.

Only CODASYL-network and extended-network systems allow multiple 1:N sets between the same two record types. Most hierarchical and shallow-network systems do not support all four types of member ordering discussed above. Some support SORTED ordering only.

4.6   SYSTEM-OWNED SETS

System is a special record type that has only one occurrence. This occurrence is automatically created by the DBMS when a database is initialized. The system record occurrence has no data values. Its purpose is to serve as a starting point for data manipulation. In a schema, there can be many 1:N sets having system as their owner; system is never the member of any set.

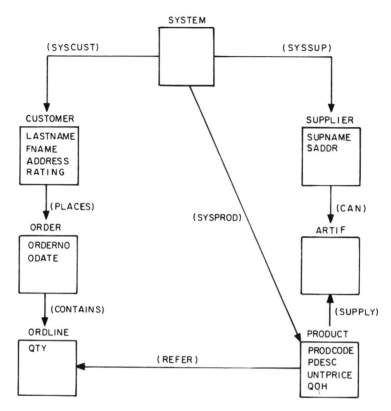

Fig. 4.22   System-owned sets.

In Fig. 4.22 three *system-owned sets* are shown: SYSCUST, SYSPROD, and SYSSUP. These have the CUSTOMER, PRODUCT, and SUPPLIER record types as their respective members. In terms of data manipulation, this means that any CUSTOMER occurrence can rapidly be found through SYSCUST. Similarly, any PRODUCT occurrence can be accessed rapidly through SYSPROD and any SUPPLIER occurrence can be accessed rapidly through SYSSUP. An ORDER occurrence can be accessed by first accessing the CUSTOMER occurrence for the customer who placed that order. If we include in our schema another system-owned set having ORDER as its member record type, then we could access an ORDER occurrence without first accessing its related CUSTOMER occurrence. Because a schema can contain many system-owned sets, we simply indicate each one by enclosing its name in parentheses next to its member record type. This is illustrated in Fig. 4.23.

As there is only one system occurrence in a database, every system-owned set

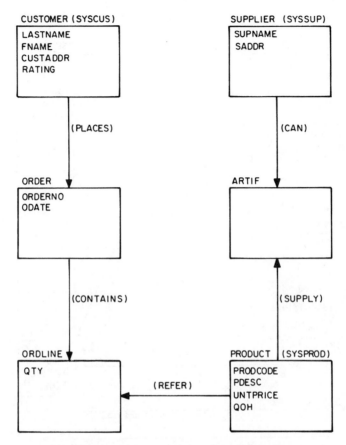

Fig. 4.23   Standard representation of system-owned sets.

represents a one-to-many relationship. Just as with any other 1:N set, the schema designer can specify a member order for a system-owned set. In fact, more than one system-owned set with the same member record type can exist in a schema. Suppose we sometimes desire to access products alphabetically based on PDESC, sometimes in sorted order based on PRODCODE, and sometimes on the basis of their unit prices, then we could declare three system-owned sets in place of the one shown in Fig. 4.23. One of these would be sorted on PDESC, another on PRODCODE, and the third would be sorted on UNTPRICE.

A system-owned set is not the only mechanism that exists for initially access-ing a record occurrence in a database. Furthermore, not all DBMSs make use of system-owned sets. However, nearly all have some comparable means for indi-cating "where" data manipulation can begin; i.e., for indicating those record types whose occurrences can be accessed without having previously accessed occurrences of other record types.

In the case of hierarchical systems, this immediate access is provided to occurrences of the record type that is not the member of any set. In some hierarchical systems, the schema can be defined to also allow immediate entry into a database through occurrences of record types further down in the hierarchical schema. In shallow-network systems, an occurrence of any record type that is the member of a set cannot be accessed unless its related owner occurrence has already been accessed. In a relational system, an occurrence of any record type can be accessed without first accessing a related occurrence of another record type. In CODASYL-network and extended-network systems, the schema designer can select any (or all) record types for immediate access.

4.7 FORMALLY SPECIFYING A SCHEMA

Once a schema has been designed in pictorial form, it must be formally specified in terms of a DDL. As explained in Chapter 3, this DDL specification is input to a program (called a DDL Analyzer or DDL Translator) that analyzes the specification and, if no errors are found, creates an internal data dictionary, and initializes the database. The analysis consists of checking for syntactic correctness of the DDL specification. It also checks to determine whether the logical data structuring rules have been observed. For instance, a DDL specification for a CODASYL-network DBMS would be rejected if it contained a 1:N set with the same record type as both owner and member.

The data description process will be illllustrated here with the MDBS DDL. MDBS is a particular DBMS of the extended-network variety. Because the MDBS DDL supports numerous data structuring features that are more advanced than those previously described in this chapter, only a *subset* of the MDBS DDL is presented here. This subset is sufficient for defining CODASYL-network, shallow-network, and hierarchical schemas; of course, relationships through data item redundancy are also allowed. The more advanced MDBS DDL features are examined in Chapters 10 and 11. These extensions involve the support of extended-network schemas, data integrity, data security, and various performance control facilities.

It must be stressed that one should not expect to find all of the MDBS DDL features in the DDL of another DBMS; nor should one expect all DDLs to have the same syntactic style as the MDBS DDL. Nevertheless, the experience of using the MDBS DDL should allow a rapid acclimation to the DDLs of most other DBMSs.

Since this book is not intended to be a reference manual, all of the possible

MDBS DDL options, abbreviations, and defaults are not discussed. Full details appear in the MDBS "Data Base Design Reference Manual"; a formal description of the language is provided in Appendix E. What is presented here is sufficient for the creation of syntactically correct MDBS DDL specifications. Unless otherwise indicated, DDL will henceforth refer to the MDBS DDL.

Rather than an abstract presentation of the DDL, we shall convey the DDL rules and syntax by means of commenting on the example DDL specification depicted in Fig. 4.24. This DDL specification is consistent with the schema picture of Fig. 4.23. The DDL specification for this schema is nearly self-explanatory. It consists of several kinds of sections. First, there is the identification section, which simply identifies the database by giving it a name. A user section follows, giving the names and respective passwords of those who are to be allowed access to the database.

```
/************************Example MDBS DDL Specification************************/
/ ***************************Database Identification ***************************/
database name is ORDERDB
/************************User and Password Definitions************************/
user is "Deb Lehr" with OBOE
user is Ferguson with "7763A TASHI"
/ ***************************Record Type Definitions ***************************/
record name is CUSTOMER
        item name is LASTNAME      string 18
        item name is FNAME         character 8
        item name is CUSTADDR      string 60
        item name is RATING        integer 1
record name is ORDER
        item name is ORDERNO       unsigned 2
        item name is ODATE         date
record name is ORDLINE
        item name is QTY           unsigned 1
record name is PRODUCT
        item name is PRODCODE      character 4
        item name is PDESC         string 25
        item name is UNTPRICE      idec 5,2
        item name is QOH           unsigned 2
record name is ARTIF
        /* no data items */
record name is SUPPLIER
        item name is SUPNAME       string 20
        item name is SADDR         string 60
/* The SYSTEM record type need not be specified, since it is always assumed to already exist */
```

```
/****************************Relationship Definitions*****************************/
Set name is PLACES          type is 1:N
        owner is CUSTOMER
        member is ORDER          order is sorted ascending (ORDERNO)
Set name is CONTAINS    type is 1:N
        owner is ORDER
        member is ORDLINE    order is fifo
Set name is REFER
        owner is PRODUCT
        member is ORDLINE    order is immaterial
Set name is SUPPLY          type is 1:N
        owner is PRODUCT
        member is ARTIF          order is immaterial
Set name is CAN             type is 1:N
        owner is SUPPLIER
        member is ARTIF          order is immaterial
Set name is SYSCUST     type is 1:N
        owner is SYSTEM
        member is CUSTOMER  order is sorted ascending (LASTNAME,FNAME)
Set name is SYSSUP          type is 1:N
        owner is SYSTEM
        member is SUPPLIER    order is lifo
Set name is SYSPROD
        owner is SYSTEM
        member is PRODUCT    order is sorted ascending (PRODCODE)
end
```

Fig. 4.24 Sample DDL source specification.

Next there appears a series of record type definitions. As each record type is specified, it is immediately followed by definitions of all data items that it contains. After all record types and their respective data items have been specified, the schema's named relationships are formally defined. There is one set section for each set in a schema. Notice that each set section describes the owner and member record types of the set, plus information about the member order.

The DDL is free-form, which means that column alignments are entirely irrelevant from the standpoint of syntactic correctness. The example schema uses some arbitrary alignments as an aid to readability. Comments can be inserted anywhere within a DDL specification as a further documentation aid. A comment begins with /* and is terminated by */.

The sequence of main DDL sections is important. The identification and user–password sections must be first and second, respectively. They are followed by all record type definitions, each of which is followed by its data item definitions.

The sequence of data item definitions for a given record type can be in any order. The sequence of record type definitions is also arbitrary. Note that a definition of the system record type is not needed, since it is always assumed to exist in any schema.

After all record types and their data items have been defined, the sets are defined. First the owner and then the member for each set is specified.

The names of data items, record types, sets, and the database are selected by the schema designer. They consist of from one to eight alphanumeric characters. A user name consists of from one to sixteen alphanumeric characters. If a user name contains a blank space, it must be enclosed in quotes (e.g., "Deb Lehr"). A password is formed by one to twelve alphanumeric characters and must be enclosed in quotes if it contains an embedded blank space (e.g., "7763A TASHI").

As each data item is defined, the type and size of its occurrences must be declared. MDBS allows nine different types of data: integer, unsigned, real, internal decimal (idec), character, string, data, time, and binary. With the exception of idec, the data item size indicates the maximum number of bytes allocated to hold a data item occurrence. In the case of an idec data item, the size indicates the number of digits that can be stored for a data value (and how many of those digits are to the right of the decimal point).

The size specified for an integer data item determines the maximum range of integer values that can be stored for that data item. For instance, the one-byte size of RATING means that its occurrences can take on any value in the range -128 to 127. Unsigned is like integer, except no negative values are allowed. A one-byte unsigned data item can have values in the range 0 to 255.

Values of real data items are floating point numbers, while values of idec data items are fixed point numbers. The number of digits to the right of the decimal point is the same (i.e., fixed) for every occurrence of an idec data item (e.g., 2 for UNTPRICE). The decimal point position in occurrences of a real data item can vary (i.e., float).

An occurrence of a character data item of size n consists of n bytes, each of which can be any legitimate character. For instance, each occurrence of FNAME consists of eight characters. A string data item is similar to a character data item with one important difference. Whereas every occurrence of a character data item has the same fixed length, occurrences of a string data item can be of varying lengths. For example, occurrences of SADDR can be of varying lengths up to a maximum of 60 bytes. Some SADDR occurrences may use only a few bytes, while others use nearly 60 bytes. Occurrences of LASTNAME can be of varying lengths up to a maximum of 18 bytes.

A data item that has been declared to be of the date type has occurrences of the form mm/dd/yyyy (e.g., 07/03/1957 for July 3, 1957). The maximum range of dates for a date data item is a 126 year period. In Fig. 4.24, ODATE occurrences can take on any value in the 126 year period beginning with 01/01/1900. January 1, 1900 is the default for the earliest date. As discussed in Chapter 10, alternative beginning dates can be declared in a DDL specification. MDBS will not allow any invalid dates (e.g., 04/31/2001, 02/29/1900, 02/29/1923) to be entered into the database as an occurrence of a date data item.

A time data item has occurrences of the form hhh:mm:ss (e.g., 015:37:12 for fifteen hr, thirty-seven min, and twelve sec). The maximum time permitted is 255:59:59. MDBS prevents invalid times, such as 207:69:83, from being entered into a database as an occurrence of a time data item. An occurrence of a binary data item represents a sequence of 0's and 1's (8/byte) that are stored in a compressed form.

Relationship definitions are straightforward. After the set name is specified, its type is indicated. The only type of set discussed so far is a 1:N set. Since the default set type is 1:N, the clause "type is 1:N" can be omitted for a 1:N set (as it is in the definitions of the REFER and SYSPROD sets). For each set, the owner record type and member record type are stated. With the exception of system, these record types must have been defined earlier in the DDL specification. When the member record type of a set is declared, the member order is also stated. When the member order is SORTED, the data item(s) that makes up the sort key must have been defined as a data item(s) in the member record type. For instance, the SYSCUST member order is SORTED with a sort key consisting of LASTNAME and FNAME. These are data items that are in the SYSCUST member record type: CUSTOMER. When a SORTED order is declared it can be based on ascending or descending values of the sort key.

A DDL specification is terminated by the word "end."

4.8 ANALYZING A DDL SPECIFICATION

A DDL specification such as the one shown in Fig. 4.24 is entered into a text file. This source DDL specification is then input to a program which analyzes the source specification for logical consistency and syntactic correctness. If an error is detected, the analysis stops and a message describing the nature of the error is displayed. The source specification can then be corrected and this corrected specification is analyzed. When a DDL specification has been successfully analyzed, the schema designer is given the option of initializing the database of the schema.

If the designer chooses to initialize the database, then the analyzer program generates the internal data dictionary and prepares the database for usage. When the initialization is complete, data can be loaded into and extracted from the database. This data manipulation is accomplished as described in Chapters 6 and 7.

4.9 SUMMARY

In this chapter we presented the fundamental constructs of logical data structuring: data items, record types, and named relationships (sets). These constructs are used to design a schema for an application system. A schema shows the structure according to which the data are logically organized in the database. All data manipulation is based on a knowledge of the logical structure of the database rather than a knowledge of where data are physically located and how they are physically interrelated.

The five major approaches to logical data structuring are relational, hierarchical, shallow-network, CODASYL-network, and extended-network (inverted file systems discussed in Appendixes A and D could be considered to be a sixth approach). These differ in terms of the methods allowed for representing relationships between record types. The relational (and inverted file) approach does not support named relationships between record types but uses data item redundancy to represent relationships. Hierarchical and shallow-network approaches impose severe restrictions on the structure of one-to-many relationships that are allowed in a schema. The CODASYL-network approach is much more flexible in its ability to represent one-to-many relationships. The extended-network approach not only permits any of the four older types of schemas (as well as inverted file structures), it also provides data structuring features that overcome drawbacks of these older approaches. These innovative features are introduced in Chapter 10.

The notions of set order (for member record occurrences) and system-owned sets were discussed. The chapter concluded with a sample DDL specification. The DDL used is the MDBS DDL. This introductory example illustrates a small (yet quite workable) subset of the MDBS DDL, which will suffice for Chapters 5–8. The reader should be aware that some DDLs are not as straightforward as the MDBS DDL and that some of the MDBS data description features are not available in other DDLs.

RELATED READINGS

ANSI X3H2, "Proposed American National Standard for a Data Definition Language for Network Structured Databases," American National Standards Institute, 1981.

R. H. Bonczek, C. W. Holsapple, and A. B. Whinston, "Foundations of Decision Support Systems," Academic Press, New York, 1981.

J. Bradley, "File and Data Base Techniques," Holt, Rinehart, and Winston, New York, 1982.

D. Gradwell (ed.), "Database—The 2nd Generation: State of the Art Report," Pergamon, Oxford, 1982.

C. W. Holsapple, "A Perspective on Data Models," *PC Tech J.* **2**, No. 1 (1984).

D. A. Jardine (ed.), "The ANSI/SPARC DBMS Model," North-Holland, New York, 1977.

J. Martin, "Computer Data-Base Organization," Prentice-Hall, Englewood Cliffs, New Jersey, 1975.

Micro Data Base Systems Inc., "MDBS Data Base Design Reference Manual," Lafayette, Indiana, 1981.

T. W. Olle, "The CODASYL Approach to Data Base Management," Wiley, New York, 1978.

EXERCISES

1. Compare five main approaches to logical data structuring via illustrated examples.
2. Describe possible relationships between the following pairs of record type names (indicate by "owner" and "member"): (a) father–son, (b) family car–car user, (c) chicken–egg, (d) clock–time, and (e) person–address.
3. Represent each relationship in Exercise 2 in terms of a data structure.
4. What is a DDL? What functions does it serve?
5. What data types can be defined in the MDBS DDL?
6. Design a schema showing relationships among the following manufacturing process record types: processor, product, process, operation, and transporter.
7. Can a schema provide information regarding the size of the database? Explain.
8. List all of the data items for the following systems: (1) football league, (2) major automobile components, (3) family unit, (4) living room furniture, and (5) art museum.
9. Define record types for the data items discovered in Exercise 8.
10. What are the major drawbacks of a relational data structuring approach?
11. Explain the concept of *data item redundancy*. Give examples. Why is data item redundancy not desirable in data structuring?
12. Can you give three examples each of cases where LIFO and FIFO orderings are appropriate?
13. Show a relational schema, a hierarchical schema, and a shallow-network schema that correspond to the schema of Fig. 4.9.
14. Repeat the previous exercise for Fig. 4.23.

15. How does the CODASYL-network approach differ from the hierarchical approach?

16. Design a database schema for an academic department including information on classes, students, and faculty. Justify your design.

17. It is possible to differentiate between two kinds of relationships between objects. One refers to data item relationships, for example, CUSTADDR (customer address) and CUSTNAME (customer name) as shown in Fig. 4.1. The other refers to relationships between record types such as a CUSTOMER record type and an ORDER record type as depicted in Fig. 4.3. Is there a general (or formal) way to classify a relationship as either kind in any particular situation? Explain with an example.

18. Give a relational schema based on the example in Fig. 4.10. Discuss the problems inherent in this approach.

19. Modify the occurrence structure in Fig. 4.17, based on a relational schema to show how connections between the occurrences of ORDER record type and those of PRODUCT record type are established.

20. In the schema shown in Fig. 4.7, the set PLACES is defined with the ORDER record type as the member and the CUSTOMER record type as the owner of the set. Discuss the desirability of replacing such a set with an artificial or a dummy record type.

21. Consider the many-to-many relationship between the SUPPLIER record type and the PRODUCT record type in Fig. 4.18. Implement this relationship using the hierarchical approach. Show corresponding occurrence structure.

22. Describe an application that needs to be supported by declaring two 1:N sets both having the same member record type and the same owner record type. Discuss the benefits and disadvantages of the situation.

23. State a general procedure for converting a CODASYL-network schema into a relational schema. State a general procedure for converting a CODASYL-network schema into a hierarchical schema. State a general procedure for converting a CODASYL-network schema into a shallow-network schema.

24. Under what real world circumstances would an owner occurrence of a 1:N set have no member occurrences? How could it be handled in a DBMS?

25. Modify Fig. 4.4 to show an example of a relational occurrence structure that does not preserve the integrity of one-to-many relationships.

26. Describe an example of a cyclic one-to-many relationship. Describe an example of a cyclic many-to-many relationship.

27. Modify Fig. 4.22 to take advantage of the extended-network approach and explain the modification.

28. Alter the schema of Fig. 4.23 so that it can also represent the fact that, at any given moment, a certain number (possibly zero) of units have been backordered from each supplier.

29. Show relational, hierarchical, and shallow-network versions of the schema derived in the previous exercise.
30. Describe how to structure a group of files to have the same information content as a database having the schema of Fig. 4.23.
31. Consider different ways of collapsing two or more record types in Fig. 4.10. Are any of these particularly desirable? Examine redundancies in each structure.
32. "It is erroneous to claim that any one among the varieties of logical structuring is more efficient than the others." Comment on this statement.
33. It is possible for two different logical views (relational versus CODASYL-network) to have practically identical underlying implementations. On the other hand, two database systems, each supporting network views, could have substantially different implementations. Discuss the implications of this statement.

PROJECT

Construct a complete list of all data items that are needed in the schema of your application system. Identify a pair of data items which have a one-to-many relationship; which is the "owner" and which is the "member?" Find four more pairs having one-to-many relationships. Identify a pair of data items which are related to each other in a many-to-many fashion. Find a pair of data items which are related in a one-to-one manner.

Chapter 5

SCHEMA DESIGN

In Chapter 4 we presented some fundamentals of logical data structuring. Clearly, there are many alternative feasible schemas that can be designed for a given application. A key to the development of a high quality application system is the design of a "good" schema. At the minimum, the schema must represent all needed data items, must correctly represent their interrelationships, and must be able to support all reports needed by the end users of the application system.

The aim of this chapter is first, to describe how to easily design a feasible and logically correct schema for an application. This schema design method is a seven-step process that results in schemas whose databases are free from redundancy of data and relationships. Refinements to a schema generated by the seven-step process are then described. The effects of these refinements with respect to various criteria mentioned above are explored. Other schema design guidelines related to the selection of a type for a data item, set order, and system-owned sets are also discussed. The entire design discussion is oriented toward generating valid CODASYL-network schemas.

5.1 FUNCTIONAL SPECIFICATION OF AN APPLICATION

It is usually desirable to design a schema that minimizes redundancy of both data and relationships. A *good* schema will also make the activity of accessing desired data convenient (for the application developer) and fast (for the end user of the application system). It is also desirable to design a schema so that the storage required for its database is minimized.

It must be emphasized that there are trade-offs among the desirable traits. A classic example is access speed versus storage: designing a schema to increase access speed very often can increase the storage cost. Such trade-offs, together with the uncertain or changing nature of some reports to be supported by an application system, make it extremely difficult to determine a generally *best* or optimal schema for an application.

Occasionally, the trade press will briefly mention some software utility package that claims to automatically generate *the optimal schema* for any application. Such claims immediately raise the (unanswered) questions of: optimal for whom? optimal with respect to what criteria and criteria weighting protocols? optimal under what set of constraints? Is the schema *optimal* from the standpoint of minimizing storage, minimizing access time needed to produce some set of reports, minimizing a developer's effort devoted to devising software to support a group of reports and data input menus, minimizing data redundancy, minimizing the time needed to create or change certain kinds of records, maximizing the ease of application system maintenance, minimizing the developer's effort that is devoted to guaranteeing data integrity, or some weighted mixture of these criteria? What report mix and relative data volumes are assumed to form the optimization constraints? Are they realistic for the application? Answers to these and other questions are crucial to any optimization effort. They rely not only on making valid judgments about just what is desirable, but also on an intimate knowledge of the implementation details of the particular DBMS that will be used and not merely the logical structuring approach that it permits.

As a prelude to schema design, the designer must acquire a clear and detailed understanding of the application. The designer may, through interaction with the end users of the application system, create the functional specifications for the application system. Alternatively, the functional specifications may be provided by a systems analyst. In either case, these specifications form a detailed statement of exactly what functions the application system is to be capable of performing.

Since this is not a book about systems analysis, a detailed treatment of methods for deriving functional specifications is not given here. Nevertheless, a few comments about the functional specification are appropriate. The value of end-user involvement in the specification process should not be underestimated. Even with this involvement, the process is likely to be an iterative one; the initial functional specification being used to implement a prototype application system. End-user feedback about the prototype is then used to arrive at a revised functional specification which is, in turn, used to modify the prototype system, and so forth.

At the very least, the functional specification for an application system should document the following:

(a)   the makeup of standard reports to be produced by the application system,

(b)   the frequency with which each report will be generated,

(c)   characterizations of classes of ad hoc reports that may be desired,

(d)   descriptions of the menus that will be presented to end users for report production, data entry, and data modification, and

(e)   the frequencies with which the various kinds of data will be entered and updated.

This list is more suggestive than it is exhaustive. Note that, with the exception of frequencies, one would normally expect to find all of this information in the end-user reference manual for the application system.

We now examine an easy seven-step procedure for the design of CODASYL-network database schemas. Now it should be clear that while relational, hier-archical, and shallow-network DBMSs are incapable of supporting schemas generated by this seven-step process, it is possible to transform a resulting schema to be compatible with one of these three structuring approaches. Such a transformation involves the replacement of named relationships with data item redundancy, data redundancy, or artificial record types. In Chapters 10 and 11, the seven-step design process is augmented to include extended-network schemas.

5.2   THE SEVEN-STEP SCHEMA DESIGN PROCEDURE

Once a designer has acquired a knowledge of an application, the schema design process can begin. A CODASYL-network schema is very easy to under-stand when its picture is seen, providing it does not have artificial record types. However, the act of designing a reasonable schema is generally not trivial, especially for nontrivial applications. It is inadvisable to attempt schema design by arbitrarily sketching out record types and their interrelationships. The struc-tured design procedure presented here is a seven-step process that has repeatedly been found to be a valuable guide for newcomers to schema design. When carefully followed, it yields a feasible schema.

Step 1

Make a list of all data items to be included in the schema of the database. These data items are typically very easy to identify by examining the reports that must be produced by the application system. For each data item, the list should include the name and description of the purpose of the data item. For example, one data item might have the name of PRODCODE and a description indicating that this data item represents code numbers used to uniquely identify products.

Step 2

If there exists a one-to-one relationship between two or more data items, aggregate them to form a record type. As each record type is formed, give it a name that is descriptive of its data items. Two data items have a *one-to-one* relationship if each occurrence of one data item is associated with no more than one occurrence of the other data item and vice versa. For instance, a product code is associated with only one product description and each product description applies to only one product code.

Relationships that are not strictly one-to-one, but which are *nearly* one-to-one are not uncommon. Consider product codes and quantities on hand. A product code does not have more than one quantity-on-hand associated with it, but it is possible for two products to have the same quantity-on-hand. However, since this is *relatively* rare, product code and quantity-on-hand are said to have a nearly one-to-one relationship. If two data items have a nearly one-to-one relationship they may be aggregated into the same record type.

Any one-to-many or many-to-many relationships between data items should be ignored in this step.

Step 3

Form a record type for each data item that has not yet been included in a record type. At the end of this step, each data item from the original data item list appears in one (and only one) record type.

Step 4

If a one-to-many relationship exists between the concepts or entities repre-sented by two record types, then create a 1:N set between the two record types. Be sure to correctly identify the owner and member of the set (i.e., draw the arrow in the proper direction). Each set should be given a name that describes the meaning of the relationship. No two sets should be given the same name. At the end of this step each one-to-many relationship will have been represented by a 1:N set.

Any many-to-many relationships between record types should be ignored in this step.

Step 5

Some unneeded 1:N sets may have been created in the previous step. They are eliminated from the schema in this step. A 1:N set is not needed if there exist two or more other 1:N sets that also represent the one-to-many relationship.

Suppose that PLACES is a 1:N set with CUSTOMER as owner and ORDER as member and that CONTAINS is a 1:N set with ORDER as owner and ORDLINE as member; this is the situation depicted in Fig. 4.7. The one-to-many relationships from customer to orders and from order to order lines implies that there is also a one-to-many relationship from customer to order lines. As a result of Step 4, a 1:N set would have been created with CUSTOMER as owner and ORDLINE as member. However, this set is unnecessary for determining which order lines are related to a customer since PLACES and CONTAINS also represent the one-to-many relationship between customer and order line. This set can therefore be omitted from the schema. For a given customer, PLACES allows us to find all related orders and, for each of the customer's orders, CONTAINS allows us to find all related order lines.

When looking at a schema it is very easy to see which 1:N sets are candidates for elimination. Figure 5.1 shows three examples.

Remember that elimination of a 1:N set is permissible only if it is a redundant representation of a one-to-many relationship (i.e., there is no loss of information by deleting it). Thus, set elimination based solely on schematic structure is not always valid. The meaning or semantics of the set must also be considered. In Fig. 5.2 for instance, the INCLUDES set (a country includes many cities) is not needed, since the CONSISTS and CONTAINS sets represent the fact that a country includes many cities. However, the CAPITAL set (a country can have many state capitals) cannot be eliminated without a loss of information. Since CONSISTS and CONTAINS tell us nothing about which cities are state capitals, the CAPITAL set is not a redundant representation of a one-to-many relationship.

Step 6

For each record type not yet participating in a 1:N set, select a record type with which it has a many-to-many relationship. Represent this many-to-many relationship with an artificial record type and two 1:N sets. The selection of this record type must be carefully made. Very often there will be several record types that have a many-to-many relationship with the unattached record type. The record type selected should be the one that is conceptually the *most closely related* to the concept or entity represented by the unattached record type. In most cases the correct selection will be obvious. However, if it is not and the choice is only narrowed to two or three alternatives, then select the alternative that allows the needed reports to be produced. When this step has been completed, all record types participate in at least one set.

Step 7

If there are many-to-many relationships needed to support the reports of the application, but which have not yet been captured in the schema, then use

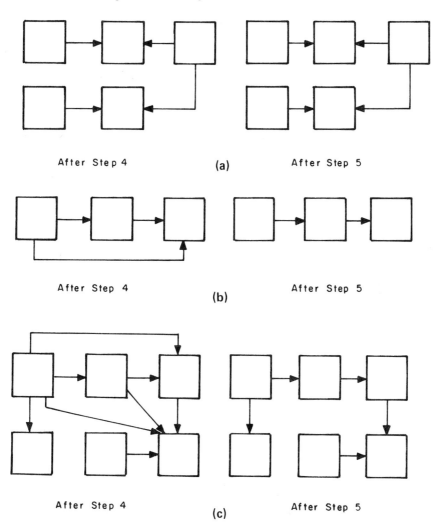

After Step 4   **(a)**   After Step 5

After Step 4   **(b)**   After Step 5

After Step 4   **(c)**   After Step 5

Fig. 5.1   Eliminating redundant relationships. (a) No 1:N sets can be eliminated, (b) one 1:N set can be eliminated, (c) three 1:N sets can be eliminated.

artificial record types to represent these relationships. Notice that at the end of Step 5 many of the many-to-many relationships will have been represented automatically. Wherever two 1:N sets have a common member record type, the many-to-many relationship between the owning record types of the sets has been automatically represented. Step 6 typically captures most, if not all, of the remaining many-to-many relationships. Nevertheless, in some cases there are many-to-many relationships that remain to be represented in Step 7.

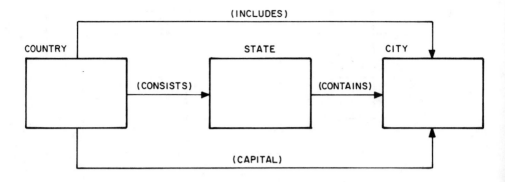

After Step 4

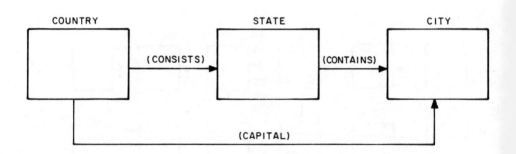

After Step 5

Fig. 5.2 Exception to set elimination in Step 5.

When the seven steps have been completed, it is advisable to examine the resultant schema to ensure that it supports all needed reports. If it does not, then an error was made at some point in the seven-step design process. The most common errors are failure to identify all one-to-many relationships in Step 4, failure to ignore many-to-many relationships before Step 6, improper selection of a record type in Step 6, and failure to recognize additional many-to-many relationships (if any additional ones exist) in Step 7.

5.3 A DESIGN EXAMPLE

We now illustrate the seven-step design process by designing a schema for a school application system. This application has been selected because most readers are familiar with school settings. A lengthy narrative description of the functional specifications of the application is therefore avoided. It suffices to indicate that we would like to be able to generate the following types of reports:

(A) **Curriculum Report,** showing the courses available in each subject area and the sections offered in each course (e.g., Algebra I is a course in the subject of Mathematics and two sections of Algebra I may be supported).

(B) **Activities Report,** showing the name and description of each activity, together with a list of students participating in that activity.

(C) **Student Information Report,** showing for each student the teacher that advises that student, the activities in which the student participates, and the course sections in which the student is enrolled.

(D) **Teacher Information Report,** showing for each teacher the students advised by that teacher and the course sections taught by that teacher.

(E) **Enrollment Report,** showing for each section the teacher of the section, the course in which the section is being offered, and all students enrolled in that section.

(F) **Student's Advisor Report,** showing for each teacher the name of every student (if any) who is enrolled in at least one section taught by that teacher. For each such student, the report should show the student's section number (and affiliated course name) for each section taught by that student's advisor.

Step 1

We first identify the data items of interest for this application.

SUBJAREA	Subject area
CTITLE	Course title
CDESC	Course description
SNUM	Section number
ANAME	Activity name
ADESC	Activity description
SNAME	Student name
SID	Student identification number
SADDR	Student address
TNAME	Teacher name
TONUM	Teacher office number

Note that if our application demands it, we could replace the SNAME data item with two data items: one for last name and one for first name. This would be

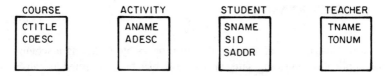

Fig. 5.3   Result of Step 2.

desirable if we frequently need to access first and last names separately, if some reports need last name first while others need first name first, if they are not simultaneously available for data entry, or if they are not always to be used together in sort keys. TNAME could also have been replaced by two data items. An occurrence of SADDR is an entire address; this too could be replaced by several data items (e.g., STREET, CITY, STATE, and ZIP). To reiterate, the functional specifications of an application should allow all data items to be easily identified.

Step 2

Now we aggregate data items having one-to-one (or nearly one-to-one) relationships into record types. CTITLE and CDESC can be combined into the same record type (call it COURSE), since a course title is not associated with more than one course description and vice versa. Similarly, ANAME and ADESC are combined to form a record type called ACTIVITY. SNAME and SADDR have a nearly one-to-one relationship with SID, so these three data items make up a record type that we shall call STUDENT. Finally, since TNAME and TONUM have a one-to-one relationship, they are combined to form a TEACHER record type. This leaves the SUBJAREA and SNUM data items, neither of which has even a nearly one-to-one relationship with any other data item. The result of this step is shown in Fig. 5.3.

Step 3

A record type called SUBJECT is formed for the SUBJAREA data item. Similarly, SNUM becomes the sole data item in a new record type called SECTION. As depicted in Fig. 5.4, we have now created all six nonartificial record types that will exist in the application's schema.

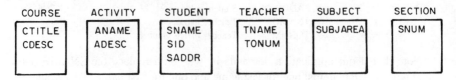

Fig. 5.4   Result of Step 3.

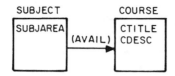

Fig. 5.5   Representing the availability relationship.

Step 4

In this step, all one-to-many relationships that exist among the six record types of Fig. 5.4 are discovered and represented by 1:N sets. Beginning with the COURSE record type, we ask whether courses have a one-to-many relationship with any of the concepts represented by the other five record types.

Can a course belong to more than one subject area?
No, assuming that we are not dealing with interdisciplinary courses.

Can a subject area have many available courses within it?
Yes (e.g., many mathematics courses may be available).

Thus, we have found a one-to-many relationship between courses and subjects. The 1:N set to represent this relationship has SUBJECT as its owner and COURSE as its member. As shown in Fig. 5.5, we call this set AVAIL.

Can a course have more than one section?
Yes.

Can a section be associated with many courses?
No, since a section of a course belongs to that course only.

Here is another one-to-many relationship involving courses. In this case COURSE is the owner of a 1:N set, with SECTION as its member. In Fig. 5.6, this set is called OFFER.

Can a course be related to more than one student?
Yes.

Can a student be related to more than one course?
Yes.

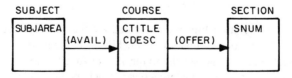

Fig. 5.6   Representing the offering relationship.

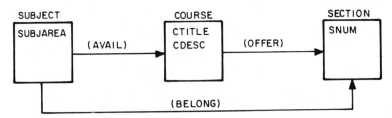

Fig. 5.7   Representing the belong relationship.

Therefore, there is not a one-to-many relationship between courses and students; a 1:N set cannot be created between COURSE and STUDENT. Similarly, courses do not have a one-to-many relationship with either teachers or activities.

Focusing on SUBJECT, do subjects have a one-to-many relationship with sections, teachers, activities, or students? We have already recognized the one-to-many relationship between subjects and courses.

Can a subject have more than one section?
Yes.

Can a section belong to more than one subject?
No.

Thus, there is a one-to-many relationship between subjects and sections which can be represented by the 1:N set BELONG as shown in Fig. 5.7.

Can a subject be associated with more than one teacher?
Yes.

Can a teacher be associated with more than one subject?
Yes.

A one-to-many relationship does not exist between subject and teacher. Nor does such a relationship exist between subject and either student or activity.

We have already found that sections have one-to-many relationships with both courses and subjects. Do sections have any other one-to-many relationships?

Can a section be associated with more than one teacher?
No, assuming that there is no team teaching.

Can a teacher teach more than one section?
Yes.

This one-to-many relationship is represented by the TEACH set in Fig. 5.8. Sections do not have one-to-many relationships with students or activities.

At this point there is one set involving the TEACHER record type, but we have yet to consider the relationship between teachers and students and between teachers and activities.

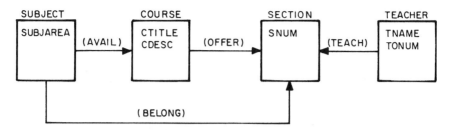

Fig. 5.8   Representing the teach relationship.

Can a teacher advise more than one student?
Yes.

Can a student be advised by more than one teacher?
No, assuming there are no advisory teams.

This one-to-many relationship is represented by the ADVISE set in Fig. 5.9. The reader can verify that there are no other one-to-many relationships for this application. Note that the sequence in which one-to-many relationships are discovered in Step 4 is irrelevant.

Step 5

This step removes any redundant one-to-many relationships that may have resulted from the previous step. From Fig. 5.9 it is clear that there is one candidate for removal, namely the BELONG set. Before eliminating BELONG, we must assure ourselves that it is indeed a redundant representation of a one-to-many relationship between SUBJECT and SECTION. The group of SECTION occurrences related to a particular SUBJECT occurrence through the AVAIL and OFFER sets is identical to the group of SECTION occurrences related to that SUBJECT occurrence via the BELONG set. The BELONG set is therefore representing a relationship that is already represented with the AVAIL and OFFER sets. We are therefore justified in eliminating the BELONG set from the schema.

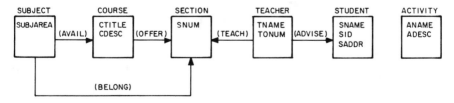

Fig. 5.9   Result of Step 4.

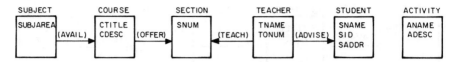

Fig. 5.10   Result of Step 5.

There is one situation where we would be justified in leaving a redundant set, such as BELONG, in a schema. If the functional specifications of the application require very rapid (perhaps sorted) access to all sections belonging to a subject, then BELONG should be left in the schema. Retaining this redundant relationship costs us more from a storage standpoint (i.e., the database will be physically larger, and the data entry time for creating SECTION occurrences will be longer), but it does provide more rapid access to a subject's sections than is afforded by the AVAIL and OFFER sets. Since the functional specifications for the school application do not require a report of all sections belonging to a subject (without also grouping sections by course), the BELONG set is eliminated from the schema as shown in Fig. 5.10.

Step 6

At this point there is one unattached record type: ACTIVITY. The concept of an activity does not have a one-to-many relationship to any of the other five concepts (i.e., subjects, courses, sections, students, teachers) represented in the schema. To integrate this unattached record type into the schema, we ask to which of the other five concepts is the notion of an activity most closely related. In light of the functional specifications, the correct choice is clear. Activities are more closely related to students than to teachers, sections, courses, or subjects (recall Reports (B) and (C)). The many-to-many relationship between students and activities is represented by two sets (DOES and IN) and an artificial record type (PARTICIP), as shown in Fig. 5.11. The reader can verify that if the many-

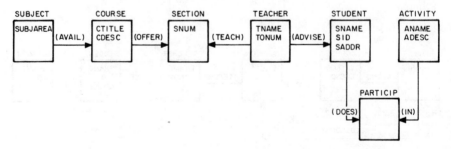

Fig. 5.11   Result of Step 6.

to-many relationship had been formed with any record type other than STU-
DENT, Reports (B) and (C) could not be produced.

In this example there was only one unattached record type. If there had been
more, each would be subjected to the same treatment as ACTIVITY. At the end
of this step, every record type participates in at least one set.

Step 7

In this step, we identify and incorporate any many-to-many relationships that
have not already been captured in the schema. Some were already captured as a
by-product of Step 4. For instance, the many-to-many relationship between
courses and teachers (a teacher can teach many courses and a course can be
taught by many teachers) is automatically represented by the two sets TEACH
and OFFER, with their intervening record type SECTION. Any course can be
associated with *many* sections (via OFFER), each of which can be associated
with a teacher (via TEACH). Conversely, any teacher can be associated with
many sections (via TEACH), each of which is associated with a course (via
OFFER). Similarly, the AVAIL, OFFER, and TEACH sets represent the many-
to-many relationship between teachers and subjects.

Step 6 captured the many-to-many relationship between students and activities. There is, however, another many-to-many relationship that is not represented in the schema of Fig. 5.11. From this schema it is impossible to know
which students are enrolled in which sections. The schema does enable us to tell,
for a particular student, all sections taught by the teacher who advises that
student (via the TEACH and ADVISE sets) and, for a particular section, all
students advised by the teacher who teaches that section (via the ADVISE and
TEACH sets). However, this will not allow us to generate Reports (C), (E), or
(F). The remedy is to represent the many-to-many relationship between students
and sections with two 1:N sets and an artificial record type, as shown in Fig.
5.12.

Notice that this addition to the schema automatically represents other many-to-
many relationships involving students. For example, it represents the facts that a
student can be taught by many teachers and that a teacher can teach many
students (with the ATTEND, CONTAINS, and TEACH sets). Similarly, this
schema allows us to find all courses in which a student is enrolled (via ATTEND,
CONTAINS, and OFFER) and all students enrolled in a given course (via OF-
FER, CONTAINS, and ATTEND). As an aid to visualizing these various relationships, it is sometimes helpful to draw sample occurrence structures for the
resultant schema.

The schema of Fig. 5.12 is a feasible schema, capable of supporting all of the
reports cited earlier. An interesting side-effect of the seven-step design process is
that it yields a schema which is also capable of supporting many other reports,
aside from (A)–(F).

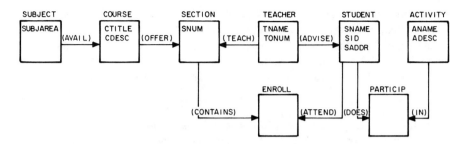

Fig. 5.12 Result of Step 7.

5.4 OTHER SCHEMA DESIGN CONSIDERATIONS

In this section we examine other design decisions that must be made before the schema can be formally specified with the DDL. These include the identification of system-owned sets, choosing a member ordering for each set, and determining the type and size of each data item.

System-Owned Sets

Recall that system-owned sets serve as entry points into a database. It is normally advisable to establish a system-owned set for any record type that is not already the member of a set. There are three such record types in Fig. 5.12: SUBJECT, TEACHER, and ACTIVITY, resulting in three system-owned sets SSUB, STCH, and SACT, respectively. These are shown in the schema of Fig. 5.13. This schema also shows two other system-owned sets (SSECT and SSTD). To understand why these are useful, consider Reports (C) and (E).

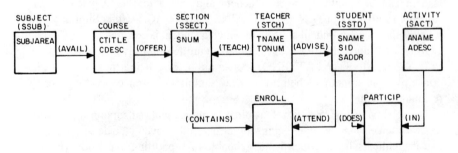

Fig. 5.13 Including system-owned sets.

To generate Report (C), we need to begin with a STUDENT occurrence, find the desired information about that student, find another STUDENT occurrence and desired information about that student, and so forth. The SSTD set makes this very straightforward. If we declare the member order of SSTD to be sorted on SID, then Report (C) is ordered by student identification numbers.

Without SSTD, we could still produce the desired report by finding students through the STCH and ADVISE sets (providing every student has an advisor). However, the students could not be accessed in sorted order. The resultant report could, of course, be later sorted by a utility sort program after all students had been accessed.

The SSECT set plays a similarly useful role in generating Report (E). To summarize, it is sometimes valuable for ease of report generation to declare system-owned sets for record types that are already members of sets. However, it is never justified to declare system-owned sets for artificial record types.

System-owned sets are very cheap (in the MDBS implementation, at least) from a storage standpoint. There is no additional storage cost incurred when creating a record occurrence for a record type that is the member of a system-owned set. A storage cost (of about four bytes) is incurred only if and when a DML command is used to connect that record occurrence to system. This implies that whenever there is uncertainty about whether to declare a particular system-owned set in a schema, it is advisable to do so. Doing so inflicts no storage penalty in the event that the system-owned set is not needed, because occurrences of the member record type need not be connected to system.

Set Order

Next we must select a member order for each of our sets. There are six alternatives: FIFO, LIFO, SORTED, IMMATERIAL, NEXT, and PRIOR. Discussion of NEXT and PRIOR ordering will be discussed Chapter 8. While deciding on the member order of a set, we must consider both the nature of reports to be produced and the relative storage and processing costs of alternative orders. These costs are dependent on the manner in which a particular DBMS implements its sets. The comments here pertain primarily to the MDBS set implementations. A comparison of the three major approaches used by DBMSs for implementing sets is presented in Chapter 11.

With MDBS, the storage costs of the alternative orders are identical, with the exception of SORTED, which requires more storage. Of greater importance are the processing costs. From the standpoint of data entry, involving the connection of a new member record occurrence to an owner record occurrence, IMMA-TERIAL is the fastest. Although the connection time for LIFO and FIFO sets is somewhat greater than IMMATERIAL, it is (on average) faster than the connection time for a SORTED set. On average, the retrieval time to find a particular randomly chosen member record is much less for a SORTED set than for any of the other member orders, because MDBS can use internal sort key indices to directly find the desired record.

SORTED sets have the added advantage that all member occurrences for an owner occurrence can be retrieved in sorted order. If a set is not sorted, all members for an owner occurrence can be retrieved and then sorted by the application program. SORTED sets incur the cost of sorting once: at data entry time, when member occurrences are connected to an owner occurrence. If a report needs to be sorted, then using a nonsorted set incurs the cost of sorting every time the report is generated.

Thus, if the member occurrences associated with an owner occurrence need to be reported in sorted order and/or if rapid access to particular member occurrences is frequently needed, then it is appropriate to declare the set to be SORTED. The sort key should be selected to allow a sorted report and/or an easy means for referencing a desired member record occurrence. For example, selecting TNAME as the sort key for STCH allows straightforward production of a teacher report, without necessitating sorting by an application program; it also provides rapid access to any TEACHER occurrence by stating the corresponding teacher's name.

FIFO and LIFO sets are appropriate where it is desired to keep track of the chronological sequence in which member record occurrences have been connected to an owner occurrence. If there is not a good reason for declaring the member order of a set to be LIFO, FIFO, or SORTED, then the IMMATERIAL order is appropriate.

It is permissible to declare more than one set for a given owner record type and a given member record type, where the only substantial difference between the sets is their member orders. For instance, we could declare two sets having TEACHER as owner and STUDENT as member, where one set is sorted on SID and the other is sorted on SNAME. It should be remembered that creating extra (nonsystem-owned) sets incurs an added storage cost and slows down data entry for member occurrences, particularly if the extra sets are SORTED.

Data Item Types and Sizes

Next, a type and size must be selected for each data item declared in a DDL specification. MDBS supports nine different types of data items. These were briefly described in Chapter 4. The size of a data item refers to the maximum length of its occurrences. As shown in Table 5.1, the smallest and largest sizes (*n*) that could be declared for a data item depend on the type of the data item. Table 5.1 also illustrates the maximum range of values for each type of data

TABLE 5.1

Data Item Type Sizes

Type	Min size (n)	Max size (n)	Storage requirement in bytes[a]	Maximum range[a]
Integer n	1	16	n	-2^{8n-1} to $2^{8n}-1_{-1}$
Real n	2	16	n	$-2^{127}(1-256^{1-n})$ to $2^{127}(1-256^{1-n})$
Binary n	1	65535	typically $<n$	Any character for each byte
Unsigned n	1	16	n	0 to 256^n-1
idec n[b]	1	30	$((n+1)/2)+1$ rounded down	$-10^{63}(1-10^{-n})$ to $10^{63}(1-10^{-n})$ if n is even $-10^{63}(1-10^{-n-1})$ to $10^{63}(1-10^{-n-1})$ if n is odd
Character n	1	65535	n	Any character for each byte
String n	1	250	typically $<n$	Any character (except control characters) for each byte
Time	—	—	3	00:00:00 to 255:59:59
Date	—	—	2	Any 126-yr period

[a]n = specified size.
[b]digits.

item. When selecting the type and size of a data item, the objective is to make a selection that permits the expected range of data values to be stored, while minimizing the storage required for the occurrences of the data item.

A data item should be declared to be integer if its data values are positive and negative integers. The proper size can be determined from Table 5.1. For instance, if the values of the data item fall in the range -70 to 124, then a size of $n = 1$ is sufficient. If they fall in the range -130 to 124, then a size of $n = 2$ is sufficient. A data item should be declared to be unsigned if its data values are nonnegative integers. If its data values fall in the range 0 to 250, then a size of $n = 1$ is sufficient. As shown in Table 5.1, a size of $n = 2$ allows unsigned data values of up to 65535.

For data items whose values are decimal numbers, the choice is between the types real and internal decimal (idec). Real uses a floating point representation, while idec uses a fixed point representation. Idec is typically selected if the target host language(s) supports fixed decimal computation and great computation precision is required to avoid small roundoff errors during host language computations.

If the values of a data item are times that are specified in terms of hours, minutes, and/or seconds, then the time type is appropriate. Values of a time data item are automatically compressed so that each value uses only three bytes of storage. If a data item represents date information in the form of month, day, and year, then it should be declared to have a type of date. Each occurrence of a date data item is automatically compressed as it is stored, so that it occupies only two bytes of storage.

For other data items, the choice is between the character, string, and binary types. As indicated in Table 5.1, there is no compression for the character type. If the values of a data item are either fairly short (i.e., $n \leq 8$) or uniform in length (e.g., always 12 symbols long), then the data item should be declared to be character.

Automatic data compression occurs when values of string or binary data items are stored. This compression is not merely a truncation of trailing blanks. Wherever there is a sequence of repeated symbols in the value being stored, it is drastically compressed (e.g., typically to about two bytes). Thus, this compression avoids storing sequences of blanks (either leading, embedded, or trailing) and other repetitive symbol sequences (e.g., the * symbol in the data value "******* SPECIAL NOTICE *******"). It should be clear that occurrences of a given string or binary data item use varying amounts of storage. Of course, decompression is automatically performed whenever a data value is retrieved.

If the nonblank portions of the values of a data item are fairly lengthy (i.e., $n > 8$) or are not uniformly the same size, then the type should be declared to be string or binary. String is generally used for representing addresses, descriptions, memos, and other textual information. Control characters are not allowed in string data values, but are allowed in binary data values. Thus the binary type is usually reserved for representing graphical images, voice patterns, and the like. Unlike string, binary data items cannot be used in sort keys.

5.5 DESIGN REFINEMENTS

A schema generated through the seven-step design procedure is typically very good from the standpoints of ease of use, minimizing data and relationship redundancy, and minimizing the developer's effort required for guaranteeing the integrity of data and relationships. Nevertheless, there are certain types of refinements that can be made to improve storage or processing efficiency of the resultant system.

In the school application suppose we need to keep track of each student's

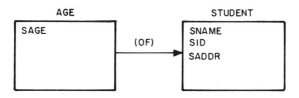

Fig. 5.14 SAGE in owning record type.

current age, then we would have a data item for that purpose. Call it SAGE. It is clear that student age does not have a one-to-one or nearly one-to-one relationship with any of the other kinds of data. However, in Step 4, we discover that it has a one-to-many relationship with other student data. Many students can have the same age, but each student has only one age. As a result of Step 4, we obtain the set shown in Fig. 5.14. With this schema, the entire database will contain only one occurrence of each possible student age.

Each of the AGE occurrences will be associated with many STUDENT occurrences. Physically, each association between an AGE occurrence and STUDENT occurrence incurs a storage cost. This storage cost per STUDENT occurrence depends on how the OF set is implemented. In the MDBS implementation, the cost would be approximately 8 bytes/STUDENT occurrence. In most CODASYL implementations, the cost would be from 8 to 12 bytes/STUDENT occurrence. A refinement to the schema, which reduces this storage cost, is to eliminate the OF set by collapsing the AGE and STUDENT record types together as shown in Fig. 5.15. Since the SAGE data item would normally be of type unsigned or integer, with size 1, the inclusion of SAGE in STUDENT adds only 1 byte of storage to each STUDENT occurrence rather than the 8 bytes required by the OF set. The significance of this savings is proportional to the number of STUDENT occurrences that the designer expects to be in the database.

Collapsing two record types together for reasons of storage efficiency is a common kind of schema refinement. Candidates for collapse are easy to identify. They are record types that are owned only by system and which have only one data item whose occurrence size is less than 8 bytes. If the data item of the owning record type can be regarded as a measurement of the concept represented

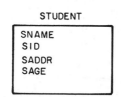

Fig. 5.15 Collapse of SAGE into STUDENT.

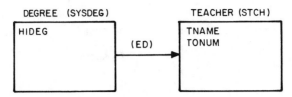

Fig. 5.16 HIDEG in owning record type.

by the member record type, then it is usually reasonable to collapse the two record types. For instance, age can be regarded as being a measurement of a student. Notice that the resultant type of data redundancy does not damage our ability to maintain data integrity, since it is rare for many students of one age to simultaneously become a different age. Furthermore, the collapse does not appreciably detract from the logical clarity of the schema.

It is not always advisable to collapse two record types whenever the owner has a short data item. Suppose that we need to keep track of the highest degree earned by each teacher and frequently produce reports showing which teachers have a particular degree. There is a one-to-many relationship between highest degree (each teacher has only one) and teachers. The design procedure yields the structure shown in Fig. 5.16. Since occurrences of HIDEG are probably very short, we may want to consider collapsing the structure as depicted in Fig. 5.17. This would save storage in the database. However, it would not allow the report of teachers with a particular highest degree to be produced as rapidly as would be allowed by the structure of Fig. 5.16. This is because the SYSDEG and ED sets, together with the DEGREE record type, have the physical effect of providing more levels of indexing than can be provided by the SDEG set. Therefore, if the fastest retrieval of member records associated with a short owning record is desired, the two record types should not be collapsed.

Another common circumstance under which it is undesirable to collapse candidate record types is if it is important to retrieve all of the different values of the short data item. This retrieval is fast and trivial provided the short data item remains in the owning record type. With the structure of Fig. 5.16, it is simple to

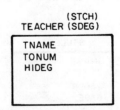

Fig. 5.17 Collapse of HIDEG into TEACHER.

XREC (SYSX)

```
X I
X2
X3
X4
```

Fig. 5.18   The XREC record type.

retrieve a list of all possible highest degrees. In contrast, the same list could be generated from the Fig. 5.17 structure only by an exhaustive search through all TEACHER occurrences. Since the number of teachers is large relative to the number of highest degrees, the collapsed structure causes much slower retrieval than the original structure.

A final caution about collapsing is its potential for schema ambiguity. Consider the record type XREC in Fig. 5.18. What relationship exists among its four data items? If we prohibit record type collapsing, then we know that there is a one-to-one relationship between each pair of data items. If the schema designer sometimes collapses record types, then there may be some one-to-one and some one-to-many relationships between the data item pairs. In other words, the schema is no longer self-documenting. Additional documentation about the nature of these data item relationships must be provided to the developer of the application system's software. A knowledge of relationships is vital for correct processing and assurance of data integrity.

A second major refinement that should be considered, for schemas resulting from the seven-step design procedure, involves the introduction of additional record types. While these record types do not increase the information content of a database, they can serve to force additional levels of indexing and thereby provide faster retrieval. Suppose that the database will contain a very large number of STUDENT occurrences and that it is important to be able to retrieve information about any given student more rapidly than is allowed by the SSTD set of Fig. 5.13. This is accomplished by replacing the SSTD set with the STINDX record type as shown in Fig. 5.19.

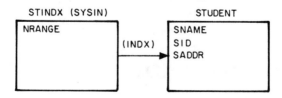

Fig. 5.19   The indexing effect.

Let the NRANGE data item be character in type with a size of 1 byte. Several occurrences of STINDX are created in the database (say A, F, L, and S). The A occurrence of STINDX will own all STUDENT occurrences having names beginning with A–E. The F occurrence will own those having names beginning with F–K, and so forth. The effect of this added record type is to provide additional levels of indexing into the STUDENT occurrences, permitting faster access to a given student's record.

This technique is not restricted to replacing system-owned sets, but can be applied to nonsystem-owned sets as well. The price that is paid for supporting faster access in this way is the storage cost of additional record occurrences and the storage cost of additional record interrelationships due to the extra set.

5.6 SUMMARY

This chapter presented a seven-step procedure for designing schemas. While this is certainly not the only approach to schema design, it is easy to use and results in correct logical structures. Schema design depends on an understanding of the functional specifications for an application system. Interestingly, the seven-step procedure can serve as a useful guide to gathering the functional specifications of an application system. It forces the systems analyst to ask crucial questions about the application area. It provides a disciplined mechanism for organizing one's thoughts about the application area.

The seven-step procedure is useful even if the application system is to be implemented using one of the non-CODASYL approaches to database management (e.g., hierarchical, relational, shallow-network) or a file management approach (e.g., an inverted-file system). Through the exercise of designing a schema with the seven-step procedure, an application developer arrives at a clear, concise representation of the conceptual structure of the application. The resultant schema can then be modified to fit within the limitations of a shallow-network, relational, hierarchical, or inverted-file system.

The issues of declaring system-owned sets and of selecting member orders, data item types, and sizes were examined. The chapter concluded with a discussion of some possible schema refinements for allowing greater storage or processing efficiency.

RELATED READINGS

R. H. Bonczek, C. W. Holsapple, and A. B. Whinston, "Foundations of Decision Support Systems," Academic Press, New York, 1981.

J. Fitzgerald, A. F. Fitzgerald, and W. D. Stallings, Jr., "Fundamentals of Systems Analysis," Wiley, New York, 1981.

Micro Data Base Systems, Inc., "MDBS Data Base Design Reference Manual," Lafayette, Indiana, 1981.

T. W. Olle, A tutorial on data modelling using entity types, attributes and relationships, *in* "Data Base Management Theory and Applications" (C. Holsapple and A. Whinston, eds.), Reidel, Dordrecht, Holland, 1982.

P. C. Semprevivo, "Systems Analysis," SRA, Chicago, 1982.

J. A. Senn, "Analysis and Design of Information Systems," McGraw-Hill, New York, 1984.

E. Yourdon and L. L. Constantine, "Structured Design," Prentice-Hall, Englewood Cliffs, New Jersey, 1979.

EXERCISES

1. Can items having a 1:1 relationship be in two different record types? Give an example.

2. What is an artificial record type? When is one needed?

3. Revise the schema of Fig. 5.13 to accommodate interdisciplinary courses.

4. Suppose that each activity has a teacher who serves as its supervisor. Is this captured in the schema of Fig. 5.13? If it is not, what modification should be made to the schema?

5. Referring to the schema of Fig. 4.23, why is it reasonable to aggregate all of the customer information into a single record type? Discuss the advantages and disadvantages of collapsing the order and customer data items into a single record type.

6. Draw the relational, hierarchical, and shallow-network counterparts of the schema in Fig. 5.13.

7. How can the schema be revised to keep track of how much credit a student receives for enrolling in a course?

8. Revise the schema of Fig. 5.13 so that the meeting room and times of each section can be stored in the database. It is important to produce a report showing room information (building, room number, capacity, audio visual aids). Reports are also needed showing which sections meet in a given room and when.

9. Write a DDL specification for the schema of Fig. 5.13, input it to the DDL Analyzer, and initialize the database.

10. Modify the schema of Fig. 5.13 to represent the fact that a course may have other courses as prerequisites, while at the same time being a prerequisite for several other courses. For any course, it is important to know its prerequisites and "postrequisites."

11.   Using the seven-step procedure, develop a schema for a department store. Start by determining the reports that you like to generate if you were the manager of the department store. List all of your assumptions.

12.   Why is it not advisable to declare system-owned sets for artificial record types?

13.   Discuss the importance of functional specification for an application system as a part of schema design.

14.   Comment on the value of end-user involvement in the functional specification process.

15.   The schema in Fig. 5.13 allows us to determine which teachers (TEACHER) teach which courses (COURSE). But it does not allow us to determine which teachers have the potential of teaching certain courses. What change should be made in the process of schema design and the resultant schema?

16.   Without SSECT in Fig. 5.13, could we still produce the desired Report (E)? Explain.

17.   Extend the schema in Fig. 5.13 so that comments or evaluation that the advising teacher made on each student are kept in the system.

18.   Consider an application in which the courses that each student has taken need to be accessed in the chronological order. Extend the schema in Fig. 5.13 to support the application.

19.   What are the potential problems with collapsing two record types, SUBJECT and COURSE, for reasons of storage efficiency in Fig. 5.13?

20.   Suggest a situation in which the member order of a set needs to be declared as FIFO in the school application system.

21.   Describe the alterations in Fig. 5.13 needed to keep track of the past-activities history for a student.

22.   Examine the schema of Figure 5.13 to ensure that it supports all needed Reports, (A)–(F).

23.   List other reports, aside from (A)–(F), which could be generated from the schema in Fig. 5.13.

24.   Enumerate the factors that must be considered in designing a database schema.

25.   Suppose that we want to produce the following reports for an airline company:

(a)   flight number associated with the pilot, departure time, arrival time, takeoff place, destination;

(b)   pilots, their home locations, the types of planes they are able to fly, and the airports nearest their homes;

(c)   a flight schedule showing number of passengers reserving a flight;

(d)   plane types, including capabilities of each type of plane.

Using schema design procedure described in this chapter, construct a schema suitable for supporting the above reports. If necessary, make (and state) reasonable assumptions needed as a basis for your design.

PROJECT

Design a schema for your application system, selecting descriptive names for its record types and relationships. Be sure to include system-owned sets in your schema. For each data item select an appropriate type and size. For each 1:N relationship choose a set order and justify your choice. Create a DDL specification for the schema you have designed. Submit it to the DDL Analyzer. Correct any errors discovered by the DDL Analyzer and proceed to initialize the database of your application system.

Chapter 6

DATABASE PROCESSING: BASIC RETRIEVAL COMMANDS

In Chapters 4 and 5, we introduced the basic concepts of database structuring and design. The three fundamental constructs—data items, record types, and set relationships—are combined in precise ways to model the data requirements of an application. In this chapter we begin to explore how to process information stored in such a data structure with a procedural data manipulation language (DML). Processing with a high-level nonprocedural query language is described in Chapter 9.

The approach of this chapter is to present DML processing commands through the use of examples. The MDBS DML commands are used here for illustrative purposes. These commands are quickly combined within program segments into workable sequences. In this way it can immediately be seen how certain commands are utilized in actual processing.

Because of this philosophy, not all commands are presented. There are eleven basic groups of DML commands in the MDBS system; these include commands for finding, assigning, retrieving, storing, building, and eliminating record occurrences. In this chapter we discuss only a subset of DML commands in the first four of these groups.

6.1 CURRENCY INDICATORS

In the course of processing information in a database system, it is necessary to be able to refer to various record occurrences, often several occurrences simultaneously. In a sequential file management system (e.g., COBOL, FORTRAN; see also Appendix A) the same problem arises; it is solved by the notion of the *current record* (occurrence). This current record is the record occurrence with which we are presently dealing, that is, the record that has either just been read or written. For each open sequential file, we would have a *potential* current record, because before the file has been used in any way, there is no current record; in other words, the current record for that file is *null*. Current record is an example of a *currency indicator*.

Because of the special nature of sequential file processing, we also can easily identify other record occurrences within the file by their relative position to the current record, as well as their absolute position within the file. Normal sequential processing makes it a simple task to determine (find) the *first* record occurrence in the file. To find the *last* record occurrence in the file, one would skip to the end of the file (through a skip-file or end-file command), and then perform a backspace command to position the file at (or find) the last record occurrence. The procedure of finding the last record occurrence of the file is equivalent to making the last occurrence the current record of the file.

Relative to the current record of the file, normal sequential processing will take us to the (physically and logically) *next* record occurrence of the file. Applying the backspace operator to the current record would typically produce the *previous* record occurrence. Note that in each of these cases, an operation is performed on the current record, which makes another record (either the next or previous) the new current record. The concept of current record is very time-dependent. Once a record occurrence has relinquished its role as a current record, it cannot again be referred to without applying a series of operators that make it again the current record. These concepts are summarized in Fig. 6.1.

Suppose that the last record occurrence in a sequential file is the current record of that file, and we now try to read (find) the next record after it. Of course there is no record occurrence that follows the last occurrence, so this case must be handled in some special manner. The common solution in file management is to assign an error indicator to some program testable variable; the error indicator would signify that an end-of-file condition has been encountered. Under normal processing conditions, the error indicator would not be set; more precisely, its value would remain constant, usually zero, until the exceptional end-of-file condition is encountered.

If we try to use the backspace operator when the first record occurrence in the file is current, then the same situation is present. Many file management systems, however, do not indicate that an end-of-file condition has been encountered; the first record simply remains the current record. In a truly symmetric organization, however, the proper response would indeed be to signify that an exceptional condition has occurred.

What is the nature of the implementation of the current record? The file management system must keep track of which record is in fact current. This

Address   Address

Address		First Record Occurrence	Once We Execute A Read Statement	Address	
1	Joe			1	Joe
2	Sally		The Currency Becomes :	2	Sally
3	Doug			3	Doug
•	•			•	
•	•			•	
•	•			•	
1733	Bill	Previous Record		1733	Bill
1734	Joy	Current Record	Previous Record	1734	Joy
1735	Kathy	Next Record	Current Record	1735	Kathy
1736	Gordon		Next Record	1736	Gordon
•	•			•	•
•	•			•	•
•	•			•	•
3841	Fred			3841	Fred
3842	Doug	Last Record Occurrence		3842	Doug

Fig. 6.1   File management currency indicators.

cannot be done by value, that is, by observing the data contained in the record occurrence. This does not work because in general file management systems each record occurrence is not required to be unique. Thus the same data values for each field (data item) in the record can appear many times in many different record occurrences.

The solution is to keep track of the location of the current record rather than the data value of the record. This is often accomplished in file management by the processing hardware itself: position of a tape or cassette, track and sector of a disk, and so on. In other systems the current record is maintained by software. In these systems the address (or location) of the current record is stored within the file management software, and is used internally by the file management system to determine the next and previous record when required.

When an address is maintained in this way, it is often referred to as a *pointer*. This is a fairly dangerous word in data processing, since it has acquired many meanings in different contexts. We will not use the term pointer (except in the discussion of implementation in Chapter 11), nor do we ever mean to imply any of its onerous characteristics.

6.2 CURRENCY INDICATORS AND DATABASE MANAGEMENT

When we make the transition from file management to database management, the number of currency indicators that one must consider increases. This is because of the greater processing flexibility offered by database management. However, the concepts and definitions are the same: *first* occurrence, *current* occurrence, *next* occurrence, and *previous* occurrence; also the end-of-information indicator (which can no longer be referred to as end-of-file). When processing with a DML, the programmer is responsible for the maintenance of the currency indicators.

The basic element of processing in database management is the set relationship, because it allows us to process related information from different record types as a unit. Because of this fact, the basic currency indicators in database management are related to set relationships.

Recall from Chapter 4 that every set relationship has two participating record types, labeled owner and member, respectively. In defining currency indicators for this relationship, we need to specify two pieces of information: which record occurrence is the owner of the set, and which record occurrence is the member of the set. Thus two currency indicators—the *current owner* occurrence and the *current member* occurrence—are associated with each set relationship in data structure.

Figure 6.2 is a database schema diagram for monitoring information about water pollution. The STATES and CITIES record types are straightforward; RIVERS refer to bodies of water being polluted; and SITES to the known sources of pollution. Observe that each site is part of only one city, and each site pollutes only one river, while each city may contain many sites, and each river may be polluted by many sites.

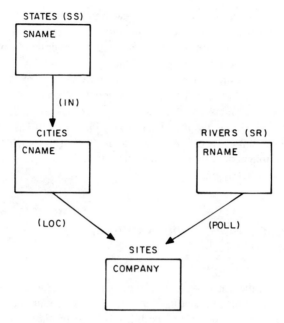

Fig. 6.2 Pollution schema.

Figure 6.3 illustrates an occurrence diagram for the pollution schema. You should check the various connections among the record occurrences to fully understand the meaning and intent of the diagram. Note especially that STATES and RIVERS have associated system-owned sets. Assume that the data occurrences shown represent the entire contents of the database at the present time.

There are five sets defined in this structure: SS, SR, IN, LOC, and POLL. Since as stated above each set defines two currency indicators, the current owner and the current member, we must have ten currency indicators for the pollution database. These five sets are summarized as follows:

Set	Current owner	Current member
SS		
SR		
IN		
LOC		
POLL		

What values should be supplied for the various indicators? In general, at the start of processing, the values of the currency indicators are *null*, that is, undefined. The single exception to this rule involves the system-owned sets. For

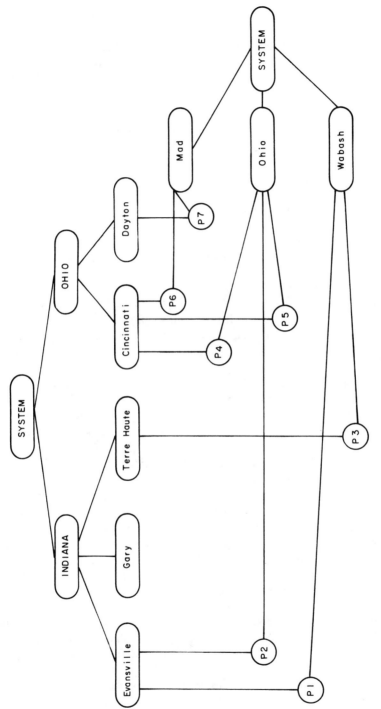

Fig. 6.3 Pollution database occurrences.

each system-owned set defined, the current owner of that set is defined to be *system*. Thus at the start of any program that uses this data structure, the currency table will look like this:

Set	Current owner	Current member
SS	(system)	
SR	(system)	
IN		
LOC		
POLL		

The values of the current indicators have been put in parentheses. This is because they represent addresses of record occurrences, and not the record occurrences themselves. It is important to remember this fact whenever we are working with database structures.

Consider for a moment the set SR. From Fig. 6.3, it can be determined that the *first member* of the set is the Mad River, while the *last member* of the set is the Wabash River. There is as yet no *current member*, nor is there a *next* or *previous* member. The *first owner*, *last owner*, and *current owner* are one and the same: the system record.

What is the first member of the set POLL? The answer is *it depends*. It depends on which river is the current owner of the set POLL. For if the Mad River is the current owner of POLL, then the first member would be P6, the last member P7; while if the Ohio River is the current owner of POLL, then (from the diagram, reading down) P4 is the first member and P5 is the last member.

When talking about system-owned sets, it is possible to explicitly identify the first and last members of the set. This is because a system-owned set is guaranteed to have but one owner record occurrence—the system record. A nonsystem-owned set may potentially have many different owner occurrences (set POLL has the rivers Mad, Ohio, and Wabash as potential owners), hence it is impossible to ascertain any information about first and last members until a specific current owner is specified.

Suppose that we are now told that the current member of the set POLL is site P2. Then without hesitation we can immediately identify the only possible non-null current owner. Why? Because there is only one owner of record occurrence P2 (or any site occurrence, for that matter). This is guaranteed by the definition of a 1:N set (Sect. 4.3). If P2 is the current member of the set POLL, then if the current owner is nonnull, the first, last, and current owners must all be the river occurrence Ohio.

Again, suppose that P2 is the current member of the set POLL. Can we identify the current owner of the set LOC? The answer is *no*. Sets and their currency indicators are completely independent of one another. Specification of any one currency indicator will have no effect on the currency indicators of any other set. Any one of the seven sites may be the current member of the set LOC while P2 is the current member of POLL; the current member of LOC could even be null.

Each set can have at most one current owner and one current member at any single point in time. It is not possible for both P6 and P7 to be current members of POLL. It is possible for one or both of the indicators to be null at any time.

Currency indicators are very much like program variables or registers. They are the entities which we are allowed to manipulate in order to achieve our goals. Virtually all DML commands use or alter the currency indicators in some way. Understanding currency indicators is fundamental to understanding database processing.

6.3 FINDING OF INFORMATION IN THE DATABASE

We are now in a position to introduce the first of the DML processing commands. And these first commands perform the task of finding information for us: they make the desired record occurrences current allowing us to subject them to further processing. This group of commands is collectively referred to as the find commands.

There is an important distinction that occurs at this point between file and database management. In the course of normal file processing, the find or positioning step is handled implicitly, that is, sequentially. There are usually several find commands available, for example, backspace and skip-file. However, most sequential processing never requires explicit finds; the operation of reading encompasses the find. In database processing, on the other hand, reading and finding are two separate operations. In this section, we discuss only the find commands; commands that transfer data from the database to a program are presented in Section 6.7.

In database management when we say that we are out to find a record occurrence, then we actually are saying that we desire the address of that record occurrence to appear in some appropriate currency indicator. Clearly we cannot expect the city Dayton to be a current owner or member of the set POLL, since POLL relates rivers and sites, and is independent of cities. To "find" the city Dayton, we must use either the member currency indicator of the set IN or the owner currency indicator of the set LOC, since only these can represent cities.

When last we left our table of currency indicators, the only nonnull entries were the current owners of the two system-owned sets. Since we also ascertained that we cannot find owners without knowing members, nor members without knowing owners, it appears that we are limited (for now) to finding records for which there are system-owned sets.

Let us consider the set SR. Earlier we identified the first member of SR: the Mad River. The first DML command we learn performs precisely this function for us:

ffm(set-name)   Find the first member of the given set with respect to the current owner of the set.

The find first member (**ffm**) command will determine, for the current owner of any set, the record occurrence positioned as the first member and make that record occurrence the current member of the set. Thus, if we issue the command "**ffm**(SR)", the current owner being the system record, the first member the Mad River, then the Mad River is made the current member of the set SR:

Set	Current owner	Current member
SS	(system)	
SR	(system)	(Mad)
IN		
LOC		
POLL		

Note several things about this table: the only currency indicator that has changed is the current member of the set SR; all of the other indicators are fixed; and (recalling our notation concerning currency indicators) the parentheses around *Mad* indicate that the address of the record occurrence, and not the data value of the record occurrence, is stored in the table.

Now let us execute another command: "**ffm**(SS)". We are trying to find the first member of the set SS, that is, the first state in the database. Since from Fig. 6.3 that state is Indiana, the table will be modified to read

Set	Current owner	Current member
SS	(system)	(Indiana)
SR	(system)	(Mad)
IN		
LOC		
POLL		

Again, the only element that changes is the current member of set SS. Examine this table for a moment. The Mad River is wholly contained in the state of Ohio. Is it rational for the Mad River to be a current occurrence at the same time that Indiana is? Of course it is. Data management systems, and computers in general, have no inherent decision-making ability. A database management system can do only what it is told to do. It will not check other set relationships to validate any operations. In fact, it is most undesirable for a database management system to do so, since it eliminates a great deal of flexibility and power from the processing tools available.

Suppose now we try "**ffm(POLL)**". Since there is no current owner of the set POLL, we saw in the previous section that it is impossible to determine a current member for the set. Thus it is an error for a program to try to execute this command. The database control system would respond by setting an error indicator to a prespecified value, indicating that there is no current owner for the set POLL. The same applies to the sets IN and LOC at the present time.

If we try "**ffm(SR)**" again, then the current member of SR will be assigned the address of the Mad River, that is, it will have the same value as it has now. There are no ill effects from such a duplicate assignment. In particular, a currency indicator need not be null before it can be assigned a value.

We now have a current member of the set SR. Thus we are in a position to consider the next and previous members of SR. In the present case there is no previous member, since the Mad River is the first member. However, there is a next member. To find that next member, we need a second command:

fnm(set-name)   Find the next member of the given set with respect to the current
                    owner *and* the current member of the set.

Find next member (**fnm**) changes the current member of the set to be the address of the present next member. In our example, executing the command "**fnm(SR)**" will produce the following effect:

Set	Current owner	Current member
SS	(system)	(Indiana)
SR	(system)	(Ohio)
IN		
LOC		
POLL		

Now the Mad River is no longer current; it has been replaced by the Ohio. It is also clear why it is necessary to use addresses rather than data values. The (Ohio) in the table refers to the address of the Ohio River, and not the State of Ohio.

Let us try some further executions of the **fnm** command:

"**fnm(SR)**"

Set	Current owner	Current member
SS	(system)	(Indiana)
SR	(system)	(Wabash)
IN		
LOC		
POLL		

"**fnm**(SS)"

Set	Current owner	Current member
SS	(system)	(Ohio)
SR	(system)	(Wabash)
IN		
LOC		
POLL		

In each case, the next member becomes the current member, and no other currency indicator is affected. The next step is to try one more "**fnm**(SR)". The problem is of course that there are no more members of the set SR. As in file management, an error indicator will be set to a prespecified value, indicating that the end-of-information (or end-of-set) has been reached. Your program can then test this indicator in order to see if the end-of-set condition is true. The current member of set SR becomes null:

Set	Current owner	Current member	
SS	(system)	(Ohio)	
SR	(system)		error = end-of-set
IN			
LOC			
POLL			

Suppose now we try yet another "**fnm**(SR)". Remember that the definition of **fnm** stated that the member is determined with respect to t oth the current owner and the current member, yet now the current member of set SR is null. In this special case, the **fnm** operates exactly as **ffm** would, that is, the current member would become the Mad River:

Set	Current owner	Current member
SS	(system)	(Ohio)
SR	(system)	(Mad)
IN		
LOC		
POLL		

As with the **ffm** command, if we were to try a "**fnm**(LOC)" command, then the data management system would return an error response stating that there is no current owner of the set LOC, and hence it is impossible to find a next member.

We have used the concepts of first member and next member to build our first two processing commands. But these were not the only concepts developed above. In a parallel and equally valid manner, we discussed the last member of a set, and the member previous to a current member. These motivate the next two commands:

flm(set-name)   Find the last member of the given set, with respect to the current owner of that set.

fpm(set-name)   Find the previous member of the given set, with respect to the current owner *and* the current member of the set.

These two commands exactly parallel the discussion of the more widely used **ffm** and **fnm** commands. Some examples will make the correspondence clear:

"**flm**(SR)"

Set	Current owner	Current member
SS	(system)	(Ohio)
SR	(system)	(Wabash)
IN		
LOC		
POLL		

"**fpm**(SS)"

Set	Current owner	Current member
SS	(system)	(Indiana)
SR	(system)	(Wabash)
IN		
LOC		
POLL		

"**fpm**(SS)"

Set	Current owner	Current member
SS	(system)	
SR	(system)	(Wabash)
IN		
LOC		
POLL		

error = end-of-set

"**fpm**(SS)"

Set	Current owner	Current member
SS	(system)	(Ohio)
SR	(system)	(Wabash)
IN		
LOC		
POLL		

ffm(set-name);
do while (found)
    { perform process-individual-occurrences;
      fnm(set-name);
    }   **Fig. 6.4** **ffm–fnm** Iteration loop.

The commands **ffm** and **fnm** (and by extension, **flm** and **fpm**) are often applied together in the course of writing application programs.† The purpose is to produce a program loop that will process all of the occurrences for a known owner of a particular set. In Fig. 6.4, the two commands are used in the kind of iteration structure that appears most frequently in programs. The logical variable found is true if the command has been properly executed, and is false if an end-of-set condition has been encountered.‡ The process-individual-occurrences procedure would undoubtedly include other DML commands.

6.4 USING THE NONSYSTEM-OWNED SETS

We have been somewhat limited in our examples of finding commands, because we need owners, and only the system-owned sets have had current owners specified. Clearly, if we are to make use of sets IN, LOC, and POLL, we must have a way of specifying which record occurrences should act as current owners, so that the previously developed finding commands will be able to work on those sets.

Referring again to Fig. 6.3, suppose we need to process (e.g., produce a report on) all of the states and cities in the database. We can use the iteration procedure of Fig. 6.4 to process all of the states. But how do we get to the cities?

As we process the individual state occurrences, what must be done is fairly clear. For a particular state, say Indiana, we must access its related cities. This would of course involve the set IN. If we consider one of those cities, say Gary, then what we must do is to have Indiana be the owner of the set IN while Gary is the member. The key is the fact that Indiana must be the current owner for some indicator.

When we start from scratch, the only nonnull currency indicators are the

---

†The syntax of the pseudo-language used for programming examples in this text is given in Appendix F; Appendix G contains information about calling sequences in some widely used computer languages.

‡This technique is a simplification of the actual processing required. See Appendix G for language-specific examples of the needed processing.

current owners of the system-owned sets. After a "**ffm**(SS)"† is performed, we have the following situation:

Set	Current owner	Current member
SS	(system)	(Indiana)
SR	(system)	
IN		
LOC		
POLL		

We want a kind of assignment statement that would assign the current owner of the set IN to the value (Indiana) or, more precisely and generally, to the value of the current member of the set SS. Using the abbreviations co and cm for current owner and current member, respectively, we would like to write

$$co(IN) = cm(SS).$$

Note the programming language convention of right-to-left assignment, that is, the *variable* on the left-hand side of the assignment receives the value of the *expression* on the right-hand side.

Because in virtually all programming languages it is impossible to write an assignment in just that form, a special DML command has been developed that provides exactly the desired function:

som(set-name-1, set-name-2)   Set the current owner of set-1 to be the value of the current member of set-2.

Set owner equal to member (**som**) is the functional form of the assignment statement given above. In our case, the form of the **som** required is "**som**(IN, SS)".

Individuals new to database management sometimes forget that the sets must be listed in the correct order in a **som** command. Remembering the proper order is really very simple because it is consistent with the idea of an assignment statement (right-to-left assignment): when using **som,** the current member is listed on the right, while the desired current owner is on the left.

If by mistake the command is entered as "**som**(SS, IN)", think of what the database control system would try to do. It would take the current member of the set IN (assuming that there was a current member) and try to make it the current owner of the set SS. Since the members of the set IN are occurrences of the record type CITIES, while the owner of the set SS is the system record, the

---

†The SS in this command is a pseudo-language variable containing the symbols "SS". See Section 8.2 and Appendix F.

database control system would be forced to respond with an error indicator, stating that the sets do not conform to the proper pattern (or the sets do not *mesh*).

We have now executed "**som**(IN, SS)", and the currency indicators should be

Set	Current owner	Current member
SS	(system)	(Indiana)
SR	(system)	
IN	(Indiana)	
LOC		
POLL		

Now that we have a current owner of the set IN, it makes sense to talk about the members of the set IN. If we were to execute a "**ffm**(IN)" the current member of IN would become (Evansville).

However, it has been observed that most of the time a **som** command is immediately followed by a **ffm.** Thus the database control system, in an attempt to save some effort for the programmer, gives **som** a *side effect.* That side effect is to automatically perform a **ffm** of set-1. In terms of our tables, from this situation:

Set	Current owner	Current member
SS	(system)	(Indiana)
SR	(system)	
IN		
LOC		
POLL		

the execution of the command "**som**(IN, SS)" will have the following effect:

Set	Current owner	Current member
SS	(system)	(Indiana)
SR	(system)	
IN	(Indiana)	(Evansville)
LOC		
POLL		

Summarizing, the **som** command assigns the value of the current member of the second set listed to the current owner of the first set listed, and then performs an automatic **ffm** of the first set listed.

```
                              ffm(SS);
                              do while (found)
                                   { perform process-state-info;
                                   som(IN, SS);
                                   do while (found)
                                        { perform process-city-info;
                                        fnm(IN);
                                        }
                                   perform other-state-processing;
                                   fnm(SS);
                                   }
```

Fig. 6.5   Processing states and cities.

Figure 6.5 illustrates the program structure required for processing states and cities. Note that the effect is to nest essentially identical loop structures. The outer loop processes each state; the inner loop processes, for each state (owner), the cities in that state (members). Study this example carefully.

As in any assignment statement, the old value of the current owner being assigned is lost, that is, replaced by the new value. And if the current member (right-hand side of the assignment) is null, the processing error indicator is appropriately signaled.

Now suppose we need to process all of the pollution sites within each city. For instance, when processing Evansville, Indiana, information on P1 and P2 is also required. Can we, with our existing tools, handle this problem? The answer is yes. Consider the last currency table above. At this point in our processing, we have located a state and a city, and are ready to find the sites within that city. What we need to do, in order to use the set LOC, is to establish a proper owner for LOC, and then use our find commands.

But this is exactly the same "problem" as trying to use IN to obtain city information. The parallels are exact in every detail. Thus the solution must be the same as well: use an appropriate form of **som** to assign to the current owner of LOC the value of the current member of IN: "**som**(LOC,IN)". The table will now read (remember the side effect):

Set	Current owner	Current member
SS	(system)	(Indiana)
SR	(system)	
IN	(Indiana)	(Evansville)
LOC	(Evansville)	(P1)
POLL		

```
ffm(SS);
do while (found)
    { perform process-state-info;
      som(IN, SS);
      do while (found)
          { perform process-city-info;
            som(LOC, IN);
            do while (found)
                { perform process-site-info;
                  fnm(LOC);
                }
            perform other-state-processing;
            fnm(IN);
            }
      perform other-state-processing;
      fnm(SS);
    }
```

                                         Fig. 6.6 Processing states, cities, and sites.

The **som** command is used in processing "downstream," that is, from owners to members. Understanding **som** is crucial for writing all but the most trivial of data management programs.

6.5   A DETAILED PROCESSING EXAMPLE

Figure 6.6 contains the program segment for processing states, cities, and sites. Let us trace the execution of this segment for a while, to reinforce our understanding of the **som–fnm** combination.

After the "**ffm**(SS)" has been executed, the currency indicators would have (Indiana) as current member of the set SS (see the second from the last table above); since this occurrence is found, we proceed into the outer loop, and process the state information. The "**som**(IN, SS)" makes (Indiana) the current owner, and (Evansville) the current member, of the set IN (see the next to last table above); since this occurrence is found, processing moves into the second loop, and the city information is processed. The "**som**(LOC, IN)" command produces the last table above; since the sites occurrence is found, processing moves into the inner loop, and the site information is processed. Next we have

"**fnm**(LOC)"

Set	Current owner	Current member
SS	(system)	(Indiana)
SR	(system)	
IN	(Indiana)	(Evansville)
LOC	(Evansville)	(P2)
POLL		

The record occurrence P2 is found, so we remain in the inner loop and process this site information.

"**fnm**(LOC)"

Set	Current owner	Current member	
SS	(system)	(Indiana)	
SR	(system)		
IN	(Indiana)	(Evansville)	
LOC	(Evansville)		error = end-of-set
POLL			

Now the end-of-set error means that a record occurrence is not found, and thus we exit the inner loop. We next perform any other processing of city information. if necessary.

"**fnm**(IN)"

Set	Current owner	Current member
SS	(system)	(Indiana)
SR	(system)	
IN	(Indiana)	(Gary)
LOC	(Evansville)	
POLL		

The current owner of LOC has not changed, since no command has yet been issued to change it. The occurrence (Gary) was found, so the second loop is re-entered. We process the city information.

"**som**(LOC, IN)"

Set	Current owner	Current member	
SS	(system)	(Indiana)	
SR	(system)		
IN	(Indiana)	(Gary)	
LOC	(Gary)		error = end-of-set
POLL			

The end-of-set error occurred because Gary has no pollution sites associated with it; thus on the implicit "**ffm**(LOC)", there were no occurrences found. It is important to remember that the **som** command can give rise to an end-of-set condition. Since an occurrence was not found, the inner loop is skipped, and we perform the other city processing.

"**fnm**(IN)"

Set	Current owner	Current member
SS	(system)	(Indiana)
SR	(system)	
IN	(Indiana)	(Terre Haute)
LOC	(Gary)	
POLL		

The city was found, so we start the second loop again, and process this city information.

"**som**(LOC, IN)"

Set	Current owner	Current member
SS	(system)	(Indiana)
SR	(system)	
IN	(Indiana)	(Terre Haute)
LOC	(Terre Haute)	(P3)
POLL		

The site was found, so we enter the inner loop, process the site information.

"**fnm**(LOC)"

Set	Current owner	Current member	
SS	(system)	(Indiana)	
SR	(system)		
IN	(Indiana)	(Terre Haute)	
LOC	(Terre Haute)		error = end-of-set
POLL			

The site was not found, so the inner loop is terminated. Other city information is processed.

"**fnm**(IN)"

Set	Current owner	Current member	
SS	(system)	(Indiana)	
SR	(system)		
IN	(Indiana)		error = end-of-set
LOC	(Terre Haute)		
POLL			

The city was not found, so the second loop is exited. Other state information is now processed.

"**fnm**(SS)"

Set	Current owner	Current member
SS	(system)	(Ohio)
SR	(system)	
IN	(Indiana)	
LOC	(Terre Haute)	
POLL		

Since the state was found, the outer loop is now repeated. We leave the processing of Ohio as an exercise.

Please note once again a trap into which the unwary or careless may fall. Even though we have finished with Indiana occurrences, if for some reason a **som** command is skipped, then the present values of the currency indicators would be used for our processing. This can lead to unfortunate results. In the present example, if, due to bad programming, the "**som**(IN, SS)" command were skipped, then Ohio would be presented as if it has no cities; even worse, all of the Indiana cities might very well be listed again, under the heading *Ohio*.

6.6   OTHER ASSIGNMENT COMMANDS

Suppose that we are starting from scratch once again. We execute (as before) the following sequence of commands:

"**ffm**(SS)"
"**som**(IN, SS)"
"**som**(LOC, IN)"

Set	Current owner	Current member
SS	(system)	(Indiana)
SR	(system)	
IN	(Indiana)	(Evansville)
LOC	(Evansville)	(P1)
POLL		

Check the currency table to see that all indicators are properly set.

Now suppose that in addition to the site information, we also need to know what river that particular site is polluting. In our example, for site P1 we need to obtain the information that P1 is polluting the Wabash River. We thus need to use the set POLL somehow.

Why can't we just use **som** again? The reason is that **som** would try to assign a value for the owner of POLL, a river. That means that we would need a river to appear as a member of some other set. And we do not have any river information at present. The side effect of **som** would be to find a first member of POLL, which again is not what is intended—we do not want just any member of POLL, we want P1.

That is the key to the solution of this problem. If we could make P1 the current member of POLL, then we might be able to access its owner to determine in fact what river it is. We now have the address of P1 as the current member of set LOC. We need an assignment of the form

$$cm(POLL) = cm(LOC).$$

Again the right-to-left convention applies.

Following the methods of the previous section, we can define a new assignment command

> **smm**(set-name-1, set-name-2)   Set the current member of set-1 to be the value of the
> current member of set-2.

Set member equal to member (**smm**) parallels **som** in a number of ways. The similarity in their names is not coincidental. In **som,** we have an owner defined by a member; in **smm** we have a member defined by a member. If the two set names do not properly mesh, an error occurs. An example would be "smm(SS, SR)"; this is an error because member records of SR are rivers, while member records of SS are states. If the current member of set-2 is null, an error occurs as well.

Just like **som,** the **smm** command has a side effect. Here **smm** will automatically find the (first) owner of set-1. Thus, in our example, the command "**smm** (POLL, LOC)" would produce

Set	Current owner	Current member
SS	(system)	(Indiana)
SR	(system)	
IN	(Indiana)	(Evansville)
LOC	(Evansville)	(P1)
POLL	(Wabash)	(P1)

Here the address of Wabash is automatically made the owner of POLL for its current member P1.

The sequence "**fnm**(LOC)" and "**smm**(POLL, LOC)" would result in

Set	Current owner	Current member
SS	(system)	(Indiana)
SR	(system)	
IN	(Indiana)	(Evansville)
LOC	(Evansville)	(P2)
POLL	(Ohio)	(P2)

Referring back to the schema diagram of Fig. 6.2, the **smm** command allows us to process "around the corner." Since such structures represent many-to-many relationships between the two *owner* record types (in this case CITIES and RIVERS), the **smm** command is vital in the processing of this important type of relationship.

Figure 6.7 is an extension to the program segment of Fig. 6.6 to include river processing. There are several things to note about this program segment. One important fact is that the use of the **smm** command here does not imply the addition of a fourth loop. This is because of the nature of our relationships. If a particular site has an associated river, then it will have exactly one such river, and never more than one. This is the assumption made in defining POLL to be a 1:N set. Thus no loop for the *other* owners is required.

The second important thing to note is the order in which the database occur-

```
ffm(SS);
do while (found)
    { perform process-state-info;
      som(IN, SS);
      do while (found)
          { perform process-city-info;
            som(LOC, IN);
            do while (found)
                { perform process-site-info;
                  smm(POLL, LOC);
                  if (found) perform process-river-info;
                  fnm(LOC);
                  }
            perform other-city-processing;
            fnm(IN);
            }
      perform other-state-processing;
      fnm(SS);
      }
```

Fig. 6.7   Process all information.

TABLE 6.1

Report from Program of Fig. 6.7

State	City	Site	River
Indiana	Evansville	P1	Wabash
		P2	Ohio
	Gary		
	Terre Haute	P3	Wabash
Ohio	Cincinnati	P4	Ohio
		P5	Ohio
		P6	Mad
	Dayton	P7	Mad

rences are processed. If the processing performed were set up to simply list in the appropriate columns the information found by the program in Fig. 6.7, the resulting report would be that given in Table 6.1. This is consistent with the example of the previous section. You should work out several lines in detail as an exercise (see also Exercise 16).

Suppose that, instead of the ordering presented in Table 6.1 (i.e., by state and city), the ordering of Table 6.2 were required. Here instead of processing by state, and then by city, processing is done by river. Can we develop the necessary program for producing this report?

To start with, we will need to process in turn each of the rivers in the database. Thus the iteration loop structure of Fig. 6.4 is of interest, using the set SR. Now suppose that we have performed a "**ffm**(SR)" to achieve

Set	Current owner	Current member
SS	(system)	
SR	(system)	(Mad)
IN		
LOC		
POLL		

We now would incorporate a second loop, using POLL to determine the pollution sites along the rivers. This two-loop structure is identical in form to that shown in Fig. 6.5, with SR replacing SS and POLL replacing IN. We should write out the program segment if we feel uneasy about the parallel development. The currency indicators after an "**som**(POLL, SR)" would read

TABLE 6.2

Alternative Ordering of Report

River	Site	City	State
Mad	P6	Cincinnati	Ohio
	P7	Dayton	Ohio
Ohio	P4	Cincinnati	Ohio
	P2	Evansville	Indiana
	P5	Cincinnati	Ohio
Wabash	P1	Evansville	Indiana
	P3	Terre Haute	Indiana

Set	Current owner	Current member
SS	(system)	
SR	(system)	(Mad)
IN		
LOC		
POLL	(Mad)	(P6)

What should happen next? We need the city of site P6. This is the "around the corner" kind of processing that **smm** was made for. What must be done is to make P6 (the current member of POLL) also the current member of LOC. Thus we execute "**smm**(LOC, POLL)". The resulting currency table is

Set	Current owner	Current member
SS	(system)	
SR	(system)	(Mad)
IN		
LOC	(Cincinnati)	(P6)
POLL	(Mad)	(P6)

Study the processing that led to this table carefully; make sure that it is understood completely before going on.

What next? We have the city, but not yet the state. We somehow need to involve the set IN. Following the lines of reasoning seen twice before, we have what we want (the city) as the owner of a set; and we want that city to become the member of the set IN. Making up the assignment, we want

$$cm(IN) = co(LOC).$$

Following the naming conventions for **som** and **smm,** this function can have only one name

smo(set-name-1, set-name-2)   Set the current member of set-1 to be the value of the current owner of set-2.

Set member equal to owner (**smo**) has many properties in common with the other DML assignment commands. The proper command for our purposes would be "**smo**(IN, LOC)", with the effect

Set	Current owner	Current member
SS	(system)	
SR	(system)	(Mad)
IN	(Ohio)	(Cincinnati)
LOC	(Cincinnati)	(P6)
POLL	(Mad)	(P6)

The **smo** again would require no loop, since each member would have at most one owner. The other rules of **smm** concerning mesh, end-of-set, and the side effect all apply to **smo** as well. **smo** is used to traverse the schema diagram upstream, that is, against the "flow" of the owner to member arrows. Figure 6.8 gives the program segment capable of producing the report shown in Table 6.2.

```
ffm(SR);
do while (found)
    { perform river-processing;
      som(POLL, SR);
      do while (found)
          { perform site-processing;
            smm(LOC, POLL);
            if (found)
                { perform city-processing;
                  smo(IN, LOC);
                  if (found) perform state-processing;
                  }
            fnm(POLL);
            }
      fnm(SR);
      }
```

Fig. 6.8   River-oriented program.

There is a fourth DML assignment command which is rarely used, called (what else but) **soo.** The definition is

> **soo**(set-name-1, set-name-2)   Set the current owner of set-1 to be the value of the
> current owner of set-2.

In our assignment notation, that is,

$$\text{co(set-1)} = \text{co(set-2)};$$

The reason that this command is less frequently used than the other three assignment commands is that **soo** uses a very weak functional relationship between the two participating member record types.

6.7 RETRIEVAL OF STORED INFORMATION

The find commands (**ffm, fnm, flm, fpm**) are used to manipulate currency indicators within a particular set relationship. The DML assignment commands (**som, smm, smo, soo**) manipulate currency indicators across two sets—the known value of the second is assigned to the first. These two groups of commands deal with addresses, not with data. As stated above, in database management it is common to separate the positioning (finding) of record occurrences and the reading (retrieval) of the information stored in those occurrences. We can now consider the latter function.

Figure 6.9 represents a simple database schema diagram for a personnel system that keeps track of employees and their respective departments. The department data items refer to the name of the department (a string of 15 characters), a

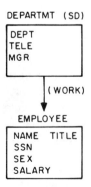

Fig. 6.9 Simple personnel schema.

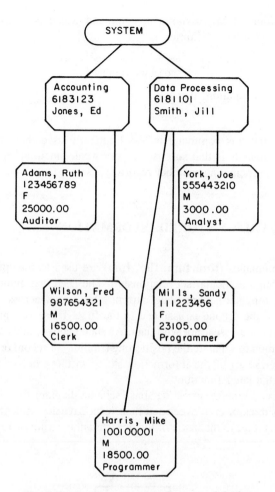

Fig. 6.10 Occurrence structure for personal database.

7 digit telephone number, and the name of the manager of the department (20 characters). The employee information includes the employee's name (25 characters), Social Security number (9 characters), sex (M or F), salary (a real number), and job title (15 characters). The occurrence diagram appears in Fig. 6.10; we will assume that this is all of the information stored in the database at the present time.

If we modify the program given in Fig. 6.5 by changing SS to SD, and IN to WORK, then the resulting program will process all employees by their departments (Fig. 6.11). We must define more clearly what kind of processing is required in the *process* routines.

```
                                       ffm(SD);
                                       do while (found)
                                          { perform process-department;
                                          som(WORK, SD);
                                          do while (found)
                                              { perform process-employee;
                                              fnm(WORK);
                                              }
                                          fnm(SD);
Fig. 6.11   Outline of retrieval program.   }
```

Fig. 6.11   Outline of retrieval program.

Suppose that all we really desired was a list of employees, by name only, listed under the proper department. The department information should consist of all three of its data items. What must go on within the process-department block?

Positioning is *not* a problem; by the time this block is executed, a "**ffm**(SD)" will have been executed, and the current member of SD will be the address of the Accounting record occurrence. The program must at this point retrieve all of the information stored in that record occurrence, and then write it to the desired output device.

Because the information we wish to retrieve belongs to an occurrence that is a current member of a set, the command involved will refer to this fact. The actual DML command that is used for this purpose is

    getm(set-name, p-record)   Get all of the data values from the current member of the given set, and store them in the program area p-record.

Get from member (**getm**) is a record-oriented retrieval command. All of the data item values are retrieved in the order that the data items are specified in the DDL. The **getm** command assumes that the specified set has a current member; if not, an error indicator is set. The **getm** command does not modify currency indicators in any way; it simply uses the current member of the specified set to determine the address of the information to be retrieved.

The p-record refers to a program data area, consisting of enough program variables to contain all of the information that is being transferred. In many computer languages, such records or data blocks can be defined naturally; these languages include COBOL, PL/I, Pascal, and C. In other languages (notably FORTRAN and BASIC), there is nothing in the language that corresponds to data blocks; these are established by the data management through the use of auxiliary commands. Refer to Appendix G for more information.

The name given to any particular p-record within a program is completely independent of the names assigned to record types in the DDL. As with any program variables, the names chosen are arbitrary and may be changed at any time. The database control system does not examine the name of the p-record; it simply transfers information from the database occurrence to the program variables.

p-record d { char dept [15];
              char tele [7];
              char manager [20]
              }

Fig. 6.12   Definition of p-record d.

Thus in our program, we need to define such a p-record. Figure 6.12 shows the necessary definition. We will call the p-record d, although any name could have been chosen. The fields of the p-record are dept, tele, and manager; note that these fields correspond in number and position to the definition of record type DEPARTMT and its items, but that the same names need not be used.†

Having defined the necessary p-record, the retrieval of the information stored in the occurrence that is the current member of set SD is accomplished by executing the command "**getm** (SD, d)", where d is the name of our p-record. No currency indicators are changed by the execution of this command. The information stored in the record occurrence is transferred to our program variables, as if the following assignment statements had been executed:

d.dept = "Accounting";
d.tele = "6183123";
d.manager = "Jones, Ed";

Now that the data values are in program variables, the values can be manipulated any way we choose. The database control system does not constrain the program in any way; it is merely an extension to the programming language. The program may continue just as if these three data values have been read from a sequential file or input from a user terminal. What is done with the data inside a program is not a concern of the database control system.

In our example, the continuation of processing after the **getm** is simply to display the retrieved values. This is done through the output mechanisms provided by the language.

We next need to list the names of the employees that work in the current department. Following Fig. 6.11, we use a **som** to set up the current member of the set WORK to be the address of the Adams record. We next arrive at the process-employees step.

We can use **getm** again at this point. We would define another p-record, consisting of variables for the five employee data items. The **getm** command would be used to retrieve all of the employee information, but only the name variable would be displayed. This approach would waste computer memory by using the additional variables in the p-record, but never otherwise referencing them in the program.

---

†The correspondences between data item types and program variable types are, of course, language dependent. The pseudo-language incorporates a simple data typing mechanism.

```
                                        ffm(SD);
                                        do while (found)
                                           { getm(SD, d);
                                             display d.dept, d.tele, d.manager;
                                             som(WORK, SD);
                                             do while (found)
                                                { gfm(NAME, WORK, emp);
                                                  display emp;
                                                  fnm(WORK);
                                                }
                                             fnm(SD);
```

Fig. 6.13 Completed retrieval program.   }

The solution to this waste disposal problem is the introduction of a new command

gfm(item-name, set-name, variable)   Get the field denoted by the given item from
                                          the current member of the given set, and store
                                          it in the given program variable.†

Get field from member (**gfm**) is used to retrieve data values of individual data items within a record type. If the item specified does not exist in the member record type of the given set, an error occurs. Otherwise all of the comments made about **getm** apply to **gfm** as well. Once information is transferred to a program variable, the program can do what it pleases with that information.

The complete program segment for this retrieval problem is given in Fig. 6.13. Tracing the execution of this program clearly conveys the logical flow of this retrieval procedure.

The **getm** and **gfm** commands are interchangeable, in the sense that **getm** can be replaced by many **gfm**s, one for each item in the record occurrence being retrieved; and **gfm** may be replaced by a **getm** and an appropriate p-record definition, although some of the information retrieved will not be used in the program. Both commands are useful for creating efficient programs in limited memory space.

There are two other DML get commands that parallel **getm** and **gfm** directly. These are

geto(set-name, p-record)   Get all of the data values from the current
                                        owner of the given set, and store them in the
                                        program area p-record.
gfo(item-name, set-name, variable) Get the field denoted by the given item from
                                        the current owner of the given set, and store
                                        it in the given program variable.

The **geto** and **gfo** commands work with the current owner record occurrence of a specified set, rather than the current member. Otherwise they are identical to

---

†Non-record oriented languages would require a p-record instead of a program variable.

getm and **gfm** respectively. The completions of the programs given in Figs. 6.7 and 6.8 both require one of these commands.

6.8 COMBINING THE FIND AND GET OPERATIONS

Consider again the personnel schema of Fig. 6.9. We wish to create a program that will accept as input (say from a terminal device) a particular department name and determine whether or not that name is the name of any department listed in the database. In other words, we must search through the list of departments until either we find the department in question, or we come to the end of the list.

Because we must process (potentially) all of the occurrences of the set SD, the program structure given in Fig. 6.4 applies. The processing required for each occurrence is to retrieve the department name and test it against the input value. The program segment required is given in Fig. 6.14. name-1 and name-2 are program variables. The "break" command is used to immediately exit the current loop (see Appendix F).

It should be clear that this segment can be modified and extended in many ways. In fact, it represents a template for finding a specific record occurrence based on the value of some data item in the member record type.

Because of the universal application of this segment, four commands exist for performing exactly the function defined by the program. The commands differ in the kinds of sets they deal with. The first command is

> **fmi**(item-name, set-name, variable)   Find the first member occurrence of the given set for which the specified item has a value equal to the value of the program variable.

Find member based item value (**fmi**) searches the members of the specified set. The set must have a current owner, or an error occurs. The members are

```
input name-1;
ffm(SD);
do while (found)
     { gfm(DEPT, SD, name-2);
       if (name-1 = name-2) then break;
       fnm(SD);
       }
if (found) then
     display "valid department name:", name-1;
else
       display name-1, "cannot be located";
```

Fig. 6.14   Finding a specific occurrence.

examined from the first member to the last. For each member occurrence, the specified data item value is retrieved and compared to the value of the given variable. The first occurrence for which there is an exact match will become the current member of the set. If no occurrence makes an exact match with the value of the variable, the end-of-set indicator is set, and the current member of the set is made null. If the specified data item name is not an item of the member record type, then an error occurs.

The loop in Fig. 6.14 can be replaced by the single command "**fmi**(DEPT, SD, name-1)". If the name exists, it will be the current member of SD. If it does not exist, then the current member of SD will be null, and the error indicator will be set to end-of-set.

fmi works on any data item and set combination. However, the values being compared must match exactly for the occurrence to be found. This is particularly troublesome when dealing with real numbers, where roundoff may be a factor. Also, **fmi** does not convert values from one type into another (e.g., integers to reals). This kind of activity must be performed in the program itself.

The **fmi** command finds the first occurrence of the specified value. To check if there are other occurrences in the set with the same data value, we can use

fnmi(item-name, set-name, variable)   Find the next member occurrence of the given set for which the specified item has a value equal to the value of the program variable.

Find next member based on item value (**fnmi**) performs the same function as **fmi,** but instead of starting its search with the first member of the set, it begins with the next member. In all other respects **fnmi** is the same as **fmi.** The **fnmi** command is used when the item being tested does not have unique values in each occurrence. If no next value exists, **fnmi** returns an end-of-set error and makes the current member of the set null. If the current member of the set is null when **fnmi** is executed, then it behaves in an identical manner to **fmi.**

These two commands, while not strictly necessary for writing application programs, can simplify the programming effort greatly. In essence, they eliminate from the main program the need to write an additional loop. Thus the structure of the program is made that much clearer.

When a set relationship is declared as sorted in the DDL, then another command can be used:

fmsk(set-name, variable)   Find the first member occurrence of the given set for which the sort key item has a value equal to the value of the specified program variable.

Find member based on sort key (**fmsk**) can be used in place of **fmi** when the set in question is a sorted set. An item need not be specified since this information is contained in the DDL. The effect of **fmsk** is similar to **fmi** in virtually all respects. However, the internal processing of **fmsk** differs greatly from that of

fmi which performs a sequential search of the occurrences, since there is no specified pattern to the information. However, when we know that we are dealing with occurrences that are maintained in a sorted order, special algorithms (e.g., binary search) can be employed that will perform the search so much faster than **fmi**. The **fmsk** command should be used whenever searching for information from a sorted set, because of the efficiency of its algorithms.

At this point, a newcomer to database management might decide that because information can be retrieved from sorted sets more efficiently than sets of a different ordering, all sets should be sorted. The problem with this decision is that maintaining a sorted set ordering can be much more expensive than maintaining nonsorted sets. The proper choice depends on the type of application and processing under consideration. If the set will be accessed frequently for retrieval, but with relatively few insertions and deletions, then sorting coupled with **fmsk** is the best choice. If the set occurrences change more frequently or are infrequently accessed, then using another ordering and **fmi** may be a better design choice. The **fmi** command has its **fnmi,** so naturally **fmsk** must have its

fnmsk(set-name, variable)	Find the next member occurrence of the given set for which the sort key item has a value equal to the value of the specified program variable.

Find next member based on sort key (**fnmsk**) is identical in behavior to **fnmi,** except that the more efficient search algorithms are employed.

The **fmsk** command has one property which differs from **fmi.** If a match occurs, then the first occurrence that matches is made the current member of the set. This is the same for both commands. If a match does not occur, then the end-of-set error occurs. This is the same for both commands. However, **fmi** will set the current member to be null. **fmsk** (and **fnmsk**) does something quite different. The current member of the set will become the record occurrence following the position where the searched-for value would go if it existed. This is referred to as a *wild card* search.

Consider again Figs. 6.9 and 6.10. Suppose that the set WORK is sorted by the data item NAME, and that the "Data Processing" occurrence is the current owner of WORK. Suppose that the value of the program variable emp is the letter "L". Now if we execute the command "**fmsk**(WORK, emp)", we will get the end-of-set indicator, because no employee's name in this set is exactly equal to "L". But the current member of the set WORK will not be null; it will be the address of the "Mills" record.

Why is this of any use? For one thing, it allows us to check in the area for possible misspellings. If we are looking for Mills, but inadvertantly typed Malls, then the current member would be in the right *neighborhood*. A recovery routine might display five or six names to either side of the error occurrence, to aid in picking out the correct name. Another use of the wild card feature is to find quickly a starting point for sublist processing, for example, display the first 20 names beginning with the letter "L".

One final note concerning **fmsk.** If the sort key of the set consists of more than one data item, then a p-record would have to be used in place of the variable in the **fmsk** command. The definition of the p-record must match precisely the definition of the sort key in the DDL.

6.9 CHANGING DATA VALUES

The title of this chapter talks about the basic retrieval commands. In no way can these next four DML commands be classified as retrieval commands. They are update commands, period. However, because of their symmetry with the get commands this is where they seem to fit best in our discussion.

In the course of database processing, if is often necessary to modify, change, or replace an existing data value. Sometimes only a single data item value need be changed; sometimes it is the entire occurrence. The put commands perform these tasks for us.

The put commands are the exact opposites of the get commands. They take information currently residing in a program variable or p-record and transfer that information from the program to a specific data occurrence, whose address is a current member or owner. For each of the four get commands, there is a corresponding put command:

putm(set-name, p-record)   Put all of the data values contained in the given p-record into the occurrence that is the current member of the given set.

pfm(item-name, set-name, variable)   Put the value of the given variable into the specified item of the occurrence that is the current member of the given set.

puto(set-name, p-record)   Put all of the data values contained in the given p-record into the occurrence that is the current owner of the given set.

pfo(item-name, set-name, variable)   Put the value of the given variable into the specified item of the occurrence that is the current owner of the given set.

None of these commands modify currency indicators in any way. In all processing respects, except the direction of the flow of data, these commands behave identically to their corresponding get commands.

When a put command is executed, data is transferred into the database. The information being replaced is lost—permanently. Some care must be exercised to ensure that, when such updating occurs, it is performed properly. One exam-

```
ffm(SD);
do while (found)
     { gfm(TELE, SD, number);
       number [1] = "2";
       number [2] = "9";
       number [3] = "7";
       pfm(TELE, SD, number);
       fnm(SD);
     }
```
                                              Fig. 6.15   Updating the telephone exchange.

ple of the use of these commands will suffice. Suppose that the telephone company has changed the exchange designator for our area. That means that the first three digits of each telephone number have been changed. In our personnel database of Fig. 6.9, we must change these digits from 618 to 297.

Our strategy is to process each department record occurrence in turn, changing the telephone numbers as we go. Thus for each occurrence we must retrieve the old number, fix the digits, and put the updated number back into the database. This is the basic loop of Fig. 6.4 again; the entire program segment is shown in Fig. 6.15. Here, number is a program variable (array of seven characters).

When a sort key item is changed by one of the put commands, then that record occurrence is automatically relocated in its (new) proper position. If in the personnel example the set SD is sorted, and the Accounting Department changes its name to Financial Welfare, we can use a **pfm** or a **putm** to accomplish the change. Then in our two department example Data Processing would become the first member of the set SD. This automatic reordering is necessary for the **fmsk** command to function properly. The reordering is logical, not physical.

6.10   SUMMARY

In this chapter we have introduced the basic concepts of data base processing with a data manipulation language. These were illustrated with the MDBS DML. The syntax and flexibility of DMLs vary from one DBMS to another. An appreciation of the MDBS DML forms a useful basis for understanding the DMLs of other DBMSs. Several other DBMS approaches to procedural data manipulation are examined in Appendixes B–D.

Currency indicators are used to refer to specific record occurrences by address rather than by ambiguous values. Each set relationship in the database gives rise to two currency indicators: the current owner of the set and the current member of the set. It may also be possible to identify a first member of a set and a last member of a set. With respect to the current member, we also can identify the next member in the set and the previous member in the set; if one or both of these do not exist, trying to process them will result in an end-of-set error.

The find commands are used to share currency indicators within a set. The commands introduced are **ffm, fnm, flm, fpm, fmi, fnmi, fmsk,** and **fnmsk.** These all have the effect of establishing a current member of a specified set.

The assign commands are used to share currency indicators between two sets. The direction of the assignment is always from right to left, that is, from the second set to the first. The four assignment commands discussed are **som, smm, smo,** and **soo.**

The get commands correspond to the reading operation in file management. Once a record occurrence has been located through the currency indicators, the data values of this occurrence may be accessed through the use of the get commands. The commands introduced are **getm, gfm, geto,** and **gfo.**

The put commands correspond to the writing operation of file management, with the significant difference that updating is done in place. Thus the *old* values are lost as soon as the put command is executed. These commands directly parallel the get commands. The commands are **putm, pfm, puto,** and **pfo.**

RELATED READINGS

R. H. Bonczek, C. W. Holsapple, and A. B. Whinston, "Foundations of Decision Support Systems," Academic Press, New York, 1981.

J. Bradley, "File and Data Base Techniques," Holt, Rinehart, and Winston, New York, 1982.

Micro Data Base Systems Inc., "MDBS Application Programmers Reference Manual," Lafayette, Indiana, 1981.

T. W. Olle, "The CODASYL Approach to Data Base Management," Wiley, New York, 1978.

EXERCISES

1. Explain why a DBMS cannot keep track of a current record occurrence by its value. Give a simple example.
2. Why should one refrain from using the word *pointer* to explain location of record occurrence in a database system?
3. Are two currency indicators sufficient for processing a set relationship? Explain.

4. What is the main difference between **fmi** and **fmsk** commands? Can one be used in place for the other and vice versa? Explain.

5. A product distribution system is defined as follows:

(a)   There are seven products in the system PROD1, PROD2, . . . , PROD7.

(b)   These products are sold in five stores STORE1, STORE2, STORE3, STORE4, and STORE5.

(c)   These products are produced in 3 plants PLANT1, PLANT2, and PLANT3.

(d)   The stores are located in two cities CITY1 and CITY2.

(e)   The plants are owned by two owners OWNER1 and OWNER2.

(f)   Plant 1 produces products 1, 2, and 3.
   Plant 2 produces products 4 and 5.
   Plant 3 produces products 6 and 7.

(g)   City 1 has stores 1, 2, and 3.
City 2 has stores 4 and 5.

(h)   Owner 1 owns plant 1.
Owner 2 owns plants 2 and 3.

(i)   Products 1 and 2 are sold at store 1.
   Product 3 is sold at store 2.
   Product 4 is sold at store 3.
   Products 5 and 6 are sold at store 4.
   Product 7 is sold at store 5.

Develop a product distribution database schema diagram for this system.
Develop an occurrence diagram for the product distribution schema.
How many system owned sets are there in this system?
How many currency indicators are there for this database?

6. For the product distribution system in the preceding exercise:

(a)   develop a program structure to process all information from an owner-orientation;

(b)   show how the report would look;

(c)   without actually writing a program structure, show how the report would look for city-oriented processing.

7. (a)   Define p-records for each of the following record types.

Given: City   →   Name and population
        Plant →   Name, No. of employees, manager
        Store →   Name, and phone no.
        Owner →   Name, and phone no.
        Product → Name, product no., selling price

(b)   Develop a record occurrence diagram and fill in appropriate values for each record occurrence. (You provide the values.)

8. For Exercise 7, develop a program to display the number of products sold in each city by each owner.
9. Referring to Exercise 7, write a program to update product selling prices.
10. (a) Write a program to find a plant that makes a given product. (b) How many ways can this be done? Explain.
11. Referring to Fig. 6.3, write a program using the pseudo-language to list the states through which each polluted river passes.
12. Suppose we have established a database for the following schema:

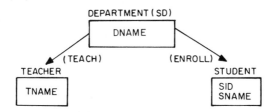

Write a pseudo-program to produce a report listing the student names of all students who are in the same department as a teacher named *D. B. Johnson*.
13. Using the schema of Exercise 12, write a program to retrieve all teachers for the departments of computer science, mathematics, statistics, and economics. All input–output must be through the terminal.
14. What kind of data structure is necessary to be able to use a **soo** command? Develop such a structure, plus an application program that includes **soo.**
15. Complete the processing of the pollution database described in Section 6.5.
16. Add to the program given in Fig. 6.7 the necessary retrieval commands to produce the report given in Table 6.1.
17. Design a program that would determine, from Fig. 6.9, all those employees whose job title included the word *computer*.
18. What commands would be affected if **putm** and **pfm** did not preserve order when modifying sort keys? Why?
19. In a hierarchical data structure, which of the commands presented in this chapter become superfluous?
20. How does the wild card search feature of **fmsk** simplify the problem of the exact matching of the data values?
21. The **fnmsk** command has a program variable as an argument. However, since it is finding the next occurrence with the same key value, it would appear that this variable is superfluous. Why must **fnmsk** have the variable as an argument?
22. It is possible to imagine a single assign command, whose arguments include an indication of which currency indicators are being set. Discuss the benefits and disadvantages of such a command.
23. The CODASYL-network model allows but a single currency indicator for

each set (see Appendix B). Discuss how the behavior of various commands presented in this chapter would have to be modified in such an environment.

24. Consider a record occurrence that has just been created, but not yet connected to any set relationship. How might your program access this occurrence?

25. Suppose that in the pollution schema of Fig. 6.2, a data item POPULATN (population) is added to the CITIES record type; set IN is still sorted by CNAME. Design a program that will determine for each state the city with the largest population. (Hint: As you iterate through the cities, where can you store the address of the current largest city?) What are the limitations of this technique?

26. It is possible to imagine a single data management command that performs both the positioning and retrieval functions. Discuss the benefits and disadvantages of such a command. Implement such a command as a subroutine.

27. Design a program that would determine from Fig. 6.2, all cities polluting a particular river in a particular state. The river and state names should be input from the terminal.

28. Design a subprogram to find the *n*th member of a set. Make the program as general as possible. What happens on successive uses of your program?

PROJECT

Devise the DML logic for generating the reports required for your application system. Embed this logic either in the pseudo-language introduced here or in another programming language with which you are familiar. These programs will be tested later.

Chapter 7

DATABASE PROCESSING: STORAGE AND UPDATE COMMANDS

Chapter 6 involved a discussion of DML commands that enable the applications programmer to perform virtually all retrieval functions. The find, assign, and get commands presented are sufficient for all but the most advanced applications. The put commands perform the important task of update in place, which of course is vital in any program that performs data modification.

All of these commands, of course, require that the database be *loaded*, that is, that record occurrences have already been created, and connected together to form sets of owner and member occurrences. In this chapter we will examine this loading process, as well as its opposite—unloading or deleting. Also, two necessary commands will be introduced, which are required in every DML program.

With the set of DML commands of this chapter and Chapter 6, completely workable applications systems can be developed.

7.1 ANOTHER CURRENCY INDICATOR

Each set relationship in a database schema gives rise to two currency indicators, called the current owner and the current member of that set. With these relationships, it is possible to process all records through the sets in which they participate. These indicators are satisfactory for the majority of database processing.

However, occasionally it is necessary to refer to record occurrences independently of any sets. For example, immediately after a new record occurrence is created, but before it is connected to any other occurrence through a set, there must be a way of referring to this new occurrence. Also, there are special types of processing that do not require the use of sets; see Chapters 10 and 12.

Because of these special circumstances, another currency indicator exists along with the current owners and members of all the sets. It is called the *current of run-unit* (cru). The name is derived from the CODASYL definitions (see Appendix B); a run-unit means a program that is running (executing). The cru, is a single currency indicator; each DML program has only one cru to manage.

Like the other currency indicators, the value of the cru is an address of a record occurrence, rather than the data value of the occurrence. The cru can be null, which is its initial value.

Many of the commands studied in Chapter 6 affect the cru, or can be extended to include the cru. The find commands all change the cru. If a find command executes without error, then the occurrence that becomes the current member of the specified set also becomes the cru occurrence. If an end-of-set error occurs during a find command, then the cru becomes null. This excludes **fmsk** and **fnmsk,** which on end-of-set makes the wild card occurrence the current member and cru.

The basic philosophy of the find commands with respect to cru is that any record occurrence that is found is automatically made the cru occurrence.

This philosophy can be extended to the assignment commands. The **som,** for example, performs an implicit **ffm**; thus the cru will be set to the first member if one is found, and to null if one is not found. Similarly, **smm, smo,** and **soo** all have an effect on cru.

In addition, there are four new assignment commands for going from set indicators to the cru and back:

scm(set-name)	Set the cru to be the value of the current member of the given set.
sco(set-name)	Set the cru to be the value of the current owner of the given set.
smc(set-name)	Set the current member of the given set to be the value of the cru.
soc(set-name)	Set the current owner of the given set to be the value of the cru.

The same naming conventions as those in Chapter 6 apply here. In the first two of these commands, the cru is being determined; thus the commands begin with **sc**. The latter two commands are assigning the cru value to other indicators; thus these commands end with **c**. As always, assignments progress from right to left.

Set current based on member (**scm**) and set current based on owner (**sco**) change only the cru indicator. An error will be returned only if the corresponding current member or owner indicator is null.

Set member based on current (**smc**) and set owner based on current (**soc**) modify a set indicator. Hence they each have the side effect of performing an automatic find. The **smc** command would automatically try to find an owner for the new member occurrence, while **soc** would automatically try to find the first member occurrence. Thus each of these commands can potentially return an end-of-set indicator. These two will also return an error if the cru occurrence does not properly mesh with the set indicator being assigned.

There is another interesting side effect to these two commands. After the execution of, for example, **soc** the current member of the set would be the first member of the owner occurrence whose address was cru. But, by finding this first member, the cru will be changed to the address of the first member. In other words, after the execution of **smc** and **soc,** the value of the cru will be different from what it was before the commands were executed.

Consider again the personnel example of Figs. 6.9 and 6.10. The initial currency configuration would be

Set	Current owner	Current member
SD	(system)	
WORK		
cru:		

Let us see the effect of executing some commands:

"**ffm**(SD)"

Set	Current owner	Current member
SD	(system)	(Accounting)
WORK		
cru: (Accounting)		

"**fnm**(SD)"

Set	Current owner	Current member
SD	(system)	(Data proc)
WORK		
cru: (Data Processing)		

The find commands set the cru to the record occurrence that is found.

"**som**(WORK, SD)"

Set	Current owner	Current member
SD	(system)	(Data proc)
WORK	(Data proc)	(Harris)
cru: (Harris)		

soms implicit **ffm** defines the cru value.

"**fpm**(SD)"

Set	Current owner	Current member
SD	(system)	(Accounting)
WORK	(Data proc)	(Harris)
cru: (Accounting)		

"**sco**(WORK)"

Set	Current owner	Current member
SD	(system)	(Accounting)
WORK	(Data proc)	(Harris)
cru: (Data Processing)		

These four new assignment commands are not that widely used. Their effectiveness lies in those few cases where the cru is required instead of the more common set-oriented processing.

The get and put commands of the previous chapter do not involve the cru in any way; they neither access nor modify the value of the cru. There are four new commands, however, which do use the cru value for retrieval or storage:

getc(p-record) — Get all of the data from the cru occurrence, and store the values in the specified p-record.

gfc(item-name, variable) — Get the value of the given data item of the cru occurrence, and store that value in the specified variable.

putc(p-record) — Put all of the data from the given p-record into the occurrence that is the cru.

pfc(item-name, variable) — Put the value of the given variable into the data item of the occurrence that is the cru.

These commands are self-explanatory. They may be used in place of the set-oriented commands, but only when we can ensure that the value of the cru will be the same as the corresponding set currency indicator.

The cru indicator is very transitory, since many commands have a direct effect on it. Generally speaking, we should not make any assumptions about the value of the cru, except in linear sequences of program code, that is, where there is no branching, iteration, or procedure invocations.

7.2 ADDING OCCURRENCES TO A DATABASE

Undisputedly, the cru indicator is most commonly used when a new record occurrence must be added to the database. Consider for a moment what processing must be performed. A new record occurrence means that space large enough to hold all of the data item values of this occurrence must be allocated in the database. Think of this space as an address that is not presently occupied. Then the data item values must be stored (or put) into this space. Finally, the new occurrence will normally need to be connected to other occurrences through the use of set relationships.

The use of the cru comes in the period after the space has been obtained and the data values stored, but before the occurrence has been connected to any other occurrences. Because the new occurrence has not been related to other occurrences, it makes little sense to refer to the new occurrence as a current owner or member of anything. Rather, when an occurrence is created, but before it is connected to other occurrences, the new occurrence is made the cru occurrence.

Perhaps, instead of using the cru indicator, we should try to establish the new occurrence in at least one set relationship immediately after the space is allocated, but before the data values are stored. But, even in this order, we must still refer to the space to be connected, and this must be done through the cru.

There is a reason why storage takes place before the new occurrence is connected to any other occurrences. In sets that have a sorted order, the value of the sort key determines the relative position in the set of the occurrence. If the occurrence is inserted into the set before the data values are stored, then the positioning of the occurrence must be done twice. The occurrence will be inserted first in a position corresponding to blank or zero data values; then after the store operation takes place, the occurrence must be logically relocated relative to the other occurrences in the set, in the position required by the new sort key value. This makes the insertion process twice as slow as necessary.

The command for creating a new record occurrence in the database is

crs (record-name, p-record)   Create a new record occurrence of the given record
                                   type, and store the values in the given p-record in the
                                   data items of the occurrence.

Create and store (**crs**) performs the first two steps discussed above, namely, the allocation of space for the new occurrence, and the storing of data values (an implicit put command) into that occurrence. The only currency indicator affected is the cru, which becomes the address of this new occurrence.

Sometimes, in the course of database processing, only a few of the data items will have known values at the time the record occurrence should be created. This is not really a problem. Using a p-record that exactly matches the DDL specification of the given record type, assign the known values to the appropriate variables in the p-record, and assign the variables corresponding to the unknown values zero or blank. Then the **crs** command will store the known values; the other data items can be updated at a later time with one of the put commands. This procedure works even if the missing values are sort keys of some set.

The p-record definition in a program must correspond to the field definitions of the given record type in the DDL in number and type. The names used for the p-record itself, and the variables in the p-record, are not important.

Figure 7.1 shows a database schema diagram for keeping inventory information on cars (units) by their model name (product), the date on which the unit is delivered to the dealership, and the date on which the car buyer takes the unit home. Each unit will be connected to its model and an arrival date, but only after it is sold will the unit be connected to the date sold. Figure 7.2 shows the present occurrence structure of the database.

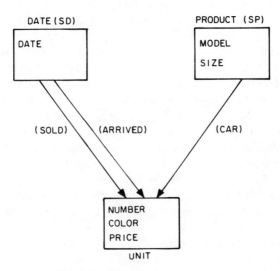

Fig. 7.1 Auto dealer inventory system.

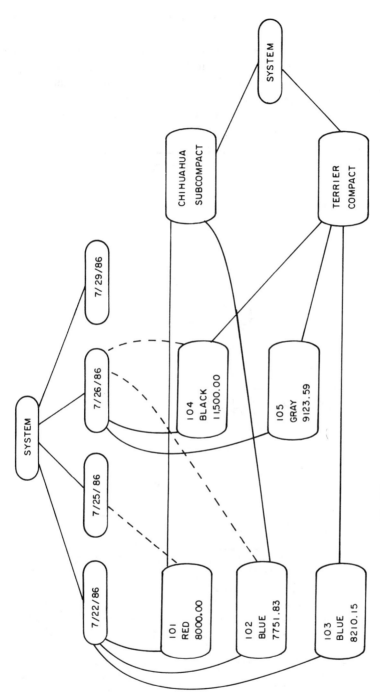

Fig. 7.2 Occurrences of inventory database. Arrived (———); sold (– – –).

Assume that we begin processing from scratch. Suppose that a p-record named auto has been defined that corresponds to the DDL definition of record type UNIT, and that the variables in auto have been assigned values for unit number 106, color green, and price $7575.00. Then executing the command "**crs** (UNIT, auto)" would create a new occurrence of UNIT as shown in Fig. 7.3. The present state of the currency indicators would be

Set	Current owner	Current member
SD	(system)	
SP	(system)	
ARRIVED		
SOLD		
CAR		
cru: (106)		

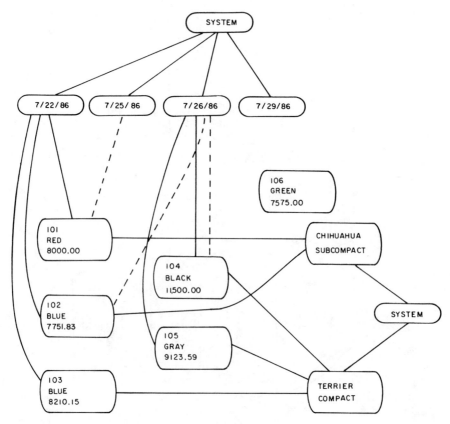

Fig. 7.3   Creating a new occurrence. Arrived (———); sold (– – –).

Notice that the occurrence is not connected to any other occurrences; this is reflected in the currency indicators as well.

Suppose that we were to get new values for the variables in the p-record auto, and execute another "**crs**(UNIT, auto)" command. Space would be allocated, the new values in auto would be stored, and the cru would be the address of this second new occurrence. Unfortunately, this is disastrous, because we have lost the address of the unit 106 occurrence and this record is not connected to any other occurrences. Thus we can never reach this occurrence by processing from system through set relationships, using the assign commands and find commands. Moreover, the only place this address was known—the cru—has just been changed. The unit 106 occurrence has just become an "orphan": the occurrence exists and takes up space in the database, but it cannot be accessed.

The moral of this story is simple: Immediately after a record occurrence is created, it should be connected to at least one other occurrence through some set. Otherwise we stand the very real chance of making an orphan of the occurrence (see Section 10.4 for a further discussion).

7.3   INSERTING OCCURRENCES INTO SETS

Thus we must quickly consider how to insert a newly created record occurrence into a set relationship. The processing involved (in terms of Fig. 7.3) is apparently straightforward—we must connect the unit 106 record with either a DATE record or a PRODUCT record. Suppose the unit 106 record occurrence has just been created. Let us first connect it to its arrival date, 7/29/86.

If unit 106 is to become a member in a set occurrence owned by the 7/29/86 record, then we must first make this DATE record the current owner of the set in question, in this case ARRIVED. This is easily accomplished: we first make the 7/29/86 occurrence the current member of the set SD (through either a **flm,** through a program loop that checks all three date fields, or more likely through **fmsk,** where all three data items are defined to be the sort key), and then make this occurrence the current owner of ARRIVED, by using **som.**

Unfortunately, this sequence of commands is also unworkable, because all of these find operations are changing the cru indicator! We have once again created an orphan occurrence. Unit 106 is no longer accessible from our application programs.

The method for solving this problem is to determine the proper owner(s) of the unit occurrence before that occurrence is created. Assuming that p-record date matches the DATE record type, and has been initialized to 7/29/86, the following sequence of commands will prepare us for inserting unit 106 into the correct set occurrence:

"**fmsk**(SD, date)"
"**som**(ARRIVED, SD)"
"**crs**(UNIT, auto)"

Set	Current owner	Current member
SD	(system)	(7/29/86)
SP	(system)	
ARRIVED	(7/29/86)	
SOLD		
CAR		
cru: (106)		

The **fmsk** made (7/29/86) the cru. The **som** made the cru null, since the implicit find would have returned an end-of-set indicator. The **crs** made (106) the cru.

We are now ready to add the 106 occurrence to the set ARRIVED. The requisite command is

> **ims**(set-name)   Insert the occurrence whose address is the cru into the given set as a member.

Insert member in set (**ims**) is the missing link. It takes the cru occurrence and adds it to the set specified under the current owner of that set. If the current owner of the set is null, an error occurs. The cru occurrence must mesh with the set, of course. The newly added occurrence also becomes the current member of this set.

In our example, we would simply write "**ims**(ARRIVED)". This would connect the 106 occurrence to its arrival date (Fig. 7.4), and make it the current member of the set ARRIVED.

We are now on fairly safe ground. As long as an occurrence is connected through set relationships to other occurrences, all the way back to the system record, then that occurrence can be accessed in the future.

Suppose now we wish to connect unit 106 with its model (a Chihuahua). If we assume that program variable model is assigned the value "Chihuahua", then we can execute

"**fmi**(MODEL, SP, model)"

Set	Current owner	Current member
SD	(system)	(7/29/86)
SP	(system)	(Chihuahua)
ARRIVED	(7/29/86)	(106)
SOLD		
CAR		
cru: (Chihuahua)		

"**som**(CAR, SP)"

Set	Current owner	Current member
SD	(system)	(7/29/86)
SP	(system)	(Chihuahua)
ARRIVED	(7/29/86)	(106)
SOLD		
CAR	(Chihuahua)	(101)
cru: (101)		

"**scm**(ARRIVED)"

Set	Current owner	Current member
SD	(system)	(7/29/86)
SP	(system)	(Chihuahua)
ARRIVED	(7/29/86)	(106)
SOLD		
CAR	(Chihuahua)	(101)
cru: (106)		

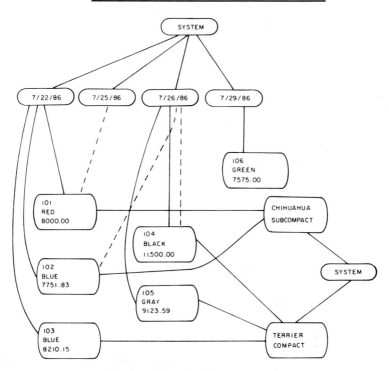

Fig. 7.4 Connecting the new occurrence.

"**ims**(CAR)"

Set	Current owner	Current member
SD	(system)	(7/29/86)
SP	(system)	(Chihuahua)
ARRIVED	(7/29/86)	(106)
SOLD		
CAR	(Chihuahua)	(106)
cru: (106)		

The **scm** command is used in this example to reassign the cru to be unit 106, the occurrence that we wish to insert as a member in the CAR set in the next statement. Occurrence 106 would now be connected to both its arrival date and its product type.

As is often the case in programming, sometimes by rearranging the command sequence some commands can be eliminated, thus producing shorter and more readable code. In this case, we could have established the Chihuahua occurrence as the current owner of the set CAR before we created the 106 occurrence. Then the **scm** would have been unnecessary, since the **crs** would have left 106 as the cru. This approach has the added benefit of making the program better struc-

```
    input auto.number, auto.color, auto.price;

/* determine date */

    input date.month, date.day, date.year;

    fmsk(SD, date);
    if (not found) then perform error-routine;
    som(ARRIVED, SD);

/* determine product */

    input model;

    fmi(MODEL, SP, model);
    if (not found) then perform error-routine;
    som(CAR, SP);

/* create and insert */

    crs(UNIT, auto);
    ims(ARRIVED);
    ims(CAR);
```

Fig. 7.5 Loading new units into the database.

tured: we find all owners, then create the new occurrence, and finally insert it into the various sets.

As a general philosophy, it is better to establish current owners for sets first, before the occurrence that is to become member is made cru. This philosophy is followed in Fig. 7.5, which presents the program developed for adding new units to our database.

When a car is sold, we must take the occurrence of that unit and connect it to the selling date. Our philosophy indicates that, because a particular DATE record will be the owner, it is best to make it the current owner of the set SOLD before we get the unit in question. Again, we are referring only to the database processing commands, not the order of data entry from the user terminal.

Figure 7.6 presents a program for indicating that a car has been sold. We will trace its execution to fully understand the techniques involved. Assume that we are starting from scratch.

The program first requests the current date (date of sale). If we enter it as 7/29/86, then after the **fmsk** and **som** commands, the currency indicators would read

Set	Current owner	Current member	
SD	(system)	(7/29/86)	
SP	(system)		
ARRIVED			
SOLD	(7/29/86)		error = end-of-set
CAR			
cru:			

The end-of-set error is irrelevant, since we are not looking for members of SOLD.

The program next asks what model of car has been sold. If the user answers ''Terrier'', then after the **fmi** and **som** our currency indicators read

Set	Current owner	Current member
SD	(system)	(7/29/86)
SP	(system)	(Terrier)
ARRIVED		
SOLD	(7/29/86)	
CAR	(Terrier)	(104)
cru: (104)		

/* date of sale */
   input date.month, date.day, date.year;

   fmsk(SD, date);
   if (not found) then perform error-routine;
   som(SOLD, SD);

/* find unit */

   input model;

   fmi(MODEL, SP, model);
   if (not found) then perform error.routine;
   som(CAR, SP);

   input number;

   fmi(NUMBER, CAR, number);
   if (not found) then perform error-routine;

/* insert */
   ims(SOLD);   **Fig. 7.6**   Indicating that units have been sold.

The program asks for the unit number; the user responds 103. After the **fmi** we have

Set	Current owner	Current member
SD	(system)	(7/29/86)
SP	(system)	(Terrier)
ARRIVED		
SOLD	(7/29/86)	
CAR	(Terrier)	(103)
cru: (103)		

Because the last occurrence found is in fact the one we wish to add to the set SOLD, the cru has the proper value without recourse to the assignment commands. The final command **ims** connects unit 103 to the present date through set SOLD; 103 also becomes the current member of SOLD. The updated occurrence diagram is given in Fig. 7.7.

The **ims** command simply requires the occurrence that is to become the new member be the cru and its owner to be the current owner. The **ims** will automatically take care of logically positioning the new occurrence according to the order of the set as declared in the DDL specifications.

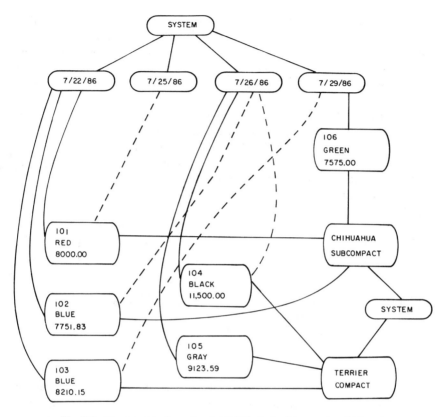

Fig. 7.7 Occurrences after sale of unit 103. Arrived (———); sold (– – –).

7.4 DELETING RECORD OCCURRENCES

At some point, record occurrences no longer convey useful information. They may report out-of-date facts, or their content may have been summarized in reports so that they are no longer needed. Thus it is necessary for such occurrences to be deleted from the database.

There is a more practical reason for deleting record occurrences. The database cannot be infinitely large. Without periodic deletions, the size of the database could well become unmanageable. There are several reasons for this. One is that commands like **fmsk** and **fmi** operate on collections of records rather than single record occurrences. The fewer occurrences that must be checked by these commands, the faster they execute, and the more efficiently the database control system operates. Another reason concerns the physical organization of the database system. Because the entire database (for even medium-sized applications) cannot all fit into the memory of the computer at one time, the database control system must search for relevant record occurrences and bring them into the memory of the machine to process a particular DML command. The greater the number of irrelevant occurrences, the slower the database control system operates.

Deletion is a rather drastic act. Once a record occurrence has been deleted, we can no longer obtain its data values. We can no longer make it the current of anything. The space it occupied in the database (its address) is returned to the pool of free space of the database. This means that future create commands can reuse this address for other record occurrences, not necessarily of the same record type. To summarize, once a record has been deleted from the database, it is gone forever.

The deletion commands are somewhat tricky, not because they are complex, but because they have a number of clever side effects. Though not unreasonable, these side effects can be extensive. If care is observed, no deleterious effects result from using the deletes. There are three delete commands

drm(set-name)	Delete the record occurrence that is the current member of the given set.
dro(set-name)	Delete the record occurrence that is the current owner of the given set.
drc	Delete the record occurrence that is the cru.

Delete record based on member (**drm**) takes the occurrence that is the current member of the given set and disconnects it from all other occurrences. In addition, if the occurrence to be deleted is the current owner or member of *another* set, that currency indicator becomes null. This applies to the cru as well. Then the occurrence is physically deleted from the database. The *next* occurrence of the specified set becomes the current member of that set and the cru; if there is no next member, the current member and cru are made null and an end-of-set error occurs. Only for the specified set is the next member made current; if the deleted record was the current owner or current member of other sets, then those currency indicators become null.

Delete record based on owner (**dro**) operates on much the same principles. If the occurrence to be deleted is current in *other* sets or is the cru, then these indicators are made null. The occurrence is disconnected from all other occurrences, and then physically deleted from the database. Because in the 1:N sets that we are using each member occurrence has at most one owner, the current owner of the specified set and the cru become null, and an end-of-set error is returned.

Delete record based on current (**drc**) has no arguments. The cru occurrence is disconnected from all other occurrences; if it is the current owner or current member of any set, that currency indicator is made null. Then the record is physically deleted from the database. The cru is also made null.

Using again the occurrence structure of Fig. 7.7, suppose that we have the following currency table:

Set	Current owner	Current member
SD	(system)	(7/26/86)
SP	(system)	(Chihuahua)
ARRIVED	(7/26/86)	(104)
SOLD	(7/25/86)	(101)
CAR	(Terrier)	(104)
cru: (Terrier)		

Let us execute a "**drm**(SD)''. The occurrence 7/26/86 appears as the current owner of ARRIVED, so this currency indicator must become null. Occurrence 7/26/86 is now deleted from the database, and the next member of the SD set, 7/29/86 becomes the current member of SD:

Set	Current owner	Current member
SD	(system)	(7/29/86)
SP	(system)	(Chihuahua)
ARRIVED		(104)
SOLD	(7/25/86)	(101)
CAR	(Terrier)	(104)
cru: (7/29/86)		

Now assume that we are back to the initial position given above, prior to **drm**. Let us try "**dro**(ARRIVED)''. Since this is referring to the same record occurrence, the effect on the database will be the same (Fig. 7.8), however, the currency indicators will not be the same:

Set	Current owner	Current member	
SD	(system)		
SP	(system)	(Chihuahua)	
ARRIVED		(104)	error = end-of-set
SOLD	(7/25/86)	(101)	
CAR	(Terrier)	(104)	
cru:			

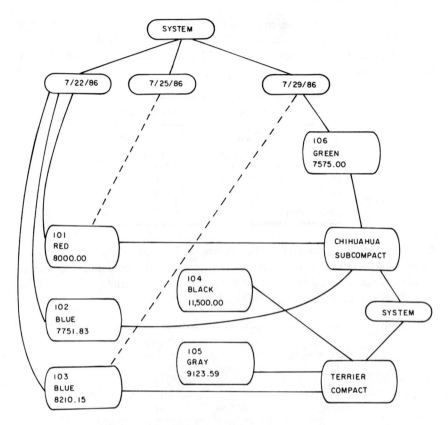

Fig. 7.8   Deleting a data occurrence. Arrived (———); sold (– – –).

The differences occur in the current member of SD and cru. In the first case, it was the member of SD that was being deleted. Thus the next member of SD became current. In the second case, the current owner of ARRIVED was deleted. Although this is in fact the very same record occurrence, because of the form of the command, the current member of SD is simply made null. Rather than being a handicap, this apparent anomoly of the delete commands can be used to great advantage when designing your application programs.

Now return the database to the state of Fig. 7.7, that is, before anything has been deleted. Note that all of the cars delivered on 7/22/86 have been sold. Thus we need to delete all of these units from our inventory database, as well as the 7/22/86 occurrence of the DATE record type.

Figure 7.9 presents a program for performing the stated task. Note that we wish to process all units (members) for a given date (owner). Thus not surprisingly the structure of the program is similar to that of Fig. 6.4. We need one

```
/* determine date */
    input date.month, date.day, date.year;
    fmsk(SD, date);
    if (not found) then perform error-routine;
    som(ARRIVED, SD);
    do while (found)
            drm(ARRIVED);
    drm(SD);
```

Fig. 7.9   Deleting the arrivals for a date and then the date itself.

iteration loop to locate each of the member occurrences. However, we do not need to include **fnm,** since the **drm** command automatically makes the next member the current member after the deletion.

After the **fmsk** and **som** have been executed, we trace the currency indicators:

Set	Current owner	Current member
SD	(system)	(7/22/86)
SP	(system)	
ARRIVED	(7/22/86)	(101)
SOLD		
CAR		
cru: (101)		

"**drm**(ARRIVED)"

Set	Current owner	Current member
SD	(system)	(7/22/86)
SP	(system)	
ARRIVED	(7/22/86)	(102)
SOLD		
CAR		
cru: (102)		

"**drm**(ARRIVED)"

Set	Current owner	Current member
SD	(system)	(7/22/86)
SP	(system)	
ARRIVED	(7/22/86)	(103)
SOLD		
CAR		
cru: (103)		

"**drm**(ARRIVED)"

Set	Current owner	Current member
SD	(system)	(7/22/86)
SP	(system)	
ARRIVED	(7/22/86)	error = end-of-set
SOLD		
CAR		
cru:		

"**drm**(SD)"

Set	Current owner	Current member
SD	(system)	(7/25/86)
SP	(system)	
ARRIVED		
SOLD		
CAR		
cru:		

The modified occurrence diagram, showing the remaining occurrences, is given in Fig. 7.10.

Deletes are very powerful commands. Because they are easy to use, they are easy to misuse. It is really quite simple to destroy or to make an orphan of a great deal of your database with just a few misguided deletes.

For example, suppose that we were to delete the 7/29/86 occurrence of the DATE record type and the Chihuahua PRODUCT occurrence from the database of Fig. 7.10. What happens to the unit 106 occurrence? It is orphaned. There is no other occurrence connected to unit 106. This problem can be compounded in larger data structures. Many hundreds of occurrences can be orphaned by a single delete. It is the responsibility of the application developer to control this activity and make sure it does not happen in his or her system.

7.5 REMOVING OCCURRENCES FROM SETS

Deletes can be thought of as the opposites of the create command. By analogy, remove is the opposite of the insert command. The remove command takes an occurrence that is part of a set out of that set. The owner occurrence will have one fewer member after the remove has occurred; however, the remove does not destroy the member record occurrence itself. Thus, the occurrence can still

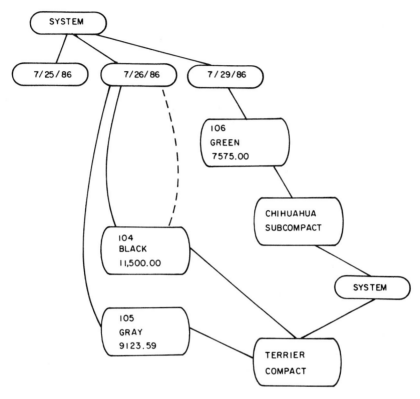

Fig. 7.10   Occurrences after deletion program. Arrived (———); sold (– – –).

function in other sets and be current in currency indicators. This command is less drastic than the deletes and does not have all of those side effects associated with record deletion.

The single remove command to be introduced is

rms(set-name)   Remove the current member from the given set.

Remove member from set (**rms**) requires a current owner and member of the specified set. The current member occurrence is disconnected from its owner occurrence. The next member record after the one that was removed becomes the current member of the set, and the cru as well. Which member record is next depends on the order of the set, as declared in the DDL specification. If there is no next member, an end-of-set error is returned.

The **rms** does not affect any currency indicators of any set other than the one specified in the command. The cru indicator may be changed.

Consider the occurrence structure in Fig. 7.10. If our currency table is

Set	Current owner	Current member
SD	(system)	(7/26/86)
SP	(system)	
ARRIVED	(7/26/86)	(105)
SOLD		(105)
CAR	(Terrier)	(105)

cru: (Terrier)

then "**rms**(ARRIVED)" produces

Set	Current owner	Current member
SD	(system)	(7/26/86)
SP	(system)	
ARRIVED	(7/26/86)	(104)
SOLD		(105)
CAR	(Terrier)	(105)

cru: (104)

"**rms**(CAR)"

Set	Current owner	Current member	
SD	(system)	(7/26/86)	
SP	(system)		
ARRIVED	(7/26/86)	(104)	
SOLD		(105)	
CAR	(Terrier)		error = end-of-set

cru:

We are on the brink of another "orphaning." If the current member of the set SOLD is changed in any way (including by terminating the current program; see the next section), then our last connection to occurrence 105 is lost forever. When using **rms,** one must pay particular attention to the order in which commands are executed, or orphaning will be the result.

Probably the most common use of **rms** is to logically move an occurrence from one owner to another. This occurs if the occurrence was originally classified incorrectly, or if the owner records represent status levels that may change over time (jobs, education, affiliations, etc.). Reverting to the occurrence structure of Fig. 7.10 once more, suppose that an audit has determined that unit 104

```
                        /* find unit */

                        input model;

                        fmi(MODEL, SP, model);
                        if (not found) then perform error-routine;
                        som(CAR, SP);

                        input number;

                        fmi(NUMBER, CAR, number);
                        if (not found) then perform error-routine;

                        /* remove from old list */

                        smm(ARRIVED, CAR);
                        rms(ARRIVED);
                        /* find new owner */

                        input date.month, date.day, date.year;

                        fmsk(SD, date);
                        if (not found) then perform error-routine;
                        som(ARRIVED, SD);

                        /* re-insert */

                        scm(CAR);
                        ims(ARRIVED);
```

Fig. 7.11 Switching arrival dates.

actually was delivered on the 25th, and not the 26th. We must change the database so that unit 104 is owned by 7/25/86 instead of 7/26/86.

The procedure is to first locate the unit in question, remove it from its present owner, and then add it to the new owner. This process is followed in the program of Fig. 7.11. Tracing the execution, after **fmi, som, fmi, som,** and **smm** we have

Set	Current owner	Current member
SD	(system)	
SP	(system)	(Terrier)
ARRIVED	(7/26/86)	(104)
SOLD		
CAR	(Terrier)	(104)
cru: (7/26/86)		

"**rms**(ARRIVED)"

Set	Current owner	Current member	
SD	(system)		
SP	(system)	(Terrier)	
ARRIVED	(7/26/86)		error = end-of-set
SOLD			
CAR	(Terrier)	(104)	
cru:			

The end-of-set can safely be ignored here. Next we execute a **fmsk, som, scm,** and **ims**:

Set	Current owner	Current member
SD	(system)	(7/25/86)
SP	(system)	(Terrier)
ARRIVED	(7/25/86)	(104)
SOLD		
CAR	(Terrier)	(104)
cru: (104)		

The key to this processing logic is the fact that after the **rms** command we still had the address of unit 104 in one of our currency indicators, in this case the current member of CAR. This enabled us at the next-to-last step to use **scm** to define the cru to be the occurrence we wished to insert. The new occurrence diagram is given in Fig. 7.12.

7.6   TWO REQUIRED COMMANDS

Computing systems can be viewed as a series of layers, or levels, where each layer views the next lower layer as "the computer." The end user of your application software believes that this program is the only function of "the computer." The application programmer is aware of the computer language, its compiler, and the database control system. In the same way, the database control system uses the level below it to perform all of its low-level, detailed processing. This multi-level view is depicted in Fig. 7.13, which most resembles "Dante's Inferno."

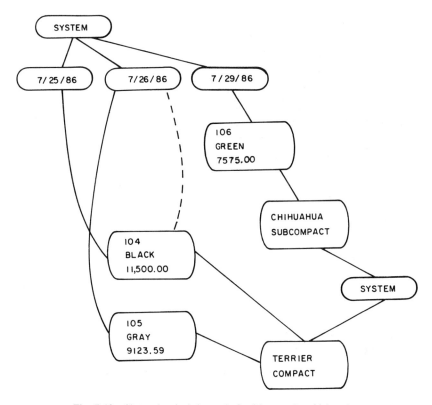

Fig. 7.12   Changed arrival dates. Arrived (———); sold (– – –).

Because of this fact, the database control system occasionally needs help in figuring out where things go. As described earlier in Chapter 4, the database appears as no more than another system file to the operating system. Thus it is necessary for the application program to identify this file to the database control system.

The database control system also needs to know certain other pieces of information, such as who is using the program and what the user's password is. Since we must communicate the password to the database control system anyway, all of this information can be set out together in a single DML command, saving time and space within the program.

There is a fourth element that needs to be specified. If the only database operations the program is going to perform are retrieval operations, then certain processing efficiencies can be realized if the database control system knows this fact. Thus, the last element is a status value, indicating whether the database will

THE WORLD (USERS)

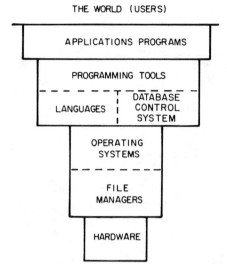

Fig. 7.13   The rings of the infernal regions.

be used for *read only* access or for possible *modification*. The required DML communication command is

dbopn(p-record)   Open the database according to the specifications given in the p-record.

The database open command (**dbopn**) is used only once in a program, and must occur before any other database processing can occur. The p-record must contain four variables. The first variable must be assigned the user name, as defined in the DDL. The second must contain the password. The third is either the string "READ", for read only access, or "MODIFY", for read–write access. The fourth variable must contain the fully qualified file name of the operating system file holding the database.

The precise form of the **dbopn** command is host language and operating system specific. Not so for the second of the required commands:

dbcls   Close the database

The database close command (**dbcls**) must occur after a program has completed its database processing to ensure that any parts of the database residing in the memory of the computer are copied back to the disk. No DML commands may be executed after a **dbcls**; *all* currency indicators are made null.

All of the program segments given in Chapters 6 and 7 must be preceded by a **dbopn,** and followed by a **dbcls**. Summarizing, **dbopn** is the "start from scratch" command, while **dbcls** signifies "all done."

TABLE 7.1

DML Commands

Find	Assign	Get	Put	Build	Eliminate	Required
ffm	**som**	**getc**	**putc**	**crs**	**drc**	**dbopn**
fnm	**smm**	**getm**	**putm**		**drm**	
flm	**smo**	**geto**	**puto**	**ims**	**dro**	**dbcls**
fpm	**soo**					
fmi	**scm**	**gfc**	**pfc**		**rms**	
fnmi	**sco**	**gfm**	**pfm**			
fmsk	**smc**	**gfo**	**pfo**			
fnmsk	**soc**					

7.7 SUMMARY

In this chapter, 16 new database processing commands have been introduced, bringing the total to 35. These DML commands allow the development of complex application programs. However, any particular procedure within a program would use only a handful of commands.

The notion of the cru indicator leads to the commands **getc, gfc, putc, pfc, scm, sco, smc, soc,** which belong to the get, put, and assign groups of the previous chapter. The cru is primarily used with the two commands of the build group: **crs** and **ims.**

The three delete commands, **drm, dro, drc,** and the remove command **rms** form the eliminating group. The deletes are characterized by their side effects. Though logical, these commands should be used with care. Injudicious use of delete and remove commands can result in orphan record occurrences, which exist in the database and consume resources, but cannot be accessed or processed.

The two required commands, **dbopn** and **dbcls,** are each used once per program. They are used primarily so that the database control system can communicate with the operating system level of the computer.

Table 7.1 contains all of the DML commands presented in Chapters 6 and 7.

RELATED READINGS

ANSI X3H2, "Overview of DBCS/Programming Language Interface," American National Standards Institute, 1982.

R. H. Bonczek, C. W. Holsapple, and A. B. Whinston, "Foundations of Decision Support Systems," Academic Press, New York, 1981.

J. Bradley, "File and Data Base Techniques," Holt, Rinehart, and Winston, New York, 1982.

Micro Data Base Systems Inc., "MDBS Application Programmers Reference Manual," Lafayette, Indiana, 1981.

T. W. Olle, "The CODASYL Approach to Data Base Management," Wiley, New York 1978.

EXERCISES

1. Explain why it is useful to have a cru currency indicator?
2. What are the side-effects of the **smc** and **soc** commands?
3. What are orphan record occurrences? Describe two ways of creating orphan occurrences. How can one avoid creating orphan occurrences?
4. In the car dealership database, the following modifications are desired. In order to keep better control of the cars, every time a car arrives it is assigned to one of the two salespersons in the dealership, namely Mr. Johnson or Ms. Smith. The next arrival goes to the other salesperson and the process continues, alternating between the two salespersons. The cars can be sold by either of the two salespersons, independently of the car assignment. That is, Ms. Smith can sell a car assigned to Mr. Johnson and vice versa. Each salesperson is identified by

   Name
   Salesperson no.   (1000001 for Johnson,
                        100002 for Ms. Smith)
   Service date   (1/1/86 for Mr. Johnson,
                        7/1/86 for Ms. Smith).

   (a) Develop a schema diagram for the modified auto dealer inventory system.

   (b) If car 101 is assigned to Ms. Smith, and if Mr. Johnson has sold cars 101 and 102, develop a record occurrence diagram showing all information (including assignments and sales). Use Fig. 7.4 as a starting point.

   (c) How many system owned sets do you have in your schema diagram?

5. The following events occur at the auto dealership. A new salesperson, Ms. Wilson, joins the dealership on 7/26/86 with a number of 100003. The car 106 is assigned to Ms. Wilson. Ms. Wilson sells cars 105 and 106 on 7/30/86.

   (a) Develop a complete record occurrence diagram reflecting the above situation.

(b) Write programs for creating the new salesperson occurrence and for connecting the new salesperson to appropriate car occurrences.

6. Write a program to produce a report showing car sales by each salesperson in a chronological sequence.

7. Write a program to switch car sales from one salesperson to another and to switch from one *sold* date to another. For instance, if car *xxx* was erroneously connected, showing that salesperson *Y* sold this car, but actually salesperson *Z* sold the car, then the car *xxx* should be disconnected from *Y* and connected to *Z*.

8. List all DML commands, including those introduced in Chapter 6, which will affect the cru.

9. Based on Fig. 7.4, write a program to delete all units which arrived at 7/22/86 and made by Chihuahua.

10. Referring to the program in Fig. 7.11, write a program which will use SD to find unit number 104, instead of using SP.

11. State the differences between the cru and currency indicators of a set.

12. Consider the following database schema. Now if we want to enter into the database the information that a student named Joan Snale with student id 901-64-2321 enrolls in the computer science department, advised by Dr. James Smith, what would be an outline of the load program?

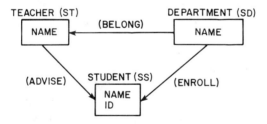

13. Indicate the difference(s) between the commands **rms**(S1) and **drm** (S1)?

14. What is the difference between **drm**(S1) and **dro**(S2), where the current member of S1 happens to be the current owner of S2?

15. What precautions should be taken when using the **rms** command?

16. Based on Exercise 12, what are the necessary steps in updating the database if we want to change a student's advisor?

17. It is possible to imagine the creation and insertion functions combined into a single command. Describe the syntax of such a command, its effect on currency indicators, and on the structure of the application programs.

18. Why doesn't the database control system check for the creation of orphan occurrences, and respond with an error indicator?

19. Using the schema of Fig. 7.1, design a computer program that will delete all records of a specified model line. The model name will be input from

the terminal. Check for, and delete, those dates which are not linked to any units.

20. Modify the program given in Fig. 7.5, so that it will create a date or model occurrence if they do not yet exist. How can spurious occurrences, due to typographical errors, be avoided?

21. The **ims** is a set-oriented command for which we did not introduce a symmetric counterpart. Describe a situation where an *insert owner into set* command could prove beneficial.

22. Design a load program for the personnel database of Fig. 6.11.

23. Suppose that, due to a clerical error, all cars in the schema of Fig. 7.2 reported as being delivered on a specified date actually arrived on a different date. Design a program that would switch arrival dates for all such units.

24. In a typical hierarchical data management system, a deletion command would not only delete the specified record occurrence, but all occurrences below it in the hierarchy. Discuss the implications of such a command in the CODASYL-network environment.

25. Can a program always be reorganized to avoid the use of a *set current* command? Is such reorganization desirable?

26. Suppose your processing is such that you need to find many occurrences before you can modify a single occurrence. What is wrong with opening the database with read access, finding the many occurrences, closing the database, and then reopening it with modify access, so that the change can be made?

27. Design a load program for the pollution database of Fig. 6.2. Is it easier to design a single program, or several shorter programs? What might the end users say?

28. Describe a situation where you would use the **dro** command.

29. Revise the program presented in Fig. 7.9 so that it uses **drc** instead of **drm.**

30. In processing a stack (LIFO set), two operations are defined. The push operation adds a new occurrence to the top of the stack, while the pop operation removes an occurrence from the stack. Write two general subprograms that perform the push and pop operations on an arbitrary LIFO set.

PROJECT

Determine which of the record types in your schema have relatively static occurrences and which have frequently changing occurrences. Also, based on your narrative description of typical transactions for the application, determine which record types and relationships are involved in each kind of transaction.

Develop sample data for occurrences of the relatively static records. Develop sample transaction data for each of the kinds of transactions.

Chapter 8

PROGRAMMING CONSIDERATIONS

We are now in a position to look at program design for database processing. We shall see that each individual program will contain only a fraction of the commands presented in the previous chapters. We shall also observe that some basic programming structures can be developed that, with simple modification, can be used in almost all circumstances. Thus the task of processing database structures can be reduced to the application of these programming structures, with customization occurring as necessary.

The main problem in presenting examples and cases in a textbook is that it is difficult to convey the essence of the discovery process required. It is rare that a problem is presented to a designer in a few paragraphs, and in a form ready for implementation. More often, the process is iterative: the designer develops the outline of a system; the user community suddenly remembers a number of details that were left out of the original description; the designer revises the original design. This process is repeated many times, until either a consensus is reached on the system, or until the economic pressures derived from not having the finished system force a completion.

In this chapter we present two cases for consideration. Not all of the elements of the DDL are incorporated into these examples; nor are all of the DML commands used. These examples do, however, provide some insights into the design process, so that when faced with more complex application situations, we will be able to apply the same strategies for design and development.

8.1   EXAMPLE 1—DISTRIBUTED COMPUTER NETWORK SCHEDULING

A distributed computer network is a collection of computing sites or centers, each connected to at least one other site through a communications system. At each site there may be zero, one, or more computers. These machines are categorized by their model number, manufacturer, and serial number. Users of the computer network each have an individual four character user ID. Databases with given code numbers can also be stored at each site. Through a remote job entry system, users submit tasks to be performed by the system. Each task is numbered; numbers are unique within a single day. Each task is assigned to a particular computer for primary processing; the computer may or may not reside at the same site as the user. Most tasks will also require some information to be accessed from one or more databases which may be maintained at remote sites. For scheduling purposes, it is necessary to know the estimated length of time that a particular database will be accessed by a particular task. It is not necessary to associate a database with a host computer at a particular site.

The schema that we design must incorporate all of these different concepts. Then programs must be developed for entering information into this data structure. Finally, report programs must be written which retrieve the data in a form usable by managers.

8.2   DESIGNING THE DATA STRUCTURE

We shall follow the schema design method of Chapter 5. The first step is to identify the data items that will be used in the schema. This is done by carefully reading the previous section. Step two is the aggregation of data items into record types. However, in reading the previous section, it becomes clear that similar items are presented together. Thus record types may also be ascertained directly from the problem description.

Table 8.1 presents a list of data items that has been extracted from the description above. With each item is a suggested name and the type and size characteristics of the item. Most of the data items are rather straightforward. The *user name* and *database description* items are included for internal control purposes, that is, to double check the accuracy of the data input process.

Now we begin to group these items into record types. Site name is not in a one–one relationship with any other items, because each site can have many users, computers, databases, and tasks. Thus it must be in a record type of its own. Computer model, manufacturer (MFR), and serial number (SERIAL) can

TABLE 8.1

Data Items for Example 1

Item description	Name	Type	Length
Site name	NAME	string	30
Computer model	MODEL	char	6
Computer manufacturer	MFR	char	15
Computer serial number	SERIAL	char	20
User name	NAME	string	20
User id	ID	char	4
Database code	CODE	integer	2
Database description	DESC	string	40
Task number	NUMBER	integer	2
Date	DATE	date	
Seconds that a task accesses a db	LENGTH	real	4

all go together in a nearly one–one fashion. If the purpose of this system was to maintain an *inventory* of hardware, users, and software (database systems), then it might be better to develop the computer related items into a schema such as the one shown in Fig. 8.1. This structure keeps track of hardware (identified by serial number) according to the model of the hardware; models are classified according to the manufacturer. However, in this application, such a detailed structure is not necessary. No anticipated processing would require knowledge of, say, "all machines built by Ace Computers." In our scheduling system we must simply have a method of referring to any particular machine. Because the processing required for this information is relatively simple, the structure we

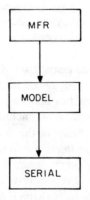

Fig. 8.1   Possible configuration of computer items.

design may itself be relatively simple. In the present case the proper solution is a single record type consisting of the three computer related items.

This is a design point that bears repeating. The database structure must only be as detailed as the processing requires. A very liberal design approach would be to make each data item its own record type and then have many set relationships among the resultant plethora of record types. This approach can be characterized as anticipating every possible combination of storage relationships and future processing. It is a quite expensive design philosophy in terms of storage overhead. A very conservative design approach is to collapse as much information into a record type as possible. This approach is quite expensive in terms of processing speed and efficiency. The best designs go to neither extreme, but incorporate the necessary relationships and make common sense assumptions on the types of processing that will occur.

User name and ID clearly form a unit, as do database code and description. The task number and date together uniquely identify the task, hence, these can be a unit as well (see also Exercise 2). Length does not fit well with any of the other items, so we must make it a separate record type. The aggregates are shown in Fig. 8.2.

We now begin the process of determining set relationships. Following the design procedure, let us arbitrarily select the SITE record type and see if we can identify any other record type that has a one-to-many relationship with SITE.

Consider first the COMPUTER record type. Each site may contain many different computers, but each computer physically is installed at only one site. This relationship precisely fits the definition of a 1:N set with owner SITE and member COMPUTER. When it comes to selecting names for set relationships, a good name can often be derived from the description of the relationship. Thus we have our first set; let us call it INSTALL.

Next, we consider SITE and USER. Each site may have many users; but is a user constrained to work from a single site? In general, of course, the answer is *no*; but perhaps in this particular system such a constraint might be desired. Whenever information is not included in the problem desciption, the designer must go back to the users of the system for clarification. The designer must not impose his or her own assumptions on the nature of the problem.

In the present case, when we ask for clarification, we are told that each user is constrained to a single site. Thus in the present case a 1:N relationship does exist with owner SITE and member USER; let us call this set WORK.

SITE and DATABASE also have a 1:N relationship. Each site may store several databases, but each individual database is stored in just one site. Set STORE will then have owner SITE and member DATABASE.

The relationship between SITE and TASK is a bit more complex. Each site may have several tasks running, and each task is run on only one computer at a site. This is a prime example of a transitive 1:N relationship. The intermediate

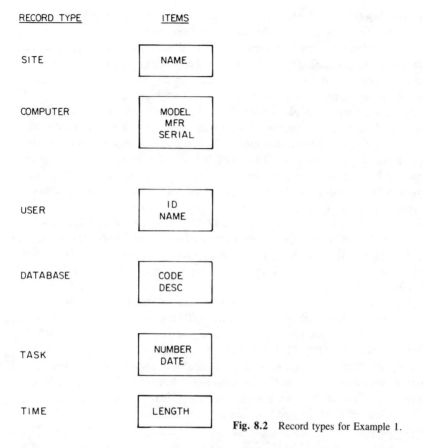

Fig. 8.2   Record types for Example 1.

record type COMPUTER is even referred to in the description. Thus we do not need to define a set between these two record types for this relationship. TASK and SITE have another apparent 1:N relationship: each site can be the point of initiation for many tasks, but each task is initiated by a single user from a single site. This is again a transitive relationship involving the record type USER.

SITE and TIME are not directly related, so we need not consider these at present. It may, of course, be necessary to revise the structure at some future time.

Now we consider the COMPUTER record type. We have already compared COMPUTER and SITE. Each computer may have many users running tasks on it, but each user may have several tasks running on different computers; thus there is no 1:N relationship between COMPUTER and USER. Because the problem description indicates that we need not associate databases with their host computers, we consider instead the access of the databases. Each computer may access many databases, but each database may be accessed by many computers, so there is no 1:N relationship here either. A computer may have many tasks running on it, and it says in the problem description that each task is assigned to a single computer. Thus a 1:N relationship exists with owner COMPUTER and member TASK; let us call it ASSIGN. COMPUTER and TIME form a 1:N relationship, but it is transitive because it involves the task.

Each user may access many databases and each database may be accessed by many users, so there is no 1:N set there. Each user may submit many tasks and each task belongs to a single user. This 1:N relationship with owner USER and member TASK will be called SUBMIT. USER and TIME form a transitive 1:N relationship through TASK.

Each database is accessed by many tasks and each task may access many databases, so there is no 1:N relationship here. Each database is accessed for many periods of time, but each length of time recorded is unique to a particular database. Thus a 1:N set ACCESS can be defined between owner DATABASE and member TIME.

Finally, each task may have many database access times, but each such time is part of only one task. Thus a 1:N set called USES is called for, with owner TASK and member TIME. The structure as defined above is given in Fig. 8.3.

We have defined a schema for which there are no unattached record types omitted. Thus we do not need to consider any other required sets. Now we must

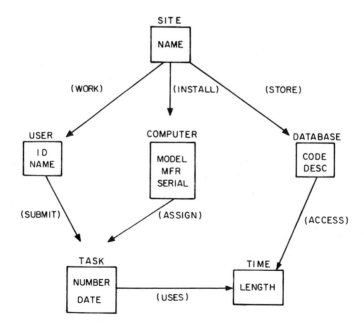

Fig. 8.3 Schema diagram for Example 1.

TABLE 8.2

Set Orderings for Example 1

Set	Order	Key	Description
WORK	SORTED	NAME	Users at a site
INSTALL	SORTED	SERIAL	Computers at a site
STORE	FIFO		Databases at a site
SUBMIT	FIFO		Tasks submitted by a user
ASSIGN	IMMAT		Tasks assigned to a computer
USES	PRIOR		Length of time a task uses a database, ordered by the database code
ACCESS	FIFO		Length of time a database is accessed
SS	SORTED	NAME	List of sites
SU	SORTED	ID	List of users
SD	SORTED	CODE	List of databases

review the structure with respect to the problem description, to make sure that the schema is sufficient to meet the needs of the application. This is left as an exercise.

Before we can turn this diagram into a formal DDL specification, we must first determine the required system-owned sets and then determine orders for all sets. The selection of system-owned sets is very much dependent upon the kind of processing that will be required. In the present case we will define system-owned sets for SITE (SS), USER (SU), and DATABASE (SD); these should prove sufficient for all of our anticipated processing.

Determining set order is also a function of the desired processing. One possible ordering plan is given in Table 8.2. Most of the orderings are straightforward with the exception of USES. The PRIOR ordering is used to obtain for each task a list of the databases required, where the list is sorted by the code number of the database. See Section 8.7 for a further discussion of this issue. A full DDL specification is given in Fig. 8.4. It is input to the DDL Analyzer to initialize the database of the application system.

Each of the programs developed for this DDL will need p-record definitions, string definitions, and a **dbopn** call (see Fig. 8.5). They must precede the DML processing in every program that uses this database. If a given p-record or string is not referenced in a program, its definition may be deleted. Also, it is often useful to have the **dbopn** information entered from the keyboard instead of hardwired into the program.

8.3 DESIGNING LOAD PROGRAMS

In programming we are often faced with severe memory restrictions. This is especially true in microcomputer and minicomputer environments. Computer

```
DATABASE name is DCNS, page is 512
USER is DOUG with CUTE
RECORD is SITE
      ITEM is NAME, string 30
RECORD is USER
      ITEM is ID, character 4
      ITEM is NAME, string 20
RECORD is COMPUTER
      ITEM is MODEL, character 6
      ITEM is MFR, character 15
      ITEM is SERIAL, character 20
RECORD is DATABASE
      ITEM is CODE, integer 2
      ITEM is DESC, string 40
RECORD is TASK
      ITEM is NUMBER, integer 2
      ITEM is DATE, date
RECORD is TIME
      ITEM is LENGTH, real 4
SET is WORK
      Owner is SITE
      Member is USER, order is SORTED by ascending NAME
SET is INSTALL
      Owner is SITE
      Member is COMPUTER, order is SORTED by ascending SERIAL
SET is STORE
      Owner is SITE
      Member is DATABASE, order is FIFO
SET is SUBMIT
      Owner is USER
      Member is TASK, order is FIFO
SET is ASSIGN
      Owner is COMPUTER
      Member is TASK, order is IMMAT
SET is USES
      Owner is TASK
      Member is TIME, order is PRIOR
SET is ACCESS
      Owner is DATABASE
      Member is TIME, order is FIFO
SET is SS
      Owner is SYSTEM
      Member is SITE, order is SORTED by ascending NAME
SET is SU
      Owner is SYSTEM
      Member is USER, order is SORTED by ascending ID
SET is SD
      Owner is SYSTEM
      Member is DATABASE, order is SORTED by ascending CODE
END
```

Fig. 8.4 DDL specification for Example 1.

```
p-record site {char name[30]}
p-record user {char id[4]; char name [20]}
p-record computer {char model[6]; char mfr[15]; char serial[20]}
p-record database {integer code; char desc[40]}
p-record task {integer number; char date[9]}
p-record time {real length}
```

```
define SITE = "SITE";                          /*Define record type names */
       USER = "USER";
       COMPUTER = "COMPUTER";
       DATABASE = "DATABASE";
       TASK = "TASK";
       TIME = "TIME";

       NAME = "NAME";                          /* Define item names */
       ID = "ID";
       MODEL = "MODEL";
       MFR = "MFR";
       SERIAL = "SERIAL";
       CODE = "CODE";
       DESC = "DESC";
       NUMBER = "NUMBER";
       DATE = "DATE";
       LENGTH = "LENGTH";

       WORK = "WORK";                          /* Define set names */
       INSTALL = "INSTALL";
       STORE = "STORE";
       SUBMIT = "SUBMIT";
       ASSIGN = "ASSIGN";
       USES = "USES";
       ACCESS = "ACCESS";
       SS = "SS";
       SU = "SU";
       SD = "SD";
```

```
p-record openrec {char user[12] ;
                  char pass[16] ;
                  char mode[6]  ;
                  char file[14]
                  }
openrec.user = "DOUG";
openrec.pass = "CUTE";
openrec.mode = "MODIFY";
openrec.file = "DCNS";
```

dbopn(openrec);

Fig. 8.5 Required program definitions.

memory is limited; further, a number of programs compete for the same memory space. These include the run-time system of the computer language, the operating system, and the database control system itself. Thus the amount of memory that any application program may use is constrained.

Often we cannot develop a single "load" program for a database. This single program would be too large to fit in the available memory. Further, it might be simpler for the user of the application system to understand the loading process if it is broken down into several steps (programs), each dealing with one record type or a few closely related record types.

Sometimes the application has evolved in such a way that the information that is entered into the database comes from forms that are already in use. Thus the data entry process must parallel these forms in their order of presentation of information. In such cases, a separate load program can be developed for each form.

It is sometimes possible to create a high level selector program, that under user control would call each of the loading *procedures* as necessary. This approach is especially useful when an operating system and the host language permit overlays. However, each procedure would be an independent load program.

Occasionally it is not clear exactly how the database structure should be partitioned for loading. In our example, this is the case. The solution in a situation like this is to arbitrarily partition the database into manageable pieces. For instance, the site and computer information could be entered together, because they both represent physical entities. Similarly, the task and time data should be entered together, because they would become known at the same time. The user and database information could be loaded in separate programs.

We have just defined four load programs for our application system: the site–computer load program, the user load program, the database load program, and the task–time load program. We shall look at all of these in turn.

8.4   SITE–COMPUTER LOAD PROGRAM

The overall structure of this program is presented in Fig. 8.6. We will be processing sites; for each site processed, we may also look at computers at that site. The site processing must handle the addition of new sites for the computer network, the deletion of sites no longer part of the computer network, and the updating of information about each site. The computer processing must handle comparable operations: addition of new computers, deletion of removed machines, and the update of existing information.

We begin by considering the site records. First we must decide if we want the program to process *every* site currently known to the system or if the user should

```
Enter site name;
Process site;
    {Enter computer serial number;
    process computer;
    }
```

Fig. 8.6   Structure of SITE/COMPUTER load program.

explicitly specify the sites to be processed. In this first case we would build a **ffm–fnm** loop, similar to that of Fig. 6.4, for processing all of the occurrences of the set SS. In the more common latter case, the user would be prompted for a site name, which would then be checked in the database to determine if the name corresponds to a known site or a new site.

To give the user the most flexibility, we should allow several sites to be processed without having to rerun the program. Thus a loop is called for. But how can the user signal that there are no more values to be entered? Some computers and computer languages have special constructs for recognizing function keys or control characters entered from the keyboard. In our pseudo-language, we shall use the more time-honored approach of a trailer symbol: we will process sites until an asterisk is entered. The start of our program is thus

```
do while ( {display "Enter a site name (or * ): ";
           input site.name;
           site.name ≠ "*"} )
```

The braces indicate a local procedure, the last line of which evaluates to either the value true or false. We will perform this loop as long as something other than an asterisk is entered; once it is entered, the loop and the program are finished.

Once a name has been entered, we must check it against the list of names already in the database to determine if this is a new site. If so, then after double checking this fact, the information should be added to the database. Since in this simple case there is only one data item in record type SITE, no additional input is required:

```
fmsk(SS, site name);
if (not found) then
   {display "Is this a new site (Y/N)? ";
   if ( not qyn( ) ) then continue;
   crs(SITE, site);
   ims(SS);
   }
```

The procedure qyn( ) returns a value of true or false, and is defined as:

```
qyn( ) /* Returns true if a capital or small letter Y is entered */
  { char a[1];
    input a;
    return (a = ''Y'' or a = ''y'');
  }
```

The continue statement above causes processing to skip to the loop control statement.

At the end of the processing of the **ims,** the new occurrence is the current member of the set SS; this is also true if the site name were found by the **fmsk** command.

Even if the site has just been created, we should display the site information so that the user may reverify that this is the desired site. Then we must give the user the option of deleting the site information. This leads to two philosophies of deletion that must be mentioned. In the common *domino theory* delete (besides deleting the site information), we would search out and delete all other record occurrences pertaining to that site. Thus, deleting the site would delete all records of the users, computers, databases, tasks, and times of that site. The *explicit reference* approach would delete the site occurrence, but leave the users, computers, and databases intact, but ownerless. This is less drastic, but potentially more dangerous, since it may result in orphan record occurrences.

We shall in our examples take a middle ground. We will not apply the domino theory, but we will not delete a site occurrence unless it has no associated users, computers, and databases. Thus the user must first delete all of the users, computers, and databases of this site before it can be deleted. This method makes the user, rather than the designers of the program (us) responsible for deleting subordinate records. This logic also avoids the possibility of orphaned records and thus leaves the database in a consistent form:

```
display ''Site name is'', site.name;
display ''Should this site be deleted (Y/N)?'';
if (qyn()) then
  {som(WORK,SS);
   if (found) then
      display ''Can't delete—still connected to users'';
   else
      {som(INSTALL, SS);
       if (found) then
          display ''Can't delete—still connected to computers'';
       else
          {som(STORE, SS);
           if (found) then
              display ''Can't delete—still connected to databases'';
           else
```

```
                {drm(SS);
                display "Site deleted";
                }
            }
        }
    }
```

Here we use the automatic **ffm** feature of **som** to tell us if our site is still connected to some other occurrence. If the **ffm** finds an occurrence, then we will not delete the current site.

Now we can begin the update portion of our load program (we are still dealing with sites; remember that we have yet to deal with computers). In order to cater to human nature, we will put the update commands within a program loop, so that the user can have as many chances as necessary to enter the correct information. Although in the present case we are dealing with but one data item, this process is clearly extendable to handle many data items:

```
        else
            {do while ({display "Are there changes to this information (Y/N)?";
                    qyn()})
                {display "Correct site name (or blank):";
                input temp;
                if (temp ≠ blank) then site.name = temp;
                putm(SS, site);
                display "Site name is now", site.name;
                }
```

Here temp and blank are program variables of type character; temp must be at least as long as site.name, while blank must be initialized to blank characters. The temp variable is required so that the NAME field of the SITE record is not modified if a blank is entered. This preserves the proper information for the **putm** command. The final display shows the user the updated information.

We have now performed all of the necessary processing for the SITE record occurrences. We can now progress to processing COMPUTER records. What must be done with these? *Exactly the same thing* that we did with SITE occurrences. We must check to see if we are dealing with a new machine or with an existing machine. If it is new, we create it and connect it to the site. In either case, we can ask for deletions and updates. Aside from some obvious changes, the only additional element required is the **som** command that allows us to use the set INSTALL.

Figure 8.7 contains the full program for loading and updating SITE and COMPUTER records. Study it carefully, for it forms the basis of virtually all future programs that we will develop.

There are several points worth mentioning in regard to this program. In the computer information section and after the **fmsk,** the "if (found)" structure is

```
/* First load site records */
do while ({display "Enter a site name (or *):";
        input site.name;
        site.name ≠ "*"})
   {fmsk(SS, site.name);
   if (not found) then
      {display "Is this a new site (Y/N)?";
      if (not qyn ()) then continue;
      crs(SITE, site);
      ims(SS);
      }
   display "Site name is", site.name;
   display "Should this site be deleted (Y/N)?";
   if (qyn ()) then
      {som(WORK, SS);
      if (found) then
          display "Can't delete—still connected to users:;
      else
          {som(INSTALL, SS);
          if (found) then
              display "Can't delete—still connected to computers";
          else
             {som(STORE, SS);
             if (found) then
                 display "Can't delete—still connected to databases";
             else
                {drm(SS);
                display "Site deleted";
                }
             }
          }
      }          /* This ends the "then" portion */
   else
      {do while ({display "Are there changes to this information (Y/N)?";
                   qyn ()})
         {display "Corrected site name (or blank):";
         input temp;
         if (temp ≠ blank) then site.name = temp;
         putm(SS, site);
         display "Site name is now", site.name;
         }
```

/* Now do computer info. Note: there are currently two open brackets—one for the outer do while loop, the second for the else before the update. */

```
        som(INSTALL, SS);
        do while ({display "Enter a computer serial number (or *):";
                    input computer.serial;
                    computer.serial ≠ "*"})
```

Fig. 8.7   SITE/COMPUTER load program.

```
{fmsk(INSTALL, computer.serial);
 if (found) then
     getm(INSTALL, computer);
 else
     {display "Is this a new computer for this site (Y/N)?";
      if (not qyn ( )) then continue;
      display "Enter model number:";
      input computer.model;
      display "Enter manufacturer:";
      input computer.mfr;
      crs(COMPUTER, computer);
      ims(INSTALL)
      }
 display "Model:", computer.model;
 display "Manufacturer:", computer.mfr;
 display "Serial number:", computer.serial;
 display "Should this computer be deleted (Y/N)?";
 if (qyn ( )) then
     {som(ASSIGN, INSTALL);
      if (found) then
          display "Can't delete—still connected to tasks";
      else
          {drm(INSTALL);
           display "Computer deleted";
           }
      }
 else
     {do while ({display "Any changes (Y/N)?";
                 qyn ( )})
          {display "Corrected model (or blank):";
           input temp;
           if (temp ≠ blank) then computer.model = temp;
           display "Corrected manufacturer:";
           input temp;
           if (temp ≠ blank) then computer.mfr = temp;
           display "Corrected serial number:";
           input temp;
           if (temp ≠ blank) then computer.serial = temp;
           putm(INSTALL, computer);
           display "Model:", computer.model;
           display Manufacturer:", computer.mfr;
           display "Serial number:", computer.serial;
           }
      }     /* else */
 }
}
}   /* Outer Loop */
```

Fig. 8.7   (*Continued*)

slightly different. A **getm** is needed for the displays that follow the **ims.** Of course, since there are more data items, there are more display statements. The only set that needs testing during deletion is ASSIGN; the rest of this section is the same.

There is an anomaly in the way in which updates are performed in this program. See Exercise 1 for more details.

8.5 LOADING USER INFORMATION

The program for entering user data is quite similar in form to that developed above, except of course it stops after one record type has been processed. In Fig. 8.8, the first part of the program for loading user information is presented. The only differences other than obvious name changes, and so forth, are the statement "perform find-site" just before the **crs** command (which is explained next), and the value-of function, which translates characters into numbers.

Before we create a new occurrence of USER, we should first determine its owner in the set WORK. This is the philosophy expressed in Chapter 7. The find-site routine will do just this for us:

```
find-site        /* find a current owner for WORK */
   {do while ({display "Enter site name:";
               input site.name;
               fmsk(SS, site.name);
               not found})
        {ffm(SS);
         display "Choose one of the following sites";
         do while (found)
             {getm(SS, site);
              display site.name;
              fnm(SS);
              }
         }
   som(WORK, SS);
   }
```

This procedure allows us to enter a site name. If the name is found, then its record occurrence is made the current owner of WORK. If the name that is entered is not found, then all known site names are displayed and we are given another chance to enter the site name.

If in this procedure the loop test were not performed on the first iteration of the loop, then the procedure would produce what is commonly called menu-driven processing. This occurs when a list of alternatives is presented to the user, who

```
/* beginning of user load program */
do while ({display "Enter a user ID (or *):";
              input user.id;
              user.id ≠ "*"})
   {fmsk(SU, user.id);
   if (found) then
       getm(SU, user);
   else
       {display "Is this a new user (Y/N)?";
       if (not qyn ()) then continue;
       display "User name:";
       input user.name;
       perform find-site;
       crs(USER, user);
       ims(SU);
       ims(WORK);
       }
   display "User ID:", user.id;
   display "    name:", user.name;
   display "Should this person be deleted (Y/N)?";
   if (qyn ()) then
      {som(SUBMIT, SU);
      if (found) then
          display "Can't delete—still connected to tasks";
      else
          {drm(SU);
          display "User deleted";
          }
      }
   else
      {do while ({display "Any changes (Y/N)?";
                  qyn ()})
          {display "Corrected user ID (or blank):";
          input temp;
          if (temp ≠ blank) then user.id = value-of (temp);
          display "          Name (or blank):";
          input temp;
          if (temp ≠ blank) then user.name = temp;
          putm(SU, user);
          display "User ID:", user.id;
          display "    name:", user.name;
          }
```

Fig. 8.8 Loading user information.

must then select one of the alternatives from the list. Menu-driven processing is best used when the user of the system is expected to have little or no knowledge of the application, the programs, or what is expected of him or her. The kind of processing performed in Figs. 8.7 and 8.8 is called scrolling, because of its effect on the user's terminal output device.

We are not yet finished, however, with the user loading program. One of the updating capabilities that this program must include is the ability of a user to migrate from one site to another. In database terms, we must allow for the case where a user has switched sites. This is similar to the processing of Fig. 7.11:

```
smm(WORK, SU);
geto(WORK, site);
display "This user's present site is", site.name;
display "Should this be changed (Y/N)?";
if (qyn()) then
   {rms(WORK);
    perform find-site;
    scm(SU);
    ims(WORK);
    }
```

Here the present site is first retrieved and displayed and the user is asked whether the information is correct or not. If the user decides to change the designated site of this user, then **rms** removes the user from the present site; find-site as before makes the new site the current owner of the set WORK; **scm** makes the user the cru again; and finally **ims** connects the user with the new site.

This processing could be put into a loop, much like the data item updates are looped, allowing the user ample opportunity to choose the correct site.

8.6 LOADING DATABASE INFORMATION

There is essentially no important structural difference in this program from the program that loads the user information. This should be apparent from the schema diagram of Fig. 8.3. If the COMPUTER, TASK, and TIME record types are removed from the database, then the remaining parts are symmetrically organized with USER on one side and DATABASE on the other. This symmetry of data structure implies a symmetry of data processing.

8.7 LOADING TASK AND TIME INFORMATION

The loading of information into these two records types differs from the preceding examples only in the sequence of the operations that are performed. Strictly speaking, loading of this information would occur at two times. First, the task and time information would be entered, but not linked through the set ASSIGN to the computer the task will run on; second, the scheduler would

```
/* Find a User */
do while ({display "Enter a User ID (or *):";
          input user.id;
          user.id ≠ "*"})
    {fmsk(SU, user.id);
    if (found) then
        {som(SUBMIT, SU);
        perform do-task;
        }
    else
        {ffm(SU)
        display "Choose one of the following users:";
        do while (found)
            {getm(SU, user);
            display user.id, user.name;
            fnm(SU);
            }
        }
    }
```

Fig. 8.9   Finding users.

```
do-task       /* Check task information */
    {do while ({display "Enter task number (or *):";
               input x;
               x ≠ "*"})
        {display "Enter Date:";
        input task.date;
        t = 0;
        fmi(DATE, SUBMIT, task.date);
        do while (found)
            {getm(SUBMIT, task);
            if (task.number = x) then
                {t = 1;
                break;
                }
            fnmi(DATE, SUBMIT, task.date);
            }
        if (t = 0) then
            {display "Is this a new task (Y/N)?";
            if (not qyn ()) then continue;
            perform find-computer;
            task.number = x;
            crs(TASK, task);
            ims(SUBMIT);
            ims(ASSIGN);
            }
        display "Task number:", task.number;
        display "    date:", task.date;
```

Fig. 8.10   Checking tasks.

assign it to a computer. However, for instructional purposes, we will connect the task to its computer as well as to its user in the present program.

We cannot begin this program as we did the user load program, because we have not defined a system-owned set for TASK. Instead, we must use either the user that submits the task (most likely) or the computer on which the task will be run (less likely), in order to arrive at the task itself.

Figure 8.9 illustrates the basic loop for finding the user that is submitting the current task. Note its similarity to the find-site procedure. Once the user has been found and made the owner of the set SUBMIT, then we can look for the task (Fig. 8.10). If the task is a new one, then we perform a find-computer (Fig. 8.11) to determine an owner of ASSIGN before the create and inserts. The delete section (Fig. 8.12) of do-task differs from previous examples in that it performs a domino delete of all associated time records. The update data and update set ASSIGN sections are structurally just like the examples above.

The processing of the TIME record occurrences is performed in a somewhat

```
find computer /* Determine an owner of ASSIGN */
   {do while ({display "Enter site name:";
               input site.name;
               fmsk(SS, site.name);
               not found})
      {ffm(SS);
       display "Choose one of the following sites:";
       do while (found)
            {getm(SS, site);
             display site.name;
             fnm(SS);
             }
       }
   som(INSTALL, SS);
   do while ({display "Enter computer serial number:";
              input computer.serial;
              fmsk(INSTALL, computer.serial);
              not found})
      {ffm(INSTALL);
       display "Choose one of the following computers:";
       do while (found)
            {getm(INSTALL, computer);
             display computer.serial, computer.model, computer.mfr;
             fnm(INSTALL);
             }
       }
   som(ASSIGN, INSTALL);
   }
```

Fig. 8.11 Finding computers.

```
display "Should this task be deleted (Y/N)?";
if (qyn ()) then
   {som(USES, SUBMIT);
    do while (found)
           drm (USES);
    drm(SUBMIT);
    }
else
    {do while ({display "Any changes (Y/N)?";
             qyn ()})
          {display "Corrected task number:";
           input temp;
           if (temp ≠ blank) then task.number = value-of (temp);
           display "          date:";
           input temp;
           if (temp ≠ blank) then task.date = temp;
           putm(SUBMIT, task);
           display "Task number:", task.number;
           display "Date:", task.date;
           }
     smm(ASSIGN, SUBMIT);
     gfo(SERIAL, ASSIGN, computer.serial);
     display "The current computer is" computer.serial;
     smo(INSTALL, ASSIGN);
     gfo(NAME, INSTALL, site.name);
     display "at site", site.name;
     display "Any change (Y/N)?";
     if (qyn ()) then
      {rms(ASSIGN);
       perform find-computer;
       scm(SUBMIT);
       ims(ASSIGN);
       }
```

Fig. 8.12   Updating tasks (continuation of do-task procedure).

different manner. Here, all existing time occurrences are displayed and for each the user is given the option of deleting the occurrence, changing its value, or leaving it alone. Once the known values have been processed, the user is given the opportunity to add new values to the database. The TIME record processing is shown in the program of Fig. 8.13 where there is a reference to a find-database procedure. This procedure is quite similar to the find-site routine presented above. However, the find-database routine incorporates the necessary processing for the set USES.

Recall that the set USES was defined to have an order of PRIOR. This ordering means that, when a new record occurrence is inserted into the set for a

```
                    som(USES, SUBMIT);
                    do while (found)
                         {getm(USES, time);
                         smm(ACCESS, USES);
                         geto(ACCESS, database);
                         display time.length, database.code, database.desc;
                         display "Do you want this occurrence to be:";
                         display " 1: Deleted:;
                         display " 2: Changed in time value";
                         display " 3: Left alone?";
                         input x;
                         if (x = 1) then
                                 drm(USES);
                         else if (x = 2) then
                             {input "Corrected time:", time.length;
                             putm(USES, time);
                             fnm(USES);
                             }
                         else if (x = 3) then
                                 fnm(USES);
                         }
                    do while ({display "Enter a new time value (or *):";
                             input temp;
                             temp ≠ "*"})
                         {time.length = value-of (temp);
                         perform find-database;
                         crs(TIME, time);
                         ims(USES);
                         ims(ACCESS);
                         }
                    }
               }
          }
```

Fig. 8.13 Loading time information (continuation of do-task procedure).

particular owner, the new member occurrence is positioned *prior* to the current member occurrence; if the current member is null, the new occurrence is added to the end of the list.

The purpose of PRIOR processing (and also the processing for the set ordering NEXT) is to provide special positioning under other than normal circumstances. The most common application of PRIOR is demonstrated in our example by the set USES: the information in the set must be ordered by the code of the database being accessed. A sorted set does not work here, since the sort information is not contained in the member record type.

The find-database procedure starts out just like the find-site procedure with essentially the same do while loop. However, the current program (Fig. 8.14) then includes a second loop designed to find the occurrence of the set USES that would logically follow the occurrence of TIME being added to the database. The **ffm/fnm** loop will iterate through all occurrences of the set USES (with respect to the present task); for each time occurrence, its database code is retrieved and compared to the desired code. If the retrieved code is bigger than the new code, then the loop is terminated; we have found an occurrence whose database code would logically follow our desired code in sequence. If the loop terminates without the break statement being executed, then the current member of USES becomes null and the new occurrence is added at the end of the list. This is consistent because no existing occurrence has a database code that exceeds the desired code.

The final **som** corresponds to the final **som** of the find-site routine. We should convince ourselves that this **som** command could not have been placed anywhere else in this routine.

PRIOR processing is not commonly used. However, it is an important technique that allows designers to get more out of their systems than might otherwise be possible.

```
find-database    /* Determine database and position for time record */
    {do while ({display "Enter database code:";
               input database.code;
               fmsk(SD, database.code);
               not found)
        {ffm(SD);
         display "Choose one of the following databases:";
         do while (found)
               {getm(SD, database);
                display database.code, database.desc;
                fnm(SD);
                }
        }
    ffm(USES);              /* Position for prior processing */
    do while (found)
          {smm(ACCESS, USES);
           gfo(CODE, ACCESS, x);
           if (x > database.code) then break;
           fnm(USES);
           }
    som(ACCESS, SD);
    }
```

Fig. 8.14   Finding the database.

8.8   RETRIEVAL OF USAGE INFORMATION

Before we leave the distributed computer network example, we will consider a programming example of a report generating program. There are few differences in style or content for report programs. One major change is that in the **dbopn** command (Fig. 8.5), the mode variable of the openrec p-record should be assigned in the value "READ". The database control system operates faster in this mode.

The particular report that we will study is a database–computer usage report calculated for each site in the network. For each site, we look at all of the databases stored at that site, then count the number of tasks that have accessed these databases. We classify the tasks by whether they executed on (were assigned to) a computer at the same site, or the task was running on a machine at a different site. This part of the report is measuring the effectiveness of the scheduling process by determining what percentage of tasks were assigned to a computer close to the necessary database.

Within each of the two groups of tasks defined above, a separate tally is made for counting those tasks that originated at the specified site as well. This part of the report indicates how much of the usage of the system is local processing, and how much is actually using the network. Thus our report will have 5 columns of output:

Site	No. of tasks that access a database at this site, and execute on a computer at this site.	No. of tasks that access a database at this site, but execute on a computer at a different site.
	Within this group, no. of tasks that were submitted from this site.	Within this group, no. of tasks that were submitted from this site.

Actually, the description of this program is longer than the program itself. The only ambiguous point in the description is how jobs that access several databases should be counted. We will assume that a job will be counted once for each database that it accesses.

The processing for this report is fairly straightforward. We will process every site; thus a loop is required for finding all members, in turn, of the set SS. Next, for each site, we look at all of the databases of that site. For each database, we determine all of the jobs that use the given database. We see which computer each such job is assigned to and where that computer is located. This gives us some of our report information. The rest of the necessary information is obtained by noting the location of the user that submitted this job. The full program is shown in Fig. 8.15.

```
/* Produce usage report; assume that headings have been printed */
ffm(SS);
do while (found)
    {getm(SS, site);
        total = 0;                          /* number of jobs that access databases */
        both = 0;                           /* jobs that both run and access */
        all-three = 0;                      /* jobs in both submitted from this site */
        sub-acc = 0;                        /* jobs submitted, not run here */
        som(STORE, SS);
        do while (found)                    /* database loop */
            {som(ACCESS, STORE);
                do while (found)            /* time loop */
                    {smm(USES, ACCESS);
                    smo(ASSIGN, USES);
                    smo(INSTALL, ASSIGN);
                    gfo(NAME, INSTALL, temp);                    /* get computer site */
                    total = total + 1;
                    smo(SUBMIT, USES);
                    smo(WORK, SUBMIT);
                    gfo(NAME, WORK, temp2);                      /* get user site */
                    if (temp = site.name) then
                        {both = both + 1;
                        if (temp2 = site.name) then
                            all-three = all-three + 1;
                        }
                    else if (temp2 = site.name) then
                        sub-acc = sub-acc + 1;
                    fnm(ACCESS);
                    }
            fnm(STORE);
            }
        display site.name, both, all-three, (total − both), sub-acc;
        fnm(SS);
    }
```

Fig. 8.15 Site usage program.

8.9 EXAMPLE 2—VOCATIONAL EDUCATION ACCOUNTING

Vocational education (VocEd) programs are of increasing importance to schools and their administrators because more specific skills are required of jobseekers in the marketplace. VocEd program receive Federal funding, so detailed records must be kept pertaining to all manners of discrimination. Information kept on students enrolled in the VocEd program must include their name, social security number (or some unique identifier), sex, date of birth, race, handicap, and disadvantaged group (if any).

VocEd programs can be divided into a number of groups; within each group are many individual programs. A program is assigned a six digit code of the form 14.0100; the first two digits represent the program group. Each program may offer courses, information on which includes the number and title, the year, and indicators of whether it is an approved course and whether it is a cooperative course. Students must select an intended program of study.

Courses are divided into individual classes: information includes the building in which the class is offered, the teacher, the classroom setting, the period number, the number of periods the class meets, the number of periods in the school day, the number of hours the class meets each day, the number of days per week the class meets, the number of weeks the class meets, and the credit hours. The teacher and setting information consist of codes and their definitions, unique to teachers and settings. Building information includes codes and definitions, the operational days of the building by quarters, and the total number of hours that the building is in operation annually.

Enrollment data for students in particular classes include: the grade level at which the student is taking the class, quarterly attendance figures (in days), quarterly grades, a final (overall) grade, and the total credit hours earned.

It should be clear that this is not a trivial application. Figs. 8.16–8.22 exhibit output reports that must be supported by the database. In other words, report programs must be written to produce the forms. Thus the database schema must be sufficiently descriptive to capture all of the intricate data relationships implied by these reports. Other required reports include lists of students, courses, approved courses, classes, and programs.

Figure 8.23 contains a schema diagram that has been developed for the VocEd application. This diagram is not a first guess, but the result of ongoing adjustment and fine tuning, as the designers learned more about the application. The principles followed in the design of this structure are consistent with the design principles of Chapter 5.

A number of considerations are worthy of discussion here. For instance, there are only three possible settings (occurrences of record type SETTING) allowed; why then is this a separate record type? The answer is that when a user of this system is entering class information, the three settings can be displayed, both the codes and types (descriptions), and the user can select the appropriate code from the displayed menu of choices. The only other way that this could be accomplished would be to build the menu into the loading program itself. This leads to difficulty if the settings ever do change—the program must be altered, rather than (as in the actual implementation) simply altering or updating occurrences in the database. As a general rule, information should be included in the database, rather than the program, whenever possible. This is a key element in adhering to the philosophy of *data independence.*

Of course, there are exceptions to this rule. The student's sex can also be

VOCATIONAL EDUCATION CLASS LIST

Instructor of record: KOEHLER, GARY
Instructor's Social Security Number: 100110001
Course Title: ENGINES
Hours per day: 1.0

School year: 1980
Buildings: NORTHERN HIGH
Setting: Mainstream/no support
Days per week: 3

Periods in school days: 4
Periods class meets: 1
Class credits: 3.00
Weeks per course: 20.0

Period: 1A Course number: 10

Students' Name	SS#	Date of Birth	Sex	Eth Grp	Dis. Code	Han. Code	Grade Level	Days enrolled in quarter				Grades in quarter					Total Credit
								1	2	3	4	1	2	3	4	F	
BACH, J. S.	999009999	/ /	M	50	0	99	9	45	0	0	0	B				B	.75
BASIE, COUNT	987654321	/ /	M	50	3	0	9	40	40	45	45	D	F	F	F	F	0.00
BEETHOVEN, L. V.	111001111	/ /	M	10	0	9	11	45	45	45	45	A	A	A	A	A	3.00
BERNSTEIN, L.	444004444	/ /	M	40	3	3	11	45	45	45	0	B	B	B	B	B	2.25
SMITH, BESSIE	555005555	/ /	F	40	0	5	11	40	40	40	45	D	D	D	B	C	3.00
WILSON, TEDDY	666006666	/ /	M	40	1	7	9	45	45	0	0	B	B			C	1.50

Fig. 8.16 VocEd class list.

INDIVIDUAL STUDENT REPORT   NORTHERN SCHOOL DISTRICT   12/29/80

HANDEL, G. F.   Birthdate: / /
11011O011   Race: White, not Hispanic   Sex: M   Hard of Hearing
                                                 Both LEP & Disadv

		Grade level	Grade received	Hours
Course	Year Teacher	12	B	100.0
PROGRAMMING	80 KOEHLER, GARY			

TOTAL HOURS: Program -   100.00   Program intent: 14.0100   EXIT: Date -   / /
           Vocational -   100.00   Accounting & Computing   Condition -

Total vocational credits -   5.00   Activity -
            G.P.A. -   3.00

                                 EXIT INTERVIEW DATA

                                 Financial: Career & Vocational:
Assistance

Contact after exit:

     Address: Supervisor:

                                                 Position:

                                                 Salary:

Employed students - address: per:

Fig. 8.17 VocEd student report.

215

INSTRUCTIONAL UNITS COMPUTATION (To be completed for vocational courses)

School: NORTHERN HIGH

School Year: 1980

NORTHERN SCHOOL DISTRICT

REVISED   FINAL

	A	B	C	D	E
Course Name	Aggregate Days Membership	# Periods Class Meets	# Perions in School day	Days School is in Session	ADM/ FTE
ENGINES	650	1	4	135	1.2037
COOKING	225	1	4	135	.4167
WOODWORKING	270	1	4	135	.5000
PROGRAMMING	120	1	4	135	.2222

TOTAL ADM/FTE: 2.3426

Fig. 8.18 VocEd FTE calculation.

ALASKA VOCATIONAL INFORMATION SYSTEM
Secondary Program Enrollment and Completion Report

This report is due July 1, and must reflect data for the program year ending June 30.

DISTRICT NAME: NORTHERN SCHOOL DISTRICT   SCHOOL YEAR: 80
Part A: Occupational Preparation Programs for 11th/12th Grade Students with Program Intent

PROGRAMS		SECTION I Enrollment				SECTION II Ethnic & Sex						SECTION III Special Needs			
		Total Enrollmt	Completr	Marketable Skills	Transfer / Work	HA	A	A	AI	BA	WA	Handcp	Disadv	Limitd	Prfcny
Accounting & Computing 14.0100	Male:	1	0	0	1	0	0	0	0	0	1	1	1	1	1
	Female:	0	0	0	0	0	0	0	0	0	0	0	0	0	0
	Total:	1	0	0	1	0	0	0	0	0	1	1	1	1	1
Auto Mechanics 17.0302	Male:	1	0	0	1	0	0	0	1	0	0	1	1	1	1
	Female	0	0	0	0	0	0	0	0	0	0	0	0	0	0
	Total:	1	0	0	1	0	0	0	1	0	0	1	1	1	1

Fig. 8.19 Enrollment report, part A.

217

ALASKA VOCATIONAL INFORMATION SYSTEM
Secondary Program Enrollment and Completion Report

This report is due July 1, and must reflect data for the program year ending June 30.

DISTRICT NAME: NORTHERN SCHOOL DISTRICT SCHOOL YEAR: 80
PART B: Occupational Preparation Programs for Students without Program Intent

PROGRAMS		SECTION I Enrollment				SECTION II Ethnic & Sex					SECTION III Special needs			SECTION IV Grade level	
		Total Enrlmt	Comptr	Mrktbl Skills	Transf W/0 Sk	Hispnc Amircn	Asian Amercn	Amercn Indian	Black Amercn	White Amercn	Handcp	Disadv	Limitd Prfcny	9th & 10th	11th & 12th
Other programs															
Business & Office 14.0000	Male:	1	0	0	1	0	0	0	0	1	1	1	1	0	1
	Female:	0	0	0	0	0	0	0	0	0	0	0	0	0	0
	Total:	1	0	0	1	0	0	0	0	1	1	1	1	0	1
Trade & Industry 17.0000	Male:	4	0	0	4	1	0	0	2	1	3	1	2	3	1
	Female:	0	0	0	0	0	0	0	0	0	0	0	0	0	0
	Total:	4	0	0	4	1	0	0	2	1	3	1	2	3	1
Prep. for Occup. of Homemaking															
Foods & Nutrition 09.0107	Male:	2	0	0	2	0	2	0	0	0	2	0	2	1	1
	Female:	0	0	0	0	0	0	0	0	0	0	0	0	0	0
	Total:	2	0	0	2	0	2	0	0	0	2	0	2	1	1
Industrial Arts 10.0000	Male:	0	0	0	0	0	0	0	0	0	0	0	0	0	0
	Female:	2	0	0	2	0	0	1	0	1	1	1	0	1	1
	Total:	2	0	0	2	0	0	1	0	1	1	1	0	1	1

Fig. 8.20 Enrollment report, part B.

ALASKA VOCATIONAL INFORMATION SYSTEM

Secondary Program Enrollment and Completion Report

This report is due July 1, and must reflect data for the program year ending June 30.

DISTRICT NAME: NORTHERN SCHOOL DISTRICT   SCHOOL YEAR: 80

PART C: Special Needs Enrollment by type of Instructional Setting and Handicapping Condition.

SPECIAL NEEDS	Mainstream/ No support		Mainstream/ Support		Separate	
	M	F	M	F	M	F
Mentally Retarded	0	0	0	0	0	1
Spec. Learning Disability	0	0	0	0	0	0
Emotionally Disturbed	1	0	0	0	0	0
Orthopedically Impaired	0	0	0	0	0	0
Speech Impaired	0	1	1	0	0	0
Visually Impaired	0	0	0	0	0	0
Other Health Impaired	1	0	0	0	0	0
Hard of Hearing	0	0	0	0	1	0
Deaf	1	0	0	0	0	0
Multi-handicapped	0	0	0	0	0	0
Deaf-Blind	0	0	0	0	0	0
Ltd.English Prof	1	0	2	0	0	0
Disadvantaged	0	0	0	0	0	1
Both LEP & Disadv	2	0	0	0	1	0

Fig. 8.21 Enrollment report, part C.

PART D: Enrollments in Cooperative Vocational Education Programs

INSTRUCTIONAL PROGRAM		TOTAL
01.00	Agriculture	0
04.00	Dist. & Marketing	0
07.00	Health Occupations	0
09.02	Occupational Home Econ.	0
14.00	Business & Office	1
16.00	Technical	0
17.00	Trade & Industry	2

Fig. 8.22   Enrollment report, part D.

processed through a menu-driven procedure, yet this can be safely implanted into a program. This is because the allowable data values for this item have not changed in over three billion years.

It is now simple to explain record types ETHNIC, DISADV, HANDICAP, TEACHER, and BUILDING. These occurrences will be used as menus, or indexes, telling the user what the allowable choices are when entering this information. The teacher and building information are much more likely to change over time than the other index record types; the more stable index record types are often called *constant* data. The various VocEd program groups and programs can also be classified as *constant* data, since these definitions have been used for years without modification.

Another interesting point is that record type STUDENT has two system-owned sets associated with it. The two sets reflect different orderings of the student information. Set SN is ordered by the student's NAME, while set SS is ordered by the student's SSN (social security number). There are three basic reasons why this occurs. One reason is that some of the input forms currently in use in this application refer to students by name, while other forms refer to students by number. This is not uncommon in applications where input is derived from several sources. The second reason is that the two sets make it easier to perform integrity checks on the data as it is being entered. The load program can find the name and number and compare the record occurrences to be sure that the same student is found each time. The final reason is that some of the output reports require students listed by name (e.g., Fig. 8.16) while others process students by number (e.g., Fig. 8.17).

The record type ENROLLMT contains a relatively large number of data items.

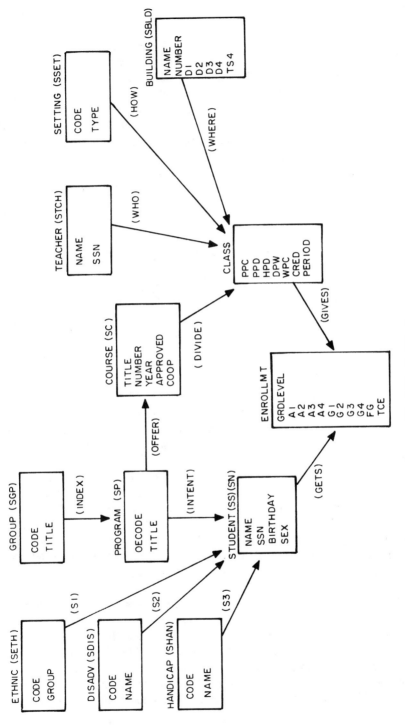

Fig. 8.23 VocEd schema.

The numbered items refer to quarterly information while the other items describe the year-long information. Since it is quite easy to split this record type into several, why was this not done? The answer is that, in a very large percentage of the cases, all of these values would be present for each student. Moreover, this enrollment information pertains to a particular student–class combination. Because the data are logically a unit and usually complete (all fields have values), separate record types would result in an unnecessary increase in the complexity of the schema and in the processing and storage overhead of the database.

As a designer, it is important to take into account the expected behavior of the data items. If this information is available, then it may be possible to significantly improve our structure. Of course, the special cases must be capable of being processed as well.

Finally, the overall schema that has been developed for the VocEd application provides an excellent example of how CODASYL-network database systems can implement inverted data structures (see Appendix A). The goal during the design phase was never to produce an inverted structure; yet all of the relationships culminate in the ENROLLMT record type, which would be the core of the underlying file in an inverted system.

8.10   VocEd LOAD PROGRAMS

In this application the designers were very much constrained by existing input forms when designing their load programs. However, there was some room for intelligent design, especially in determining which records should best be loaded together.

As noted above, many record types represent *constant* data. The occurrences of these record types are rarely subject to change. Thus it makes sense to load these records at the same time. Thus the first program developed, called FIRST, loads records for the constant record types GROUP, PROGRAM, ETHNIC, DISADV, HANDICAP, and SETTING. All of these involve only system-owned sets, except for GROUP and PROGRAM, which are related by the set INDEX. The loading of this information is quite straightforward, and follows directly the principles of the programs discussed earlier.

Since the information contained in these record types is prespecified, when the disks containing the programs were distributed to the various school districts, they also contained a data file. The contents of this data file were the values of these constant record occurrences. The load program FIRST reads the data file rather than taking input from the user's terminal.

The next set of records to be loaded are the COURSE, TEACHER, and BUILDING record types. These, although independent of one another, are grouped together since they are all basically administrative in nature (this second program is called ADMIN), and all would be updated with approximately the same frequency. The third load program loads class information (and is called CLASS). This program must first identify a course, a teacher, and a building, because nothing in the CLASS record type can be used as a unique identifier of any particular class. The outline of this load program is given in Fig. 8.24.

STUDENT record occurrences are entered next (program SDP). This program is similar in form to the program of Fig. 8.8 plus its continuations, although many find procedures (find-ethnic, find-disadv, etc.) must be used instead of the one required in the figure. Finally the ENROLLMT information is entered (program CEP). The outline of this program is presented in Fig. 8.25. The notable feature of this program is the selection of the appropriate class occurrence. This

```
input course.number, teacher.ssn, building.number;
fmsk(SC, course.number)
if (not found) then perform error-process;
fmsk(STCH, teacher.ssn);
if (not found) the perform error-process;
fmsk(SBLD, building.number);
if (not found) then perform error-process;
som(DIVIDE, SC);
do while (found)
    {smm(WHO, DIVIDE);
    gfo(SSN, WHO, temp);
    if (temp ≠ teacher.ssn) then
      { smm(WHERE, DIVIDE);
        gfo(NUMBER, WHERE, x);
        if (x ≠ building.number) then continue;
        perform update-class-info;
        }/* this is the typical update section, including
            a possible delete, and possible setting changes */
    fnm(DIVIDE);
    }
som(WHO, STCH);
som(WHERE, SBLD);
do while ({display "New class for this combination (Y/N)?";)
            qyn ()})
    {perform enter-class-info;
    perform find-setting;
    crs(CLASS, class);
    ims(DIVIDE);
    ims(WHO);
    ims(HOW);
    ims(WHERE);
    }
```

Fig. 8.24 Loading class information.

```
do while ({display "Enter teacher (or *):";
           input teacher.name;
           teacher.name ≠ "*"})
   {fmi(NAME, STCH, teacher.name);
    if (not found) then
       {display "No such teacher";
        continue;
        }
    t = 0;
    som(WHO, STCH);
    do while (found)
       {gfm(PERIOD, WHO, per);
        smm(DIVIDE, WHO);
        geto(DIVIDE, course);
        smm(HOW, WHO);
        geto(HOW, setting);
        smm(WHERE, WHO);
        gfo(NAME, WHERE, bname);
        display course, per, setting, bname;
        display "Is this the right class (Y/N)?";
        if (qyn ()) then
           {t = 1;
            break;
            }
        fnm(WHO);
        }
    if (t = 0) then
       {display "No more classes for this teacher";
        continue;
        }
    do while ({display "Enter student SSN (or *):";
               input ssn;
               ssn ≠ "*"})
       {fmsk(SS, ssn);
        if (not found) then
           {display "No such student");
            continue;
            }
        t = 0;
        som(GIVES, WHO);
        do while (found)
           {smm(GETS, GIVES);
            gfo(SSN, GETS, temp);
            if (temp = ssn) then
               {t = 1;
                break;
                }
            fnm(GIVES);
            }
```

Fig. 8.25   Entering ENROLLMT data.

```
            if (t = 0) then
                    perform add-new-enrollmt-occurrence;
            else
                    perform update-existing-enrollmt-occurrence;
            }
      }
```

Fig. 8.25   *(Continued)*

is done by presenting all of the classes taught by a particular teacher, one at a time, and continuing the display until the user indicates the desired class is being displayed. This kind of sequential menu processing is appropriate when the information required in each menu entrée is voluminous.

8.11 VocEd REPORT PROGRAMS

For the most part these programs are rather simple retrieval and report programs. The report defined in Fig. 8.16 is a good example of this kind of report. It simply summarizes all of the known information for students in a particular class. The teacher can review this report, make additions, deletions, and corrections, and return it to the administration. Then the corrections noted on the form can be entered. Such an output form is referred to as a *turn-around document*.

The individual student report (Table 8.17) has elements of this retrieval type report in listing the student's information and courses taken by that student. However, some of the items in this report have not simply been retrieved, but have been calculated by the report program itself. Examples are the two total hours values and the student's grade point average (GPA). It would have been a simple matter to have a data item called, for example, GPA which would be updated every time a final grade was assigned. However, it was decided that the individual student report would be processed much less often than final grades would be assigned. Thus in terms of the total processing effort, calculating the GPA when the report is requested is less total computing effort than calculating and storing the GPA in the STUDENT record type. The instructional units report (Fig. 8.18), for similar reasons, calculates the ADM/FTE value when the report is requested.

The remaining reports (Figs. 8.19–8.22) are basically retrieval reports counting the number of students that fall into the designated categories. In determining these categories, as much as possible, the information defining the category is obtained from the database rather than programmed into the report itself. This means that, should at some future time the definitions of these categories change, then little or no reprogramming effort would be required. This is an especially important consideration, since the original designers may no longer be available for program maintenance; and it is extremely difficult for anyone to modify someone else's programs.

8.12 SUMMARY

In this chapter the design of computer programs using the MDBS data manipulation languages is presented. The basic forms, or structures, of these programs is given through examples. These forms are transportable, in the sense that they generally fit most database structures; the forms are also expandable, in the sense that they are easily modified to fit any local application requirements or eccentricities.

The load programs of the distributed computer network system were fully developed to show how the forms are used in practice. In the VocEd case, the load programs were not written out, although in several cases outlines were presented. When a qualified programming staff is available, this is really all that a designer or analyst should need to specify.

With DBMS facilities and methods examined to this point in the text, very extensive application systems can be designed and implemented. The subset of features that have been discussed are complete, that is, no other features are necessary for building application software. However, the remaining chapters of this text present more advanced and sophisticated DBMS features. With these additional facilities, more compact and efficient application systems can be developed. They can also save considerable time and effort in the course of developing an extensive application system. The basic programming structures presented in this chapter do not change; rather we will augment them with new structures for taking advantage of the new DBMS facilities.

RELATED READINGS

D. Ferris, Micro DBMS, *Comput. Decisions* **15,** No. 5 (1983).
Micro Data Base Systems Inc., "MDBS Application Programming Reference Manual," Lafayette, Indiana, 1981.
Micro Data Base Systems Inc., "MDBS Data Base Design Reference Manual," Lafayette, Indiana, 1981.

EXERCISES

1. Consider the site–computer load program of Fig. 8.7. Without changing the program, how can a computer be switched from one site to another? Is

any information lost in performing this switch? Modify the program of Fig. 8.7 to allow straightforward site changes.

2. Suppose it became necessary, in the distributed computer network system, to maintain a record of tasks by date as well as by user and computer. How must the data structure and the task load program be revised?

3. In the distributed computer network system, modify the data structure to allow users to be associated with multiple sites; you must record the time and date that the user accessed the system at each site.

4. Why should the user's name and password be entered on the terminal before opening the database?

5. Modify the find-site procedure of Section 8.5 so that it provides a menu of sites. How can the user easily select the proper site?

6. Write out the program that loads and updates the database record occurrences in the distributed computer network schema.

7. In the distributed computer network system, suppose that the set SU had not been defined. Revise the user-load program for this situation.

8. Revise the find-database routine of Fig. 8.14 so that it would work if the set USES had been defined with NEXT order.

9. In the find-database routine of Fig. 8.14, explain why the final **som** command could not have occurred earlier in the routine.

10. Suppose we want to generate a user account information report. For each user we want to indicate the times that have been spent. Prepare a program to do this.

11. Design a load program for the ethnic record occurrences of the VocEd application.

12. Design the report program necessary for generating the output shown in Fig. 8.20 from the VocEd schema of Fig. 8.23. In Section I, a completer is a student who has finished at least 500 course hours in courses offered by the student's declared program of intent; marketable skills is defined similarly, but with total hours between 250 and 499. Assume that the categories of Sections II and III reflect the actual occurrences of the corresponding record types.

13. How, in the VocEd schema of Fig. 8.23, are class periods uniquely identified? Suggest an alternate method of identifying class periods, that would simplify the processing of Fig. 8.24. How is storage affected by the change?

14. Scrolling and menus are two common types of input processing. Another is form-oriented data entry. In this technique the terminal screen is formatted in a manner similar to a printed form; the user just fills in the blanks on the screen (i.e., form). Design a screen form for entering the site and computer occurrences of the distributed computer network system. How would the load program of Fig. 8.7 have to be modified?

15. Describe a situation where the creation, update, and deletion of record occurrences should not be performed in the same program.
16. What other kinds of processing could be performed after a negative response to the question ''Is this a new occurrence (Y/N)?''
17. The township of Little USA comprises many families. The parents and children of each family are members of this township. There are many schools in Little USA. Children are free to go to the school of their own choice. Each child of a family is assigned a different teacher–advisor who works in his or her school. Each child participates in at least one team sport. The members of his or her team are always his or her classmates. The child's circle of friends consists entirely of his or her teammates. For each child's birthday, the parents throw a party and invite the child's teacher–advisor and friends. Each family has parents and may or may not have any children.

(1) Parents can be a single member or two members. They are identified by mother's full name, father's full name, street address, and telephone number.

(2) Each child is characterized by name, sex, birthdate, and age.

(3) A school is identified by school name, street address, and telephone number.

(4) A teacher is identified by name, street address, and home telephone number.

(5) A child's class is identified by grade number and the number of students in the class.

(6) Each student in a school is identified by student name, student number, class, teacher–advisor, and participation in team sports.

(7) Each team sport is characterized by its name, the number of different teams, and the name of each team.

(8) Each team is characterized by the name of the team, total number of players on the team, student numbers of all of these players, and the class represented by the team.

(9) Each party is identified by the name of the child for whom the party is given, age, birthdate, friends, teacher–advisor, brothers and/or sisters, parents, the time of party, the day of party.

(10) Assume that all children of Little USA attend school.

(a) Develop a list of data items for this application. For each item, provide its name, type, length, and a brief description.

(b) Develop a schema for this application.

18. For the Little USA township of Exercise 17:

(a) Develop a program for loading parent–children information.

(b) Develop a program for loading information regarding school–teacher–student–class–team sports–and team information.

(c)   Develop a program for entering birthday party data.

(d)   Write a program to find members of a particular team.

(e)   Write a program to update a student's school, class, teacher–advisor, team sports, teams and friends when a student changes schools.

(f)   Write a program for listing all the parents of the community, their children, children's ages, and children's friends.

(g)   Write a program to produce for a given school, a student report listing student's name, id, birthdate, sex, teacher–advisor, class, team sports, and teams for which the student plays.

19.   Show the relational, shallow-network, and hierarchical counterparts to the schema of Fig. 8.3.

20.   Transform the schema of Fig. 8.23 into a relational schema, into a hierarchical schema, or into a shallow-network schema.

PROJECT

Devise a program or programs to load sample data into the database. Test the retrieval programs developed earlier for report generation.

Chapter 9

SEMI-STRUCTURED DATA MANIPULATION TOOLS

In Chapters 6–8, we examined the basic programming tools used for effective design of application system software. The database control system is an essential complement to these application programs, enhancing the programming language environment so that efficient well-structured application systems can be developed.

We present in Chapter 9 two additional tools for the application developer, both of which benefit the developer by being *interactive*. The user of these tools is provided with immediate feedback on the operations just performed. Another benefit is that the tools are programming language independent, making it possible to pretest and posttest the logic of application software without writing programs. These progress checks can even be made by nonprogrammers (individuals not versed in the host language of the design project).

Both tools are easy to use. One of the tools needs relatively little explanation because it is simply an interactive version of the DML commands described in Chapters 6–8; this is presented first. The remainder of the chapter concentrates on the second tool; though even easier to use, it involves a high-level nonprocedural language quite different from the DML and so requires a more extensive explanation.

9.1 INTERACTIVE DATA MANIPULATION

This add-on package to the basic database management system gives an application developer the ability to interactively use all of the data manipulation commands discussed in Chapters 6–8 (and those to be discussed later in Chapters 12 and 13 as well). This facility provides the programmer with a very powerful tool for checking the validity of application program logic during both the design and debugging phases of program development. It also provides a convenient way of making ad hoc one-shot modifications to database contents without necessitating an investment in the design of a computer program.

The interactive data manipulation language (IDML) is an independent program, executed directly under the operating system of the computer. The IDML software includes all aspects of the database control system needed to interactively execute DML commands. At the inception of execution, IDML requests the name of the operating system file that holds the database about to be processed, a user name, and a password. These elements are of course just those supplied with the **dbopn** command when it is invoked in an application program. The IDML automatically will invoke **dbopn,** specifying "MODIFY" access. Figure 9.1 illustrates a sample dialogue for entering this information. The prompt "I:" indicates that IDML is awaiting further instructions.

The IDML user now has available all of the DML commands. These can be entered one at a time for immediate execution. The form of entry is simple: to find the first member of the set SS, one need only enter "**ffm** SS" or "**ffm,** SS". The appropriate currency indicators will be set. There is no distinction between upper and lower case letters; thus another equivalent rendition of the above command is "**FFM** ss".

If IDML detects any error condition while executing a DML command, then the corresponding error number will be displayed on the screen with a brief description of the problem. This of course includes the end-of-set condition. An error response of zero (that is, no error has occurred) is not displayed; instead the "I:" prompt reappears, indicating the successful completion of our command.

DATA BASE FILE NAME: file

USER NAME: user

PASSWORD: pass

I:

Fig. 9.1 Opening the IDML session.

There are no p-records in the IDML. Instead, values are retrieved directly to the screen and entered directly from the keyboard. Prompts are automatically issued for the necessary values when data need to be entered. When data values are output to the screen they are automatically labeled with their appropriate data item names. Thus every DML command that requires a p-record or variable for processing will, within IDML, either ask for additional information or present the retrieved values on the screen.

Suppose that set SS is sorted by a data item named NUMBER and we wish to find the record occurrence whose value of NUMBER is 273. The appropriate sequence of IDML entries is shown in Fig. 9.2. Note that in the first line we do not specify a p-record, as the definition of **fmsk** requires; instead the IDML prompts us to enter the desired value of NUMBER. We respond by typing 273. The **getm** command provides an example of the retrieval process. The values for all fields of the current member of SS are displayed on the screen. The **getc** command would have had the same result here.

There are essentially three uses of the IDML for application developers. The first is its importance as a tool for simply becoming familiar with the database management system and the effects of its individual DML commands. All of the examples of Chapters 6 and 7 can be performed using the IDML. Other combinations of DML commands can be explored as well, checking the user's knowledge and understanding of the DML operations and logic. Further, by typing a question mark (?) after a DML command, the IDML system immediately displays the full syntax of that command. For example, entering "**fmi**?" would produce "**fmi** item set (data)" The "(data)" means that the user will be prompted for the necessary data values.

The second use of the IDML concerns the validation of program logic without taking time to write or compile test programs. This validation can be done at two distinct times. During program design, the sequencing of data manipulation commands can be simulated via the IDML, thus aiding in the design of application programs that are logically correct from a DML standpoint. We could check the logic of any of the Chapter 8 programs in this way. During application program debugging, the IDML can be used to examine the effects of an applica-

                 I: **fmsk** SS
                          enter NUMBER: 273

                 I: **getm** SS
                          NAME: Smith, Jan
                          NUMBER: 273

                 I:

Fig. 9.2   Prompting for p-record information.

tion program on the database by checking on the data loaded by the program as well as check the relationships established among the record occurrences. This is undoubtedly the most important utilization of the IDML tool.

Finally, the application developer can use the IDML to perform small-scale data processing. This is particularly useful when a few records are in error or otherwise require updating, and the expense of developing an appropriate update program, however short, is quite large. The application developer may even opt not to write maintenance programs for several types of records, utilizing the IDML solely for that purpose. In the VocEd application discussed in Chapter 8, the "menu" record types could easily be maintained in this way.

The only other knowledge required to use the IDML is that to exit this package when finished with interactive processing, the command **quit** should be entered. Internally, this command automatically invokes **dbcls;** thus **dbcls** is not directly available as part of the IDML.

9.2   ADDITIONAL IDML FACILITIES

There are four extra IDML facilities that can aid an application developer. The first of these is the **display** command. This command allows an IDML user to examine nearly any aspect of the internal data dictionary for the database being processed.

Through the use of **display,** an IDML user can obtain information on the record types, data items, and set relationships that have been defined in the DDL specification. In this way the user of the IDML need not have the DDL specification or schema diagram at hand during an IDML session. Two of the most useful **display** options available to an IDML user are

    display r   Display all record types, with their associated data item names and the sets
               in which they participate.
    display s   Display all sets, with owner, member, and set order.

Two other options exist; **display** i shows detailed information about specific data items, while **display** a shows information about database areas (see Chap. 11).

Specifying a set name after the **display** s produces the same information as **display** s, but just for the set specified. Specifying a record type name after the **display** r produces the same information as **display** r plus the type and length information for each data item of the record type specified. Figure 9.3 illustrates two examples, drawn from the VocEd database of Fig. 8.23. The command **display** can be abbreviated as **disp.**

The second additional IDML facility is the ability to use an input source other than the keyboard for commands. In particular, one or more interactive data manipulation commands can be written on a disk file and later can be input to the

```
I:   display r PROGRAM
     PROGRAM
          title:         (none)
          synonyms:      (none)
          owned by:      SP
                         INDEX
          owner of:      OFFER
                         INTENT
          items:         OECODE CHAR 6
                         TITLE STR 25

I:   display s INTENT
     INTENT
          title:         (none)
          synonyms:      (none)
          type:          1:N
          owner:         PROGRAM
          member
          insertion:     MANUAL
          member
          order:         SORTED
          members:       STUDENT

I:
```

Fig. 9.3   Using the data dictionary.

IDML through the command **read.** When this command is invoked a file name is specified as its argument. The IDML accesses this file, interprets each record of the file as a command to be processed by the IDML, and proceeds to execute each of these IDML commands.

The benefits of such off-line preparation of commands are many. If a command sequence is linear (that is, it requires no iteration structure or other programmatic control elements), then the sequence can be stored in a command file and executed directly using the **read** command. Thus the application developer can bypass the usual programming and compilation steps, defining the appropriate "program" as a simple IDML command sequence. Initially such a sequence would most likely be debugged interactively and then committed to the disk file. The commands on the file can be any valid IDML command, including **quit** and **display,** although not another **read.**

The third feature of the IDML is related to the concept of reading a prepared command file. It is possible to have such a file executed immediately when the IDML is invoked, without the step of entering a **read** command. Such a file of commands is called a *startup file.* Any file can be designated as a startup file simply by passing the name of the file to IDML when the IDML is loaded into the memory of the computer. Otherwise, the IDML will look for a file name STARTUP from which to read commands. The actual forms of these invocations are operating system dependent.

The startup file differs from command files used by **read** in one regard. The first line of the startup file must contain the **dbopn** information for the IDML. The form of such a line is

> START   "file name"   "user name"   "password"

Following this line, any number of IDML commands (including **display** and **quit,** but excluding **read**) may appear.

Thus a linear command sequence as discussed above can be executed directly, without the user of the IDML ever needing to know about the operation of the IDML. By preparing a startup file whose last record is the command **quit,** the application developer need only instruct the users on the proper operating system instructions for running the IDML with the startup file.

It should be noted that both the read and startup files may interact with the user terminal through the DML commands requiring data entry. For example, a **putm** command in a **read** or startup file would issue prompts for the user to specify the associated data values.

The fourth adjunct of the IDML is the **define** command. Through this feature we are able to build sequences of IDML commands, including **display** and **quit,** that are stored in the database itself, rather than in a disk file. Such sequences are referred to as *macro* definitions. In fact, disk files accessed through the **read** command may themselves include macro references.

A macro is simply a name which refers to one or more lines of text. Such text may consist of one or more terms. Thus a macro need not define an entire IDML command, but perhaps just a fragment of one. At the other extreme, a macro text could consist of many IDML commands. Figure 9.4 shows how two such macros are defined in an IDML session. The first consists solely of two set names (see the VocEd database of Fig. 8.23). This SNG macro could be used in the IDML command "**som** SNG". The IDML would expand this command line into "**som** GETS SN", and execute this expanded result. The second macro (BIG) would be used by itself as an IDML command line. Each of the individual commands listed in the text for BIG would be atomically performed in sequence by IDML.

Furthermore, macros can be parameterized. A macro definition can include up to nine parameters which are indicated in the macro text as an ampersand (&) followed immediately by a single digit (1–9).

For example, a macro named RDI that retrieves a specified data item value from the current member of the set SN might be defined as the text

> **gfm** &1,sn

The parameter designation (&1) appears in the proper position for the name of the data item whose value is to be retrieved. Two examples of RDI usage are

I: define
          Macro Definition Utility
     Macro/Synonym Functions
          (A)   Add a Macro
          (C)   Change a Macro
          (D)   Delete a Macro
          (I)   List Index of Macro/Synonym Names
          (L)   List Macros and Synonyms
          (?)   Print This Command List
          (Q)   Quit Define Mode
     Function? A
     Name? SNG
     Enter text below (terminate with an empty line)
     * GETS SN
     *

     Function? A
     Name? BIG
     Enter text below (terminate with an empty line)
     * **fnm** SN
     * **getm** SN
     * **som** GETS SN
     * **flm** SN
     * **smm** GIVES GETS
     * **smo** DIVIDE GIVES
     * **gfo** TITLE DIVIDE
     *

     Function? Q
I: **Fig. 9.4**   Defining macros.

                              RDI(NAME)
                              RDI(BIRTHDAT)

These would be expanded into "**gfm** name,sn" and "**gfm** birthdat,sn", respectively.

It is possible to specify default values for parameters, so that if the user decides to leave out a value, the default is automatically used. To specify that the NAME data item should be used as a default value in the RDI macro, one would define it as

                         gfm &1=NAME,sn

Then the usage RDI ( ) would be equivalent to RDI(NAME).

Macro definitions have all of the advantages that files accessed through the **read** command do, plus the advantage of being an integral part of the database itself. Thus no additional files are required; further, the users of the IDML need not have knowledge of such additional files. As far as an IDML user is concerned, all previously defined macros can be viewed as native IDML commands or command fragments. The **define** command provides editing capabilities for the macro definitions, making the macro facility independent of other required processing.

As a general rule, the application developer would construct frequently used sequences of data manipulation commands into macros. The **read** facility can be used to better effect for command sequences that are very long or that are still undergoing development (that is, for command sequences not yet in a final form for incorporation into the data base).

9.3   QUERY LANGUAGES

The previous sections have extolled the many virtues and uses of the IDML. However, the IDML is a relatively *low-level,* procedural language that requires a knowledge of the DML. In using IDML, we build command sequences, much as we would if we were actually writing an application program. This kind of language is usually called low-level, since as developers we must pay attention to the details of command sequence structure.

The alternative would be a *high-level* language, one not requiring the developer to consider the intricacies of the data manipulation commands, but rather the overall relationships among the data elements. Such a language is *non-procedural,* in that the user does not construct a sequence of commands for accomplishing some complex data processing task. Instead, the task is requested by stating a single command. High-level, nonprocedural languages are called *query languages.*

With a single query command, a user can generate a desired report derived from many records of many different types. The user of a query language need not be a programmer. The benefits of a query language appear to be immense. If the database can be accessed without programming, then all of the design structures presented in Chapter 8 can be discarded, and the entire design process in a sense automated. Of course this cannot be so; the reasons help to further define the query language concept.

A query language is primarily a tool for information retrieval. There do exist query languages that allow certain trivial updating to be performed. But in general, for even moderately complex applications the database loading and update process is much more demanding than the retrieval process. If we contrast the programs required for loading or updating several record types (e.g., Fig. 8.7) with those that retrieve the same information, the differing degrees of complexity are readily apparent. The well-designed, user-friendly load program will not be replaced by the existence of a query language.

Further, the well-designed report program will not be replaced either. A report program such as that given in Fig. 8.15 contains far too much programming logic for a query system to easily incorporate. A query system could provide the raw data for the report of that figure; the required table would then be generated by hand or by another program. But this procedure, if anything, has increased the complexity of the retrieval task.

Query languages are typically general: the query processor is capable of retrieving many different kinds of record occurrences through long chains of set relationships. Because of the generality, the query processor incurs inefficiencies with respect to the well-written report program. If processing efficiency is a factor in our application, then this becomes an important issue.

The proper role of a query language in an application system is to be a supplement to the set of programs developed for the application. Routine loading and updating would be performed through application programs. Standard, periodic reports would also be produced through application programs. The IDML could be used in special circumstances to supplement these programs, as described in the previous sections. The query language would be used primarily for generating ad hoc reports, that is, handling those unexpected requests for additional information that end users of application systems always seem to require.

A query language can be an important aid to application developers. Like the IDML, the query language can greatly facilitate the task of application program development, allowing the developer to easily check out the effects of application programs as they are being written and revised. Although not stressed by many vendors of query languages, this aspect may be the most important use of a query system.

Typically a query system has two major aspects. The first of these is the query language itself which is used to describe the nature of the report to be generated from a database. The second aspect is the actual software that interprets a query, performs the necessary retrieval, and presents the resultant report in suitable format. The Query Retrieval System (QRS) of MDBS that we shall examine here provides extremely flexible and powerful retrieval mechanisms. Although it gives modest control over the formats of generated reports, the QRS is by no means a report writer system. However, a simple technique exists for interfacing the QRS with an independent report writer programs (see Sect. 9.7). The automatic generation of elaborately formatted reports is discussed in Chapter 14. Of course, the specification of elaborate formats requires more user effort than a simple query statement.

9.4 PROGRAMMERS, NONPROGRAMMERS,
AND QUERIES

As noted above, the user of a query language need not be knowledgeable of low-level data manipulation commands. Nor do we have to be conversant in a programming language. Because a query language is nonprocedural, there is no flow of control as there is in the procedural pseudo-language. However, the effective use of a query language and the effective writing of queries does require a modicum of skill. As with programming, repeated use of and practice with a query language will make the programmer and nonprogrammer alike better able to fully utilize the power of the query language.

Query languages are designed for casual computer users in the sense that most of them attempt to be English-like in nature. Rather than using the highly structured syntax of a programming language, they use a looser syntax that incorporates English keywords. This does not imply that a person can walk off the street and into the computer room and immediately access the database through the query language.

In particular, the user of any query language must have some knowledge of the logical data structure. For example, the user must know the names of the data items whose values are to be retrieved. Further, if data item values are being retrieved for more than one record type, the user must know about the relationships that exist among the record types. Knowledge of the logical structure of a database is necessary for the successful use of query system, regardless of the data model being used.

9.5 BASIC QRS EXPRESSIONS

The QRS examples presented in this chapter involve the database whose schema is shown in Fig. 9.5. Each division of our corporation has many employees housed (possibly) in different buildings; each employee has one office and is assigned to one division at any point in time. Divisions also initiate projects. An employee can be loaned to projects belonging to divisions other than the one for which he or she works. The estimated number of hours per week each employee will spend on a particular project is also recorded. Figure 9.6 illustrates the record occurrences that are presently loaded into this database. The system-owned set occurrences are not depicted.

Each query consists of a minimum of three parts. The first of these parts is a command keyword. This tells the QRS the basic kind of processing that is being requested. The most commonly used command keyword is **list** which produces a table of values retrieved from the database. There are a number of options available with the **list** command; these are discussed below.

The second element of the query specifies what information is to be retrieved from the database, that is, what values should be listed. The most common form is to specify one or more data items. The (partial) query

list CODE

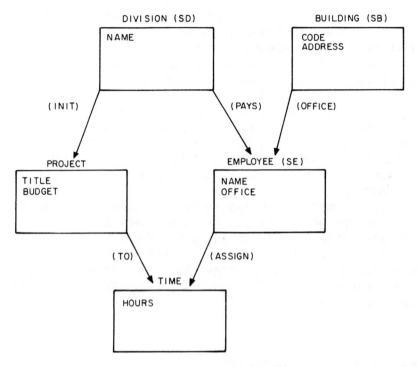

Fig. 9.5 Project data structure.

produces a one column table consisting of an automatically generated heading
followed by all of the known building codes

CODE

C158
J477

The query

list CODE, ADDRESS

produces a two column report

CODE	ADDRESS
C158	1 Main
J477	3 South

Each specified data item produces a column in the output table and each retrieved
occurrence is placed on a separate row.

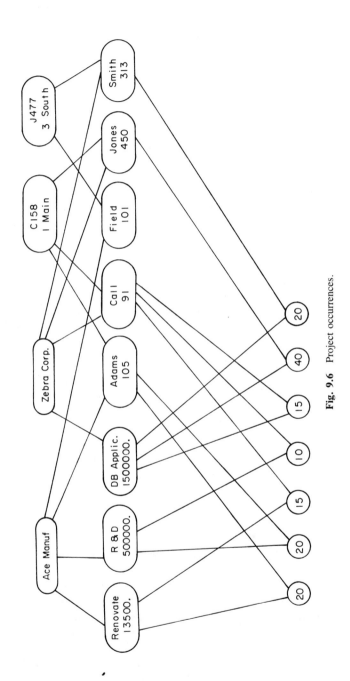

Fig. 9.6 Project occurrences.

As with the IDML, the QRS is indifferent toward upper and lower case letters. Thus the last query could equally well have been entered as

list code, address

or even

LIST code, ADDRESS

The data items must be unambiguously specified. The (partial) query

list NAME

may be ambiguous, since it is unclear whether the division name or the employee name is intended. The solution is to use the name of the intended record type as a prefix for the data item name in the following way:

list DIVISION.NAME

The period (.) serves the same function here as it does in our pseudo-language p-records, identifying the individual parts of the record type.

Data items are not the only things that can be listed. Numeric and character (string) constants can be listed along with retrieved information. A string must be enclosed within a matching pair of quotes (''). The (partial) query

list CODE, ''is located at'', ADDRESS

produces essentially a three column report:

CODE	TERM 2	ADDRESS
C158	is located at	1 Main
J477	is located at	3 South

Characters appearing within the quotation marks appear as literals in the output report. This is the one exception where the case (upper or lower) of alphabetic characters is strictly observed by QRS.

For numerical data items, expressions can be constructed using the normal arithmetic operators $+$, $-$, $*$, $/$, and parentheses. To produce a report of the minutes worked by an employee, we would use the expression HOURS $*$ 60. The usual programming language rules of operator precedence and expression evaluation apply.

The final element of the basic query specifies the relationships among the retrieved data items. This is equivalent to specifying the sets to be used to answer the query and also the order in which the sets are to be used. The sets selected will have a direct impact on what values are retrieved and the order in which occurrences are displayed.

The start of the relationship section is signalled by the keyword **thru.** The examples presented above have the following completions:

> **list** CODE **thru** SB
> **list** CODE, ADDRESS **thru** SB
> **list** DIVISION.NAME **thru** SD
> **list** CODE, ''is located at'', ADDRESS **thru** SB

Sets are specified in the same order in which they would be used in a sequence of IDML steps for retrieval or in an application program. Thus the first set following the keyword **thru** must be a system-owned set.

The query

list CODE, EMPLOYEE.NAME **thru** SB, OFFICE

produces the following two column report:

CODE	NAME
C158	Adams
C158	Call
C158	Jones
J477	Field
J477	Smith

Note how the specified sets (often collectively called the query *path*) control the order of the listed occurrences. The retrieval is equivalent to a **ffm/fnm** loop on the set SB, with an **som/fnm** loop on OFFICE nested within it. Of course, the query user does not need to understand DML commands or logic.

A different path will produce a different ordering of the occurrences. The query

list CODE, EMPLOYEE.NAME **thru** SE, >OFFICE

produces

CODE	NAME
C158	Adams
C158	Call
J477	Field
C158	Jones
J477	Smith

Here we begin our processing at the sorted set SE. The > symbol preceding the set name OFFICE indicates that the set is to be processed from the member occurrence to the owner occurrence (that is, in DML processing terms, using an **smm** command). Thus for each employee, **smm** is used to ascertain the associated building for that employee.

The sequence in which data items appear in a query statement controls the sequence of the *columns* in the output report. The path, however, specifies the ordering of the *rows* (occurrences) in the report. It is important to keep this distinction in mind.

The following queries each produce different output reports:

(1) **list** CODE, EMPLOYEE.NAME, DIVISION.NAME **thru** SB, OFFICE, >PAYS
(2) **list** CODE, EMPLOYEE.NAME, DIVISION.NAME **thru** SD, PAYS, >OFFICE
(3) **list** CODE, EMPLOYEE.NAME, DIVISION.NAME **thru** SE, >PAYS, >OFFICE
(4) **list** CODE, EMPLOYEE.NAME, DIVISION.NAME **thru** SB, OFFICE, ASSIGN, >TO, >INIT

The last of these queries produces a list of building codes, employees who have offices in those buildings, and the division that the employees are associated with through initiated projects. The output for each of these queries is given in Fig. 9.7. Note that the **thru** clause gives us a concise and extremely powerful way of clearly indicating the semantics of the desired report.

There is one restriction on the form of paths. A path may not form a closed loop, that is, circle back on itself. The path SD, PAYS, ASSIGN, >TO, >INIT is not valid, since the record type DIVISION occurs in two places, as member of SD and owner of INIT. (For a relaxation of this restriction, see Sect. 9.9).

Paths need not be linear. The query

> **list** EMPLOYEE.NAME, CODE, TITLE **thru** SE, >OFFICE, ASSIGN, >TO

is a valid query producing

NAME	CODE	TITLE
Adams	C158	Renovate
Adams	C158	R & D
Call	C158	Renovate
Call	C158	R & D
Call	C158	DB Applic
Jones	C158	DB Applic
Smith	J477	DB Applic

Note here that the proper name and code data values appear for each retrieved title. Also note that the path is not a straight line in this case. Finally, note that the employee whose name is Field is not listed at all in the output table. This is because Field has no project assignment at the present time (Fig. 9.6); thus there is no associated project occurrence from which to retrieve a title; hence Field is not listed.

One final feature of path specification should be noted. If a set name is preceeded by a minus sign (−), then instead of the usual internal **ffm/fnm** processing being performed on that set, a **flm/fpm** loop is executed instead. This is particularly useful for obtaining reversed lists from sorted sets. Thus

> **list** EMPLOYEE.NAME **thru** −SE

gives

(1)	CODE	NAME	NAME	(2)	CODE	NAME	NAME
	C158	Adams	Ace Manuf.		C158	Adams	Ace Manuf.
	C158	Call	Zebra Corp.		J477	Field	Ace Manuf.
	C158	Jones	Zebra Corp.		C158	Call	Zebra Corp.
	J477	Field	Ace Manuf.		C158	Jones	Zebra Corp.
	J477	Smith	Zebra Corp.		J477	Smith	Zebra Corp.

(3)	CODE	NAME	NAME	(4)	CODE	NAME	NAME
	C158	Adams	Ace Manuf.		C158	Adams	Ace Manuf.
	C158	Call	Zebra Corp.		C158	Adams	Ace Manuf.
	J477	Field	Ace Manuf.		C158	Call	Ace Manuf.
	C158	Jones	Zebra Corp.		C158	Call	Ace Manuf.
	J477	Smith	Zebra Corp.		C158	Call	Zebra Corp.
					C158	Jones	Zebra Corp.
					J477	Smith	Zebra Corp.

Fig. 9.7 Outputs for various path specifications.

NAME

Smith
Jones
Field
Call
Adams

In a linguistic sense, the path specification is used to make a query unambiguous. A good query system should allow the user to easily specify which relationships are of interest for producing the desired report. With the exceptions of hierarchies and shallow networks, this is true regardless of the data model used for logical structuring. Because hierarchies and shallow networks do not support multiple relationships between a pair of record types, there are no multiple choices. The specification of a path can also eliminate data item ambiguities. We saw that the data item NAME is ambiguous, since it could refer to data items in two separate record types. However, in the query

list NAME **thru** SE

the data item NAME is no longer ambiguous, for on the specified path there is only one record type, namely EMPLOYEE, that contains a data item NAME. Thus the qualification of data items with record type names is also a function of the path selected.

9.6 CONDITIONAL RETRIEVAL

One important aspect of any query language is the ability to retrieve subsets of the database. In programming terms, this is the equivalent of performing conditional statements (i.e., ifs) that control the operation of the program. In the QRS, this process is automatically performed using a conditional retrieval mechanism.

Between the list of items being retrieved and the path specification in a query, we may optionally include a conditional specification. This part of the query is introduced by the keyword **for**. The condition itself most closely resembles the conditional portion of the *if* statement of a programming language. Any of the usual six relational operators (= or eq, ≠ or ne, < or lt, > or gt, ≤ or le, ≥ or ge) can be used to compare data items with constants, data items with expressions, data items with other data items, expressions with constants and expressions. The logical operators [and, or, xor (exclusive or), not] plus parentheses, can be used to form arbitrarily complex logical expressions.

The query

list NAME, OFFICE for OFFICE < 200 thru SE

contains a simple conditional expression; we are looking for people assigned to low-numbered offices. The report generated by this query is

NAME	OFFICE
Adams	105.00000000
Call	91.00000000
Field	101.00000000

We assume that the OFFICE data item is a numeric data item. Note that the path still controls the row ordering of the report. Any data item along the specified path may be used in a conditional expression. Often the data item used does not appear in the report itself. The query

list NAME for CODE = "J447" thru SB, OFFICE

produces

NAME

Field
Smith

The building code appears in quotes to indicate that this is a character constant. Also note in the last two examples the unambiguous use of the data item NAME for the given paths.

The conditions specified can become complex, and the length of the query will grow proportionately. For example, suppose that we need to know those employees with office in building C158 who are also currently working on projects for Ace Manufacturing. One possible query to answer this is

list EMPLOYEE.NAME for CODE = "C158", DIVISION.NAME = "Ace Manuf."
    thru SD, INIT, TO, >ASSIGN, >OFFICE

Here the two conditions must both be satisfied for the name to be retrieved. The report is

NAME

Adams
Call
Adams
Call

What happened? The list appears to be retrieved twice. As always, though, the path specification holds the clue to row ordering. Both Adams and Call work on two separate projects for Ace Manufacturing. The QRS saw these two employees twice, in iterating first through divisions, second through projects, and finally through the times.

This situation arises because of the implied many-to-many relationship between the EMPLOYEE record type and DIVISION along the specified path. If we desire to eliminate this effect, we might try beginning at the other starting point, using the path SB, OFFICE, ASSIGN, >TO, >INIT. This would yield

NAME

Adams
Adams
Call
Call

Now the names come together, but it should not be surprising that we still see each name listed twice. We are actually obtaining one row of output for each TIME occurrence that is connected to the proper building and division. There are four such occurrences of TIME, two for each of the employees Adams and Call. By listing the project and time information as well, the total relationships become clear:

list EMPLOYEE.NAME, TITLE, HOURS **for** DIVISION.NAME = "Ace Manuf.",
    CODE = "C158" **thru** SD, INIT, TO, >ASSIGN, >OFFICE

NAME	TITLE	HOURS
Adams	Renovate	20.00000000
Call	Renovate	15.00000000
Adams	R & D	20.00000000
Call	R & D	10.00000000

As another possibility the path SE, >OFFICE, ASSIGN, >TO, >INIT would iterate through all employees once, checking for the building and then the project of each; but there are still two TIME occurrences to be dealt with for each employee.

This particular path has an important drawback: it produces less efficient processing than either of the first two alternatives. Generally speaking, it is better to place conditional expressions as close to the beginning of the path as possible to ensure the quickest processing of the query.

To summarize, when a path specification requires several sets not otherwise involved in the solution to the stated problem (in our example, TO), it is often wise to display one or more data items from each of the record types involved. This practice makes it easy to interpret a query's output table.

There is potential problem lurking in this example. In the specification of the condition on the division name, the exact form of the name stored in the database must be known. The *equals* operator means just that, exactly equals. The QRS provides a technique for handling situations where the exact value being sought (e.g., the exact division name) is not completely known.

Within a character constant, the asterisk (*) symbol is processed in a special way. This symbol will match any sequence of characters of any length. Thus the conditional expression in our example could have been written as DIVISION.NAME = "A*". Assuming that we know the only division whose name begins with the letter A is Ace, then this expression will find just that.

The query

list NAME **for** NAME = "*e*" **thru** SE

will produce a list of employees whose names contain anywhere in them the letter lower case e:

NAME

Field
Jones

This kind of matching is referred to as *match-string* or wildcard processing. The match string symbol may be changed (see Sect. 9.7). Wildcard processing is very useful in situations where there is uncertainty about how a name is spelled.

A refined version of match string processing is *match-one* processing. When used in character constants, the dollar sign ($) will match any single character. For example, to find employees whose names contain da as the second and third letters, we use the conditional expression NAME = "$da*". The $ matches any first letter; then the next two must be da; the * allows for any completion of the name. This match-one symbol can also be altered (see the next section).

9.7   THE QRS ENVIRONMENT

A number of features are built into the QRS to provide capabilities beyond mere retrieval. Generally speaking, these features involve interfaces with the QRS and its environment. This includes the interface between QRS and the user.

The three additional commands discussed in Section 9.2 for IDML are also available in the QRS. The **display** command can be used in precisely the same manner as indicated there to obtain the data dictionary information. Figure 9.3 shows a typical use. The **read** command can be used to process a set of queries written onto a disk file. The startup concept applies as well. Finally, the **define** command can be used to build macro definitions of queries. As in the IDML, a macro could be a fragment of a query (say a path specification) or could include many queries spread over several lines of text. Parameterized macros are especially useful in QRS.

To enhance the flexibility of the QRS, there are a number of additional elements that define the QRS environment. There is a set of *environmental parameters*. These can be interrogated by the use of the "**display** e" command (Fig. 9.8). Many of these parameters are self explanatory, for example, console depth and console width. Others are quite esoteric, for example, printer close. We shall discuss some of the commonly used parameters next.

The M1 and MS parameters define the symbols to use for match-one and match-string (wildcard) conditionals, respectively. To alter these values, the QRS **set** command is used. For example, to change the match-one variable to have the value of a semicolon, we would say

set M1 ";"

The column spacing variable CS defines the number of blank columns inserted between the columns of output produced by a query. The TL parameter defines a title to be printed at the top of each output page; an example would be

```
-->disp e
        CN      class negation       ^
        CD      console depth      24
        CP      console page eject      0
        CW      console width      80
        M1      match one char      $
        MS      match string      *
        OC      open class      [
        CC      close class      ]
        OF      output format      89
        PC      printer close      0, 0, 0, 0
        PD      printer depth      60
        PM      printer margin      0
        PO      printer open      0, 0, 0, 0
        PP      printer page eject      0
        PW      printer width      120
        CS      column spacing      2
        SF      scale factor      0
        TL      title
        FN      list file name
```

Fig. 9.8 Environment parameters.

set TL "This is the title line for the report"

The output format parameter OF specifies the manner in which values of numerical data items and expressions are to be displayed. The OF variable has a two digit value. The first of these digits defines the number of symbols to be used for the display of the integer part of the numeric value. The second digit defines the number of symbols to be used for the decimal point plus any fractional digits to be displayed. Thus the command

set OF xy

defines a total width of an output for numeric data of $x+y$ symbols, with x symbols to the left of the decimal point, and $y-1$ symbols (i.e., digits) to the right.† The maximum value that can be specified for the OF parameter is 89. Note that the OF parameter applies to all values being listed. Thus there is only one numeric output format that can be applied for any particular query.

The FN parameter is used to specify the name of a disk file. This is particularly important when used in conjunction with a new command: **write.** The **write** command operates in much the same manner as **list** with the exception of sending the report not to the terminal screen, but to the disk file specified in the FN parameter. The form of this output is somewhat different from that of the **list** command. Instead of rows and columns, the information is written as one value per line.

The purpose of the **write** command is to allow other programs to access information retrieved by the QRS. Thus it is conceivable that an application designer could use the QRS to extract information from the database into a disk file, and then a program would read that file to produce an elaborately formatted report. The person writing that report program need not be cognizant of database management, since that program is simply accessing a sequential file.‡

A number of *environment options,* which can be turned on and off by the set command are also available. The current settings of these options can be seen by entering the command "**display** o" (Fig. 9.9). Many of these options need no further explanation. Option 3, when turned off, causes the information displayed on the terminal screen to be printed on a line printer. The option should be turned on to suppress printer output.

Turning the options on and off is accomplished through the use of the **set** command. We can be explicit, as in "**set** opt 3 on" and "**set** opt 3 off", or we can use the feature of toggling the option: "**set** opt 3" changes the value of the option from its present state to its alternate state.

Option 4 permits the retrieved information to be automatically entered into a disk file. The file name is specified in the FN parameter. This allows standard

---

†The equivalent FORTRAN format specification would be $F(x+y).(y-1)$.
‡The format of this file is a text file under the specific operating system.

```
--->disp O
OPTION     STATUS              MEAN IF ON
   1        OFF      interactive I/O echo to printer
   2        ON       report output displayed on console
   3        ON       suppress printer output
   4        OFF      spool printer output to disk (FN)
   5        OFF      echo alternate input
   6        OFF      write output to console
   7        OFF      print output from WRITE
   8        OFF      echo one term per line
   9        OFF      supress column headings
  10        OFF      supress value labels
  11        OFF      supress macro recognition
  12        OFF      echo macro expansion output
  13        ON       supress printer form feed
  14        OFF      perform sort on query output
  15        OFF      pause after each report page
  20        OFF      print record access count
  21        ON       print number of observations
  22        ON       print maximum observation
  23        ON       print minimum observation
  24        ON       print sum of observations
  25        ON       print mean of observations
  26        ON       print variance of observations
  27        ON       print std dev of observations
  28        OFF      supress statistics (opt21..27)
```

Fig. 9.9 Available environment options.

output tables of information to be routed to disk, rather than having the information in the 1 value/line format of the **write** command. This is useful for offline printing, that is, printing the results of a query after the query session has been terminated, or for executing a program that uses the retrieved information as input.

When option 14 is on, the rows of data produced by a **list** command automatically appear in sorted order. QRS does this by performing a dynamic line sort on the output before it is actually displayed. Thus the most significant fields must appear in the left-most columns of the report. Of course sorting at retrieval time results in a slower retrieval process.

Options 21–27 define the statistical information that may be computed during retrieval. For nonnumeric information, the only statistic that applies is the number of observations (rows). The others will be calculated and displayed immediately following the retrieved information, if the corresponding option is on. Option 28 provides a quick way to turn off all of the statistics. If on, no statistical information will be displayed.

Another command, **stats,** operating in the same manner as **list,** but with a different output effect, only displays the statistics about the data retrieved. A table of retrieved values does not appear. This kind of processing is important in those situations where only summary statistical information is needed. The **stats** command is sensitive to the status of options 21–28.

The QRS automatically supplies column headings for output tables, which are either the name of the data item being listed or a heading such as "TERM n", where n is the number of the column, and a calculated value is being listed in that column. It is possible to supply your own column headings through the use of the "**set** ch" command. Recalling our example schema of Fig. 9.5, the query

   list DIVISION.NAME, EMPLOYEE.NAME **thru** SD, PAYS

would produce a two column report with the headings

          NAME   NAME

This is probably undesirable. Before executing that query, it would be better to define column headings that are more explicit:

          set ch "DIVISION", "EMPLOYEE"

When the query is executed, the two column headings specified will be used in the output report.

However, headings set in this manner do not go away after the query has been run. Thus if we next execute

          list CODE ADDRESS **thru** SB

the headings for this two column report will be DIVISION and EMPLOYEE. Thus it is imperative to remove column headings after they are no longer needed. To perform this task, the command "**set** ch" with no headings specified can be employed.

It is also important to note that the size of the data values being listed define the space available for column headings. This applies both to the default headings (data item names) and those established by "**set** ch". For example, suppose that a one character data item called SEX has been defined in the EMPLOYEE record type. The query

          list NAME, SEX **thru** SE

would produce the headings

          NAME   S

Only the first letter of the data item appears, since SEX is a field whose values are only one character long.

There is a trick that can be employed in such a situation. In the example the solution is

          set CS 0
          set ch "NAME", " SE", "X"

```
list NAME, "          ", SEX thru SE
set CS 2
set ch
```

The first command establishes the intercolumn spacing as zero. The second defines three column headings. As can be seen, the second column heading contains two spaces plus the letters SE. The third column contains just the letter X. The **list** command produces a three column report. The first column is the employee name, the second column a literal constant of 4 spaces, and the third column the value of the SEX data item. Because the intercolumn spacing is zero, the columns are concatenated; thus the second and third column headings combine to form SEX, while the literal constant is used to supply actual spacing between the NAME and SEX information. The last two commands simply restore the environment to its original configuration.

One final environmental element exists in the QRS. The **compute** statement provides a simple calculator capability. Any constants can be used with any of the usual arithmetic operators. A single accumulator exists, and is referenced by #. The interesting facet of this is that the accumulator can be used in subsequent queries. For example, suppose we needed to know the percentage of the budget allocated to each project supported; administrative costs not included in the database, are 8% of the budgeted amount, plus a fixed cost component of $32,500. The processing (assuming the occurrences of Fig. 9.6) might be

```
-→ set OF 83
-→ stats BUDGET thru SD, INIT
   BUDGET:
       no of observations:    3
       2135000.00  sum
       1500000.00  max
        135000.00  min
        711666.67  ave
       ********.**  var
        706683.56  std
-→ compute
C:   2135000*1.08 + 32500
                                 2338300.00
C:   Q
-→ list TITLE, BUDGET*100/# thru SD, INIT
```

We could also have defined column headings that better reflect the information being listed.

9.8   A CLASSIFICATION TECHNIQUE

Often when data is retrieved from a database, it is necessary to present that data in a form that represents some classification scheme. For example, we might need to know the people who are assigned to projects in a particular division, plus the total hours associated with that division. The QRS provides a classification method, using a breakpoint mechanism. A breakpoint is typically a change in a data value for some data item. Whenever an occurrence of that item is reached where the value of the item differs from that of the previous occurrence, a break occurs. Using the QRS breakpoint facility, statistical information is displayed for each such break.

The problem specified above is simply solved using the query

> **list**   EMPLOYEE.NAME, HOURS, TITLE, DIVISION.NAME **by** DIVISION.NAME
> **thru** SD, INIT, TO, >ASSIGN

Four data items are being listed. The breakpoint is specified by the keyword **by:** whenever a new occurrence of DIVISION.NAME is reached, whose value differs from the previous value of DIVISION.NAME, a break will occur.

The output for this query is given in Fig. 9.10. Note that headings are printed for each new value of DIVISION.NAME. Two types of statistics are displayed. The first set refers to the break, that is, to that group of occurrences just listed. The second set refers to the cumulative values, that is, statistics on all retrieved occurrences.

Breakpoints are used in primarily two circumstances. The first, by far the most common, has the data item which defines the break occurring earlier in the path specification than the data being listed. This is the case in the previous example. The problem statement referred to employee names and hours assigned; the division name (the breakpoint data item) is accessed before these two items in the course of processing records along the path. The project is listed solely for convenience of the person reading the output.

It is, however, always a good idea to list the breakpoint data item in the report. Consider the report of Fig. 9.10 if the division had not been listed. The same information in the first three columns would have been displayed, along with the same statistics. However, we would be unable to identify which division corresponded with each break group.

The other time it makes sense to use breakpoints involves the items being listed occurring in the same record type as the breakpoint data item, but the set being used for that record type is sorted on the breakpoint data item. For example, if we augment the schema of Fig. 9.5 to include in record type EMPLOYEE a data item SEX and define a system owned set SX sorted on both the SEX and NAME data items, then the following query would produce a classification of employees by their sex:

> **list** NAME, SEX, HOURS **by** SEX **thru** SX, ASSIGN

Although none of the examples presented in this section include them, it is permissible to use a conditional expression in queries that utilize breakpoints. This fact provides a great deal of flexibility to the user of the QRS.

NAME	HOURS	TITLE	NAME		
Adams	20.00	Renovate	Ace Manuf.		
Call	15.00	Renovate	Ace Manuf.		
Adams	20.00	R & D	Ace Manuf.		
Call	10.00	R & D	Ace Manuf.		
	no of observations;		4		
	65.00				sum
	20.00				max
	10.00				min
	16.25				ave
	22.92				var
	4.79				std
NAME	HOURS	TITLE	NAME		
Call	15.00	DB Applic.	Zebra Corp.		
Jones	40.00	DB Applic.	Zebra Corp.		
Smith	20.00	DB Applic.	Zebra Corp.		
	no of observations;		3		
	75.00				sum
	40.00				max
	15.00				min
	25.00				ave
	175.00				var
	13.23				std
	no. of observations;		7		
	140.00				sum
	40.00				max
	10.00				min
	20.00				ave
	91.67				var
	9.57				std

Fig. 9.10   Using breakpoints.

9.9   ADVANCED CONDITIONAL CONSTRUCTS

The first of the advanced features to be discussed refers only to character type information. The conditional section of a query allows for exact character matches to be identified. The match-one and match-string symbols can be used to liberalize the matching process. However, sometimes these two concepts match too much.

For example, suppose that we wish to find all employees whose names begin with the letter S. The appropriate conditional expression is simply **for** NAME = ''S*'', where the asterisk is of course the wildcard match-string symbol. Now, however, suppose that we need to identify those employees whose names begin with an S and who have a vowel for the second letter. This processing is much more difficult. Using the techniques already established, the only possible solution is

> **for** NAME = ''Sa*'' or NAME = ''Se*'' or NAME = ''Si*''
> or NAME = ''So*'' or NAME = ''Su*'' or NAME = ''Sy*''

While not difficult to comprehend, this conditional expression is cumbersome to enter. Thus, a shorthand notation for this kind of processing would be desirable.

The particular shorthand adopted is to use *character classes*. These classes are defined by left and right brackets [ ]. The problem stated above can be solved using character classes with the conditional expression

> **for** NAME = ''S[aeiouy]*''

Any of the symbols appearing within the character class definition can be used to match the second character of the data item NAME.

Character classes are a restriction of the match-one process, since a subset of values is being specified for matching purposes. The class definition must appear with a string constant; nesting of character classes is undefined. An additional shorthand can be used to specify ranges of characters. To select those buildings whose codes have a digit in the first position, we can say

> **for** CODE = ''[0–9]*''

The notation ''0–9'' implies all symbols between the symbols 0 and 9, inclusive.†

It is also possible to choose values not in a specified class. To obtain a list of employees whose names begin with ''S'' followed immediately by a consonant, one could enter

> **for** NAME = ''S[bcdfghjklmnpqrstvwxz]*''

A simpler technique is to say

> **for** NAME = ''S[^aeiouy]*''

The '' ^ '' stands for class negation, that is, select only those characters *not* appearing in this class. This notational convenience simplifies the query construction process and shortens the queries produced.

The character class defining symbols can be changed by using the set command to alter environment parameters OC and CC (see Fig. 9.8). The class negation symbol can also be changed by modifying the parameter CN.

The character class concept has a generalization beyond the specification of single characters. Groups of constants can be defined in much the same manner as character classes. This generalization allows numerical constants as well as string constants to be specified. In conjunction with these groups, a new operator must be defined for processing. That operator is ''in.''

---

†The symbols included in a range of characters depend upon the character set of the underlying hardware.

Suppose we need to know the employees with offices in buildings N205, J477, or T007. One query that can be used to solve this problem is

> **list** NAME **for** CODE = ''N205'' or CODE = ''J477'' or CODE = ''T007''
> **thru** SE, > OFFICE

The in operator simplifies this query substantially:

> **list** NAME **for** CODE in [N205, J477, T007] **thru** SE, >OFFICE

The query is not only shorter, but more readable, because the query statement more closely resembles the original problem statement.

When character constants are used in groups that are processed by the in operator, the constants need not be enclosed in quotation marks. The quotes are necessary if the string constants within the groups include match-one, match-string, or character class constructs. For example, the conditional expression

> **for** CODE in [N205, J477, ''T[0–5]07'']

would match eight different building codes: N205, J477, T007, T107, T207, T307, T407, and T507. Character classes and constant groups can be used in conjunction with any of the other QRS elements of course. The richness of expression available from such features increases the retrieval power of the query language.

The concepts of grouped constants and the in operator have their own generalization. Rather than forcing the user to explicitly specify constants in the group to be matched, it would be beneficial if those values could be obtained from the data base. In other words, the group of values processed by the in operator should be allowed to consist of values retrieved from the database by another query. This kind of processing is called *query nesting*.

Suppose we need a list of employees who have offices in the same building as employee Field. One solution is to execute a query that identifies the building for Field and then execute a second query that incorporates the retrieved information:

> -→ **list** CODE **for** NAME = ''FIeld'' **thru** SE, >OFFICE
> CODE
> J477
> -→ **list** NAME **for** CODE = ''J477'' **thru** SB, OFFICE
> NAME
> Field
> Smith

This kind of processing requires the QRS user to devise the statement of the second query as it is entered; thus this kind of processing is difficult when using the **read** command or the macro facility. The nested query approach combines these queries into a single statement:

list NAME **for** CODE in [**select** CODE **for** NAME = ''Field'' **thru** SE, OFFICE]
   thru SB, OFFICE

The new element is the command **select** which specifies that the results of the nested query will be used as input to the in operator. Note also that each query is complete, that is, it consists of a command, a retrieval list, conditions (as always, optionally), and a path. In the nested query, only one data item can be selected and breakpoints are not allowed. It is possible to have **select** commands within **select** commands to a maximum of 6 levels of nesting.

The nested query is used whenever standard query processing is incapable of providing the desired report. This most commonly occurs when one or more sets involved in the query must be processed twice; alternatively, a record type must be referenced in two different contexts. In the last example, record type EMPLOYEE is accessed through set SE to identify the Field occurrence and later through the set OFFICE to identify Field's coworkers. One characterization of the use of query nesting is that the total path involved contains a loop.

9.10 SUMMARY

The application developer often needs recourse to application development aids during the design and implementation of a project. The tools described in this chapter provide a basis for examining in an interactive manner the results of data manipulation commands.

The IDML is used to see the effects of the data management commands, during both program design and debugging. It can also be used for direct infrequent data updating. The **read** command and the macro facility provide flexibility to the application designer, because certain programs may be eliminated through the use of the IDML.

The QRS performs many of the same functions as the IDML, but at a level far beyond that of the IDML. The user of the QRS need not be knowledgeable in the intricacies of DML programming and command structures; only knowledge of the database schema is necessary for successful utilization of the QRS.

The QRS also serves the application developer in its ability to retrieve information in different formats and write that information onto a sequential disk file. This file can later be used for a variety of purposes such as elaborate report formatting, loading a spreadsheet system, generating a KnowledgeMan relational table for interrogation and graphics display, and so forth. The QRS syntax includes many powerful techniques for selecting and organizing the retrieved information. Whenever possible, the QRS stresses flexibility of retrieval over elaborate report formatting. These are important considerations when comparing the QRS to other retrieval systems.

RELATED READINGS

Micro Data Base Systems Inc., "Interactive Data Manipulation Language Reference Manual," Layfayette, Indiana, 1982.

Micro Data Base Systems Inc., "Query Retrieval System Reference Manual," Lafayette, Indiana, 1982.

EXERCISES

1. Describe what is meant by a query language. What traits should it have? List important benefits of a query language. What are the concerns if we are going to use the query language instead of writing relatively complex programs?
2. How can a query language benefit causal computer users?
3. Describe a startup file. Why is it useful?
4. Consider the VocEd system presented in Chapter 8. Which of the reports shown in Figs. 8.16–8.22 could be produced by the query system?
5. Build an IDML startup file for modifying the values of the user occurrences in the distributed computer-network system of Chapter 8.
6. List three major uses of the IDML. As an application developer, which one of these would you find most useful? Explain your answer.
7. Discuss the relative merits of the IDML and QRS as program debugging aides. Under what circumstances would you choose one over the other?
8. For the distributed computer-network system of Chapter 8, devise queries that tell

   (a) what databases exist;

   (b) what databases have been accessed by a user named Smith;

   (c) what tasks were run at each site;

   (d) what tasks were submitted from and assigned to computers at size *XYZ;*

   (e) which databases are located at sites which have DEC or IBM computers installed;

   (f) an activity report for both users and sites on the number and average length of tasks submitted;

   (g) all the computers in the network system;

   (h) the computers that have been required to execute all tasks submitted by John Howard;

   (i) the users that have used a particular database on a specific date;

   (j) all the users have task numbers less than 2000;

   (k) all the users with last name Brown;

   (l) the users whose time usage of a particular database in a particular task exceeds 2 min.

9.   Devise a query sequence that will approximately produce the output given in Table 6.1. How would the outputs differ?

10.   Devise a query sequence that will approximately produce the output given in Table 6.2. How would the outputs differ?

11.   What are macro definitions? What are the advantages of macros?

12.   Discuss the relative merits of command files versus macro definitions. Under what circumstances would you choose one over the other?

13.   For the VocEd application of Chapter 8, devise queries that tell

(a)   minority students (i.e., nonwhite) taking classes in programs labelled 09.1xxx;

(b)   teachers who instruct classes with a setting code of 2, classified by buildings;

(c)   the average classroom contact hours each course provides;

(d)   the average attendance by quarters in each school;

(e)   all other teachers of those students taught by M. Jones;

(f)   all teachers of those students whose social security numbers have both their first and last digits being given numbers.

14.   In the car dealership application of Chapter 7, devise a query that could be used daily to produce a sales report. How would the users make use of this query?

15.   For the project schema of Fig. 9.5, devise queries to

(a)   find all projects in which Adams is involved;

(b)   find all employees who are involved in a project whose title contains the word RENOVATE;

(c)   find all projects in which the division Zebra is involved.

16.   Why must a query include a path clause? Could the QRS select a path for the user if one is not specified? Should the QRS do this? Explain the problems inherent in a query system that does not permit users to state desired relationships.

17.   In the personnel schema of Fig. 6.11, how many different retrieval queries can be developed without using conditions, breakpoints, or nesting? What happens if we do allow conditions?

18.   For the VocEd application of Chapter 8, develop a query that involves two levels of query nesting. Can such queries be easily characterized?

19.   How can one use an input source other than the keyboard for commands with the help of IDML?

PROJECT

Use the query system to generate ad hoc reports from the database of the application system.

Chapter 10

ADVANCED LOGICAL STRUCTURING

The fundamentals for schema building were presented in Chapter 4. In this chapter we examine the more advanced logical structuring facilities that are available to an application developer. They are more advanced in the sense of being more powerful, capable of reducing the work of an application developer. Furthermore, their power is more fully appreciated in the light of a working knowledge of data manipulation, as presented in Chapters 6–8. The logical structuring facilities presented here are by no means more difficult to use or understand than the fundamentals. Indeed, most of them arose in an effort to make the application developer's task easier. In addition, several of the advanced facilities have a favorable impact on storage or access efficiency.

We begin by examining the notion of a repeating data item. We then explore the extended-network approach to logical structuring, concentrating on its advances relative to the older approaches described previously. The chapter concludes with an explanation of data security and data integrity conditions that can be stated with the DDL and which are automatically enforced by the DBCS during all data manipulation. As each new feature is introduced, its impact on schema design is discussed and its DDL syntax is presented.

10.1 THE REPEATING DATA ITEM

A data item can be declared to be a repeating data item, meaning that each of its occurrences consists of many data values. The number of repetitions must be

Fig. 10.1   PASTSAL as a repeating data item.

specified in the DDL. If a repeating data item has *m* repetitions, then each of its occurrences consists of *m* values. For instance, the data item PASTSAL (past salaries) in Fig. 10.1 could be declared to be a repeating item in the DDL:

item name is PASTSAL   idec 7,2   occurs 4 times

The *occurs* clause indicates that each occurrence of PASTSAL consists of four idec values (each of size 7,2). Thus within each TEACHER occurrence we can store the teacher's last four annual salaries.

Note that the relationship between a teacher and his or her past salaries is one-to-many. Thus the seven-step design procedure would have yielded the structure shown in Fig. 10.2 where the PAID set has either a FIFO or LIFO member order. In comparing the two structures, the same amount of storage is needed by each for storing the salary data itself. However, the PAID set incurs an additional storage cost (about 8 bytes/occurrence of PAST) for connecting TEACHER and PAST occurrences. The structure of Fig. 10.1 accommodates the same information as the alternative shown in Fig. 10.2. In fact, the former can be regarded as a design refinement of the latter.

In Section 5.5 we saw a design refinement in which two record types were collapsed, eliminating the set between them, if the owning record type had only one short data item and was not the member of a nonsystem-owned set. A repeating data item can be used to accomplish a comparable type of collapse. If a schema contains two record types related by a set such that the member record type participates in no other sets, has the same (small) number of occurrences connected to each owner occurrence, and has a single data item, then the two record types can be collapsed into one and the single data item becomes a repeating data item in the remaining record type.

It is inadvisable to make this collapse unless *all* of the conditions just stated are

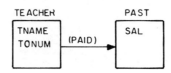

Fig. 10.2   Alternative schema without a repeating data item.

satisfied; this is a situation only occasionally encountered in practice. Generally, the only reasons ever to use a repeating data item are for increased efficiency or to handle a string data item exceeding 250 bytes (recall Table 5.1). A similar collapse could be made for a many-to-many relationship, eliminating two sets and an artificial record type. With respect to ease of data manipulation, repeating data items are handled comparably to regular data items. The only difference is that, since an occurrence of a repeating data item is an array of values, the p-record used in retrieval would contain a corresponding host language array.

Repeating data items are supported in extended-network and CODASYL-network systems. With the exception of the relational, they are also supported in many implementations of the other types of database approaches. To permit a repeating data item would violate the flat file view required by the relational approach.

10.2 THE EXTENDED-NETWORK APPROACH TO LOGICAL STRUCTURING

All logical structuring facilities previously described are available in extended-network DBMSs. Beyond these the most notable schema building facilities are: M:N sets, 1:1 sets, recursive sets, and forked sets.

M:N Sets

An M:N set is a named relationship between two record types. One record type is called the owner and the other is called the member. Any occurrence of the owner record type can be associated with many ($N \geq 0$) occurrences of the member record type. Conversely, any occurrence of the member record type can be associated with many ($M \geq 0$) occurrences of the owner record type. Thus, an M:N set can be used to *directly* represent a many-to-many relationship.

Pictorially, an M:N set is represented by a two-headed arrow as shown in Fig. 10.3. Just as with a 1:N set, the arrows always point from the owner record type to the member record type; further, an arrowhead is always positioned where the "manyness" occurs. For an M:N set, there can be both many owner occurrences per member occurrence and many member occurrences per owner occurrence. Therefore, two arrowheads are used, one positioned next to the owner record type and the other positioned next to the member record type. In Fig. 10.3 SUPPLIER is the member record type, so both arrowheads point toward SUP-PLIER. When specifying an M:N set during schema design, the selection of one record type as owner and the other as member is entirely arbitrary.

Fig. 10.3   An M:N set.

Notice that an M:N set is an alternative to an artificial record type for representing a many-to-many relationship. It can readily be used in place of artificial record types in the last two steps of the seven-step design procedure. Rather than the CODASYL-network schema of Fig. 5.12, we would obtain the extended-network schema depicted in Fig. 10.4. The selection of ACTIVITY as the owner of PARTICIP is arbitrary. STUDENT could have been chosen instead, with no adverse effect. Similarly, the selection of STUDENT as the owner of ENROLL is arbitrary.

Just as with 1:N sets, a member order can be declared for M:N sets. However, an *owner order* can also be specified for an M:N set. Since any member record occurrence can be related to many owner occurrences, we can use the owner order to specify the logical access order of those owners. Permissible owner orders are SORTED, FIFO, LIFO, NEXT, PRIOR, and IMMATERIAL. If an owner order is SORTED, then the sort key for the owner order consists of one or more data items from the owning record type. Suppose we want each student's sections to be sorted by section number and each section's students to be sorted by name and identifier, then the owner order of ENROLL is SORTED (on SNAME and SID) and the member order is SORTED (on SNUM). The EN-ROLL set is formally specified in the MDBS DDL as follows:

```
set name is ENROLL type is M:N
          owner is STUDENT order is sorted ascending (SNAME,SID)
          member is SECTION order is sorted ascending (SNUM,
```

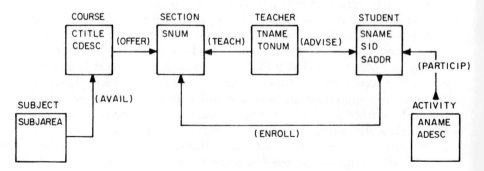

Fig. 10.4   Using M:N sets rather than artificial record types.

An M:N set is superior to an artificial record type in every respect. From a physical standpoint, it needs substantially less storage to represent a many-to-many relationship among record occurrences. Significantly faster access is permitted from an occurrence of one record type to related occurrences of the other record type. The owner and member orderings, which are so easily handled with an M:N set, have no straightforward counterpart with the artificial record type approach. From an application developer's viewpoint, schemas like those of Fig. 10.4 are simpler than those involving artificial record types and they allow simpler DML logic.

N:1 Sets

An N:1 set is named relationship in which any occurrence of the owner record type is related to no more than one occurrence of the member record type. However, an occurrence of the member record type can be related to many owner occurrences. An N:1 set between two record types is pictured in Fig. 10.5, where STUDENT is the owning record type. An owner order can be specified for an N:1 set. For instance,

```
set name is ADVISED type is N:1
    owner is STUDENT order is FIFO
    member is TEACHER
```

is the DDL specification for the set shown in Fig. 10.5. The availability of N:1 sets is mentioned here only for the sake of completeness; there is no advantage to using N:1 sets in designing a schema.

1:1 Sets

A 1:1 set is a named relationship between two record types in which any occurrence of the owner record type is related to at most one member record occurrence and any occurrence of the member record type is related to at most one owner record occurrence. The seven-step design procedure does not yield a schema with 1:1 sets. However, it is sometimes useful to refine the schema to include 1:1 sets. This is accomplished by splitting a record type into two record

Fig. 10.5 An N:1 set.

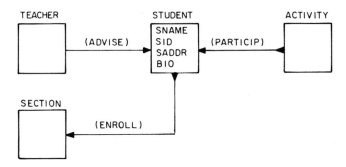

Fig. 10.6   Incorporation of the BIO data item into STUDENT.

types having a 1:1 set between them. The usual justification for such a refinement is increased processing efficiency.

As an example, suppose for the school application of Fig. 10.4 we need to
keep track of a biographical description for each student. The seven-step design
procedure would have yielded the STUDENT record type shown in Fig. 10.6.
Since the length of biographical descriptions vary widely from one student to
another (from a few bytes to perhaps 200 bytes), we might declare BIO to be a
string data item of size 200. Inclusion of BIO in the STUDENT record type
causes STUDENT occurrences to be up to 200 bytes longer than if BIO were not
included. Whenever a STUDENT record is accessed (i.e., transferred to central
memory), the biographical information is carried along, incurring an added
processing cost. If biographical information is only occasionally needed for
reporting purposes, then it would be desirable, from an efficiency standpoint, to
exclude BIO from STUDENT. Nevertheless, we still want to preserve the integrity of the one-to-one relationship between students and biographies and we still
want to be able to retrieve the biographical information pertaining to a particular
student.

The solution is to split the STUDENT record type as shown in Fig. 10.7. The
1:1 set HAS is denoted by centering the arrowhead (''manyness'' does not occur
either for students or biographies). The direction of the arrowhead points from
the owner to the member. Of course, owner order and member order do not apply
to 1:1 sets. When the split is performed, the new record type consisting of the
less frequently used data is usually declared to be the member record type.

The HAS set is formally specified with the DDL by

set name is HAS type is 1:1
owner is STUDENT
member is BIOGRPH

This causes a student's biographical data to be physically separate from the
student's other data. The result is generally faster access to the nonbiographical

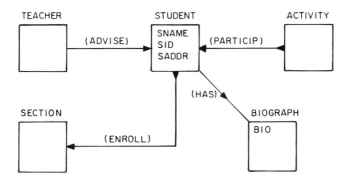

Fig. 10.7   Using A 1:1 Set to associate BIO with STUDENT.

data. Nevertheless, the biographical data for a given student is easily accessed through HAS and the integrity of the one-to-one relationship is assured.

Aside from processing efficiency, there are also situations for which a 1:1 set can be used to reduce storage costs. If the seven-step design procedure yields a record type having some data items which will be valueless for an appreciable number of occurrences of that record type, then the designer should consider placing those data items in a separate record type. A 1:1 set would connect this new record type with the original record type. As an example, consider the CUSTOMER record type shown in Fig. 10.8. The COMPANY data item refers to the company for which a customer submits orders. The AGENT data item represents a customer's purchasing agent, who approves orders. BILLADDR is used for the customer's billing address, in those cases where it differs from the mailing address (CUSTADDR).

If there are many (say, 25% or more) customers that are not ordering for a company and therefore do not have purchasing agents or a separate billing address, then many occurrences of CUSTOMER will not have data values for the COMPANY, AGENT, and BILLADDR data items. The schema of Fig. 10.8 forces storage space to be allocated for each of these data items for each CUS-

Fig. 10.8   A record type with data items that are not always used.

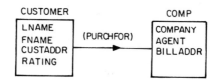

Fig. 10.9   An alternative schema using a 1:1 set.

TOMER occurrence. If these are not string data items, then 25% or more of the CUSTOMER occurrences will have considerable wasted space. This wastage is avoided by separating the three data items into a separate record type and using a 1:1 set as shown in Fig. 10.9.

The 1:1 set is available in extended-network systems. Although it is not supported in the formal CODASYL-network model, there is at least one CODA-SYL implementation that has been enhanced to allow 1:1 sets. Other data models do not support 1:1 sets. In the MDBS implementation, 1:1 sets are relatively cheap from the standpoint of storage cost.

Recursive Sets

Extended-network systems allow sets (either 1:1, 1:N, or M:N) to be used recursively. This means that the record type that owns the set is also the member record type of the set. For extended-network systems, Step 4 of the seven-step design procedure is modified to identify not only one-to-many relationships between concepts represented by two different record types, but also any one-to-many relationships that a concept may have with itself. As an example, suppose we have an EMPLOYEE record type and we need to keep track of which employees (if any) each employee manages. This is a one-to-many relationship. One employee can manage many employees, but no employee is managed by more than one employee.

This relationship is represented by a 1:N set as shown in Fig. 10.10. It is specified in the DDL by

```
set name is MANAGE type is 1:N
    owner is EMPLOYEE
    member is EMPLOYEE order sorted ascending (SSN)
```

Here, the member order is sorted based on the SSN data item.

For extended-network systems, the final step of the seven-step design procedure is extended to include many-to-many relationships that a concept may have with itself. Consider a document archival application for which it is important to keep track of which documents refer to which other documents. There is a many-to-many recursive relationship, since one document can refer to many documents and

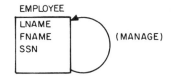

Fig. 10.10   Using a 1:N set recursively.

can also be referred to by many documents. This is very concisely represented by the M:N set as shown in Fig. 10.11. The DDL specification is

> set name is REFER type is M:N
>> owner is DOCUMENT order sorted ascending (DATE)
>> member is DOCUMENT order sorted ascending (TITLE)

Here, the owner order is sorted by DATE and the member order is sorted by TITLE.

From a data manipulation standpoint, recursive sets are operated on by the same DML commands that are used for nonrecursive sets. Each recursive set has the two usual currency indicators: current owner and current member. To find which documents are referred to by the document with an ID of 8393, we make document 8393 the current owner of REFER (e.g., with **som**). We then invoke the desired find member commands (e.g., **fnm, fmsk, fmi**), using REFER in the argument list. Extensive data manipulation examples involving recursive sets are presented in Chapter 12.

Recursive sets are not supported in the original CODASYL DBTG specifications of 1971, and existing CODAYL-network implementations do not support this valuable feature. CODASYL-networks can indirectly represent one-to-many and many-to-many recursive relationships with artificial record types and extra 1:N sets as shown in Figs. 10.12 and 10.13. Similarly, relational systems can indirectly represent such relationships with additional record types and redundant data items as shown in Figs. 10.14 and 10.15. In the case of Fig. 10.14, there must be one occurrence of MANAGE for each employee that has a manager; each occurrence consists of an employee's identifier and his or her manager's identifier. In the case of Fig. 10.15 there is for each document (e.g., 8393) an

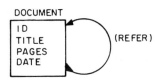

Fig. 10.11   Recursive use of an M:N set.

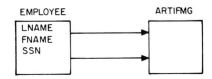

Fig. 10.12   CODASYL-network representation of a one-to-many recursive relationship.

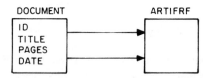

Fig. 10.13   CODASYL-network representation of a many-to-many recursive relationship.

Fig. 10.14   Relational representation of a one-to-many recursive relationship.

Fig. 10.15   Relational representation of a many-to-many recursive relationship.

occurrence of REFER for each of the documents to which it (i.e., document 8393) refers. Hierarchical and shallow-network architectures are also unable to directly represent recursive relationships; they too force the application developer to resort to cumbersome redundancy.

Forked Sets

With an extended-network system, an application developer can declare *multiple member record types* for a single set. Such a set can be a 1:1, 1:N or M:N set. The seven-step design procedure does not yield sets of this kind. However, they are easily constructed as a design refinement. Such sets are very useful for naturally representing forked (i.e., nonbinary) relationships that exist in the application world being modeled. They are also valuable for reasons of storage efficiency and processing convenience.

As an example, consider an application where it is important to keep track of the hourly and salaried employees of each department. The seven-step design procedure yields the schema shown in Fig. 10.16. Although they have some kinds of data in common, hourly and salaried employees do not share all of the same kinds of data (e.g., hourly and overtime rates versus salary and pay periods). The schema of Fig. 10.17 shows an alternative approach to representing the same situation. The EMPLOY set forks into two member record types and is specified in the DDL as follows:

> set name is EMPLOY type 1:N
>> owner is DEPT
>> members are (HOURLY, SALARY) order is sorted ascending (ENAME)

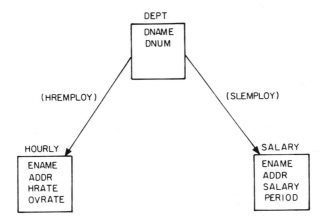

Fig. 10.16   Schema for hourly and salaried employees.

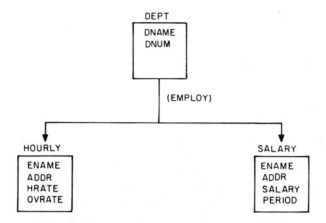

Fig. 10.17   Multiple member record types for a 1:N set.

The multiple member forked set has three advantages. First, it is a more natural way of representing what is conceptually a single relationship among three different types of entities. Second, it is less expensive in terms of storage requirements, because it represents with a single set what would otherwise require two sets. Third, it allows uniform access to employees regardless of whether they are salaried or hourly. Chapter 12 presents data manipulation examples involving a multiple member forked set. The member order for the EMPLOY set can be any of the usual orderings. If it is sorted, then it must be sorted on data items that the member record types have in common (e.g., ENAME). The sort can also be based on the names of the member record types (in addition to data items). To sort first by ENAME and then by record type name, the DDL specification is

members are (HOURLY,SALARY) order is sorted ascending (ENAME,record)

Figure 10.18 presents a forked M:N set with multiple member record types. This set can have both an owner order and a member order. The owner order might be IMMATERIAL and the member order could be sorted on TITLE, for instance. For any author, this schema enables us to obtain a sorted list of writings, a sorted list of books, and/or a sorted list of articles. For a given article, we can find its authors and the book written by each. For any book, we can obtain its authors and the other writings of each.

Forked sets with *multiple owner record types* are analogous to those with multiple member record types. The example shown in Fig. 10.19 indicates that a class can contain many different models. When keeping an inventory of parts, it is vital to know the quantity of a part that is on hand for either a model or a class of models. A quantity is owned by a class if the part is interchangeable across all

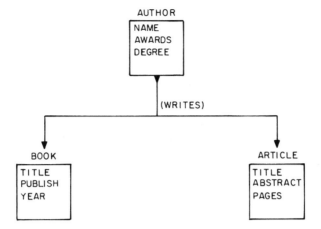

Fig. 10.18   Multiple member record types for an M:N set.

models in a class, otherwise a quantity must be owned by a model. This schema allows us to easily determine, for any model, how many of each part is on hand. For a given class, we can find which parts are interchangeable among the models of the classes and how many of each are on hand. The forked AVAILABLE set is specified in the DDL by

> set name is AVAILABLE
>   owners are (CLASS,MODEL)
>   member is Q order is immaterial

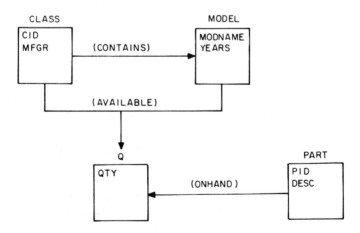

Fig. 10.19   Multiple owner record types for a 1:N set.

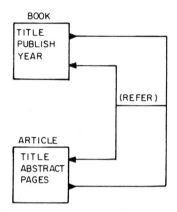

Fig. 10.20   Multiple owner/member recursive M:N set.

It is permissible to define a set with both multiple member record types and multiple owner record types. Moreover, this set could be M:N and even recursive. Suppose that we need to keep track of which books and articles are referred to by other books and articles. This is a many-to-many recursive relationship. A book or article can refer to many other books and/or articles and can be referred to by many other books and/or articles. This relationship among books and articles is very concisely represented by the REFER set shown in Fig. 10.20. For any book we can find all books and articles to which it refers.

The extended-network model supports all of the foregoing kinds of forked sets. The only kind of forked set permitted by the CODASYL-network is a 1:N set with multiple member record types. The other data models do not support any kind of forked set.

$SYSSET

In addition to automatically defining a record type named system, the MDBS extended-network system also defines a special set named $SYSSET. This set is configured automatically as a 1:N, system-owned, multiple member set, with every defined record type declared as member. The member order of $SYSSET is FIFO.

The $SYSSET is special in the way in which it is handled by the database control system, too. At the end of the current processing session (run-unit), the member occurrences of $SYSSET are all disconnected from the system record. That is, after the call to **dbcls** in a program, $SYSSET will have no member occurrences. Thus $SYSSET is not used for maintaining lists of data across run-units.

The purpose of $SYSSET, and typical examples of the kinds of processing for which it is designed, are given in Chapter 12.

Set Insertion Mode

In the DDL specifications of an extended-network system, a set insertion mode can be declared for the owner record type(s) and the member record type(s) of a set. The two permissible modes are *automatic* and *manual*. If the membership of a set has been declared to be automatic, then whenever a member occurrence is created it is automatically connected to the current owner of the set. No **ims** command is needed following the **crs** command. If the membership of a set is manual, then the creation of a member record occurrence does not result in its automatic connection to an owner occurrence for the set. Manual membership is the default. All examples in previous chapters used this default.

The ownership of a set can also be declared to be automatic or manual. If it is automatic, the creation of an owner record occurrence results in its automatically being connected to the current member of the set. No automatic connection occurs in the case of manual ownership. Manual ownership is the default and was used in all examples in Chapters 6–8.

Suppose that we desire the AVAIL set in Fig. 10.4 to have automatic member insertion. The appropriate DDL specification is

```
set name is AVAIL
    owner is SUBJECT
    member is COURSE auto order is FIFO
```

Automatic membership (ownership) is indicated by the word *auto* following the name of the member (owner) record type. Manual insertion is indicated by specifying either *manual* or nothing.

As a schema is designed, the application developer must eventually select a set insertion mode(s) for each set. For 1:N sets, membership should be manual if there are to be member occurrences that are not connected to any of the owner occurrences of the set. Otherwise, automatic membership should be considered; if, whenever a member occurrence is created, the owner occurrence to which it is to be connected is known, then there is no disadvantage to choosing automatic membership. It does save a programming step, although it makes little difference in terms of processing speed.

The choice of automatic or manual set insertions for a 1:1 set is typically based on the guidelines that are used for 1:N sets. In the case of M:N sets it is recommended that both ownership and membership be allowed to default to manual. Manual set insertion always offers more processing flexibility at the same processing cost as automatic insertion.

In every case, though, automatic insertion only refers to insertion when a *new* record occurrence is created. Existing occurrences are removed and reinserted into sets independent of the specified insertion mode. The behaviors of the insertion commands themselves are not affected by the set insertion mode; only **crs** is affected.

CODASYL-network systems allow an application developer to choose between automatic and manual membership for a 1:N set. Hierarchical and shallow-network systems generally force the use of automatic membership. In the relational approach there is no notion of owners and members; a connection between two records (of different record types) is established by giving them the same value for a common field(s).

Synonyms and Titles

As with most DBMSs, synonyms and titles can be specified for data items, record types, and sets in the MDBS DDL. A synonym is an alternative name that can be used (e.g., in QRS) instead of the primary name. For instance, we could define DNO as a synonym for DEPTNUM by declaring

item name is DEPTNUM character 8 syn DNO

In stating a query, DNO can be used interchangeably with DEPTNUM. Synonyms *cannot* be used in application programs in place of the actual schema names.

A title may be regarded as a comment, which can be displayed along with other data dictionary information. An example is

item name is QTY unsigned 3
title "quantity of a part on back order from a supplier"

The title is enclosed in quotes. Note that the extensive use of titles can significantly increase the size of the data dictionary.

10.3   DATA SECURITY

Three kinds of data security can be employed by an application developer using MDBS: passwords, data encryption, and access codes. As shown in Chapter 5, each user (or user group) is assigned a *password*. A user is unable to open a database for processing if that user's correct password is not passed as an argument to the **dbopn** command. Most DBMSs have a comparable password mechanism.

The existence of user passwords does not prohibit a nonuser from accessing a database directly from the operating system by using an operating system command to scan the contents of auxiliary memory. Since data values of a record occurrence are typically stored contiguously, there is a danger that sensitive data could be directly viewed by nonusers (e.g., a person's name and salary). With MDBS this possibility is easily precluded by declaring selected data items to be *encrypted*.

When a data item has been declared to be encrypted, each of its data values is stored in an encrypted form. When encrypted data values are accessed through application programs or QRS, they are automatically decrypted. Any data item can be declared to be encrypted by including the word *encrypted* following the data item name in the DDL specification. For example,

item name is SALARY encrypted idec 8,2

or

item name is SALARY idec 8,2 encrypted

Many DBMSs do not support an encryption facility.

A third kind of security allows the application developer to restrict a bona fide database user's access privileges to only a certain portion of a schema. DBMSs that support this type of security differ primarily in terms of how they define the portion of a schema that can be accessed. With MDBS this is accomplished by making *access code* assignments.

It is important, no matter what the method, to distinguish between read access and write access. If a user has read access to a portion of the database, then that portion of the database can freely be used for data retrieval. If a user has write access to a portion of the database, then the user can modify that portion of the database.

Sixteen access codes (*a, b, c, . . . , p*) are available to an application developer using MDBS. The application developer can assign any combination of one or more of these codes to a user, thereby establishing that user's read access privileges. The developer can also assign any combination of access codes to a data item to establish its read access protection. If a user's read access combination has any access code in common with the read access combination of a data item, then that user has read access to the values of that data item. Otherwise, the user does not have read access to those values.

An application developer can also assign a write access code combination to each user and to each data item. The user has write access only to those data items whose write access combinations have an access code in common with the user's write access combination.

Read and write access code combinations can also be assigned to record types and sets. The read access combination of a data item must be a subset of the read access combination of its record type. The same convention must also hold for write access combinations. Furthermore, the read access combination of a record type must have an access code in common with the read access combination of each set for which it is an owner or member; the same is true for write access combinations. The MDBS DDL specifications presented to this point contain no mention of access codes. When no access codes are included, all bona fide users have unrestricted read and write access privileges.

As part of the schema design process, an application developer can make access code assignments. The following procedure makes this assignment process very straightforward. The procedure is applied once to make write access code assignments. It is also applied once to make read access code assignments. The two are not mixed together; thus in the description of the assignment procedure, the word *access* can mean either read access or write access, but not both.

The assignment procedure has five steps:

(1)   Partition the users that are to be specified in the DDL into groups, such that all users in a group are to have the same access privileges. In other words, if a data item is accessible by one user in a group, then it should be accessible by all other users in the group. No two groups should have the same access privileges (if they do, they should be considered as one group). A user is in exactly one user group. We refer to these groups as $U_1, U_2, \ldots, U_k$, where k is typically less than 17.

(2)   Partition all data items of a schema into groups, such that all data items in a group are to have the same degree of access protection. In other words, if a user has access to one data item in a group, then that user should also have access to all other data items in the group. No two groups should have the same access protection (if they do, they should be considered as one group). A data item is in exactly one data item group. We refer to these groups as $I_1, I_2, \ldots, I_h$, where h can be very large.

(3)   Form a matrix with $U_1, U_2, \ldots, U_k$ as columns and $I_1, I_2, \ldots, I_h$ as rows. For each user group U_i that is to have access to a data item group I_j, place a mark at the intersection of column U_i and row I_j.

(4)   Assign access code a to U_1, access code b to U_2, access code c to U_3, and so forth. The result is that every column has a unique access code assigned to it.

(5)   The access code combination of each row is now assigned to consist of the access code of every column for which that row has a mark.

A sample access code assignment matrix is shown in Fig. 10.21. In this example there are 5 user groups and 18 data item groups. The X marks show which users are to be granted access to which data items. For instance, users in the first group (U_1) should be permitted to access data items in groups $I_1, I_2, I_3,$ $I_4, I_7, I_{12}, I_{15},$ and I_{16}. Data items in I_5 should be accessible by users in U_2 and U_5. Data items in I_{12} are to be accessible to all users. Access to data items in I_6 should be restricted to users in U_4.

	U_1	U_2	U_3	U_4	U_5	Item access code combinations
I_1	X		X			ac
I_2	X	X				ab
I_3	X	X			X	abe
I_4	X		X	X		acd
I_5		X			X	be
I_6				X		d
I_7	X					a
I_8		X		X	X	bde
I_9			X	X		cd
I_{10}				X	X	de
I_{11}			X	X	X	cde
I_{12}	X	X	X	X	X	abcde
I_{13}		X	X			bc
I_{14}			X	X	X	cde
I_{15}	X				X	ae
I_{16}	X	X	X		X	abce
I_{17}		X	X	X		bcd
I_{18}		X		X		bd

User access codes   a   b   c   d   e

Fig. 10.21   Access code assignment matrix.

User access code assignments (Step 4) are shown at the bottom of the matrix. The derived access code combinations (Step 5) for the various data item groups are shown along the right side of the matrix. In row I_9 we see X's in the third and fourth columns. The access codes assigned to these columns are c and d, respectively. Therefore, the access code combination for I_9 is c and d. The access code combinations of the other rows were derived similarly.

The assignments resulting from the five-step procedure are not the only feasible assignments for providing the desired access protection and privileges. However, they are very easy to obtain. The five step procedure does not handle situations where there are more than sixteen distinct user groups. If there are more than 16 user groups and fewer than 17 data item groups, the procedure should be modified to place data item groups in columns and user groups in rows. In Step 4, then, access codes are assigned to the item groups rather than user groups. In the relatively rare case of more than 16 distinct user groups and more than 16 distinct data item groups, feasible access code assignments can still be made (though not with the simple five step procedure).

In a DDL specification, every user in the same user group is given the same access code and every data item in the same data item group is given the same access code combination. Suppose that the user *shipping clerk* has a read access code of g and a write access code of b, then the DDL specification for that user is user "shipping clerk" with "pass sc3" read access g write access b

Suppose that the PONUMB data item has a read access combination of *c, d, e, g,* and a write access combination of *b, m, p,* then the DDL specification for this data item is

item name is PONUMB unsigned 3 read access (c–e,g) write access (b,m,p)

Note that whenever more than one access code is involved in an access code combination, those access codes are enclosed in parentheses.

Once the user and data item access code assignments have been made, record type and set access code assignments should be considered. There is a simple approach to handling a record type. If an access code is specified for any of its data items, then include that access code in the access code combination of the record type. If any of the data items of a record type has the same access code combination as the record type, then it need not be specified for the data item. This is because the access code combination of a data item defaults to be the same as that of its record type. The appropriate DDL specification for a record type having read access of *a, b, c, e,* and write access of *b* is

record name is EXMPL read access (a–c,e) write access b

A straightforward way to determine a feasible access code combination for a set is to include all access codes of all record types that participate in the set. This allows any user who has access to any data item in the owner or member record type of the set to have access to the set. In the case of read access, this means that the user can find any owner or member record occurrence through the set. Of course, data can be retrieved from the found record only for those data items (if any) to which the user has read access. In the case of write access to a set, the user can connect and disconnect owner and member records.

The method of set access code assignment described in the preceding paragraph implies that any user with access to a data item of any record type involved in a set will have access to that set. If this is not desirable, access codes can be either omitted from or added to the access code combination of the set. Four alternative cases are shown in Fig. 10.22. It is assumed that there are four distinct user groups, each having one of the access codes *a, b, c, d.*

Case 1 allows all users to have access to both sets. In the event of a read access any user can find all students taught by any teacher, all students advised by any teacher, the advisor of any student, and the teachers of any student. In the event of write access, all users can connect and disconnect teachers and students for either the ADVISE or TEACH set. Assuming that both read and write access are *a, b, c, d,* the DDL specification for Case 1 is either

set name is ADVISE type 1:N read access (a–d) write access (a–d)

or

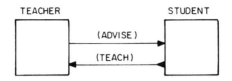

Access code assignments for the TEACHER and STUDENT record types:

TEACHER	ad
STUDENT	bcd

Example access code assignments for the ADVISE and TEACH sets:

	Case			
	1	2	3	4
ADVISE	abcd	d	ac	ace
TEACH	abcd	abcd	ab	d

Fig. 10.22 Alternative set access code combinations.

set name is ADVISE type 1:N access (a–d)

In Case 2, only users with access code *d* have access to both sets. Just as in Case 1, all users have access to the TEACH set. If these are read access codes then only users with code *d* will be able to find the students advised by a given teacher and to find the advisor of a given student. In the event of write access codes, only users with write access code *d* are able to connect and disconnect STUDENT and TEACHER occurrences for the ADVISE set.

The assignments shown in Case 3 are valid, but probably not very useful. For both ADVISE and TEACH there is one access code in common with each record type. In a read access context, users with access code *a* have access to some data items of TEACHER and can use DML find commands to discover students advised by a given teacher. However, data cannot be retrieved from any of the found students, because these users do not have access to STUDENT records. Users with access code *c* can access some STUDENT data items and can use the ADVISE set to find a student's advisor. However, these users are unable to retrieve data from TEACHER occurrences.

Suppose that we want only some users with access code *d* to have access to the ADVISE set. To these users we assign another access code (e.g., *e*) in addition to *d*. In Case 4, these users have access to the ADVISE set, while those user's with only *d* access do not. The *a, c, e* access combination for ADVISE is valid, since it has a code in common with both record types. As in Case 3, the users with codes *a* and *c* cannot make effective use of ADVISE, even though they have access to it. Their access could be prevented by adding *e* to the TEACHER and

STUDENT access code combinations, while eliminating *a* and *c* from the AD-
VISE access code combination. This valid assignment preserves the access privileges of users with both codes *d* and *e*.

The access code approach to data security is not available with DBMSs other
than MDBS and the Knowledge Manager, although IMAGE (a shallow-network
system) utilizes a somewhat similar approach involving access ranges. Nevertheless, there are other security approaches that allow a user's access privileges
to be restricted to only certain portions of a schema. Most notable is the definition of CODASYL *subschemas*.

A subschema is that portion of a CODASYL-network schema that remains
after zero, one, or more data items, records types and/or sets have been eliminated. The restrictions on this elimination are that all record types in the remaining subschema must be connected to each other and for each remaining set its
owner and member record types must also be in the subschema. For instance, we
could not eliminate ORDLINE from the schema of Fig. 10.23 without also
eliminating the REF and CONTAINS sets, and also eliminating either the
PRODUCT record type or the CUSTOMER PLACES ORDER structure. Figure
10.24 illustrates four legitimate subschemas for the schema of Fig. 10.23.

Most implementations of the CODASYL approach to database management
allow a password to be specified for each subschema. In CODASYL systems an
application program is restricted to processing only the data that is represented by
a single subschema. Beyond a subschema password, there is typically no further
restriction on the processing that can be performed by a program with respect to
its subschema. For instance, an application program using the first subschema of

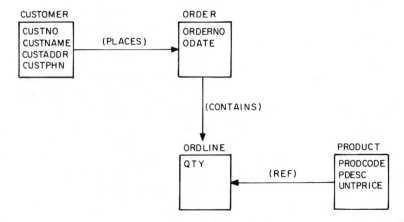

Fig. 10.23 Example CODASYL-network schema.

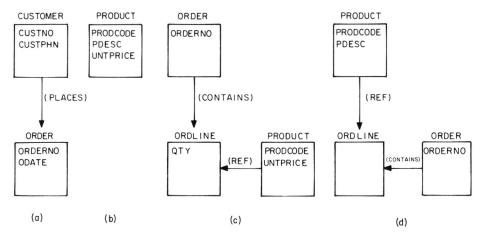

Fig. 10.24   Four example subschemas.

Fig. 10.24 cannot be restricted to have only read access to CUSTOMER and PLACES, while having both read and write access to ORDER.

Thus in most CODASYL implementations, a user's (i.e., application programmer's) access privileges are defined by the subschema passwords which that user knows. While this approach does not provide security control of the same flexibility or refinement as the access code approach, it is nevertheless fairly powerful. Furthermore, it must be pointed out that the CODASYL proposals suggest more powerful security control features than those generally available in current CODASYL-network implementations. Among hierarchical and shallow-network systems there is no uniform approach to data security, beyond requiring a password to open the database. Similarly, there is no standard approach to data security for relational systems.

10.4   DATA INTEGRITY

Professional, high-quality application software must be able to guarantee the integrity of *data values* and *data interrelationships*. An application developer has two choices: build the integrity guarantees into each piece of application software or build the application software with a DBMS that automatically enforces desired integrity conditions (as stated in the DDL specification). DBMSs vary considerably in terms of the integrity conditions they are able to enforce. The relatively extensive integrity facilities of MDBS are described here. The reader should not expect to find all of these integrity features available in every DBMS.

Data Value Integrity

Perhaps the most significant feature a DBMS can have for assuring data value integrity is its capacity to store data nonredundantly. If a given data value exists only once in the data base, rather than repeatedly, the application developer does not need to be concerned with maintaining consistency among the redundant values. CODASYL-network and extended-network logical structuring approaches are the only two that allow redundancy to be completely controlled. Redundancy of data values is a prominent characteristic of most current implementations of the other three data models where it is commonly used as a mechanism for indicating data interrelationships. In these cases it is generally the task of an application developer to guarantee consistency.

In DBMSs that support a sorted ordering of records of one type that are related to a record of another type, it is useful to have a mechanism for disallowing duplicate sort key values. Such a facility exists in CODASYL-network systems for the member order of a set and in extended-network systems for both member and owner sorted orderings. In MDBS, duplicate values of a sort key are automatically prohibited by including the word "nodup" after the sort key in a DDL specification. For instance, in Fig. 10.4 duplicate sort key values among the owner occurrences of ENROLL are prohibited by declaring

owner is STUDENT order is sorted ascending (SNAM,SID) nodup

If an attempt is made to insert (or alter) a STUDENT record having a sort key value that already exists in the database, the attempt is thwarted and an appropriate command status message is issued.

MDBS rejects any attempt to create or alter a date value that is invalid. Examples of invalid dates are 01/32/1983, 13/05/1942, 09/31/1926, 02/29/1957, and 02/29/1900. Invalid time data values are also rejected; examples include 023:52:65 and 055:75:02. Alphabetic characters are rejected for integer data items and so forth.

Many DBMSs allow the application developer to specify a range of feasible values for a data item when it is defined with the DDL. In MDBS this is allowed for any of the nine different types of data items with the exception of binary data items. An attempt to create or modify a data value that is outside of the range of feasible values of its data item is not permitted. The feasibility range of a data item is specified in the DDL along with the type and size of the data item.

As an example, to prohibit salary values of less than 9000 and greater than 83000, we define the SALARY data item as

item name is SALARY idec 7,2 range 9000.00 to 83000.00

Range values for string and character data items must be enclosed in quotes, as the following example illustrates:

item name is ENAME string 25 range "A" to "ZYZZZ"

The lower bound on ENAME values is an A, followed by 24 blanks. The upper bound is ZYZZZ, followed by 20 blanks. The maximum ranges that can be specified for each type and size of data item are shown in Table 5.1.

Finally, it should be noted that the access code described earlier also helps to guarantee integrity. The ability to declare write access protection for a data item further secures its values from unauthorized assaults (both intentional and accidental) on their integrity.

Data Relationship Integrity

The importance of data relationship integrity cannot be overemphasized. In most application areas, the majority of relationships between record types are one-to-many in nature. The integrity of these one-to-many relationships can always be automatically guaranteed in extended-networks by simply representing them with 1:N sets. With the exception of recursive one-to-many relationships, this is also true for CODASYL-networks.

In comparing Figs. 10.12 and 10.13, it is clear that the same logical structure is employed for representing both one-to-many and many-to-many recursive relationships. Unlike the logical structure of Fig. 10.10, the CODASYL-network structure of Fig. 10.12 does not prevent a many-to-many relationship among employees; the application builder must build the necessary integrity checks into application software.

Since the hierarchical and shallow-network approaches place severe limitations on the usage of 1:N sets, an even greater amount of integrity checking must be performed by the application developer. Such checking is required wherever redundancy (e.g., ORDLINE1 in Fig. 4.11) or artificial record types (e.g., DUM in Fig. 4.14) are used to represent one-to-many relationships. In ORDLINE1 of Fig. 4.11, there is nothing that structurally forces the desired one-to-many relationship between PRODCODE and QTY. Similarly, in Fig. 4.14 the DUM record type (along with the D1 and D2 sets) does not structurally enforce the desired one-to-many relationship between CUSTOMER and ORDER.

Although the relational approach represents all one-to-many relationships with redundant data items, it can nevertheless provide the same degree of automatic enforcement of one-to-many integrity as the CODASYL-network approach. This is true as long as, for every one-to-many relationship, the relational DBMS implementation automatically guarantees that the redundant data item(s) in one record type is the unique identifier of the other. There are few (if any) micro relational implementations that provide such a guarantee. In Fig. 4.3 for instance, as long as a DBMS guarantees that CUSTNO is the unique identifier of

CUSTOMER, the one-to-many relationship between CUSTOMER and ORDER is assured.

In addition to automatically enforcing the integrity of one-to-many relationships, the integrity of all one-to-one relationships between record types is also guaranteed by MDBS. Generally, this guarantee is not available in systems that do not allow the application developer to explicitly specify 1:1 sets in a schema. An exception would be a relational DBMS implementation that guarantees that the unique identifier of one record type is also the unique identifier of another record type whenever a one-to-one relationship is to be represented.

Another aspect of relationships that is important from an integrity standpoint is permanency. Once two record occurrences become related (i.e., logically connected) to each other, can they later be disconnected or should the logical connection be permanent? If the application developer decides that a connection is to be permanent, the set can be declared to have *fixed retention* in the DDL specification.

```
set name is CONTAINS type 1:N fixed
     owner is COUNTRY
     member is STATE
```

Declaring a set to have fixed retention means that once a member occurrence is connected to an owner occurrence, that connection can never be removed without deleting the owner occurrence or member occurrence from the database. This type of integrity facility is also available with CODASYL-network systems and some hierarchical systems.

Finally, it should be noted that the ability to declare write access protection for a set further secures record occurrence connections from unauthorized assaults (either intentional or unintentional) on their integrity.

Recovery

A crucial element of any DBMS is the ability to recover from situations where integrity of the database has been compromised. Recovery facilities are discussed in depth in Chapter 14.

10.5 SUMMARY

We introduced those aspects of extended-network data structuring that go beyond the structuring capabilities of the older hierarchical, shallow-network, relational, and CODASYL-network approaches. The impact of each of these new features on database design procedures was examined. The advantages of extended-network schemas, in terms of simplifying an application developer's tasks and offering greater efficiencies, were described and illustrated. Most notable among the extended-network advances are direct representations of many-to-many, recursive, and forked relationships.

Other important database management facilities discussed in this chapter included the automatic enforcement of data security and automatic guarantees on the integrity of both data values and data relationships.

Chapters 12 and 13 contain further examples of the features introduced in this chapter, along with illustrations of data manipulation for extended-network schemas.

RELATED READINGS

S. Atre, "Data Base: Structured Techniques for Design, Performance, and Management," Wiley, New York, 1980.

R. H. Bonczek, C. W. Holsapple, and A. B. Whinston, "Foundations of Decision Support Systems," Academic Press, New York, 1981.

D. Gradwell (ed.), "Database—The 2nd Generation: State of the Art Report," Pergamon, Oxford, 1982.

W. H. Inmon, "Effective Data Base Design," Prentice-Hall, Englewood Cliffs, New Jersey, 1981.

Micro Data Base Systems Inc., "MDBS Data Base Design Reference Manual," Lafayette, Indiana, 1981.

T. W. Olle, "The CODASYL Approach to Data Base Management," Wiley, New York, 1978.

N. Vetter and R. N. Madison, "Database Design Methodology," Prentice-Hall, Englewood Cliffs, New Jersey, 1981.

EXERCISES

1. Modify the seven-step design process described in Chapter 5 to take advantage of the extended-network features.
2. Can you suggest a special case in which using N:1 set is better than 1:N set?
3. Under what circumstances would you prefer to split a record type into two record types related by a 1:1 set? What advantages result from this split? What extra work needs to be done by the DBMS because of this splitting?

4. Revise the schemas of Figs. 10.18–10.20 to conform with the CODASYL-network approach to data structuring.
5. Revise the schemas of Figs. 10.18–10.20 to conform with the relational approach to data structuring.
6. Revise the schemas of Figs. 10.18–10.20 to conform with hierarchical data structuring.
7. Revise the schemas of Figs. 10.18–10.20 to conform with the shallow-network data structuring approach.
8. Show how to handle the schemas of Figs. 10.18–10.20 with an inverted file approach to data structuring.
9. List the advanced structuring features available with the extended-network approach and briefly describe the nature and value of each.
10. Compare M:N sets and artificial record types. Discuss the relative merits of each.
11. How are the owner and member record types chosen for M:N sets? Develop a simple 2 record M:N example and compare it to having two 1:N sets with each record *owning* one of the two sets.
12. Discuss the kinds of relationships that can exist among entities in the real world, independent of data modeling methods. Give an example of each.
13. Describe three real world applications which could make effective use of recursive sets.
14. Develop a schema having a set with more than two record types. Specify this in terms of DDL statements.
15. In what situations would you use a repeating data item?
16. Explain how inverted file systems can be simulated with a subset of the extended-network capabilities. Explain how the ADABAS notion of coupling (Appendix D) can be simulated.
17. Describe applications where a user should have

   (a) read access to an item, but not write access;
   (b) read access that is a subset of some other user's read access privileges;
   (c) read access privileges that partially overlap with another user's read access privileges;
   (d) read access privileges that are entirely different from those of another user;
   (e) write access, but not read access, to a data item;
   (f) read access to data items in two record types, but not to the set relating those two record types.

18. Suppose the read access of various users with respect to various data items are desired to be as follows:

   user A: items 1, 3, 5
   user B: items 1, 5

user C:	item 3
user D:	items 1, 3
user E:	items 2, 4
user F:	items 1, 2
user G:	items 1, 4
user H:	items 2, 5
user I:	items 4, 5
user J:	items 3, 4, 5
user K:	items 2, 3

(a)   Derive access code assignments for data security control. Show the access code(s) for each item and the access code(s) for each user.

(b)   Let record type R1 include items 1, 2, 3, 4; record type R2 contains items 5, 6, 7; record type R3 contains 8, 9, 10, 11; Complete access code assignment for record types.

(c)   What access code(s) would you assign for the set relationship between record type R1 and type R2?

19.   Given an extended-network schema, what additional commands beyond those of Chapters 6 and 7 would be useful to facilitate data processing?

PROJECT

Revise the application schema to take advantage of the advanced logical structuring facilities presented in this chapter. Make access code assignments as warranted by the application.

Chapter 11

PHYSICAL CONSIDERATIONS
AND PERFORMANCE CONTROL

Chapters 1–10 do not delve into the internal physical details of a database. Where are record occurrences stored, how does the DBMS keep track of record occurrences, how are named relationships actually implemented? As we have seen, an understanding of such issues is not necessary to be able to use MDBS in developing application systems. However, it is important for judging the quality of a DBMS for evaluating the care and effort that went into its design and implementation, and for assessing its relative efficiency.

As discussed in Chapters 5 and 10, storage and processing performance are greatly affected by the nature of logical structuring facilities furnished by a DBMS. Even for a given DBMS, performance can vary widely depending on how skillfully the database designer uses the logical structuring facilities of the system. Furthermore, two different physical implementations of the same database management approach can differ substantially in performance. The major implementation methods are described in this chapter. In addition to physical considerations, this chapter examines the related topic of performance control facilities.

The MDBS performance control facilities enable a skilled application developer to govern the physical structure of the contents of the database for purposes of improving both storage and processing efficiencies. This control is exercised in the DDL specification for the database. It is not a concern of the application

programmers. Based on the data dictionary contents, the MDBS software automatically performs the desired physical structuring during creation, modification, and deletion of data and data relationships. As each performance control
facility is described, its corresponding DDL syntax is presented.

11.1 DATABASE PAGES

A database resides in auxiliary memory. Before an application program (or
QRS) can utilize a data value from the database, that value must be brought into
main memory. Similarly, when the data of an application program needs to be
stored into a database, those data must be transferred from main memory to
auxiliary memory. The database control system (DBCS), handles the data transfer between auxiliary and main memory. However, this transfer does not take
place one data value at a time.

The smallest unit of a database that can be transferred between auxiliary and
central memory by a DBCS is called a *page.* A page is a contiguous group of
bytes that exists in auxiliary memory, that can contain many record occurrences,
and that the DBCS can transfer as a whole between auxiliary and main memory.
A portion of main memory, called the *page buffer region,* is reserved to hold
pages as they are transferred into main memory.

Each page in a database has a unique identifier that allows it to be randomly
(i.e., quickly) accessed by the DBCS. When a DML command is invoked, the
DBCS checks to determine whether the page(s) needed to carry out the task of
that command is in the page buffer region. With a **getm** command, for instance,
the DBCS determines whether the page containing the needed record occurrence
(i.e., the current member of the indicated set) is in the page buffer region. If it is,
then the task proceeds. If it is not, then the DBCS must bring the needed page
into the page buffer region. This page replaces one of the pages that was already
in the page buffer region. The replaced page is transferred back to auxiliary
memory, if its contents have changed since it entered main memory.

Figure 11.1 illustrates a paging example. This database has fifty pages (in
auxiliary memory). The page buffer region (in main memory) is large enough to
hold six pages at a time. The asterisk on pages 3 and 44 indicate that their
contents have changed since they were transferred to main memory. Now suppose that page 50 is needed to carry out some DML task. Because it is not in
main memory, the DBCS randomly accesses page 50 and deposits it in the page
buffer region. In this example it replaces page 3 in main memory. Because page
3 has changed since entering the page buffer region, its contents are not the same
as the contents of page 3 in auxiliary memory. Thus before page 50 is actually
transferred into the page buffer region, the new page 3 is transferred to auxiliary

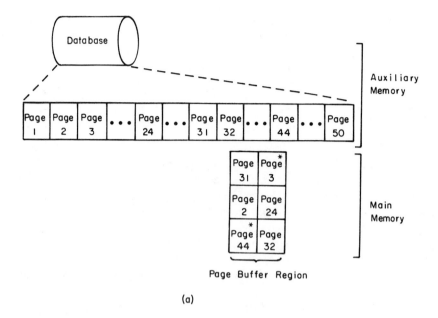

(a)

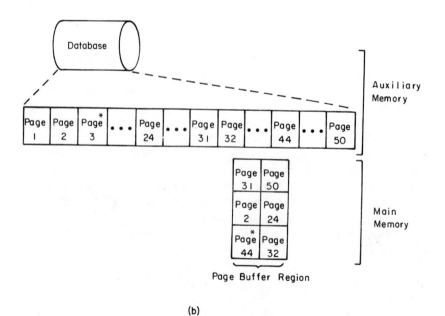

(b)

Fig. 11.1   The paging process. (a) Before page 50 is needed, (b) after replacing page 3 by 50.

memory (overwriting the old page 3). If page 3 had not changed since entering main memory, there would have been no need to transfer it back to auxiliary memory; both images of page 3 would have been identical.

When the DBCS needs a page that is not resident in main memory, a *page fault* is said to have occurred. In the previous example, when page 50 was needed but was not in the page buffer region, a page fault occurred. Whenever there is a page fault the DBCS must determine which page in main memory should be replaced. A commonly used rule for making this choice is to replace the least recently used (LRU) page. The rationale for this is that the least recently used page is usually least likely (among the pages in main memory) to be needed by future DML commands. An LRU approach is used by MDBS.

11.2   RECORD OCCURRENCE IMPLEMENTATION

Each record occurrence is typically stored as a contiguous group of bytes on a database page. The DBCS assigns a unique identifier, called a *database key* (dbk), to each record occurrence. The dbk for a given record occurrence indicates the location of that record in the database. This location can be indicated directly or indirectly. In the direct case, a dbk involves a page identifier (for the page on which the record is stored) and an offset on the page. The offset is a number showing how many bytes the start of a record is away from the start of the page. For instance, 0791023 is the dbk for a record that begins with byte 1023 on page 79. An indirect dbk does not directly show the location of a record; it does show where in a table the DBCS can look in order to find the location of the record.

The direct technique offers both faster access and lower storage overhead than the indirect technique. The indirect technique makes it easier for the DBCS to change the location of an individual record; the only change needed, aside from moving the record, is to revise the location that was formerly assigned to the indirect key of the record in the table that associates dbk's with locations. Most DBMS, including MDBS, use the direct technique.

A dbk is not the value of a data item. It is the DBCS, not an application developer, that is concerned with the dbk of a record occurrence. The DBCS uses dbk's not only to determine where a needed record is, but also to keep track of which records are current. Physically speaking, the current of run-unit is a cell in main memory whose value is always the dbk of the record that is the current of run-unit. Other currency indicators also take on dbk's as their values.

In an MDBS database, record occurrences of the same type can vary in length. This is due to the automatic data compression that is performed for certain types of data items. Many DBMSs do not support variable length records. It is much easier to implement a DBMS that uses only fixed length records. In such systems, every occurrence of a given record type has the same length and the length of a record occurrence does not change as long as it remains in the database. This, of course, can be quite inefficient storage-wise when compared against systems that allow variable length records.

Aside from efficiency, variable length records have another advantage. They provide an inexpensive flexibility that allows the definition of *phantom* data items. These are string and binary data items whose usage is unknown at the time that the schema is designed. Although these data items appear in a DDL specification, no (nonblank) values for them appear in the database itself. The advantage is that they incur very little storage cost, but can later be used to store nonblank data values. In other words, defining an extra data item(s) for a record type conveniently provides for a subsequent need to include unanticipated data in the occurrences of that record type.

A final point about physical aspects of a record occurrence concerns its creation and deletion. When a record occurrence is created, the DBCS must find a page with sufficient free (i.e., unused contiguous bytes) space to accommodate that record occurrence. Each group of contiguous unused bytes on a page is called a *hole*. A page can have zero, one, or more holes of varying sizes. Two holes are never adjacent to each other. As part of free space management, the DBCS keeps track of the holes (and their sizes, in bytes) that exist on each database page. When a record is created, the hole information is updated by the DBCS to reflect the fact that one of the holes is either smaller or has disappeared. Conversely, when a record is deleted, the DBCS revises the hole information to reflect the fact that either an existing hole is now larger or a new hole has appeared. The space previously occupied by a deleted record is thus available for reuse as more new records are created.

When a DML command is issued to create a record, the DBCS must choose from among the many available holes that are sufficiently large to hold the record. In some DBMSs the application developer has no control over the choice that is made. As explained in subsequent sections of this chapter, the application developer using DBMS has a considerable degree of control over record placement. This control is accomplished with simple clauses in the DDL specification and can have a highly significant positive impact on processing efficiency of the resultant application system. The control over record placement as specified with the DDL occurs automatically when records are created; it is not a concern of application programmers using DML commands.

11.3   NAMED RELATIONSHIP
IMPLEMENTATION

We begin by examining traditional methods for implementing 1:N sets, proposed in the CODASYL DBTG Report of 1971: chaining and pointer arrays. The

MDBS implementation method is then described for 1:N, M:N and 1:1 sets. The set implementation method employed by a DBMS has very strong impacts on both the storage and processing efficiencies of the system. Furthermore, some implementations prohibit certain kinds of DML processing.

Chaining

The most common method for implementing 1:N sets is *chaining*. With this method, pointers are embedded within record occurrences. A *pointer* is simply a dbk; a pointer therefore *points to* a record occurrence by giving the DBCS all the information that it needs to access that record.

With chaining, each owner occurrence of a set contains a pointer to (i.e., the dbk of) its first member record occurrence. Determining which member is first depends upon the set ordering convention specified in the DDL. Embedded within the first member occurrence for a particular owner occurrence is a pointer to the next member of that owner occurrence. In fact, each member record owned by a particular owner record contains a pointer to the next member record owned by that owner. This chain of pointers is depicted in Fig. 11.2, which shows two set occurrences. In each case the owner record has a first pointer (F) and each member record has a next pointer (N). Notice that the next pointer of the last member record in each set occurrence is null, though in some implementations it points back to its owner record.

The forward chaining shown in Fig. 11.2 means that once a DBCS has accessed an owner occurrence of a set, it has found out how to access that owner's first member record. Of course, the first member may reside on a physically separate page. Once a DBCS has accessed a member record of a set, the next pointer in that record indicates how the next member record (if any) can be accessed.

Backward chaining can also be used. As depicted in Fig. 11.3, it is the reverse of forward chaining. Each owner record occurrence for a set has a pointer (L) to

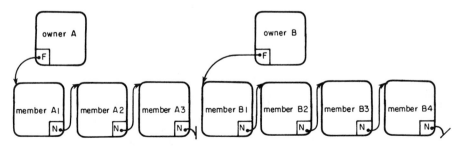

Fig. 11.2 Chaining with first–next pointers.

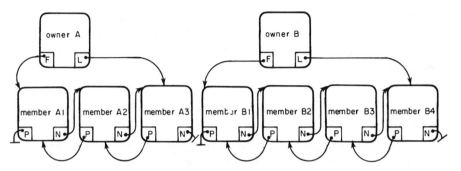

Fig. 11.3 Chaining with last–prior pointers.

its last member record and each member record contains a pointer (P) to its prior
record within a set occurrence. The meaning of *last* and *prior* depends solely
upon the member order of the set as specified with the DDL. Without backward
chaining, certain kinds of DML processing are prohibited. The DBCS would be
unable to rapidly find which member record precedes another member record in a
set occurrence (**fpm**) or which member record is last in a set occurrence (**flm**).

A third aspect of chaining embeds in every member record a pointer to its
owner record. This is shown with the O pointers in Fig. 11.4. When a member
record is accessed, the owner pointer indicates to the DBCS how the owner
record of that member can be accessed. Without owner chaining, the DBCS
would be unable to rapidly find the owner record for a given member record.

Many CODASYL implementations require the application developer to
choose (at DDL specification time) some combination of the three chaining
mechanisms for each set. For reasons of processing flexibility, all three mechanisms are typically selected for each set. Such a selection also allows application

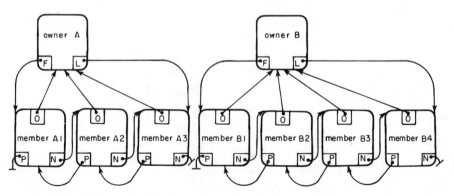

Fig.11.4 Chaining with owner pointers.

programmers to be unconcerned with set implementation, since all set-oriented DML commands would be usable for all sets. If backward chaining were not used for a particular set, then the DML command to find the prior member in a set occurrence could not be used with that set. Some CODASYL implementations give no choice, but automatically use all three chaining mechanisms for all sets.

The preceding examples have described chaining with respect to one set. Since a record type can be involved in many sets, its record occurrences will contain pointers for each set in which it participates. As an example, suppose that a given record type is the member of three sets and the owner of two sets. Each occurrence of this record type will contain space for thirteen pointers:

> two first pointers (one for each set the record type owns),
> two last pointers (one for each set the record type owns),
> three next pointers (one for each set of which the record type is a member),
> three prior pointers (one for each set of which the record type is a member),
> three owner pointers (one for each set of which the record type is a member).

Of course, an application programmer is not directly concerned with all of these pointers. They are used internally by the DBCS for accessing records.

When a record occurrence is created, the DBCS allocates sufficient space to hold all of its data and all of its embedded pointers. The relative positions of data values and pointers is governed and managed by the DBCS. It is possible for an owner record occurrence to be without member records for some set. Nevertheless, it still contains space for a first and last pointer; but these two pointers are null. Similarly, a set may have member records that are not associated with any owner occurrence. Such a member record contains space for next, prior, and owner pointers. However, these are null until the member record is connected to an owner (e.g., with the **ims** command).

When a new member record is connected to its owner, the DBCS handles all details of placing that new record at the appropriate place in the chain. These details involve finding where to break the existing chain, revising the next pointer of the record before the break so that it points to the new record, revising the prior pointer of the record after the break so that it points to the new record, setting the prior pointer of the new record to be the dbk of the record before the break, setting the next pointer of the new record to be the dbk of the record after the break, and setting the owner pointer of the new record to be the dbk of its owner.

For LIFO and FIFO orderings, the breaking point is easy to find since the new record is added to front or end, respectively, of the member chain. The break occurs between the owner and first member or between the owner and last member, respectively. For NEXT and PRIOR ordering, the programmer finds the breaking point by properly setting the current member indicator of the set. For SORTED ordering, the DBCS must extract the sort key data value from each record occurrence in the member chain until it finds the first member record whose sort key value exceeds the sort key value of the new record. The break occurs prior to this point, as the DBCS welds the new record into the chain.

Pointer Arrays

The second method proposed by the CODASYL DBTG for implementing 1:N sets utilizes *pointer arrays*. However, there are few CODASYL implementations that give an application developer the opportunity to use pointer arrays. This may be because pointer arrays are more difficult to implement than chaining mechanisms. Unlike chaining, owner records do not contain first and last member pointers. Also, the member records do not contain next and prior pointers.

A pointer array is simply an array of pointers. For a given set there is one pointer array for each owner record occurrence. A pointer array need not be physically within an owner record. Instead, an owner record may contain a pointer (PA) to its pointer array as illustrated in Fig. 11.5. The pointer array itself contains a pointer to each of the member records owned by the owner record.

The ordering of pointers within a pointer array is consistent with the member order of the set as declared in the DDL specification. If the member order is FIFO, then the first pointer in a pointer array is the dbk of the first member record that was connected to the owner record. As new members are inserted into the set occurrence, their dbk's are appended to the end of the pointer array. LIFO member ordering is handled similarly. In the cases of NEXT, PRIOR, and SORTED orderings, the DBCS must be able to insert a new dbk into the interior of a pointer array.

Notice that the pointer array implementation (Fig. 11.5) supports all of the same kinds of processing that are supported by the chaining implementation (Fig. 11.4). For any member record, the DBCS finds its owner with the owner (O) pointer. To perform **ffm–fnm** processing, the DBCS scans a pointer array from beginning to end. To perform **flm–fpm** processing, the array is scanned from end to beginning.

For **fmsk** processing, the DBCS can perform a binary search on the pointer array. At each chop in the binary search, the DBCS accesses the sort key value of the record occurrence whose dbk is at the midpoint of the remaining portion of the pointer array. On average, this is more efficient than **fmsk** processing where chaining is used. With chaining, a DBCS must access every record occurrence until the one with the desired sort key value is found. This superiority of the pointer array method over chaining becomes very pronounced as the number of member records per owner record increases.

Record insertion into a sorted set implemented with pointer arrays can also take advantage of binary searching. The DBCS performs a binary search on the

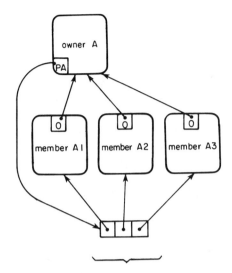

pointer array for owner A

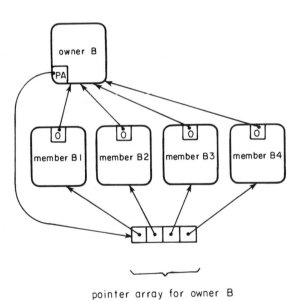

pointer array for owner B

Fig. 11.5 Set implementation using pointer arrays.

pointer array of the owner of the new record until it determines where in the array the dbk of the new record is to be inserted. Member records are accessed only for each chop in the binary search. On average, chaining requires many more record accesses to determine where to insert the new record (particularly for large set occurrences).

As Fig. 11.5 illustrates, the pointer arrays for a given set can vary in length. If an owner occurrence has no members, its PA pointer is null and its pointer array has a length of zero (i.e., it does not have a pointer array). Another owner occurrence in the same set may have a hundred members. The pointer array for this owner record contains a hundred database keys. The first of these points to the first member record, the second points to the next member record, and so forth.

Even though the pointer array method supports all of the same processing as the chaining method (and does so more efficiently), the pointer array method is less expensive from a storage standpoint. Fewer pointers are required when representing a relationship with pointer arrays. This is easily seen by contrasting Fig. 11.5 with Fig. 11.4. The former uses space for only 16 pointers, while the latter has space allocated for 25 pointers. Furthermore, if a member record is not connected to an owner record, only the storage cost of an owner pointer is incurred with the pointer array mechanism. With chaining, space is allocated for three times as many pointers (owner, next, and prior).

The preceding examples have described pointer arrays with respect to one set. Because a record type can participate in many sets, its record occurrences will contain pointers for each set in which its record type is involved. Suppose that a given record type is the owner of two sets and the member of three sets. Then with the pointer array implementation, each occurrence of this record type will contain space for five pointers:

> three owner pointers (one for each set of which the record type is a member),
> two pointer array pointers (one for each set the record type owns).

In addition to pointers in the record occurrence, there may be as many as two pointer arrays, one for each set the record type owns. If the record occurrence has no members for either set, then it has no pointer arrays. If it is connected to member records for one set only, then the record occurrence has only one pointer array. Two pointer arrays exist only if the record has member records with respect to each set.

Multi-level Balanced Indices

MDBS departs from the traditional methods of implementing 1:N sets, by utilizing *multi-level balanced indices* for sorted sets. In this implementation, each owner occurrence for a set contains a pointer to an index. There is one entry in the index for each member occurrence associated with the owner occurrence. Each entry consists of the sort key value of a member record, together with the dbk of that record. The DBCS maintains the index in sorted order on the basis of its sort key values. As with pointer arrays and chaining, each member record contains a pointer to its owner record (if any).

The indexing approach is illustrated by the example shown in Fig. 11.6. From an application programmer's vantage point, indexing supports all of the same DML commands as pointer arrays or chaining. Internally, however, the DBCS processes indices differently from chains or pointer arrays. For instance, **fmsk** causes the DBCS to perform a binary search of an index in order to obtain the dbk of the desired record (making it the current member and current of run-unit). Since sort key values of the current owner's members are in an index, the DBCS need not access any record occurrences in order to perform the **fmsk.**

With chaining, an **fmsk** typically requires many record accesses. Beginning with either the first or the last record, each member record is accessed until the one with the desired sort key value is found. This type of processing can cause numerous page faults. With pointer arrays, there are generally fewer page faults because (on average) fewer member records need to be accessed. In the indexing

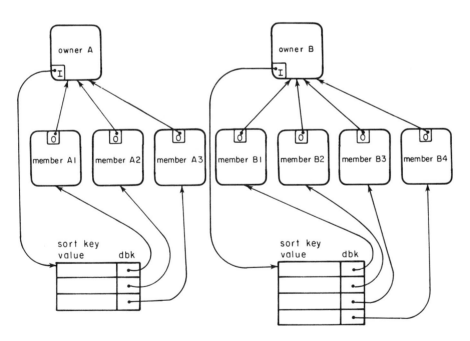

Fig. 11.6 Set implementation with indices.

implementation, there are no page faults involving member record access. If the index becomes large, causing it to be physically fragmented over more than one page, then some (but relatively few) page faults may occur due to index processing. Large fragmented pointer arrays can cause similar page faults.

The processing efficiency of indexing is also superior to the other two implementations during the insertion of member records into a set occurrence. With indexing, the DBCS does not need to access member records when performing an **ims.** There are therefore no page faults due to record access. The sort key value and its associated dbk are inserted into the index for the current owner record of the set. With chaining, the DBCS must access records in the member chain until it discovers where the break in the chain is to be made, to accommodate insertion of the new record. On average, the pointer array implementation requires fewer record accesses (and page faults) than chaining, but more than indexing.

Although it provides greater processing efficiency, the indexing implementation does have a higher storage cost than the pointer array implementation. This is because sort key values are stored along with dbk's. Using MDBS, an application developer can control how much of a sort key value is actually used in the indices of a sorted set. This is accomplished when the sort key is declared in the DDL specification. For instance, if PARTNO is a sort key, the application developer can limit index entries to, say, the first three characters of PARTNO values by specifying

sorted by ascending PARTNO index width is 3

for the sort clause of a set in a DDL specification.

If PARTNO is also the sort key for another set, the index of that set could be declared to have the same (3) or a different width. If an application developer desires to force the set to be implemented as a pointer array, then an index width of zero is declared for the sort key of the set. The ability to declare an index width is an important performance control facility. Generally, it is advisable to choose the smallest possible width which still provides a fairly high degree of differentiation (i.e., uniqueness) among the truncated sort key values that are to be associated with an owner record.

The foregoing description of the indexing approach to 1:N sorted set implementation is a simplification of the actual approach used by MDBS. Although precise details of the MDBS implementation cannot be given here, we can point out one other aspect beyond the general principles already described. Each index that exists for a set is not merely a sequential list of [sort key value, dbk] pairs. As the number of members associated with an owner record increases, the index of the owner record becomes an n-ary multi-level balanced tree of indices. This technique allows much faster index searching than the utilization of a binary search on an index that is physically held as a simple list of [sort key value, dbk] pairs.

The indexing approach to 1:N set implementation is pertinent only for 1:N sets whose member order has been declared to be SORTED. Other member orders (e.g., LIFO, FIFO, etc.) cannot use this method, because they have no sort key as a basis for index formation. In MDBS, 1:N sets with these other member orders are implemented as *n*-ary multilevel balanced pointer arrays. Physically, this is like the indices of a sorted set whose index width has been declared to be zero.

For an M:N set, the relationship between an owner record and its members is implemented identically to an MDBS 1:N set. The exception is that a member record does not contain an owner pointer, because a member record can have many owners. The relationship between a member record and its owners is implemented in an exactly analogous manner to the relationship between an owner and its members. A simple example is illustrated in Fig. 11.7, for a set having FIFO member order and SORTED owner order. Of course, application programmers are unconcerned with such physical implementation details.

A 1:1 set is implemented quite simply in MDBS. Since no owner record is associated with more than one member record (and vice versa), each owner record contains space for a pointer to its member and each member record contains space to hold a pointer to its owner. This is shown in the example of Fig. 11.8. Using these pointers, a DBCS can find any member's owner and any

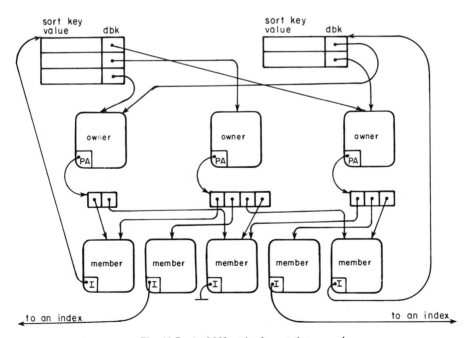

Fig. 11.7 An M:N set implementation example.

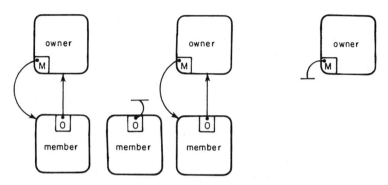

Fig. 11.8 A 1:1 set implementation example.

owner's member. If an owner record has no member record, then its member pointer (M) is null, and vice versa.

In MDBS, system-owned sets are implemented somewhat differently from other 1:N sets. A member occurrence of a system-owned set does not contain an owner pointer to the system record occurrence. This means that system-owned sets are quite inexpensive from a storage standpoint. No storage is used for a system-owned set until a member record is connected to the system record occurrence (e.g., with the **ims** command). This has several implications.

Physically, a system-owned sorted set is identical to a secondary key index, as used in inverted file systems. Of course, there may be many such sets for a given record type, just as there can be many secondary key indices for an inverted file. Thus MDBS can be used to closely emulate inverted file systems, if so desired, by ignoring its capability of supporting named relationships between record types and its capacity to handle nonsorted (e.g., FIFO) system-owned sets.

If there is uncertainty during schema design as to whether a particular system-owned set is really needed, then it is advisable to include it in the schema. This is because there is essentially no cost incurred by including it and ignoring it until needed (if ever). Such a set should not be declared to be automatic.

An extra system-owned set can be very valuable when an application demands that an application system keep track of a particular (and perhaps changing) subset of occurrences for a given record type. For example, if we need to track all customers whose accounts receivable exceed $25,000, then these customer records could be made members of a system-owned set. Customer records with receivables of $25,000 or less would never be members in the system-owned set. Of course, membership in this set would change over time. The result is that the system-owned set can be used to very rapidly access (process or monitor) the customers of greatest concern. The storage cost is only about 4 bytes/customer record included in the set. System-owned sets used for this purpose should be declared to be manual, rather than automatic.

11.4   DATABASE AREAS

A database can be partitioned into one or more named *areas,* each consisting of many pages. Each database page must exist in exactly one area. Every schema example presented so far in this book has used the default of one area per database. When a database name is specified in a DDL specification, the DDL Analyzer automatically establishes a database area having the same name. This area, called the *main area* of the database, physically resides on the disk file stated in the DDL specification. For instance,

> data base name is INVNTRY
>   file name is "INV.DB", size is 2000 pages,
>   page size is 1024 bytes

defines a main database area named INVNTRY which is assigned to a disk file named INV.DB. This area consists of 2000 pages, each with a size of 1024 bytes.

Beyond the main area, up to 15 additional areas can be defined for an MDBS database. These area definitions appear in the DDL specification immediately after the user declarations and immediately before the record type declarations. Each extra area is declared with the following kind of statement:

> area name is INVA
>   file name is "AR1.DB", size is 725 pages,
>   page size is 1024 bytes

In this example, the name of the extra area is INVA. It consists of 725 pages, of 1024 bytes each, and is assigned to a disk file named AR1.DB.

The name of the file to which an area is assigned must be a fully-qualified file name for the host operating system. This means that the file name can be qualified by the number (or letter) of the drive on which the area will reside while on-line. If a drive is not specified, the default drive is assumed. Thus the application developer can assign some areas to fast devices (e.g., hard disk drives) and other areas to relatively slow devices (e.g., floppy disk drives). Two or more areas can be assigned to the same medium and/or device.

Within each area a few pages, called system pages, are reserved for use by the DBCS. System pages within the main area contain the data dictionary. No record occurrences are stored on system pages. Nonsystem pages within an area can hold record occurrences and/or indices (and pointer arrays). The application developer has extensive control over what is held in the nonsystem pages of an area.

When declaring an extra area in a DDL specification, the developer can optionally specify that the DBCS will not be allowed to put any indices or pointer arrays in the pages of that area. This is accomplished by appending the optional clause pointers are not allowed

to the definition of the area. This clause cannot be used for the main area.

The developer can also control which record occurrences are stored in an area. As each record type is defined it can be assigned to one or more areas. All occurrences of the record type will be placed *only* in the area(s) to which it is assigned. The record type PART is assigned to the area INVA by stating

                              record name is PART in INVA

or it could be assigned to the areas INVA and INVB by stating

                          record name is PART in (INVA, INVB)

A record type can be assigned to many areas and many record types can be assigned to any given area. If no area assignment is made when a record type is defined, the DBCS is free to place its occurrences in any area.

This control over record placement allows an application developer to force frequently accessed records to be in areas on relatively fast access devices. Seldom-accessed records can be forced to areas on relatively slow devices. This control over record placement also allows certain portions of a database to be off-line while an application program is operating on the database. If the application program does not utilize occurrences of the record types assigned to a particular area, then that area need not be on-line, provided it does not contain any indices or pointer arrays.

It should also be noted that the record occurrences of a database can be entirely segregated from its indices and pointer arrays if desired. For instance, the developer might prohibit indices and pointer arrays from all extra areas, while assigning all record types to extra areas only.

11.5 RECORD CLUSTERING

Another important performance control feature permits the application developer to force logically related occurrences of different record types to be physically clustered. In situations where the processing of an owner record occurrence often necessitates processing its members, it would be highly advantageous if the member occurrences of an owner record were physically clustered. Clustering of this kind results in fewer page faults (i.e., faster processing), than if an owner's member occurrences were scattered over many pages. As an example of MDBS clustering, the DDL specification

                             record name is STUDENT
                           in area of owner of ADVISE

causes all students advised by a teacher to be clustered together. Here, STU-DENT is the member record type of a set (ADVISE) owned by a TEACHER record type. The clustering takes place in the area(s) to which the TEACHER record type has been assigned. When clustering is declared, the area(s) in which STUDENT record occurrences can be stored is not explicitly stated.

If records to be clustered are large relative to the size of a page, then it is more difficult for the DBCS to cluster records as effectively. In such a situation the designer should consider forming smaller records, by breaking the record type into two record types that are related by a 1:1 set.

When clustering is declared for a particular record type with respect to a set, it is generally advisable to exclude uninvolved record types, indices, and pointer arrays from the area(s) where clustering will occur.

11.6   RECORD CALCULATION

When clustering is the location mode for a record type, the DBCS determines the location of where a record is stored based on physical proximity to logically related records. An alternative location mode is one in which the DBCS calculates the location where a record is to be stored. This is called the *calc* location mode. If a record type is declared to have a calc location mode, a calc key must be specified for the record type.

A calc key consists of one or more of the data items of the record types. As an occurrence of a calced record type is stored, the calc key value of the occurrence is input to an algorithm that calculates the page on which that record occurrence will be stored. Of course, the calculated page is one that exists in an area to which the record type has been assigned.

In the MDBS DDL a record type is declared to have a calc location mode, as follows:

> record name is CUST
> in CUSTAREA calc key is (CUSTNUM) nodup

In this example, occurrences of CUST are stored in pages of CUSTAREA. CUSTNUM is a data item in CUST and serves as the calc key. Because a calc key is specified, the location of a CUST record is calculated, based on the customer number of that record. If the optional word *nodup* is used in the calc key clause, the DBCS disallows any attempt to create a CUST record having the same calc key value (i.e., customer number) as an already existing CUST record. When the nodup integrity condition has not been specified, the DBCS permits records with the same calc key values.

The DBCSs calc algorithm can be used not only during the creation of a record, but during subsequent accesses to that record. DML commands to accomplish this kind of access are fully described in Chapter 12. Declaring a record type to be calced allows very rapid access to any of its occurrences without using a set, provided the calc key value of the occurrence is known. The DBCS does not need to perform a binary search on an index or pointer array.

An application developer is justified in declaring a record type to be calced if very rapid access to any of its occurrences is desired. The same record type can also participate in (and be accessed through) numerous sets, including system-owned sets.

Calcing is the database management counterpart of hashing in file management. Database pages are comparable to buckets in a hashed file. If two records of a given type are calced to the same page, they are referred to as synonyms. The treatment of synonyms is important for calcing, just as it is important for hashing. It is desirable to avoid overflow situations, in which so many synonyms exist for a page that the page does not have sufficient room to hold them. Large numbers of overflows can slow down the calced access speed.

Although the calc algorithm of MDBS is robust in terms of spreading calced records evenly throughout available pages, the application developer can take several steps to further minimize the incidence of overflow. First, indices and pointers should not be permitted in areas containing calced records. If they are allowed, then fewer synonyms can be held on a page. Second, the page size for the area(s) containing occurrences of a calced record type should be large enough to hold several occurrences. Otherwise, frequent overflow is nearly inescapable. If records containing calc keys are relatively large, consider breaking the record type into two record types related by a 1:1 set. Third, the developer should, if at all possible, avoid assigning other record types to an area that already has a calced record type assigned to it.

Both the clustering and calcing location modes are performance control mechanisms which an application can optionally use. Each provides relatively fast record access for a particular kind of processing. If neither clustering nor calcing is specified as the location mode for a record type, the DBCS determines where its occurrences are physically placed within the area(s) to which the record type is assigned. CODASYL-network systems also support clustering and calcing.

11.7 PAGE SIZE

Some versions of MDBS allow pages in one area to have size different from pages in another area. In any event, the page size declared for an extra area cannot exceed the page size declared for the main area. An application developer using MDBS can allow page size to default (e.g., 512 bytes under many operating systems). Alternatively, the developer can, with the DDL, exercise explicit control over the page size within each area.

A large page size allows relatively few pages to simultaneously reside in central memory. A small page size allows more pages to simultaneously reside in central memory. In either case, essentially the same percentage of the database is resident in central memory. This percentage is a function of the page buffer region, rather than the page size. Nevertheless, in choosing a page size it is important to realize that both very small pages and very large pages have significant disadvantages. As page size becomes larger, page faults become much more expensive; that is, the disk input–output needed to write a page to auxiliary memory and read a page into central memory increases as larger page sizes are used. On the other hand, a page size that is very small defeats the clustering and calcing performance control features.

It is therefore advisable to select the page size of an area in the range of 256 to 1024 bytes. Another valuable rule-of-thumb is to select a page size that allows at least eight nondictionary (i.e., nonsystem) pages to simultaneously reside in central memory. When an MDBS database is initialized, the DDL Analyzer reports how many bytes of the page buffer region will be needed by the DBCS for holding system pages (i.e., pages with data dictionary information). It should be obvious that, regardless of page size, a larger page buffer region will yield faster processing than a small page buffer region. However, once a page buffer region goes beyond a 15–20 page capacity, the marginal value of each added page of capacity diminishes (though the marginal value is still positive).

An aid in assessing the effect of a given page size (for a given page buffer region) on processing, the **dbstat** DML command can be used. This command returns five values into host language variables:

(a)   the number of pages that can be held in the currently allocated buffer region;

(b)   the number of times, since opening the database, that the most recent page access was made to a page different from the preceding page access;

(c)   the number of page transfers that have occurred from auxiliary memory into main memory since opening the database;

(d)   the number of page transfers, not caused by page faults, that have occurred from main memory into auxiliary memory since opening the database;

(e)   the total number of page transfers that have occurred from main memory into auxiliary memory since opening the database.

Nonfault page transfers mentioned in (d) can be caused by the **dbsave** DML command (see Sect. 14.8). Using the **dbstat** command is a convenient way to compare the effects of different page size alternatives. It is also useful in seeing the effects of other performance control options (e.g., record clustering) previously discussed in this chapter.

The foregoing issues of page size selection are concerned with processing speed. A final consideration involves effective utilization of storage space on a page. If one record type (or a few record types having occurrences of roughly the same size) is assigned to an area for which indices and pointer arrays are disallowed, the page size of the area should be selected so that it avoids large amounts of unusable space. Suppose the occurrences of the record types are 200 bytes apiece and the page size is 256 bytes. The result is about fifty unused bytes per page (20% unused space). Such a situation is avoided by declaring a larger page size (e.g., 1024 bytes), by splitting the record type into two (say, 80 and 120 bytes) related by a 1:1 set, by assigning a record type with small occurrences (e.g., 40 bytes) to the same area, or by allowing indices and pointer arrays in the area.

11.8   AREA ACCESS CODES

Each extra area declared in a DDL specification can be given read and write access code combinations. A user has read access to the contents of an extra area only if the user has a read access code in common with the read access code combination of the area. A user's read access to the contents of an area is further constrained by read access restrictions on data items, record types, and sets (as described in Chapter 10). For instance, a user may have read access to an area but might not have read access to the occurrences of a record type that is in the area. Write access for an area is treated in the same way. Access code combinations are not specified for the main area of a database.

The choice of access codes for an area must be consistent with the access code combinations for record types assigned to that area. The read (write) access combination of a record type must have at least one access code in common with the read (write) access combination of each area to which that record type has been assigned. If a record type has a calc key, then all areas to which it is assigned must have one or more read (write) access codes in common and the read (write) access combination of the record type must be a subset of those common read (write) access codes.

11.9   SUMMARY

The implementation and performance control issues examined in this chapter are of vital importance to serious application developers. In selecting a DBMS, its method for implementing relationships should be closely considered. The implementation method has a very significant impact on the storage and processing efficiencies of application software built with the DBMS. The three major implementation approaches were presented: chaining, pointer arrays, multi-level balanced indices. In general, chaining is the least efficient of the three. For the most part, application programmers are unconcerned with the underlying implementation of relationships. Conceivably any of the three approaches could be used in implementations of data models (e.g., the relational) that rely on field redundancy for representing relationships. However, this is rare among micro DBMSs; their implementations tend to be based on data value redundancy.

Aside from underlying implementation, the extent of performance control features offered by a DBMS is also important to an application developer. A variety of performance control facilities were described in this chapter, including extensive controls over record placement, record access speed, index–pointer array placement, index width, and page sizing. The performance control capabilities are exercised (if so desired) by an application developer at design time. With the exception of calcing, these features are of little concern to an application programmer, because they are carried out by the DBCS according to the developer's design specifications.

RELATED READINGS

J. Bradley, "File and Data Base Techniques," Holt, Rinehart, and Winston, New York, 1982.

CODASYL, "Data Base Task Group Report," Assoc. Comput. Mach., New York, 1971.

J. Martin, "Computer Data-Base Organization," Prentice-Hall, Englewood Cliffs, New Jersey, 1975.

Micro Data Base Systems Inc., "MDBS Application Programming Reference Manual," Lafayette, Indiana, 1981.

Micro Data Base Systems Inc., "MDBS Data Base Design Reference Manual," Lafayette, Indiana, 1981.

T. W. Olle, "The CODASYL Approach to Data Base Management," Wiley, New York, 1978.

EXERCISES

1. As they relate to a microcomputer, what are auxiliary and main memories?
2. What is a memory page and what limits are placed on its size? How is page size specified?

3. Discuss the advantages and disadvantages of a large page size.
4. Describe two methods of implementing named relationships.
5. What is meant by forward and backward chaining? Illustrate each with an example.
6. What is the price paid for using forward and backward chaining instead of just forward chaining? What is the price paid for using only forward chaining?
7. For forward and backward chainings, devise algorithms to handle the updates (record insertions and deletions) for FIFO, LIFO, NEXT, PRIOR, and SORTED orderings.
8. What are pointer arrays and in what ways are they more efficient than chaining mechanisms?
9. How do system owned sets differ in their implementation from other named sets? What is the reason(s) for the difference?
10. A difficulty in implementing a pointer array is that if the maximum number of member record occurrences for an owner record occurrence cannot be predetermined, then space for the pointer array cannot be properly preallocated. Suggest a solution to this problem.
11. A truncated sort key in an indexing implementation has a problem of not being able to differentiate a record occurrence from others with the same key value. Devise a method to solve this problem.
12. In an *n*-ary multi-level balanced tree of indexing, how is balance maintained when inserting or deleting a member record occurrence?
13. How is a record occurrence physically implemented? Briefly describe this, making sure that the concepts of dbk's and variable length records are discussed.
14. In a page fault condition, the DBCS must decide which page in main memory to replace. On what basis does it make this decision and do you agree with the rationale?
15. Describe the physical ramifications of the **getm** DML command.
16. A FIFO page replacement policy has been proposed. Compare the relative merits of this policy to the LRU page replacement policy.
17. Partitioning a database into areas can be most helpful in implementing large databases. What specifications are needed in the DDL and how are the areas physically implemented on a microcomputer?
18. Define a calc key and give an original example of its use. When is a calc key needed?
19. Discuss security considerations in the context of areas.
20. What is a *phantom* data item and why is it valuable?
21. Describe a situation where it would be desirable to have part of a database off-line while another part of it is being processed.

22. Explain the problems created for an application developer when data value redundancy is the method used to implement relationships between record types.

PROJECT

Incorporate peformance control aspects into the DDL specification of the application as appropriate. Also include the schema changes made in the preceding stage of the project. Use the DDL Analyzer to initialize a new database.

Chapter 12

ADVANCED PROCESSING COMMANDS

Chapters 10 and 11 have presented extensions to the data structuring capabilities of the DBMS. In the present chapter we will see the corresponding processing commands for these structures. Examples of the use of these commands will also be presented.

It is almost inconceivable for any single application system to use all of this added flexibility. However, across the universe of applications the value of such flexibility is undeniable. Experience shows that an application system can usually be partitioned into several independent modules, each involving only a subset of the full arsenal of data structuring facilities and corresponding commands. The fact that a rich assortment of features are available should not distress, but rather comfort the application developer. Selecting the appropriate subset of features necessary for solving a specific application problem is usually not a difficult task. It is certainly simpler than trying to overcome limitations inherent in relatively impoverished development tools.

Once the appropriate features have been selected, use of the processing commands is straightforward. Some of the basic DML command structures for performing this processing are presented in this chapter.

12.1   PROCESSING 1:1, N:1, and M:N SETS

The 1:1 set is quite simple to process. None of the loops described in Chapters 6 and 7 need be used, there will be at most one occurrence at the other end of the set. The assignment commands are all that are needed to find a record through a 1:1 set; of course, if there is no occurrence, an end-of-set indication will result.

To summarize, the 1:1 set behaves in almost an identical manner to the 1:N set, except that no processing loops are required.

The N:1 set is in many ways the converse of the 1:N set. Here the processing loops are required for the owner occurrences, rather than the member occurrences. We can easily adapt the programs of Chapters 6 and 7 to process owners instead of members, but we need some commands that operate on owners instead of members. For the gets and puts, we have already discussed the necessary owner commands. The assignment commands also allow us to process from owner to owner, by using **smo** instead of **som,** and **soo** instead of **smm.** The create command **crs** only creates an occurrence, so that will function as before too. The deletes include **dro.**

The other DML command groups are the finds, inserts, and removes. For each member-oriented command in these groups, we will now define a corresponding owner-oriented command. The processing is strictly symmetrical: the owner command performs the same series of operations as the respective member command, except at the other end of the set. The new owner-oriented commands are:

Member command	Owner command	Function
ffm	**ffo**(set-name)	Find first owner
fnm	**fno**(set-name)	Find next owner
flm	**flo**(set-name)	Find last owner
fpm	**fpo**(set-name)	Find previous owner
fmi	**foi**(item, set, variable)	Find owner based on item
fnmi	**fnoi**(item, set, variable)	Find next owner based on item
fmsk	**fosk**(set, variable)	Find owner based on sort key
fnmsk	**fnosk**(set, variable)	Find next owner based on sort key
ims	**ios**(set)	Insert owner into set
rms	**ros**(set)	Remove owner from set

These new commands are exact counterparts of the corresponding member commands. The discussions of Chapter 6 and 7 apply for all aspects, including the effects on currency indicators. Figure 12.1 illustrates how the find first–find next loop of Fig. 6.4 would be converted to handle the N:1 case. All of the other programs would translate in a similar mechanical manner.

Three commands have an additional side effect on N:1 sets, that make them consistent with the corresponding member-oriented processing. The **smm** and **smo** commands perform an automatic **ffo** (recall that **soo** and **som** perform an automatic **ffm**). And the command **dro** makes the next owner in the specified set the current owner. In other words, these three owner-oriented commands behave exactly as their member-oriented counterparts.

```
ffo(set-name);
do while (found
        {perform process-individual-occurrences;
        fno(set-name);
        }
```

Fig. 12.1   The **ffo/fno** iteration loop.

Sets that are defined to be N:1 are not often used in data structures. The evolution of data management favored the use of 1:N sets. However, the distinction is completely arbitrary; either may be used to achieve the effect of a one-to-many relationship.

The M:N set relation is more than a combination of a 1:N and an N:1 set. Each owner record occurrence can have many member occurrences associated with it, while at the same time each member record occurrence may have many owner occurrences associated with it. The M:N relationship is the most general kind of relationship that can be defined in database management.

All of the commands discussed to this point work equally well with M:N sets. The basic concepts do not change for M:N sets. When processing from owner occurrences to member occurrences, we use the member-oriented commands (e.g., **fnm, ims, getm, drm**). When processing in the other direction, that is, from members to owners, then the owner-oriented commands should be employed (e.g., **fno, ios, geto, dro**).

The M:N set processing is just as easy as 1:N set processing, but more options must be considered. For instance, as a general rule M:N sets are defined in a DDL specification to have a MANUAL insertion mode for both owners and members. This is because a record occurrence being inserted for an M:N set will most likely to connected to several other records. Thus a single insert procedure can be utilized, rather than first determining an occurrence for the automatic insertion and then entering a loop for the other insertions. In other words, the application program is generally shorter and simpler if the M:N set is declared to be MANUAL for both owners and members.

Figure 12.2 depicts a fairly simple logical data structure for keeping track of products and the parts used in the manufacture of the products. The set USES is

Fig. 12.2   Product/part schema.

```
do while ({display "Enter product number (or *):";
             input product.number;
             product.number ≠ "*"})
  {fmsk(SPR, product.number);
   perform load-and-update-product-as-usual;
   som(USES, SPR);
   do while ({display "Enter part number (or *):";
                input part.number;
                part.number ≠ "*"})
     {fmsk(SPA, part.number);
      perform load-and-update-part-as-usual;
      /* The desired part should be the cru at this point */
      ims(USES);
      }
```

Fig. 12.3   Loading products, then parts.

an M:N set, since each product can use many parts and each part can be used in many products. The indicated data items are obvious.

How would data be loaded for this schema? There are (at least) two ways. One method would be to load information about products, and then the parts they use; the outline of this procedure is given in Fig. 12.3. The two system-owned sets have automatic insertion for members; the M:N set is manual for both owners and members. The second method loads part information first and then associated products; this is outlined in Fig. 12.4. The two load and update procedures involve only their respective system-owned sets.

Comparing these two program structures, it is easy to see how symmetrical they are to one another. Which one is correct? They both are correct, since they both perform the desired function, namely entering the product–part information

```
do while ({display "Enter part number (or *):";
             input part.number;
             part number ≠ "*"})
  {fmsk(SPA, part.number);
   perform load-and-update-part-as-usual;
   smm(USES, SPA);
   do while ({display "Enter product number (or *):";
                input product number;
                product.number ≠ "*"})
     {fmsk(SPR, product.number);
      perform load-and-update-product-as-usual;
      /* The desired product should be cru at this point */
      ios(USES);
      }
```

Fig. 12.4   Loading parts, then products.

```
input product.number;
fmsk(SPR, product.number);
if (found) then
    {display "Parts for product", product.number;
    som(USES, SPR);
    do while (found)
        {getm(USES, part);
        display part.number, part.cost;
        fnm(USES);
        }
    }
```

Fig. 12.5 Listing parts for a product.

into the database. Which is better? The answer is, "it depends." Perhaps the information is presently organized by product; then the first method is the better. If on the other hand the information is derived from receiving, then it might be organized by part and the second program would best suit our needs (see also Exercise 15).

One fairly obvious report program would be to list the parts used in the manufacture of a given product. This program is shown in Fig. 12.5. Another report, depicted in Fig. 12.6, produces a list of products for which a given part is used.

If we decide to delete a particular part from the database (and presumably from our inventory of parts), then all associated products can no longer be built. Thus a domino deletion procedure is called for. This processing is outlined in Fig. 12.7 (see also Exercise 18).

Suppose we are going to discontinue a product. Should the associated parts be deleted? Not if the parts are used to manufacture other products as well. Thus in this case the semantics of our application imply somewhat different processing.

Before an associated part can be deleted, we must see if that part is used in

```
input part.number;
fmsk(SPA, part.number);
if (found) then
    {display "Products for part", part.number;
    smm(USES, SPA);
    do while (found)
        {geto(USES, product);
        display product.number, product.type, product.price;
        fno(USES);
        }
    }
```

Fig. 12.6 Listing products for a part.

```
input part.number;
fmsk(SPA, part.number);
if (found) then
   {smm(USES, SPA);
   do while (found)
           dro(USES);
   drm(SPA);
   }
```

Fig. 12.7   Deleting a part and its product.

other products. Although this can be accomplished using commands already introduced, a new command will make this task much easier:

goc(set-name, variable)   The number of owner occurrences for the current member occurrence of the given set is returned in the given integer variable.

Get owner count (**goc**) calculates how many owner occurrences there are for the current member occurrence in this set. No currency indicators are changed by this command. It may be used with any type of set (e.g., N:1). It has a corresponding member-oriented command,

gmc(set-name, variable)   The number of member occurrences for the current owner occurrence of the given set is returned in the given integer variable.

Get member count (**gmc**) may also be used with other types of sets, especially 1:N sets.

Returning to our example, we need to delete a part when it is owned by (associated with) no other products, that is, when the number of owners is only one. Figure 12.8 gives the necessary DML logic for this deletion process.

```
input product.number;
fmsk(SPR, product.number);
if (found) then
   {som(USES, SPR);
   do while (found)
       {goc(USES, x);
       if (x > 1) then
          fnm(USES);
       else
             drm(USES);
       }
   drm(SPR);
   }
```

Fig. 12.8   Deleting a product and singly used parts.

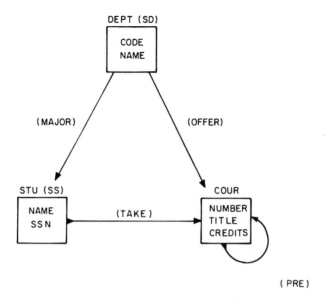

Fig. 12.9   University schema diagram.

Next consider the schema diagram given in Fig. 12.9, which stores informa-tion about university departments, the students that major in those departments, and the courses offered by the departments and taken by the students. The TAKE set is clearly M:N. In fact, students majoring in one department can take courses in any other department. The M:N recursive set PRE represents prerequisite courses, that is, courses that should be taken before another course. This set is M:N, because accounting may be a prerequisite of both finance and auditing, while auditing may require both accounting and programming as prerequisite courses. To make the present example more interesting, let us also assume that the course number data item contains only the numerical portion of the course designator (the 201 of MGMT 201), while the department code is used for the prefix (MGMT).

There is little difference in processing recursive sets versus nonrecursive sets. Loading the various record occurrences is a straightforward exercise in adapting the generic program segments already presented. Suppose that departments, courses, and students have been entered and connected through the sets OFFER, MAJOR, and TAKE. Let us now examine the process of determining (and updating) prerequisites for a particular course.

To load and update the prerequisite list of a given course, we must first enter the department for that course and then the course number itself. Once the course has been located, we can update the existing prerequisites; this updating consists solely of pruning the list of courses no longer required. After all existing prereq-

uisites have been displayed, new courses are accepted as prerequisites. Naturally, the set PRE is declared to have manual insertion for both owners and
members.

The program for editing prerequisite courses is shown in Fig. 12.10. Through
the first two **fmsk** commands the course is determined. The first loop displays

```
display "Enter department.code:";
input dept.code;
fmsk(SD, dept.code);
if (found) then
   {som(OFFER, SD);
    display "Enter course number:";
    input cour.number;
    fmsk(OFFER, cour.number);
    if (found) then
       {som(PRE, OFFER);
        do while (found)
            {getm(PRE, cour);
             smm(OFFER, PRE);
             gfo(CODE, OFFER, dept.code);
             display dept.code, cour.number, cour.title;
             display "Should this be removed as a prerequisite (Y/N)?";
             if (qyn ()) then
                 rms(PRE);
             else
                 fnm(PRE);
             }
        do while ({display "Do you want to add another prerequisite (Y/N)?";
                   qyn ()})
            {display "Department code:";
             input dept.code;
             fmsk(SD, dept.code);
             if (not found) then
                {display "No such department:"
                 continue;
                 }
             som(OFFER, SD);
             display "Course number:";
             input cour.number;
             fmsk(OFFER, cour.number);
             if (not found) then
                {display "No such course";
                 continue;
                 }
             ims(PRE);
             }
        }
   }
```

Fig. 12.10   Editing prerequisites.

the existing prerequisites, removing from the set those so indicated by the user. Note how the automatic **fnm** of **rms** is employed in the example. Also note that currency indicators for the set OFFER has been disturbed; possibly both its current owner and current member are different from what they were after the two **fmsk** commands. However, the course we found first is still the current owner of PRE; because that indicator is not changed, we are able to perform our desired tasks.

The second loop allows new courses to be listed as prerequisites for the given course. The department code of the new prerequisite is entered and found and then the course number of the prerequisite is entered and found. Once this course occurrence has been found, it is the cru occurrence; so the **ims** command adds it to the set PRE.

Suppose that, for a particular student, we would like to determine the highest numbered course taken by that student in each department. For example, if student X has taken 12 management courses and 5 computer science courses, then 2 courses would be listed: the highest numbered management course and the highest numbered computer course taken by this student. We will assume, for simplicity, that member occurrences of the set TAKE are sorted by ascending course numbers.

One solution for this problem is to process each course taken by a particular student. For each such course, we could determine its department. Then we could look through the remainder of the list of courses, checking the department of each. If the departments match, then the present course is not the highest numbered; thus it should not be listed. If no department matches, then this course must be the highest numbered course in the given department taken by this student.

Consider the occurrences shown in Fig. 12.11. Suppose that we are processing student Y. The first course is numbered 100; the department is English. Now let us run through the rest of the list of Y's courses to see if any other English courses have been taken. The third member of TAKE is also an English course. Thus ENGL 100 would not be listed for Y. Now we must find Y's next course. Which one should it be? It should be the next record occurrence after 100; not the next one after 200 or English would be skipped; and not the 200 occurrence directly, because MGMT 100 would not be processed, and this might be the highest numbered management course.

Once an occurrence of TAKE has been determined (100 above), we need to save that occurrence so that we can restore it as a current member after the search is finished. We can use any unused set to do this; in this case we have the set PRE. By incorporating a command like "**smm**(PRE, TAKE)" before we run through the list, we save the current member of TAKE as the current member of PRE. Thus we will almost be able to restore it as the current member of TAKE afterwards.

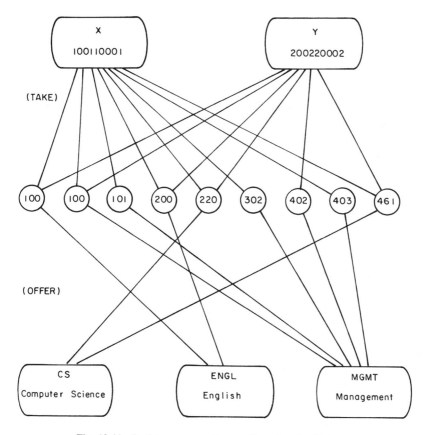

Fig. 12.11   Partial occurrence diagram for university database.

At first glance we might try to make the restoration with "**smm(TAKE, PRE)**". However, this has the additional effect of finding the first owner of the set TAKE, which in this case would lead us to the wrong student (X). This is unworkable, since students X and Y have taken different courses. What we would like to do is restore the current member of TAKE *without* performing that automatic **ffo.** The solution is a new command,

> **sme**(set-name)   Set the current member of the given set to be the same record as the cru, except do not perform an automatic **ffo.**

Set member exceptionally (**sme**) is an assignment command that uses the cru value to determine the new member of the set. The current owner of the M:N set specified must be a valid owner for the given member; otherwise an end-of-set condition occurs. There is of course a parallel owner-oriented command,

soe(set-name)   Set the current owner of the given set to be the same record as the cru,
                  except do not perform an automatic **ffm.**

The operation of the set owner exceptionally (**soe**) command is analogous to **sme.**

The solution of the restoration problem is given in Fig. 12.12. Note how the set PRE is used to save the current member and how **sme** is used to restore this value. The preceding **scm** makes the saved value the cru.

Note also that, because the automatic find-first operation has been suppressed, the cru value will not change. This is in direct contrast to **smc** and **soc** (Sect. 7.1).

Before leaving this section we introduce two additional commands from the remove category. These commands do not exclusively apply to M:N sets, but can be used with any type of set. The commands are

```
display "Enter student number";
input ssn;
fmi(SSN, SS, ssn);
if (found) then
{   som(TAKE, SS);
    do while (found)
    {   smm(OFFER, TAKE);
        gfo(CODE, OFFER, code);
        smm(PRE, TAKE);                    /* Saving the current member */
        t = 0;
        fnm(TAKE);
        do while (found)
        {   smm(OFFER, TAKE);
            gfo(CODE, OFFER, temp);
            if (temp = code) then
            {  t = 1;
               break;
            }
            fmn(TAKE);
        }
        scm(PRE);                          /* Restore the current member */
        sme(TAKE);
        if (t = 0) then
        {   getm(TAKE, cour);
            display code, cour.number, cour.title;
        }
        fnm(TAKE);
    }
}
```

Fig. 12.12 Listing highest numbered courses.

rsm(set-name)	With respect to the current owner of the given set, remove all member occurrences of that set.
rso(set-name)	With respect to the current member of the given set, remove all owner occurrences of that set.

Remove set members(**rsm**) and remove set owners (**rso**) will disconnect an entire group of records for the specified set. For **rsm,** all member records are disconnected from the current owner of the set and the current member of the set becomes null. For **rso,** all owner records are disconnected from the current member and the current owner becomes null.

These commands are not everyday commands. They can be used in situations where we quickly need to undo a lot of work. In our previous example, we might include an option to disassociate all prerequisites from a particular course. This can be accomplished with a single **rsm** command, rather than with the program loop shown in Fig. 12.10. Though that program works quite well, the additional complexity of including the extra user dialogue and associated commands is (in many cases) not worth the effort.

12.2 PROCESSING AREAS IN THE DATABASE

Chapters 4–10 we were able to consider database management without explicitly considering areas. The query and DML commands examined earlier do not depend on how many areas a database has. However, there are a few additional DML commands that can be used to special advantage in the event of multiple areas.

If multiple areas are to be used, then each area must be opened for access within the program before it is used. The **dbopn** command opens the main database area for processing. The opening of other areas is implicitly performed by the DBCS as those areas are needed by the application program. Alternatively, the program can explicitly open areas. The form of the DML command for explicitly opening an area is

dbopna(area-name, variable)	Open the area specified by the given area-name; if the value of the variable is a nonblank, then use this as the name of the operating system file holding the area.

The open an area (**dbopna**) command tells the DBCS that a particular area should be made available for use by the program. If the value of the specified variable is a string of blanks, then the area is assumed to exist on the file indicated for it in the DDL specification. Otherwise, the variable is assumed to contain a valid file name, which then overrides the name given in the DDL.

Before an area is opened, the file to which the area is assigned must be on-line. If several areas are to be used but not all areas are required at a time, then it is possible to explicitly close an area, issue instructions to the user on how to physically change disks, and then execute a **dbopna** for the newly loaded area. The command for explicitly closing an area is

> **dbclsa**(area-name)   Close the specified area.

The close an area (**dbclsa**) command allows the file holding a particular area to be taken off-line while other areas remain open for processing. The database close command **dbcls** automatically closes all open areas.

If a program attempts to access a record occurrence in an unopened area, the DBCS will automatically try to open that area using the file name and drive specified with the DDL. In either the implicit or explicit case, the opening of an area will be transparent to the users provided the file holding that area is on-line. Otherwise an error indicator is set to which the program must respond. For purposes of both documentation and control, it is often advisable to explicitly open those areas a program might use.

Any record type can be assigned to several different areas in the database. Sometimes, though, it may be desirable to force a particular record occurrence into a specific area. It might be desirable to group the record occurrences by data value or some other characteristic. Using **crs,** the record occurrence would be placed in one of the areas declared for the record type in the DDL specification, according to the criteria stated. To force the particular occurrence into a particular area, a new command can be used,

> **cra**(record-name, area-name, p-record)   Store the p-record information into a newly created occurrence of the record type, within the given area.

The create record in area (**cra**) command is identical in function to the much more commonly used **crs,** except that it forces the new record occurrence to be stored in a particular area. If this area is full, then an error indicator is set. The **cra** command will not attempt to add the occurrence anywhere else. Using **cra,** a developer can directly control the placement of record occurrences into areas, so that only appropriate areas need be on-line for various processing operations. When initially loading large volumes of data (e.g., 5–20 megabytes) into a multi-area database, the **cra** command can be used to achieve much faster loading than **crs** by partitioning the input data to force load one area at a time. As each area is filled, the area argument of **cra** is changed to load the next set of input data into a new area.

One common use of an area is to reserve it for a record type declared to have a calc location mode. Two commands are required for processing records that have been calced; these commands are quite similar to **fmi** and **fnmi.** They assume that the appropriate area or areas into which records can be calced are open:

> **frk**(record-name, variable)   Find the first record occurrence whose calc key value matches the value of the specified variable.

fdrk(record-name, variable)   Find another record occurrence whose calc key value
                                     matches the value of the specified variable.

The find record based on calc key (**frk**) command will set the cru to the first
occurrence of the indicated record type whose calc key value *exactly* matches the
value of the specified variable. No other currency indicators are affected. If no
match is found, an end-of-set condition occurs. The find duplicate record based
on calc key (**fdrk**) command changes the cru to be another occurrence (other than
the present cru occurrence) whose calc key value exactly matches the value of the
specified variable. Repeated use of **fdrk** will find all records having the same
specified calc key value. When there are no further records with the duplicate
calc key value, an end-of-set condition occurs.

Because the cru is set by these commands, calc record processing can be used
to find particular record occurrences in much the same way as (say) **fmsk** will
find a particular occurrence. Then the other assignment commands can be employed to utilize sets in the usual way.

If the calc key consists of more than one data item, then a p-record would be
used in place of the variable in each of these commands. The p-record must
conform to the specification of the calc key as declared with the DDL.

One word of caution must be issued here concerning data items that participate
in calc keys: their values *cannot* be changed by any put command. Information
that is accessed via **frk** is assumed to be very stable in nature. Should a data
value for a calc key item require updating, the proper processing would be to
delete the existing occurrence, and then create a new occurrence with the updated
values. The new occurrence must be reinserted into the appropriate sets, of
course.

Two much more esoteric commands exist for sequentially processing the
records stored in areas of the database. These are

ffs(area-name)   Find in a sequential manner the first record occurrence within the
                       specified area.
fns(area-name)   Find in a sequential manner the next record occurrence within the
                       specified area.

The find first sequential (**ffs**) command sets the cru to the dbk of the physically
first record occurrence within an area. If the area is empty of occurrences, an
end-of-set condition occurs. The find next sequential (**fns**) command sets the cru
to be the physically next record occurrence existing in the area. If there are no
more occurrences, an end-of-set condition occurs.

These two commands can be used to sequentially and exhaustively examine
the entire contents of a database area. One reason for doing so would be to
process all occurrences of a particular record type in situations where no system-
owned set exists for that record type. Another reason would be to discover
orphan record occurrences; this process is usually referred to as *garbage collection*. An example of this process is given in Section 12.4.

One problem that can arise when processing records sequentially is that, in cases where areas contain occurrences of several different record types, we need to identify the record type of the occurrence that is the cru. Two commands come to the rescue,

gtc(variable) 	The name of the record type of the cru occurrence is returned in the specified variable.

tct(record-name) 	Check the record type name of the cru occurrence against the given record type name.

The get the type of the cru (**gtc**) command retrieves the record type name of the cru occurrence. This could then be used as a decision variable within an application program.

The test cru type (**tct**) command determines whether the cru record is an occurrence of the specified record type. If it is, then no error condition occurs; if it is not, then an "invalid record type" error results.

The last four commands presented are very rarely used in an application system. We present them only for completeness. Typical applications, even quite complex applications, can manage quite nicely without any of these.

12.3   PROCESSING FORKED SETS

When a set relationship has more than one owner or member record type (or both), all of the DML find commands behave in their customary ways. However, once a record has been found we need a method for determining its type. Consider for a moment the schema of Fig. 12.13. Keywords can be used in books and journal articles; we can assume that the set IN has its member occurrences sorted by ascending authors.

In providing a list of references for a particular keyword, we need to determine what kind of record occurrence is being processed (is it a book or a journal?), in order to use the proper p-record for processing. To do this we can employ one of the following commands:

gtm(set-name, variable) 	Get the record type name of the current member record of the given set and assign that name to the given variable.

tmt(record-name, set-name) 	Test the current member of the given set to determine if it is an occurrence of the specified record type.

The get type of member (**gtm**) and test member type (**tmt**) commands operate in a similar manner to the **gtc** and **tct** commands presented in Section 12.2. The **gtm** command returns the name of the current member's record type. The **tmt** command determines whether the current member of the indicated set is an

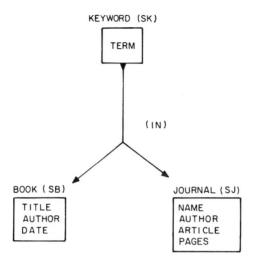

Fig. 12.13   Multiple member set.

occurrence of the specified record type. If it is not, then an "invalid record type" error results. Naturally, for multiple owners, there are

gto(set-name, variable)   Get the record type name of the current owner record of
                                     the given set and assign that name to the given vari-
                                     able.

tot(record-name, set-name)   Test the current owner of the given set to determine if it
                                     is an occurrence of the specified record name.

The get type of owner (**gto**) and test owner type (**tot**) commands behave analo-
gously to **gmt** and **tmt.**

To produce a list of references for a specified keyword, the program of Fig.
12.14 first locates the keyword, then iterates through the member occurrences of
the set IN. If the occurrence is a book, then the appropriate p-record is used;
otherwise it must be a journal and a different p-record is used. This kind of
processing is all these commands are designed to do. The commands **gtc** and **tct**
can be used to test occurrences in this case as well.

12.4   PROCESSING USER-DEFINED CURRENCY INDICATORS

Recall for a moment the processing in Section 12.1 that led to the introduction
of the command **sme.** There we were finding the highest numbered classes taken

```
display "Enter Keyword";
input term;
fmsk(SK, term);
if (found) then
{   som(IN, SK);
    do while (found)
    {      tmt(BOOK, IN);
          if (no error) then
          { getm(IN, book);
            display book.author, book.title;
            }
          else
          { getm(IN, journal);
            display journal.author, journal.title, journal.name, journal.pages;
            }
          fmn(IN);
          }
}
```

Fig. 12.14   List references for a single keyword.

by a student. In the course of our processing, we used the set PRE to temporarily remember the current member of the set TAKE, which we later restored through the **scm** and **sme** pair.

What could we have done if the set PRE had not been so conveniently present and available? All of the other currency indicators were being utilized. To help alleviate problems like this, another group of currency indicators can be defined within the program. These are completely under the control of the program and are not affected by any database processing (other than a **dbcls**). These indicators are referred to as the user-defined indicators (udi).

Just how many of these user-defined indicators are there? There are at least four. That is, four such indicators are predefined by the DBCS for our use. What if we need more than four? We can use the following command:

aui(variable)   Allocate enough space to maintain user defined indicators, the number of which is determined by the value of the given variable.

The allocate user indicators (**aui**) command reserves enough computer memory for the number of indicators specified by the variable. This memory is stolen from the memory used by the DBCS for disk operations (paging); hence it is important to keep the number of udi's to a minimum.

For example, if the variable x is assigned the value 10, then executing the command "**aui**(x)" would allocate a total of 10 udi's. For convenience, we shall refer to these udi's as udi(1), udi(2), . . . , udi(10).

The maximum number of udi's that may be defined for a program is 255. It is possible to use **aui** repeatedly in a program to vary the number of defined indicators. It is also possible to deallocate all of the udi's, by assigning the value 0 to a variable, say x, and executing the command "**aui** (x)".

Because udi's are used as temporary storage of currency indicators, the main commands that apply to udi's are assignment commands. There are seven new assignment commands:

suc(variable)	Set udi(variable) to be the same as the cru.
sum(set-name, variable)	Set udi(variable) to be the same as the current member of the given set.
suo(set-name, variable)	Set udi(variable) to be the same as the current owner of the given set.
suu(p-record)	Assuming the p-record to contain two variables, v-one and v-two, then set udi(v-one) to be equal to udi(v-two)
scu(variable)	Set the cru to be the same as udi(variable).
smu(set-name, variable)	Set the current member of the given set to be the same as udi(variable).
sou(set-name, variable)	Set the current owner of the given set to be the same as udi(variable).

These commands allow assignment to and from the udi's. Error conditions occur if the values being assigned are null, if the udi number given in the variable is too large or small, or in the last two commands if the udi occurrence does not mesh with the specified set. The last two commands also perform the usual automatic find firsts.

As mentioned above, a udi could be used in place of the set PRE in the example of Fig. 12.12. Another udi usage involves **ffs/fns** processing. Figure 12.15 gives an example of a simple form of garbage collection. Here we sequentially search area AA, looking for occurrences of the record type OOPS. These occurrences should be deleted, because they represent (for our purposes) orphan occurrences. Once an OOPS occurrence is located, its address is saved in udi(1). The next sequential occurrence is located; its address is saved in udi(2). The OOPS occurrence is then made the cru again and quickly deleted. The next sequential occurrence is restored from udi(2) and processing can continue.

The udi also comes in handy for another kind of processing. Consider again the university database of Fig. 12.9. Suppose now we want a list of students that have taken at least one prerequisite of a particular course. To process this information, we could iterate through the students, iterate through their courses, and for each course, check the value of the course number and its department code (through the set OFFER). This processing is depicted in Fig. 12.16. A drawback of this processing approach is that for each course taken we must check the data values for the course number and department code. This can be a long and tedious process both for the programmer to implement and for the computer to execute.

```
ffs(AA);
do while (found)
{      tct(OOPS);
       if (no error) then
       {   v = 1;
           suc(v);
           fns(AA);
           t = found;
           if (t) then
           {   v = 2;
               suc(v);
               v = 1;
           }
           scu(v);
           drc( );
           if (t) then
           {   v = 2;
               scu(v);
           }
           found = t;
       }
   else
       fns(AA);
}
```

Fig. 12.15   Trashing OOPS occurrences.

However, if we could avoid checking the data value of the course, but check only its address, then we can presumably make the program more efficient to write and to execute. To do this we need a method of comparing database keys (i.e., currency indicators),

   ccu(variable)   Compare the cru value with the value of udi(variable).

The check current against user indicator (**ccu**) command returns an end-of-set error when the specified user indicator does not match the cru. An error condition will occur if the variable specifies a value too large or negative. If there is a match, then no error is returned by **ccu.**

The revised program incorporating **ccu** is shown in Fig. 12.17. The primary savings come from playing with the set OFFER and its associated data values only once outside of any loop. This, in addition to the fact that the currency indicators can usually be compared much faster than the data values can be retrieved and then compared, makes the second version of the program considerably more efficient.

```
                    display "Department code:";
                    input code;
                    display "Course number:";
                    input num;
                    ffm(SS)
                    do while (found)
                    {      t = 0;
                        som(TAKE, SS);
                        do while (found)
                        {      smm(PRE, TAKE);
                            do while (found)
                            {      gfo(NUMBER, PRE, x);
                                if (x = num) then
                                {      smo(OFFER, PRE);
                                    gfo(CODE, OFFER, temp);
                                    if (temp = code) then
                                    {  getm(SS, STU);
                                        display stu.name, stu.ssn;
                                        t = 1;
                                        break;
                                        }
                                    }
                                fno(PRE);
                                }
                            if (t = 1) then break;
                            fnm(TAKE);
                            }
                        fnm(SS);
                        }
```

Fig. 12.16 Using data values for report.

12.5 BOOLEAN OPERATIONS

Consider for a moment the database structure shown in Fig. 12.18. This structure tells which shipments from a particular supplier went to a particular warehouse. Suppose that we want to list all of the shipments from supplier ABC, Inc. to warehouse no. 93.

This is a very simple problem; one solution is given in Fig. 12.19. Here we make the supplier occurrence the value of udi(1), and then iterate through the shipments of no. 93, checking the suppliers of those shipments with **ccu**. This could also be accomplished at higher cost by data value checking within the loop.

Of course, this is a very symmetric problem. We could have started with the warehouse as udi(1), and then iterated through the supplier's shipments. This

```
display "Department code";
input code;
fmsk(SD, code);
if (not found) then perform error-process;
som(OFFER, SD);
display "Course number:";
input num;
fmsk(OFFER, num);
if (not found) then perform error-process;
v = 1;
sum(OFFER, v);
ffm(SS);
do while (found);
{      t = 0;
    som(TAKE, SS);
    do while (found);
    {    smm(PRE, TAKE);
        do while (found);
        {    ccu(v);                      /* cru is current owner of PRE */
            if (no error) then
            {  getm(SS, stu);
                display stu.name, stu.ssn;
                t = 1;
                break;
            }
            fno(PRE);
        }
        if (t = 1) then break;
        fnm(TAKE);
    }
    fnm(SS);
}
```

Fig. 12.17   Using indicators for report.

program is given in Fig. 12.20. Comparison of the two show the parallel nature of the processing.

Both of these programs are correct, because they both will provide the desired list. But there are differences, too. One difference is the order in which the list will be printed. In the first program the order of the output list is a function of the set ordering for members of the set FROM. In the case that the output report requires a particular ordering, then this may be the deciding factor in selecting between the programs.

The other important difference is the efficiency of the two programs. Generally speaking, the set (TO or FROM) with the fewer number of members will provide the more efficient processing. This is because fewer occurrences have to

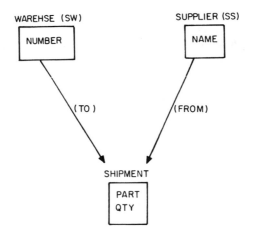

Fig. 12.18 Warehouse database.

```
display "Enter supplier:";
input name;
fmsk(SS, name);
if (not found) then perform error-process;
v = 1;
sum(SS, v);
display "Enter warehouse:";
input num;
fmsk(SW, num);
if (not found) then perform error-process;
som(TO, SW);
do while (found);
{      smm(FROM, TO);
       ccu(v);
       if (no error) then
       {   getm(TO, shipment);
           display shipment.part, shipment.qty;
           }
       fnm(TO);
       }
```

Fig. 12.19 Processing by shipments received.

```
display "Enter warehouse";
input num;
fmsk(SW, num);
if (not found) then perform error-process;
v = 1;
sum(SW, v);
display "Enter supplier:";
input name;
fmsk(SS, name);
if (not found) then perform error-process;
som(FROM, SS);
do while (found);
{    smm(TO, FROM);
     ccu(v);
     if (no error) then
     {   getm(FROM, shipment);
         display shipment.part, shipment.qty;
     }
     fnm(FROM);
}
```

Fig. 12.20   Processing by shipments sent.

be processed, which implies fewer accesses of the database, implying fewer disk operations. Thus, to ensure the most efficient processing of this information, a program structure such as that outlined in Fig. 12.21 could be employed.

Let us examine the conceptual processing in these programs more closely. In each case we are trying to isolate those occurrences of SHIPMENT that have a particular owner in FROM (ABC, Inc.), *and* a particular owner in TO (No. 93). If we think for a moment of the member occurrences in FROM for owner ABC, Inc., and the member occurrences in TO for owner No. 93, as mathematical sets, then we are trying to find which occurrences appear in both (mathematical) sets. This operation is called a *set intersection* in mathematics.

The MDBS DML provides a single command for performing an entire set intersection. The command is

> **amm**(set-1, set-2, set-3)   Perform a set intersection (logical and) of the members of set-1 and the members of set-2 and connect the common records as members of the system-owned set, set-3.

The and members with members (**amm**) command is also referred to as a Boolean command, since this is another term for mathematical set operations. The **amm** command is different from the other commands that we have studied in one important respect: **amm** does not reference the currency indicators of the first two sets specified in the command. Rather, the particular owner occurrence of set-1, whose members we are considering, must have its dbk stored in udi(1),

```
/* Collect warehouse and supplier, do fmsk for each */
som(TO, SW);
gmc(TO, x);
som(FROM, SS);
gmc(FROM, y);
v = 1;
if (x > y) then
{    sum(SW, v);
        .

        .

        .

     /* Process as in Fig. 12.20 */
     }
else
{    sum(SS, v);
        .

        .

        .

     /* Process as in Fig. 12.19 */
     }
```

Fig. 12.21   Guaranteeing efficient processing.

while the particular owner occurrence of set-2 must have its dbk stored in udi(2). The reason for this will be explained later.

The common occurrences found by **amm** become members of the specified system-owned set, set-3. However, there is a side effect to **amm** that must always be kept in mind: **amm** performs an *automatic* "**rsm**(set-3)". In other words, all of the present members of set-3 are removed from that set *before* the common occurrences are inserted.

If we happen to have an unused system-owned set lying around (i.e., if during the design of the schema we anticipated the use of **amm,** and so declared an additional system-owned set for the record type that set-1 and set-2 have as a common member), then that set can safely be used as the set-3 for **amm.** The set order defined in the DDL specifications will apply to its new member occurrences generated by **amm.**

If we do not have such a set, then we may use the set $SYSSET. This special system-owned set is predefined by the data management system for use in exactly this circumstance. Its order is FIFO, which means that the order in which occurrences appear in $SYSSET is dependent upon their order in the two input sets.

If either set-1 or set-2 (or both) is a system-owned set, then we need not worry about the contents of udi(1) or udi(2), respectively. In fact, set-1 or set-2 could be the output set from a previous **amm** operation. One of them could be $SYSSET. On completion of **amm,** the current member of set-3, plus the cru, are made null.

In Fig. 12.22, the solution to the above problem is given using **amm.** The two owner occurrences are found and they are assigned to the proper udi's. Then **amm** is executed, the results of which go into $SYSSET. Finally a simple **fnm** loop is used to process the occurrences of $SYSSET. The automatic **rsm($SYSSET)** ensures the $SYSSET is empty of occurrences before the intersection is computed.

Generally speaking, **amm** is more efficient than any of the other solutions discussed earlier. This is because in determining the desired group of records it does not need to access even a single record in the database. The command **amm** is particulary useful when the occurrences forming the intersection must be processed repeatedly.

The input sets need not be 1:N sets as in our example. They could be N:1 or M:N sets as well (using a 1:1 set is allowable, but just plain silly). Thus for symmetry we also have

> **amo**(set-1, set-2, set-3)   Perform a set intersection of the members of set-1 and the owners of set-2 and connect their common records as members of the system-owned set, set-3.

The and members with owners (**amo**) command requires the desired owner for set-1 to be assigned to udi(1), and the desired member for set-2 to be assigned to udi(2).

> **aom**(set-1, set-2, set-3)   Perform a set intersection of the owners of set-1 and the members of set-2 and connect the common records as members of the system-owned set, set-3.

```
display "Enter supplier:";
input name;
fmsk(SS, name);
if (not found) then perform process-error;
v = 1;
sum(SS, v);
display "Enter warehouse";
input num;
fmsk(SW, num);
if (not found) then perform process-error;
v = 2;
sum(SW, v);
amm(FROM, TO, $SYSSET);
ffm($SYSSET);
do while (found)
{     getm($SYSSET, shipment);
      display shipment.part, shipment.qty;
      fnm($SYSSET);
      }
```

Fig. 12.22   Using set intersection.

And owners with members (**aom**) requires the desired member for set-1 to be assigned to udi(1) and the desired owner for set-2 to be assigned to udi(2).

aoo(set-1, set-2, set-3)   Perform a set intersection of the owners of set-1 and the owners of set-2 and connect the common records as members of the system-owned set, set-3.

The and owners with owners (**aoo**) command requires the two desired members to be assigned to udi(1) and udi(2), respectively. For each of the Boolean commands, the currency indicators of set-1 and set-2 are neither accessed or modified. The automatic **rsm**(set-3) is always performed. The sets set-1 and set-2 must mesh in the usual way, as must set-3 if $SYSSET is not used. $SYSSET provides only a short term memory capability. The **dbcls** command performs an automatic "**rsm** ($SYSSET)", effectively disconnecting all occurrences from this set. Thus $SYSSET is not being used to maintain occurrences across different programs (run-units).

A Boolean command performs a great deal of processing. They usually replace an otherwise large portion of a program. Because of this, their execution time can appear to be longer than other DML commands. Just keep in mind the fact that with this single command we are performing the work that would otherwise require many DML commands in a large program loop and we are performing that work more efficiently in terms of total elapsed processing time.

Let us return to our university database in Fig. 12.9. Suppose that we wish to determine the common prerequisites of three courses. The conventional (non-Boolean) DML processing required is quite messy (Exercise 16). However, with **amm** the processing is quite straightforward (Fig. 12.23). First we determine the intersection of two of the courses; then, if that intersection is not empty, we intersect it with the prerequisites for the third course.

This example indicates why the set currency indicators are inadequate for the Boolean commands: we often need to intersect an M:N set with itself in order to find common members (in this case) or owners (if we ever use **aoo**). Having the udi's around make such operations possible.

Let us now try to solve the real problem of registering a student for a particular class. Before we allow the student to take the class, we must first check the prerequisites for the course to see if the student has taken all of the prerequisites. The conventional processing required for this is not trivial (Exercise 17).

Consider how an intersection command can help here. We can determine the courses in common between those taken by the student and those required as prerequisites for the given course. If the number of these common occurrences is equal to the number of prerequisites, then the student must have taken all of the prerequisites. This is one solution to the problem. However, we cannot tell from this which prerequisites a student has not taken. Further conventional processing would be required.

```
perform find-course; /* input dept and course, make it cm (OFFER) */
v = 1;
sum(OFFER, v);
perform find-course;
v = 2;
sum(OFFER, v);
amm(PRE, PRE, $SYSSET);
ffm($SYSSET);
if (not found) then exit ( );
perform find-course;
v = 2;
sum(OFFER, v);
amm($SYSSET, PRE, $SYSSET);
ffm($SYSSET);
do while (found)
{      gfm(NUMBER, $SYSSET, num);
       smm(OFFER, $SYSSET);
       gfo(CODE, OFFER, code);
       display code, num;
       fnm($SYSSET);
}
```

Fig. 12.23   Three-way, single set intersection program.

Mathematically, the problem we are considering is one of *set difference*. We would like to know the difference between the group of prerequisites for a course and the group of prerequisites taken by the student. If this difference is empty, then the student has all of the required prerequisites. Otherwise the occurrences that form the difference are those prerequisites yet to be taken by the student.

Figure 12.24 explains the notion of set difference in terms of an example. Using the standard mathematical notation of "$-$" for difference, the effect of the difference operations can be seen. Notice that difference is not reflexive: $A - B$ is not necessarily the same as $B - A$. The difference $A - B$ is the set of items in A that are not in B. Another way to say this is that $A - B$ is what remains of A if we take away all of the items in the intersection of A and B.

Difference is often called for in data processing. Whenever we need to ask what portion of a group of requirements has not been filled, we are talking about a difference operation. The DML provides four difference commands paralleling the intersection commands:

xmm(set-1, set-2, set-3)	Perform the difference "members of set-1" $-$ "members of set-2."
xmo(set-1, set-2, set-3)	Perform the difference "members of set-1" $-$ "owners of set-2."
xom(set-1, set-2, set-3)	Perform the difference "owners of set-1" $-$ "members of set-2."
xoo(set-1, set-2, set-3)	Perform the difference "owners of set-1" $-$ "owners of set-2."

$$A = \{a, b, c, e, h\}$$

$$B = \{b, d, e, f, g, h\}$$

$$A \text{ intersect } B = \{b, e, h\}$$

$$B \text{ intersect } A = \{b, e, h\}$$

$$A - B = \{a, c\}$$

$$B - A = \{d, f, g\}$$

Fig. 12.24   Examples of Boolean operations.

To avoid confusion the letter **x** is used for difference, because the letter **d** was previously used for delete. We can think of these commands as excluding from the first group all that it has in common with the second group. Note that the difference is always calculated as "set-1" − "set-2" and not the other way around. We are finding those occurrences which appear in set-1, but *not* in set-2. This is the definition of the difference operation.

These commands behave in much the same way as the Boolean intersection commands. The desired owner–member of set-1 must be assigned to udi(1) and the desired owner–member of set-2 must be assigned to udi(2). The currency indicators of set-1 and set-2 are in no way affected. The set-3 must be a system-owned set. The sets must properly mesh. An automatic **rsm**(set-3) is performed.

Our problem was to determine if a student has the necessary prerequisites for a given course. Figure 12.25 shows how a Boolean difference command can be used to solve this problem. Again, note that the order in which the sets appear is very important when finding the difference; the command "**xmm**(TAKE, PRE, $SYSSET)" would find the courses taken by the student that are *not* prerequisites of the given course.

Difference can also be used to determine those students that have taken one course but not another. This program is given in Fig. 12.26.

Intersection and difference are the only Boolean operations provided by the DML. Mathematical set theory has several other operations, though. One of these is *set union*, that is, all of the elements of both mathematical sets. There is no need for the DML to provide this as a separate command; merely process every occurrence in each list.

Another operation that is sometimes defined in mathematical theory is the *exclusive union*, where items are part of the exclusive union if they are in one set but not the other. This concept, similar to the *exclusive or* of logic, can easily be performed using difference. The exclusive union of sets A and B is simply the regular union of $(A - B)$ and $(B - A)$. Thus a series of commands will produce the effect of exclusive union.

```
perform find-course;    /* input dept and course, make it cm (OFFER) */
v = 1;
sum(OFFER, v);
perform find-student;   /* input name, make it cm (SS) */
v = 2;
sum(SS, v);
xmm(PRE, TAKE, $SYSSET);
ffm($SYSSET);
if (not found) then     /* student make take class */
{   som(TAKE, SS);
    scm(OFFER);
    ims(TAKE);
}
else                    /* missing prerequisites */
{   display "The following prerequisites must first be taken:";
    do while (found)
    {       gfm(NUMBER, $SYSSET, num);
            smm(OFFER, $SYSSET);
            gfo(CODE, OFFER, code);
            display code, num;
            fnm($SYSSET);
    }
}
```

Fig. 12.25 Check prerequisites.

The final set theory operation is *complement*. The complement of a set *A* is *all* of the elements not in *A*. In database terms, the complement of a set of member occurrences would be all of the other member occurrences of that set. There is really no way that the DBCS could ever determine the complement of a set of occurrences without resorting to an exhaustive search of all relevant database

```
perform find-course;  /* get course x */
v = 1;
sum(OFFER, v);
perform find-course;  /* get course y */
v = 2;
sum(OFFER, v);
xoo (TAKE, TAKE, $SYSSET);
ffm($SYSSET);
do while (found)
{       getm($SYSSET, stu);
        display stu.name, stu.ssn;
        fnm($SYSSET);
}
```

Fig. 12.26 Students in course *x,* but not course *y.*

areas. In certain circumstances this can be accomplished manually within a program, though. Thus there are no commands for directly finding complements.

Boolean DML commands are extremely advanced features. They are in no way required for developing useful application software. However, because they can be used to replace a large body of complex code, when appropriately used they improve the efficiency and organization of our programs.

12.6 SUMMARY

Corresponding to advanced data structuring and performance control features described in Chapters 10 and 11 are advanced DML processing techniques. This chapter explained those techniques by function.

The processing required for more powerful relationship types led to the introduction of several new commands. In particular, we added the owner-oriented find commands, insert command (**ios**) and remove command (**ros**). Processing for the M:N set is similar to processing discussed in earlier chapters for 1:N sets; however, commands like **goc** and **gmc** can simplify that processing greatly.

When it becomes necessary to turn off the automatic find-first feature of the assign commands, we can use **soe** and **sme** in conjunction with the cru value. Finally, the **rsm** and **rso** commands can quickly "disconnect" a set, if that kind of processing is called for.

For database area processing, it is necessary to first open the area (**dbopna**) and sometimes close it (**dbclsa**). To place a record occurrence in a specific area, the **cra** command can be used in place of **crs.** To locate calced information, the find commands, **frk** and **fdrk,** must be employed. The sequential commands, **ffs** and **fns,** are used less often.

To determine what kind of occurrence we have found when using sets with multiple owner and/or member record types, the get and test commands **gtc, gtm, gto, tct, tmt,** and **tot** can be used.

User defined currency indicators are useful when we need to save a particular indicator, and have no available, unused sets for the occasion. The **aui** command will allocate user indicators; a full set of assignment commands are also available. The very useful **ccu** command permits the checking of record addresses without resorting to data values.

There are two types of Boolean commands, intersection and set difference. These also use the user-defined indicators. The results (outputs) of these commands form a system-owned set, either one of our sets defined in the DDL or the dynamic set $SYSSET.

All of the MDBS commands discussed to this point are listed, by category, in

TABLE 12.1

Data Management System Commands

Find	Assign	Get	Put	Build	Eliminate	Required	Tests	Boolean
ffm	som	getc	putc	crs	drc	dbopn	tct	amm
fnm	smm	getm	putm	cra	drm	dopna	tmt	amo
flm	smo	geto	puto		dro		tot	aom
fpm	soo			ims		dbcls		aoo
fmi		gfc	pfc	ios	rms	dbclsa	(aui)	
fnmi	scm	gfm	pfm		ros		ccu	xmm
fmsk	sco	gfo	pfo					xmo
fnmsk	smc				rsm			xom
ffo	soc	gmc			rso			xoo
fno		goc						
flo								
fpo	suc	gtc						
foi	sum	gtm						
fnoi	suo	gto						
fosk	suu							
fnosk	scu							
frk	smu							
fdrk	sou							
ffs	sme							
fns	soe							

Table 12.1. The 82 commands listed provide the software designer with enough flexibility to easily prepare application products.

It is important to note that use of $SYSSET is not restricted to the Boolean commands. It is a properly defined system-owned set, with FIFO member ordering and manual insertion and every database record type is declared as a member of $SYSSET. It is especially useful in those situations where occurrences are being manually identified for later processing; such occurrences could be inserted into $SYSSET and processed afterwards. When the database is closed, however, an automatic **rsm** is performed upon $SYSSET. Thus information carried by $SYSSET is lost at the termination of the run-unit.

RELATED READING

Micro Data Base Systems Inc., ''MDBS Application Programming Reference Manual,'' Lafayette, Indiana, 1981.

EXERCISES

1. List all new *find* commands introduced in this chapter and illustrate their use via the product–part schema. Indicate the logical and physical sequence of events, including changes to various currency indicators.
2. How can a program determine when an end-of-set condition occurs?
3. When **dro** is invoked, what happens to the cru?
4. When is it convenient to use the *exceptional* commands **sme** and **smo**? Give an example.
5. In general, compare the effects of the delete and remove commands both logically and physically.
6. Present a program segment and physical structure to illustrate the use of calc keys. Use both the **frk** and **fdrk** commands. Describe an alternative (i.e., noncalc) method of accomplishing the same result.
7. Using the test commands and user indicator capability, test each occurrence in the Oldfil area to determine whether it is an occurrence of record type A, B, C, or D. Separate the occurrences into two files: Newfil1 and Newfil2. Newfil1 should contain all A and C records. Newfil2 should contain all B and D records. If an occurrence of a type other than A–D is found, then it should be copied to Errfile.
8. Use the Boolean commands to solve the problem of finding the highest numbered courses as in Fig. 12.12. Which program is better? Why?
9. Referring to Fig. 12.9, suppose we want to create a new course that has some existing courses as its prerequisite. The new course is itself a prerequisite of other courses. How would you construct a program to achieve this?
10. Suppose we want to determine if student A is senior to student B, that is, all courses taken by student B are also taken by student A. Write a program to do this with respect to the database schema of Fig. 12.9. Do not use Boolean commands.
11. What is the precondition for executing Boolean commands?
12. Why is the **dbopna** command used?
13. Why are user indicators valuable?
14. A student majoring in accounting can graduate if
(a) he has at least 21 credits for courses offered by the department of accounting,
(b) among these, at least 15 credits must be from courses above the 400 level, and
(c) he has at least 30 total credits.
    According to the database schema in Fig. 12.9, write a program to determine whether or not the student named *John Hansen* could graduate.

15. With respect to the schema of Fig. 12.2, design a load program which first loads all of the product occurrences, next loads all of the part occurrences, and then connects the products and parts together.
16. With respect to the schema of Fig. 12.9, write a program that determines the common prerequisites of any three courses, without using Boolean commands.
17. With respect to the database of Fig. 12.9, write a program that determines if a student has taken all of the prerequisites of a particular course, without using Boolean commands.
18. In the processing of Fig. 12.7, we may be deleting a product which used parts unique to that product. Modify the program so that such parts are also deleted.
19. Why must recursive sets be defined with manual insertion?

PROJECT

Devise load, update, and retrieval programs for the new schema, taking advantage of the advanced processing commands introduced in this chapter.

Chapter 13

A CASE STUDY

Chapter 13 combines all of the previously studied material into a single, large example. Incorporating many of the features discussed in previous chapters, the schema is designed according to the methodology of Chapters 5 and 10. Programs for processing the information are direct and simple extensions of the examples given in Chapters 6, 7, and 12. One thesis of the authors is that the use of a DBMS as a development tool can simplify the entire system design process.

13.1 THE SCENARIO

The USA Car Rental company is in the process of building a new computer system to take care of its inventory of automobiles. A database schema, and accompanying programs, are required for processing this inventory. The data analysis has taken place and is summarized in the following paragraphs.

One problem that USA has had in the past is that it never really knew just where any of its cars were at a particular time. The new system must be able to track cars as they are rented to customers, as they sit in parking lots or garages, or as they are in one of the regional service centers of the company.

When a customer complains about a malfunction in a particular car, the sales person handling the complaint must call the manager of the nearest service center to request pickup of the faulty unit. From that moment the car is assigned to the service center. In the service history information for the car the sales person records the date of the complaint and summarizes the complaint. When the service center releases a car to a sales location, the release date is noted in the service history and the actions taken by the service center are listed. The name of the service representative making the entry must also be entered. This control permits management to track down faulty service work and terminate the persons involved.

Another problem that USA has had in the past is keeping all of their cars properly licensed and registered. Thus the new system must keep track of the license number of each unit, the state in which the license is issued, and the date of renewal for that license.

The serial number of the car is used to uniquely identify each unit. The sales personnel also need to know the make, model, and year of the auto so that customers will know what they are renting. Cars are also classified by a somewhat arbitrary size class (subcompact, compact, midsize, etc.). This is useful information during the reservation process.

Rate information is quoted by size class, but there can be several different prevailing rates for each class, representing different rental plans. For example, a weekend plan for compacts and subcompacts might be $23/day and unlimited free mileage with the restriction of "pickup Thursday–Saturday, return by Sunday." On the other hand, the normal compact rental rate might be $19/day, $0.14/mile, 50 free miles. Customers also have the option of buying insurance coverage for collision and other damage; this must be noted in the rental agreement.

One major problem that USA must face is getting cars to the sales locations where the demand is. Each numbered location must have an address and telephone number listed so that other locations can call if demand is unexpectedly heavy. In large metropolitan areas, the various sales locations can pool their resources into a single super-location; this location would maintain the local inventory of cars, which would be delivered as needed to the sales locations. For demand balancing, it is necessary to know when and where cars will be returned by the customers.

Each location can also apply up to three special discounts on the basic rate. Thus the actual rental rate charged for a particular class of service will vary from location to location.

Customer information is maintained for promotional reasons as well as to accelerate the processing of reservations for repeat customers. The customer's name, address, and telephone number are stored. Each new customer is automatically given an account number, which happens to be identical to the customer's credit card number. When applicable (85% of the time), the customer's company name and address are also recorded. This allows the marketing people to periodically scan the customer information to identify those companies that could benefit from a corporate rental plan.

Each customer may have an associated discount based upon frequency of renting, credit rating, and other promotional gimmicks. There is also the USA Super-Renter's Club, which provides faster check-out and check-in at all service locations. The membership fee for the club is $100/year and provides an additional 10% discount on the basic rental rate (in addition to other services). The club member's driver's license number and whether the member desires the additional insurance coverage must be recorded so that the rental contract can be automatically generated. The renewal date for club membership and whether the member authorizes an automatic charge to the member's credit card for the membership fee must also be recorded. Not more than 10% of USA's customers belong to the Super-Renters Club.

This is the summary of the data characteristics of USA's application system. Processing would include making reservations, recording counter transactions, providing the service history of each auto, providing sales personnel with all of the relevant rate information, predicting demand at each sales location so that inventories can be shifted, and so forth. Periodic reports would include marketing reports on the types of cars being rented, the locations at which cars are rented, the customers and their companies, performance reports for the service centers and so on.

13.2   DESIGNING THE SCHEMA

Step 1.

The first step in the schema design process is sometimes the hardest: determining the collection of data items. This is because a concept that appears at first to be a data item sometimes turns out to be best represented by a set relationship or by a program computation; further, in the course of program development, it can become apparent that the introduction of another data item can produce simpler programs. Thus this step is not final in choosing the data items; it is simply a first iteration.

Bearing this in mind, an analysis of Section 13.1 produces the list of data items shown in Fig. 13.1. These are all derived from the descriptions given, in the order they were stated. It is possible that we missed some data items. These may be found during subsequent development efforts. However, we certainly have a nice large group of items to work with at this initial stage.

Steps 2 and 3.

Next, in the design procedure comes the aggregation of data items into record types. Here we try to identify the 1:1 and nearly 1:1 relationships between data items. This has been done in Fig. 13.2.

Data Item	Description
LOCATION	Where the car is at any time
TELE	Phone number of service center
MANAGER	Manager of service center
COMPDATE	Date of complaint: service history
COMPLNT	Complaint: service history
RELDATE	Release date: service history
ACTIONS	Maintenance: service history
NAME	Who performed the maintenance: service history
LICENSE	Auto license number
STATE	State in which car is registered
RENEWAL	Date of registration renewal
SERIAL	Serial number of car
MAKE	Manufacturer of car
MODEL	Model of car
YEAR	Model year of car
SIZE	Size class of car
PERPERD	Rental rate per time period
PERMILE	Rental rate per mile
MILEAGE	Number of free miles
RESTRICT	Rate restrictions
INSURNCE	Chose the insurance option (Yes or No)
NUMBER	Sales location number
ADDRESS	Sales location address
TELE	Sales location telephone
SUPER	Number of super-locations for this location
OUTDATE	Reservation date
OUTTIME	Reservation time
OUTLOC	Reservation location
INDATE	Return date
INTIME	Return time
INLOC	Return location
DISC1	Location discount 1
DISC2	Location discount 2
DISC3	Location discount 3
NAME	Customer name
ADDRESS	Customer address
TELE	Customer telephone
ACCTNUM	Account (credit card) number
CARDNAME	Credit card name
COMPANY	Company name
CADDRESS	Company address
DISCOUNT	Customer discount
LICENSE	Driver's licence no. (club members)
INSURNCE	Buy insurance (Yes or No; club members)
DATE	Club membership renewal date
AUTOCHRG	Automatically charge membership to credit card (Yes or No)

Fig. 13.1 Data items.

SERVICE CENTER:	RATE:	CUSTOMER:
TELE	PERPERD	NAME
MANAGER	PERMILE	ADDRESS
	MILEAGE	TELE
	RESTRICT	ACCTNUM
SERVICE HISTORY:		CARDNAME
COMPDATE		COMPANY
COMPLNT		CADDRESS
RELDATE	SALES LOCATION:	DISCOUNT
ACTIONS	NUMBER DISC1	LICENSE
NAME	ADDRESS DISC2	INSURNCE
	TELE DISC3	DATE
	SUPER	AUTOCHRG
CAR:		
LICENSE		
STATE	RESERVATION:	
RENEWAL	OUTDATE	LOC:
SERIAL	OUTTIME	LOCATION
MAKE	OUTLOC	
MODEL	INDATE	CLASS:
YEAR	INTIME	SIZE
	INLOC	
	INSURNCE	

Fig. 13.2 First aggregation.

Several facets of this aggregation deserve mention. The first data item of Fig. 13.1, LOCATION, does not really fit with any other group, so it becomes its own record type (Step 3). This is also true of the SIZE data item. The first INSURNCE data item seems to best belong with the other reservation information. We apply the nearly 1:1 test in the remaining cases.

Steps 4 and 5.

From this group of nine record types, we can begin to establish the 1:N relationships. Beginning with the service center, each center will fill out many histories, but each history entry comes from a single center; this yields a 1:N set. Each car may have many history reports, but each report refers to a particular car; another set. Drawing in a number of these obvious 1:N sets provides the partial schema of Fig. 13.3. At this point each record type is related to at least one other record type except for LOC. Transitivities are not included in the figure.

Now, consider the data item OUTLOC of RESERVATION. This gives the sales location number of where the car would be picked up. But actually, this information could just as well have been represented by a set, since many cars will be picked up at each location. Thus the item OUTLOC can be replaced by a

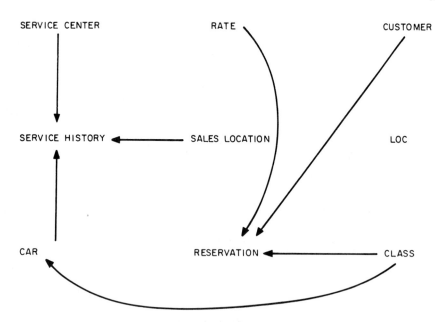

Fig. 13.3 Making up sets.

1:N set from SALES LOCATION to RESERVATION. Similarly, the INLOC data item can also be replaced by a 1:N set from SALES LOCATION to RESER-VATION. And for SALES LOCATION itself, the data item SUPER can be replaced by a 1:N (recursive) set from the SALES LOCATION that is the super location to the member locations of that car pool. The situation is now given in Fig. 13.4

Now consider LOC. Each LOCATION can have many cars at any one time, but a car can be in just one location. Thus we are not really talking about an M:N set here. What are the possible locations in which a car can be? The car can be assigned to one of the service centers, it can be available at a sales location, or it can be rented to a customer. Obviously, the car can be in only one of these places at any one time. In database terminology, each service center can have many cars, each sales location can have many cars, each customer could have many cars, but each car is assigned to either one service center *or* one sales location *or* one customer. This fits the definition of a 1:N forked set with multiple owner record types: SERVICE CENTER, SALES LOCATION, and RESERVATION (rather than customer). The data item LOCATION is actually replaced by this set relationship, thereby eliminating LOC as a record type. Figure 13.5 shows this latest development.

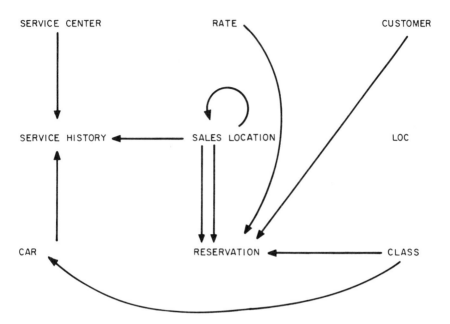

Fig. 13.4   Modifying the structure.

Steps 6 and 7.

We now have no unattached record types. Thus it is time to review the structure and problem description to determine whether the structure is fully capable of supporting the application needs.

Several questions arise at this point. The first we encounter deals with car registration. If keeping cars properly registered is a problem, we should perhaps make a separate index for the states in which the cars were bought. On the other hand, it might be simpler to add a system-owned set sorted by the renewal date of the registration; this set could be periodically checked to see which cars required renewal. We will adopt the second alternative.

Can we tell what rental rates apply to the various classes in the present structure? The answer is no. We need to directly relate the rate and class record types, so that sales persons can be prompted with the prevailing rates for the particular class of car being rented. What kind of relationship is this? The example given above suggests that the relationship is M:N—each size class can have several rate plans, while a particular rate might apply to several size classes (compact and subcompact in the example above). Thus we can draw an M:N set between RATE and CLASS, arbitrarily choosing RATE to be the owner.

It might be desirable to separate the customer's company name and address

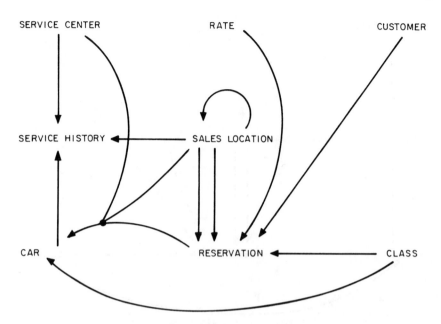

Fig. 13.5 Eliminating LOC.

from the CUSTOMER record type, since this is what the marketing department is interested in for their corporate sales program. This is a hard decision for a designer to make without consultation with the system users. In this case, the users tell us that it is not necessary to separate out the company information.

However, the users also tell us that it is important for the sales people to have the car make and model separated from the car information. This is because, in defining one of the size classes, the sales person would like to access the list of makes and models for that class to better inform the customer as to the likely choices of automobiles. Clearly, each class can have several makes and models, while each make and model belongs to just one class; and each car is just one make and model, while a make and model might refer to many individual cars. Thus two 1:N sets support this structure.

Finally, we note that less than 10% of the customers are Super-Renter Club members. Carrying the data items for the club in the customer record type would result in a considerable amount of wasted storage in the database. A better course of action would be to separate these items into a CLUB record type related to CUSTOMER through a 1:1 set. Thus space for club information is only used for those customers who are in the club. Is it necessary to have a data item in CUSTOMER to indicate club membership? No, since the existence of a CLUB record related to a CUSTOMER record implies club membership. This situation is outlined in Fig. 13.6.

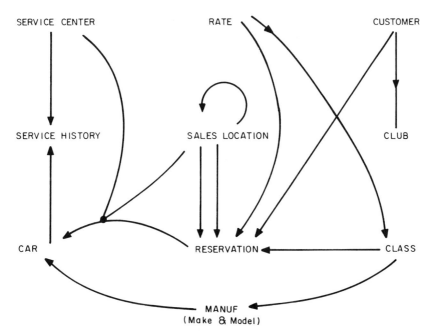

Fig. 13.6 The chosen sets.

The developer (in consultation with end users) should now carefully review the logical structure, to ensure that no wrong assumptions have been made in the design of the structure, nothing of importance has been omitted, and finally, the data item, record type, and set names selected are consistent with the terminology of the application. It is not uncommon to have the users rename many items at this stage.

In Fig. 13.7, the data items reflect names suggested by the users rather than those made up for Fig. 13.1. It also might take several tries to draw the schema diagram in such a way that there are no crossed lines, all lines are relatively short and the concepts built into the structure are clear. Fig. 13.7 is the second try: the users also added the CENTERNO data item for identifying service centers.

13.3   CONSTRUCTING THE DDL

Now that the designers and users are both fairly happy with the logical data structure, we can begin to construct the DDL specification for the system. This effort essentially consists of four parts. The first is specification of the environment in which the system will operate. This would include defining database

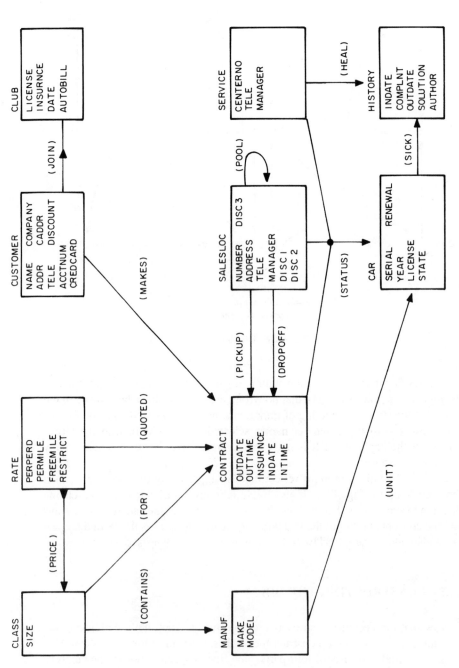

Fig. 13.7 Redrawn schema.

areas, assigning them to operating system files, and defining users, along with their different passwords and security codes. For simplicity then we shall define only three users: "Mgmt", "Sales", and "Service". "Mgmt" should have universal read and write capability. "Sales" will have universal read access to information, but write access to only CUSTOMER, CLUB, CONTRACT, and HISTORY record types. "Service" can read only SERVICE, CAR, and HISTORY and can write only the last three items of HISTORY.

Because this first stage of DDL design includes the specification of database areas, we must now examine whether we need to use areas in our processing in any way. We choose not to use the clustering option in this case. However, there may be some good applications of calc here. Recall that calc is used for relatively static information that must be retrieved very, very quickly. Two relevant situations that come to mind in this application involve the CUSTOMER record occurrences and the SALESLOC occurrences. In the latter case, the calc key would merely be the NUMBER data item of SALESLOC. In the former case, we have a choice. The best choice is probably the ACCTNUM data item, since this is a unique identifier for each customer; furthermore, it is information that each customer would have available. As a backup direct access technique, a system-owned set listing customers alphabetically could also be employed.

Thus we would, for processing reasons, define at least two database areas, for calc purposes. The beginning of the DDL specification is given in Fig. 13.8. To indicate calc keys in our database diagram, we place asterisks by the data items that participate in the keys. This helps to remind us that calc processing may be employed.

The next section of the DDL specification consists of the record type and data

```
DB name is USA, size is 1000 pages
                page size is 1024 bytes

USER is Mgmt with CARGO, Access is (a-c)
USER is Sales with RENTEM, Read access is a
                                 Write access is b
USER is Service with FIXEM, Access is c

AREA name is CUST, size is 500 pages
                   page size is 1024 bytes, pointers not allowed
                   access is (a, b)

AREA name is SLOC, size is 100 pages
                   page size is 512 bytes
                   read access is (a, c), pointers not allowed
                   write access is a
```

Fig. 13.8   Environment section of DDL.

item definitions. Thus the next phase of the DDL design process is the specification of the details of the data items. Often the decisions are simple to make: items OUTDATE, INDATE (of CONTRACT), INDATE, OUTDATE (of HISTORY), RENEWAL, and DATE are all of type date—the range information would specify a safe starting date, for example, 1-1-80. Similarly, OUTTIME and INTIME are of type time; PERPERD, PERMILE and the discount data items would all be real numbers; FREEMILE, NUMBER, CENTERNO, and YEAR would all be integers.

The harder decisions come with the character data items. In particular, what sizes should be specified for character data items? When possible, the data items should be declared as strings rather than characters. In all, a bit of common sense should prevail.

Interesting questions are raised by telephone numbers and by *yes/no* data items (such as AUTOBILL). How is a telephone number best entered into the database? The shortest (in terms of database storage) would be to store it as a long integer; but many programming languages do not support 10 digit integers. Another solution is to store the number as three 2 byte integers; this is extremely confusing to a user who might need to refer to the database diagram—why are there three data items for a single telephone number? The other alternative is to store the number as ten characters. This may not be as efficient as the first two in terms of data storage, but it is transportable (will work with any programming language) and it is easily understandable (for maintenance programmers). This is the alternative we choose to implement.

The *yes/no* data item poses the question of how best to represent this information. The choices range from 0, 1 values for an integer type item to Y and N values in a character item. Both would require 1 byte of storage; the second has the advantage of being simpler for another individual to interpret. Thus the *best* solution is to code such data items as character, length 1 byte, and store the values of either Y or N.

The sections of DDL defining the record types are given in Fig. 13.9. Note how the items and record types are assigned to security classes in order to match the requirements of our three users.

The third part of the DDL specification is the declaration of sets; and in particular, the selection of set orders. As pointed out earlier defining many sets to be sorted sets is not always good practice, since sorting will slow down the data entry processing although it does speed up the retrieval processing. Thus a balance must be struck. Figure 13.10 gives the set sections of the DDL specification.

The final part of the DDL specification has the definition of system-owned sets. Two such sets have been described above. Other system-owned sets are defined if the anticipated processing will require such sets. It is perfectly permissible to add the system-owned sets as the programs are written; indeed, the

Record CUSTOMER
     Within CUST, key is ACCTNUM, NODUP allowed, access is (a, b)
    Item is NAME, CHAR 25
    Item ADDR, STR 50
    Item TELE, CHAR 10
    Item ACCTNUM, CHAR 20
    Item CREDCARD, CHAR 4
    Item COMPANY, STR 30
    Item CADDR, STR 50
    Item DISCOUNT, REAL 4

Record CLUB, in USA, access is (a, b)
    Item LICENSE, CHAR 15
    Item INSURNCE, CHAR 1
    Item DATE, DATE, range is 01/01/1980 to HIGHEST
    Item AUTOBILL, CHAR 1

Record RATE, in USA, access is a
    Item PERPERD, REAL 4
    Item PERMILE, REAL 4
    Item FREEMILE, INTEGER 2
    Item RESTRICT, STR 30

Record CLASS, in USA, access is a
    Item SIZE, CHAR 12

Record CONTRACT, in USA, access is (a, b)
    Item OUTDATE, DATE, range is 01/01/1980 to HIGHEST
    Item OUTTIME, TIME, range is LOWEST to 23:59:59
    Item INSURNCE, CHAR 1
    Item INDATE, DATE, range is 01/01/1980 to HIGHEST
    Item INTIME, TIME, range is LOWEST to 23:59:59

Record MANUF, in USA, access is a
    Item MAKE, CHAR 6
    Item MODEL, CHAR 12

Record SALESLOC,
    Within SLOC, key is NUMBER, NODUP allowed
    read access (a, c), write access a
    Item NUMBER, INTEGER 2
    Item ADDRESS, STR 50
    Item TELE, CHAR 10
    Item MANAGER, CHAR 16
    Item DISC1, REAL 4
    Item DISC2, REAL 4
    Item DISC3, REAL 4

Fig. 13.9   Record section of DDL.

Record SERVICE, in USA, read access (a, c), write access a
    Item CENTERNO, INTEGER 2
    Item TELE, CHAR 10
    Item MANAGER, CHAR 16

Record CAR, in USA, read access (a, c), write access a
    Item SERIAL, CHAR 25
    Item YEAR, INTEGER 2
    Item LICENSE, CHAR 8
    Item STATE, CHAR 2
    Item RENEWAL, DATE, range is 01/01/80 to HIGHEST

Record HISTORY, in USA, access is (a-c)
    Item INDATE, DATE, write access is b, range is 01/01/80 to HIGHEST
    Item COMPLNT, STR 80, write access is b
    Item OUTDATE, DATE, write access is (a, c)
    range is 01/01/80 to HIGHEST
    Item SOLUTION, STR 120, write access is (a, c)
    Item AUTHOR, CHAR 16, write access is (a, c)

Fig. 13.9   (*Continued*)

Set PRICE, M:N, access is a
    Owner is RATE, manual, LIFO
    Member is CLASS, manual, FIFO

Set JOIN, 1:1, access is (a, b)
    Owner is CUSTOMER
    Member is CLUB, auto

Set CONTAINS, 1:N, access is a
    Owner is CLASS
    Member is MANUF, auto, FIFO

Set FOR, 1:N, access is (a, b)
    Owner is CLASS
    Member is CONTRACT, auto, IMMAT

Set QUOTED, 1:N access is (a, b)
    Owner is RATE
    Member is CONTRACT, auto, IMMAT

Set MAKES, 1:N, access is (a, b)
    Owner is CUSTOMER
    Member is CONTRACT, auto, FIFO

Set PICKUP, 1:N, access is (a, b)
    Owner is SALESLOC
    Member is CONTRACT, Auto, SORTED by ascending (OUTDATE, OUTTIME)

Fig. 13.10   Set section of DDL.

Set DROPOFF, 1:N, access is (a, b)
    Owner is SALESLOC
    Member is CONTRACT, Auto, SORTED by ascending (INDATE, INTIME)

Set POOL, 1:N access is a
    Owner is SALESLOC
    Member is SALESLOC, manual, IMMAT

Set UNIT, 1:N, access is a
    Owner is MANUF
    Member is CAR, auto, SORTED by ascending SERIAL

Set STATUS, 1:N, access is (a-c)
    Owners are CONTRACT, SALESLOC, SERVICE
    Member is CAR, manual, SORTED by ascending SERIAL

Set HEAL, 1:N, read access is (a-c), write access is (a, b)
    Owner is SERVICE
    Member is HISTORY, auto, FIFO

Set SICK, 1:N, read access is (a-c), write access is (a, b)
    Owner is CAR
    Member is HISTORY, auto, FIFO

Fig. 13.10   *(Continued)*

entire structure may be revised as the programs are written. In the present case, we can anticipate the need to list the available class sizes, so a system-owned set will be defined for CLASS. Also, to provide a list of service centers, a system-owned set will be defined for SERVICE. Additional sets may be added as necessary. The DDL definition of the system-owned sets appears in Fig. 13.11; the revised schema diagram is given in Fig. 13.12.

13.4   THE STOCK LOAD PROGRAM

The first load program is used to maintain the physical inventory information about the cars themselves. We must be able to enter, update, and delete information pertaining to individual units as they are bought, licensed, and either sold or wrecked. In examining the schema the sets most likely to be used for this process would be the system-owned set CLA, CONTAINS, and UNIT. Thus this program should also take care of the CLASS and MANUF information.

There is nothing very special about the processing required for each of these record types. The processing is similar to that performed in Chapters 7 and 8 for similar (linear) structures. First we find and process a CLASS occurrence; then,

Set CLA, 1:N, access is a
    Owner is SYSTEM
    Member is CLASS, auto, FIFO

Set CUS, 1:N, access is (a, b)
    Owner is SYSTEM
    Member is CUSTOMER, auto, SORTED by ascending NAME

Set SER, 1:N, read access is (a-c), write access is a
    Owner is SYSTEM
    Member is SERVICE, auto, SORTED by ascending CENTERNO

Set LEGAL, 1:N, access is a
    Owner is SYSTEM
    Member is CAR, auto, SORTED by ascending RENEWAL

Fig. 13.11   System-owned set section of DDL.

through CONTAINS, we find and process one or more makes and models; for each of these, we can process through UNIT one or more CAR occurrences. The outline of this processing is shown in Fig. 13.13. The program parallels the processing of Fig. 8.7 with a third set added.

The importance of this load program is not the fancy features that it includes, but that it is so simple to construct. Once the basic load program structures have been mastered, the construction of load programs becomes a relatively simple task, regardless of the nature of the application system.

13.5   THE SITES LOAD PROGRAM

The next load program loads information about the physical sites used by USA. These are, of course, the sales locations and service centers. These two are independent of each other, so that two separate program blocks can be developed.

The outline of the basic program is presented in Fig. 13.14. We determine which type of information is needed; then we branch to that particular process. The service center load program is identical to many that we have already studied. The sales location program has two additional features that make it worthy of discussion.

The first of these features is the fact that SALESLOC does not have a system-owned set, but instead is calced. Thus, instead of using **fmsk** or a related command to search for a particular sales location, we use **frk.** This processing is shown in Fig. 13.15.

The delete portion of this program would make sure that the sales location is

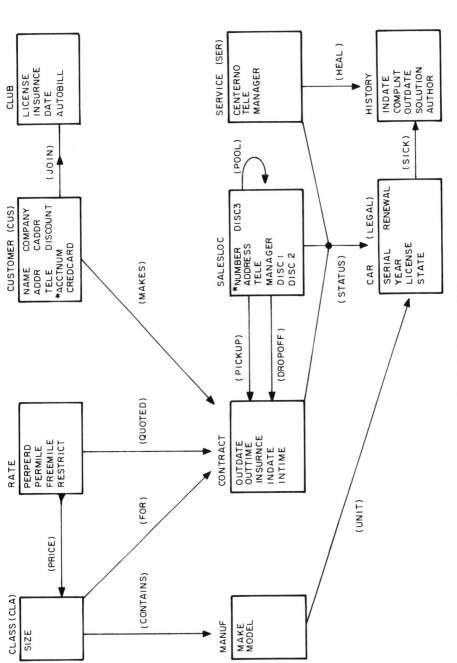

Fig. 13.12 Final schema for USA application.

```
do while (
⋮
/*create, delete and/or update a CLASS record thru CLA */
⋮
som(CONTAINS, CLA);
do while (
    ⋮
    /* create, delete and/or update a MANUF record thru CONTAINS */
    ⋮
    som(UNIT, CONTAINS);
    do while (
        ⋮
        /* create, delete and/or update a CAR record thru UNIT */
        ⋮
```

Fig. 13.13 The stock load program.

not connected to other occurrences through any sets before the delete could occur. This would apply to the service center occurrences as well.

The second interesting feature is the processing of the recursive set POOL. This (it turns out) is no different from the processing of any other 1:N set (for example, the set WORK in Fig. 8.8 and the ensuing discussion). The only major difference between the two processes is that, because SALESLOC is calced, we must first save the cru occurrence somewhere. In Fig. 13.15 the saving place is udi(1); it just as easily could have been the current owner of DROPOFF or any other currently unused set.

13.6 THE MARKETING (RATE) LOAD PROGRAM

The purpose of this program is to establish rates for the various classes of cars. Thus the information being loaded and updated are the RATE occurrences. But,

```
x = 0;
do while (x ≠ 3)
  { display "Do you wish to process:";
    display " 1: Sales Locations";
    display " 2: Service Centers";
    display " 3: Terminate Program";
    display "Choose by number:";
    input x;
    if (x = 1) then
        perform load-sales-locations;
    else if (x = 2) then
        perform load-service-centers;
  }
```

Fig. 13.14 Main program for sites loading.

```
load-sales-locations
{
do while ({display ''Enter Location Number (or -1):'';
            input x;
             x > 0})
   {frk(SALESLOC, x);
    if (found) then
        getc(salesloc);
    else
     {. . . /* collect information, perform crs */
       }
     .
     .
     .
    /* Delete Section */
     .
     .
     .
    /* Update Date Items Section */
     .
     .
     .
    /* Check on POOL */
    smc(POOL);
    if (found) then
      {    geto(POOL, salesloc);
           display ''Current Pool Site is,'' salesloc.number, salesloc.address;
           }
    else
           display ''Not in Pool Area'';
    display ''Any change (Y/N)?'';
    if (qyn ( )) then
        {    v = 1;
             sum(POOL, v);
             if (found) then rms(POOL);   /* found is set above by smc */
             perform find-pool-owner;
             scu(v)
             ims(POOL);
             }
```

Fig. 13.15   Loading sales locations.

upon examination of the schema and DDL specifications, we see that there is no direct access to the RATE occurrences. The shortest route would be via CLASS, using sets CLA and PRICE.

Is this a problem? It could very well be. A difficulty may arise because PRICE is an M:N set. Processing through CLA and PRICE requires that a size class must first be specified in order to find any particular rate. A better solution might be to add another system-owned set for RATE that would allow rates to be processed directly.

In many applications, that last suggestion would be the proper course of action. In this case, the users have decided that they would rather be forced to indicate a particular size class before dealing with rates; in particular, this is the way their forms are laid out. Thus we do not need to introduce another system-owned set.

The users anticipate fewer than 10 size classes and fewer than 12 rate plans in effect for any particular size class. Thus this load program can be designed with menus. To select a particular size, all of the known sizes will be displayed; the user will select from this list the desired class. For that class, the set of current rates will be displayed; the user will select from that list a desired rate. Then, for the user's information, all of the size classes to which rate pertains will also be displayed for verification and update.

The load program is given in Fig. 13.16. Note how the set CLA is used to generate the first menu (in routine pick-class-from-menu). The user selects a particular size by number (this is simpler for the user and the user is less likely to err); then that number is used to relocate the desired occurrence (in routine find-class-from-y). This processing is repeated using the set PRICE to find a particular RATE occurrence.

The delete rate and update rate data items sections involve the customary processing. The update connections section is similar to that of Fig. 12.10, and is left as an exercise. The udi(1) is used to keep track of the first class found at the start of processing, since subsequent processing also requires the use of the set CLA. The udi is used just as a temporary storage location.

The three programs discussed so far could only be run by one of our three users, namely "Mgmt". The other two users do not have sufficient write access for these record types and sets, and their attempts to execute these instructions would result in error indicators being set.

13.7   THE RESERVATION LOAD PROGRAM

Handling reservations is one of the most important functions of the USA system. This application program must be capable of updating the CUSTOMER and CLUB record occurrences and of also completely specifying a CONTRACT occurrence for a customer. The program should also be able to give rate information to the customer.

We will start by first identifying the customer. If the customer has an account with USA and knows the account number, then **frk** can be used to quickly locate the correct CUSTOMER occurrence. Otherwise the set CUS can be used. For new customers all information must be entered. Customers should be invited to join the Super-Renter's club; if they choose to do so, then that information must

```
do while ({perform pick-class-from-menu;
             y > 0});
    {if (y > x) then continue;
     perform find-class-from-y;
     v = 1;
     sum(CLA, v);
     do while ({smu(PRICE, v);
                   perform pick-rate;)
                   y < x + 2})
         {if (y = x + 1) then /* new rate */
             {perform create-new-rate;
              ios(PRICE);
              display "Does this rate apply to any other classes (Y/N)?";
              if (qyn ()) then
                      do while ({perform pick-class-from-menu;
                                   y > 0 and y < x})
                          {perform find -class-from-yj
                           ims(PRICE);
                           }
              }
         else
             perform find-rate-from-y;
         .
         .
         .
         /* Delete Rate Section */
         /* Update Rate Data Items Section */
         /* Update Connections to Classes Section */
         .
         .
         .
         }
pick-class-from-menu
    {display "Select by number a size class (or enter 0):";
     x = 0;
     ffm(CLA);
     do while (found)
        {gfm(SIZE, CLA, size);
         x = x + 1;
         display x, size;
         fnm(CLA);
         }
     input y;
     }
find-class-from-y
    {t = 1;
     ffm(CLA);
     do while (t < y)
```

Fig. 13.16   Marketing load program.

```
                    {t = t + 1;
                    fnm(CLA);
                    }
             }
        pick-rate
          {display "Select By Number One of the Following:";
           x = 0;
           ffo(PRICE);
           do while (found)
              {geto(PRICE, price);
               x = x + 1;
               display x, price.perperd, prce.permile, price.freemile, price.restrict;
               fno(PRICE);
               }
           display x + 1, "Create new rate";
           display x + 2, "Finished with these rate";
           input y;
           }
        find-rate-from-y
           {t = 1
            ffo(PRICE);
            do while (t < y)
               {t = t + 1;
                fno(PRICE);
                }
            }
```

Fig. 13.16   (*Continued*)

also be entered. This much of the load program is outlined in Fig. 13.17. More detail could be added to this program.

Next, the user must determine the sales location for pickup and the size class desired to be able to quote rental rates to the customer. The sales location is required, because the local discounts must be applied to the rates before they are displayed. The individual and club discounts (if applicable) must also be included.

However, there is a problem. If the person taking the reservation knows the location number (e.g., the customer wants a local reservation), then all is well. But what happens if the sales person does not know the number of the desired site? The number could be looked up in a book, but why bother in this case to have a computer system? What is really needed is a mechanism for identifying the sales location by address.

After consultation with the users, we decide to add a system-owned set SL to the DDL specifications. This set would be sorted by ascending ADDRESS. Moreover, the users will enter addresses in the form:

```
display "Enter customer account number:";
input num;
frk(CUSTOMER, num);
if (not found) then
    {display "Enter customer name:";
     input name;
     t = 0;
     fmsk(CUS, name);
     do while (found)
          {getm(CUS, customer);
           display customer.addr, customer.tele;
           display "Is this the correct person (Y/N)?";
           if (qyn ()) then
                {t = 1;
                 break;
                 }
           fnmsk(CUS, name);
           }
     if (t = 0) then
     perform process-new-customer;
}
soc(makes);
```

Fig. 13.17   Processing customers.

ST:City:Address

where ST is the two letter state code and city is the city name (the alternative of using three data items was discussed, but the users did not feel the extra complexity was necessary).

Finding the sales location is now similar to finding customers. We use **frk** if possible, but resort to **fmsk** and a menu if necessary. The processing is shown in Fig. 13.18. Procedure display-rates-with-discounts is similar to pick-rate above, except the local and individual discounts would be factored in.

All that remains, should the customer wish to place a reservation, is to establish the dropoff location and collect the data values for the CONTRACT data items. Then the CONTRACT occurrence can be created.

What happens when a customer wishes to change a reservation? That CONTRACT occurrence must be located, the information displayed, and then updates performed. The simplest way to find the contract is to intersect the set of contracts for the customer (MAKES) with the PICKUP sales location; using $SYSSET, these occurrences can then be checked and updated as necessary. This processing is outlined in Fig. 13.19.

```
display "Enter location number (or 0):"
input n;
if (n = 0) then
  {display "Enter ST:city-";
   input temp;
   fmsk(SL, temp);
   sales.address = temp;
   display "Choose by location number the proper location:"
   do while (temp = sales.address)
      {getm(SL, salesloc);
       display sales.number, sales.address;
       fnm(SL);
       }
   input n;
   }
frk(SALESLOC, n);
if (not found) then perform oops;
soc(PICKUP);
perform pick-class-from menu;   /* The Makes and Models within a class should */
perform find-class-from-y;      /* also be displayed for convenience */
smm(PRICE, CLA);
perform display-rates-with-discounts;
```

Fig. 13.18   Displaying rate information.

```
perform find-customer; /* As in Fig. 13.17 */
v = 1;
suc(v);
perform find-location; /* As in Fig. 13.18 */
v = 2;
suc(v);
amm(MAKES, PICKUP, $SYSSET);

do while (found)
   { getm($SYSSET, contract);
     display contract.outdate;
     display "Is this the right date (Y/N)?";
     if ( qyn ( ) ) then break;
     fnm($SYSSET);
     }
if (not found) perform no-contract;
smm(MAKES, $SYSSET);
⋮
/* Perform Usual Deletes and Data Item, Set Owner Updates */
⋮
```

Fig. 13.19   Locating existing contracts.

13.8   THE COUNTER LOAD PROGRAM

When a customer walks up to a sales counter, several things may be happening. The customer may want to rent a car. If there is no reservation for that customer, then a contract must be filled out. Once a contract has been agreed upon, a particular car must be located of the size class desired by the customer. If no such unit is available, then the customer may be given the next larger size car at the quoted rate.

Alternatively, the customer may be returning a car. The sales person must determine if the car may be rented out again after a cleanup or if the car should be sent to a service center for repairs.

The outline of the main programs are given in Fig. 13.20. For rentals, if there is no reservation, the previously described programs are called in order to fill out the contract. If there is a reservation, **amm** is used to find the reservation. The customer is then assigned a car of the appropriate class; the CAR occurrence is moved from that sales location to the contract in the set STATUS.

For the returns, the CAR record is removed from the CONTRACT record and reconnected to either a SALESLOC or SERVICE record. In the latter case the service history entry is begun.

```
/* Assume this location is current member of SL */
display "Today's Date:";
input date;
display "Is this a (1) Rental or (2) Return?";
input n;
if (n = 1) then                              /* RENTAL */
  { input "Is there a reservation (Y/N)?"
    if ( qyn ( )) then
      { perform find-customer;
        v = 1;
        suc(v);
        v = 2;
        sum(SL, v);
        amm(MAKES, PICKUP, $SYSSET);
        fmi(OUTDATE, $SYSSET, date);
        if (not found) then perform oops-1;   /* Find By Some Other Means */
        smc(Makes);
        }
    else
        perform make-contract;
    perform find-a-car;
    rms(STATUS);
    som(STATUS, MAKES);
```

Fig. 13.20   Counter processing.

```
            scm(UNIT);
            ims(STATUS);
            }
        else
        { perform find-customer;
          v = 1;
          suc(v);
          v = 2;
          sum(SL, v);
          amm(MAKES, DROPOFF, $SYSSET);
          fmi(INDATE, $SYSSET, date);
          if (not found) then perform oops-2; /* Find by Some Other Means */
          som(STATUS, $SYSSET);
          if (not found) then perform error;
          smm(UNIT, STATUS);
          rms(STATUS);
          display "Does this car need service (Y/N)?"
          if (qyn( ) ) then
              { display "Enter service center #: ";
                input x;
                fmsk(SER, x);
                if (not found) then perform oops-3; /* Try Again */
                getm(SER, service);
                display "Call" service.tele, service.manager;
                som(STATUS, SER);
                scm(UNIT);
                ism(STATUS);
                som(HEAL, SER);
                som(SICK, UNIT);
                history.indate = date;
                display "Symptoms are:";
                input history.complnt;
                crs(HISTORY, history);
                }
        else
            { som(STATUS, SL);
              scm(UNIT);
              ims(STATUS);
              }
        }
```

Fig. 13.20   *(Continued)*

13.9 OTHER APPLICATION PROGRAMS

One program that must be developed is the program that forecasts demand for cars at each sales location for a particular day. This program would be used to instigate transportation of units from one location to another to meet the antici-pated demand. The demands would have to be computed by size class. Another program is required to note the release of automobiles from service centers to sales locations including the completion of the service history report.

One report program already discussed would determine, for a particular date, those cars due for license renewal within a certain period following that date. Another similar program would prepare lists of club members who do not permit automatic billing of membership fees and whose membership must be renewed.

Other report programs would summarize the service histories of various makes and models of cars for future purchase planning. This kind of analysis would spot the lemons very quickly and management might be able to put off future pur-chases of these models. Service histories can also be used to evaluate the repair record of the service centers by noting how many cars become repeaters for service.

Processing the customer records for marketing purposes has already been discussed. Trend analysis of customer rentals could also be used to predict future demand for the different classes of cars. Analysis could also be performed on the various rate plans to determine the more popular features within each size class.

13.10 SUMMARY

The example discussed in this chapter is not designed to provide an exhaustive enumeration of DBMS features nor is it especially designed to show how car rental companies operate. Rather, the purpose is to provide a more complex and less stylized example of the problems of design and implementation that can arise in the development of nontrivial application systems. In particular, it may be useful to depart from formal algorithmic schema design techniques when con-fronted by complex real world problems. This is especially true as the developer becomes more experienced and adept at schema design. The design process is typically iterative and subject to a variety of refinements.

The programs are all extensions of the previous examples and methods. In many cases it is not even necessary to specify what the processing is; so greatly does it follow the developed patterns. In designing application programs, a sense of time is important: knowing in which sequence data are made available is a most useful guide in the design of load programs.

The security system is used in the example to prohibit certain users from accessing and modifying certain data values. The security system is worth mas-tering, since the internal controls it provides are sufficient to minimize exposures in many instances.

RELATED READINGS

Micro Data Base Systems Inc., "MDBS Application Programming Reference Manual," Lafayette, Indiana, 1981.
Micro Data Base Systems Inc., "MDBS Data Base Design Reference Manual," Lafayette, Indiana, 1981.
TLB Associates, "Solomon III," Computech Group Inc., Frazer, Penn., 1983.
ADP, "Cash Express Workstation User Manual," Detroit, 1984.

EXERCISES

1. Suppose you have only a relational DBMS. Design a schema for the car rental application, which is capable of supporting all reports that can be generated from the extended-network schema.
2. Using inverted file techniques, design a system that can support all aspects of the car rental application.
3. Develop a hierarchical schema capable of supporting the car rental application.
4. Convert the extended-network schema for the car rental application into a shallow-network structure.
5. Suppose you have only a CODASYL-network DBMS. Design a schema for the car rental application, which is capable of supporting all reports that can be generated from the extended-network schema.
6. Explain why it is undesirable to have OUTLOC, INLOC, and SUPER (Fig. 13.1) as data items in the car rental schema.
7. Explain why it is inappropriate to represent LOCATION in terms of an M:N set.
8. Describe 10 ad hoc reports that might be needed by a user of the car rental system. For each, show the QRS query that can generate that report.

Chapter 14

OTHER DEVELOPMENT ISSUES

In preceding Chapters 4–13 we have examined the central and essential components of a DBMS. Now that the reader has acquired considerable expertise in the usage of database management for application system development, we shall take up a few miscellaneous development issues which are of interest to most application developers.

First we delve into the construction of convenient end–user interfaces to an application system that is based on database facilities. This includes a discussion of how a developer can use QRS to define virtual tables. These virtual tables serve as tabular end user views which support direct ad hoc interrogation of a database by end users. Another variety of user-friendly interface is the application software built for routine repetitive data processing tasks. As explained in Chapter 2, screen handling tools play a crucial role in constructing such an interface. Here we examine the highlights of a very extensive screen handler called SCREEN MASTER and a report writer called RDL.

After exploring the construction of user-friendly interfaces with developer-friendly tools, we address the issues of physical and logical data restructuring. Finally, there is a discussion of mechanisms that can be built into a database control system to guard against database inconsistencies in the event of abnormal termination of application software. Other built-in mechanisms that allow recovery from an inconsistent state or physical database destruction are also described.

14.1   TABULAR END-USER VIEWS†

The very developer-friendly QRS language was introduced in Chapter 9. It enables a developer to effortlessly produce any of a wide variety of output tables (i.e., flat files) on the spur of the moment. We have seen that each query can be stated in terms of an extended-network schema. An application developer can readily understand logical structures of the extended-network variety.

QRS is also quite friendly for end users. Extended network logical structures are by no means beyond the comprehension of nontechnical end users, for their pictorial forms are very similar to conceptual schemas of the entity-attribute-relationship (EAR) variety.‡ End users can conceive of rectangles as entities, data items as attributes of entities, and arrows as relationships that are 1:1, 1:N, N:1, or M:N in nature. Thus queries can be posed in terms of entities, attributes, and their relationships. Of course, the end user who poses such queries is entirely unconcerned with the physical representation of data in the database.

Despite of the elegance and conceptual simplicity of extended-network schemas, there are those who advocate that end users should be restricted to tabular views of data; they should conceive of data as being organized according to a schema of disjoint tables. The macro definition facility of QRS can be used to define tabular views of the database. An end user can then use QRS to state queries in terms of a tabular logical structure. This means that with an extended-network DBMS, a developer has extensive flexibility with respect to the kinds of logical views that can be presented to end users. These range from various tables (i.e., flat files) to hierarchical, shallow-network, and CODASYL-network sub-sets of the overall logical structure to conceptual schemas.

What the End User Sees

A variety of distinct logical views is shown in Fig. 14.1. All of these views are supported by QRS. Note that a user of any of these views is never concerned with physical access paths, indices, pointer chaining, or file handling. Figure 14.2 illustrates a few of the many possible tabular views that can be defined for the comprehensive extended-network schema of Fig. 14.1. To obtain a report, the end user chooses an appropriate table and submits a query describing what data are desired. This end user is unconcerned with the alternative logical views.

---

†This section is partially based on "A Multipurpose Query System for End Users and Application Developers" by C. W. Holsapple, 1982.

‡See, for example, "A Tutorial on Data Modelling Using Entity Types, Attributes and Relationships" by T. W. Olle in *Data Base Management: Theory and Applications* (C. W. Holsapple and A. B. Whinston, eds.), Reidel, Dordrecht, 1983.

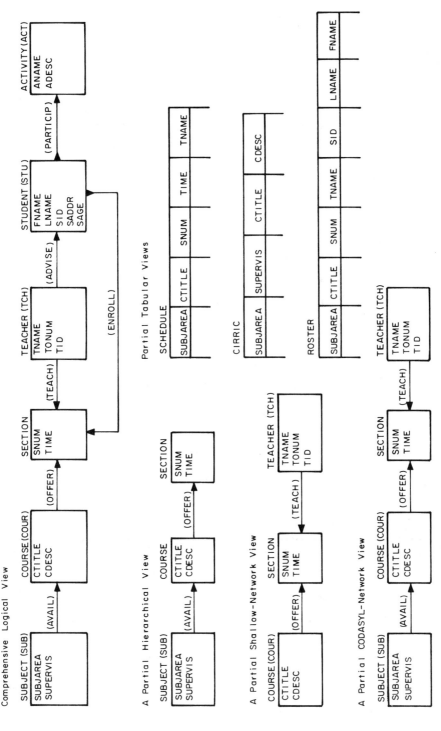

Fig. 14.1 A variety of logical views.

SCHEDULE

SUBJAREA	CTITLE	SNUM	TIME	TNAME

TEACHES

TNAME	TONUM	TID	LNAME	FNAME	SID

CIRRIC

SUBJAREA	SUPERVIS	CTITLE	CDESC

ADVISES

TNAME	TONUM	TID	LNAME	FNAME	SID

ACTIV

ANAME	ADESC	FNAME	LNAME	SID	SADDR	SAGE

ROSTER

SUBJAREA	CTITLE	SNUM	TNAME	SID	LNAME	FNAME

STCOUR

SID	LNAME	FNAME	SADDR	SNUM	TNAME	TIME	CTITLE	SUBJAREA

STSTATUS

LNAME	FNAME	SID	SADDR	SAGE	TNAME	ANAME

Fig. 14.2   Example end-user tabular views.

For instance, to obtain a report showing teacher names and identification numbers of the students they advise, the end user enters:

> **list** TNAME,SID **from** ADVISES

For more selective retrieval, the end user can specify conditions. The following query produces a report of the names and identification numbers of all students *advised* by O. G. Fitzgerald.

> **list** LNAME,FNAME,SID **for** TNAME= "O.G.FITZGERALD" **from** ADVISES

For a report showing all students *taught* by this teacher, the query is identical except the TEACHES table is used instead of the ADVISES table:

> **list** LNAME,FNAME,SID **for** TNAME= "O.G.FITZGERALD" **from** TEACHES

Note that table names are selected to be descriptive of the nature of the relationships among their data items. For instance, the TEACHES and AD-VISES tables have the same data items. A developer defines the TEACHES table for representing teachers and the students whom they teach. The ADVISES table is defined to represent teachers and the students whom they advise. Of course, in the underlying database there is no redundancy of teacher or student information.

The ability of QRS to support tabular end user views, means that an end user sees only the tables and need not realize that they are virtual. When stating a query, an end user needs to consider only one table. Because of the flexibility that a developer has in defining virtual tables, an end user need not think about the complexity of combining data from various tables based on redundant fields.

The truly innovative aspect of all of this is that it is based on an extended-network DBMS. This means that a developer need not sacrifice the power and flexibility of the extended-network approach to provide a tabular appearance. There is no sacrifice in the convenience of conceptual data structuring and associated data manipulation that is furnished with the extended-network approach. Nor is there a sacrifice in the relatively efficient storage and processing performance achievable with the extended-network approach. Also, there is no sacrifice in the ease of guaranteeing data integrity and security.

Defining Virtual Tables

By now the reader may have guessed how a developer can use the macro definition facility of QRS to support table-oriented queries. First, we define a macro named **from** having **thru** as its text. The virtual tables themselves can be defined very concisely in terms of the desired relationships between the fields of the table. Just as a sequence of relationships is used in a **thru** clause to indicate a desired output table, a relationship sequence can be used to define a virtual table.

The name desired for a virtual table is defined to be a macro name. The text of this macro is a sequence of relationship names. Like any other macro, a virtual table can be defined whenever desired.

As an example, the ADVISES table is defined as being a sequence of two named relationships: TCH,ADVISE. Once this definition has been made, an end user can ask queries about the ADVISES table shown in Fig. 14.2. For instance, the end user might state

list TNAME,TONUM,LNAME,FNAME **from** Advises.

This table-oriented query yields the same result as the QRS query

list TNAME,TONUM,LNAME,FNAME **thru** TCH,ADVISE.

Internally, the processing logic of the two queries is identical. Figure 14.3 depicts the relationship sequences used to define the tables shown in Fig. 14.2.

Interestingly, the ADVISES table as defined above can be presented to an end user in forms other than that shown in Fig. 14.2. As shown in Fig. 14.4, the ADVISES table could be presented as supersets or subsets of the ADVISES table shown in Fig. 14.2. Regardless of which of these versions of ADVISES is (or are) presented to an end user, QRS queries are stated in the usual manner. A query can refer to any fields within the presented table and the query ends with the clause "**from** ADVISES". All QRS selective retrieval features are allowed as are control breaks.

Note that there is always a maximal table with respect to a sequence of relationships. It consists of all fields of all record types belonging to the relationship sequence. For instance, the second form of ADVISES shown in Fig. 14.4 is the maximal table for TCH,ADVISE. Any query that can be posed for any subset of a maximal table can also be posed (with no alteration) for the maximal table. This suggests that, to avoid a large number of tables, the developer may want to present only maximal tables to an end user.

For security reasons, it may happen that an end user has access to some, but not all, fields of a maximal table. If an end user is presented with such a maximal

SCHEDULE	SUB, AVAIL, OFFER, >TEACH
TEACHES	TCH, TEACH, >ENROLL
CURRIC	SUB, AVAIL, OFFER
ADVISES	TCH, ADVISE
ACTIV	ACT, >PARTICIP
ROSTER	SUB, AVAIL, OFFER, >TEACH, >ENROLL
STCOUR	STU, ENROLL, >TEACH, >OFFER, >AVAIL
STSTATUS	STU, >ADVISE, PARTICIP

Fig. 14.3   Defining tables with relationship sequences.

ADVISES

TNAME	TONUM	TID	LNAME	FNAME	SAGE	SID

ADVISES

TNAME	TONUM	TID	LNAME	FNAME	SID	SADDR	SAGE

ADVISES

TID	SID

ADVISES

TNAME	TID	LNAME	FNAME	SADDR

Fig. 14.4   Alternative presentations of the ADVISES table.

table, attempts to access restricted fields are automatically thwarted. From the standpoint of user-friendliness, it is advisable for a developer to present the end user with a maximal secure table rather than the maximal table. A maximal secure table contains only those fields of the maximal table which are accessible by an end user. Clearly, there can be many maximal secure tables for a given maximal table, depending on variations in end users' security clearances.

The left-to-right order of fields within a table presentation is, of course, irrelevant to QRS. Nevertheless, it can be important to an end user. It is recommended that the fields be presented in the same order in which they are encountered through the relationship sequence that defines the table. This protocol was followed for the tables presented in Fig. 14.2. The value of observing such a protocol can be seen from a simple example. Consider the two maximal tables shown in Fig. 14.5. Although these tables have the same fields, they have different definitions and therefore different names (ADVISES and ADVISED).

The left-to-right arrangement of fields in ADVISES suggests that as we examine the table we are interested in looking first at a teacher and then at the students that the teacher advises. Very natural queries to ask for the ADVISES table include

ADVISES

TNAME	TONUM	TID	FNAME	LNAME	SID	SADDR	SAGE

where ADVISES is defined to be TCH, ADVISE

ADVISED

FNAME	LNAME	SID	SADDR	SAGE	TNAME	TONUM	TID

where ADVISED is defined to be STU, >ADVISE

Fig. 14.5 Alternative definitions of similar tabular forms.

list SID,LNAME **for** TID=123456789 **from** ADVISES
list TNAME,LNAME,FNAME **from** ADVISES.

The arrangement of fields in ADVISED conveys a very different impression. Its organization suggests that it is convenient for looking first at a student and then at that student's advisor. Very natural queries to ask for the ADVISED table include

list TNAME,TONUM **for** SID=987654321 **from** ADVISED
list LNAME,FNAME,TNAME **from** ADVISED.

An end user naturally thinks of obtaining a report from the ADVISES table that is organized by teacher or conditioned by teacher data. Similarly, one naturally thinks of obtaining a report from the ADVISED table that is organized by student or conditioned by student data. Now suppose an end user, upon examining the ADVISED table, wants a list of student identifiers and last names for the teacher whose identifier is 123456789. The query is

list SID,LNAME **for** TID=123456789 **from** ADVISED

and the result that QRS generates for this query is comparable to the result that is generated for

list SID,LNAME **for** TID=123456789 **from** ADVISES.

However, the former is considerably slower, which is exactly what an end user would intuitively expect. If the end user were to answer the query by visually

scanning an ADVISED table filled with data, it would take longer than a visual
scan of a comparable data-filled ADVISES table (an exhaustive scan versus a
limited scan).

Thus a left-to-right presentation of fields, consistent with the relationship
sequence, has the desirable effect of intuitively guiding the end user into using
the table that will yield the fastest processing. It also has the effect of avoiding
confusion that would result if two presented tables were (aside from the names of
the table) identical in appearance.

There is a class of virtual tables that always exists. None of the virtual tables in
this class ever need to be explicitly defined by a developer. Each maximal table
in this class consists of all fields of a system-owned record type. For the Fig.
14.1 schema, this means that five maximal virtual tables always implicitly exist.
These are shown in Fig. 14.6. Notice that the table names are identical to the

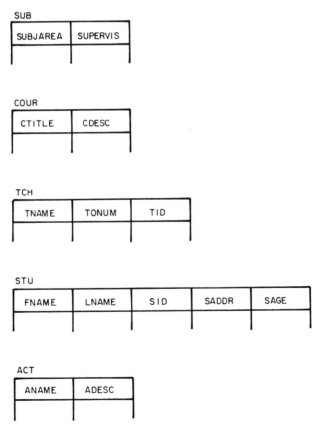

Fig. 14.6 Implicit virtual tables.

names used for the system-owned relationships shown in Fig. 14.1. The table-oriented query

> list FNAME,LNAME,SAGE **from** STU

is functionally identical to the QRS query

> list FNAME,LNAME,SAGE **thru** STU.

Of course, the developer can choose to explicitly specify an alternative virtual table name (e.g., STUDENT rather than STU) to present to an end user in place of the implicit name.

In cases where a given record type has more than one system-owned relationship, there is an implicit virtual table for each such relationship. Since all of these implicit virtual tables (in their maximal forms) have the same fields, it is important to choose their names in such a way that their content differences are readily apparent to an end user. For example, the COURSE record type might be involved in two system-owned relationships, one for all courses in a catalog and the other for all courses being offered in the present semester. The names CAT-COUR and NOWCOUR might be used for the implied virtual tables in order to make it clear to an end user that the two tables differ in content, even though they may have the same fields. Of course, in this dual-table situation there is no data redundancy, since the tables are merely logical views.

Defining Virtual Fields

In addition to supporting virtual tables, QRS can also be used to support virtual fields in the virtual tables. That is, the developer can define a field which does not actually exist in the database, but which appears just like any other field to an end user. A virtual field is a macro defined by an arithmetic expression involving one or more actual fields.

Consider the schema fragment in Fig. 14.7, paying particular attention to the CSALES (company sales) and DSALES (division sales) fields. The developer might define virtual item called RATIO as being the ratio of division to company sales (DSALES/CSALES). Figure 14.8 illustrates the two virtual maximal tables for this schema, augmented by the virtual field RATIO. As far as an end user is concerned, RATIO is a field in each table. As far as QRS is concerned, ratios are computed as needed to answer a query. Thus virtual field values are always up to date and consistent with values of actual data items. Example queries involving RATIO are

> list DNAME,RATIO **for** CNAME="XYZ,Inc." **from** COMPANY

or

> list DNAME,RATIO **from** DIVISION.

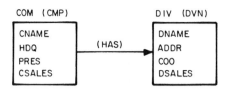

Fig. 14.7   Company-division schema fragment.

Note that the formula of a virtual item can be redefined at any time and that virtual items can also be used with nontabular logical views.

14.2   A SCREEN MANAGEMENT SYSTEM

The importance of screen handling in developing interactive, user-friendly application systems was previously discussed in Chapter 2. There are a number of screen handling tasks that are typical of interactive application software. Screen elements (i.e., titles, prompts, pictures, *slots* for data display and entry) must somehow be properly positioned on each screen that is displayed to an end user. The desired display characteristics of these screen elements must be obeyed when display takes place. These characteristics include sizes, color (foreground and background), intensity, blinking, underlining, bell sounding, and so on. A variety of data entry checks must be performed when accepting input from an end user. These integrity checks include feasibility range checking, completion

COMPANY

CNAME	HDQ	PRES	CSALES	DNAME	ADDR	COO	DSALES	RATIO

where COMPANY is defined to be CMP, HAS

DIVISION

DNAME	ADDR	COO	DSALES	RATIO	CNAME	HDQ	PRES	CSALES

where DIVISION is defined to be DVN, >HAS

Fig. 14.8   Virtual tables with virtual fields.

checking, and positional value type checking. To make the system user-friendly, there should be automatic editing of data entered by an end user, such as case conversion and fixed character insertion. The software should also allow an end user to edit data as it is being entered (e.g., to correct a typographical error).

Still another important screen handling task is the output of data held in program variables to the screen. Menus must be constructed and represented to end users as needed and an end user's response to a menu must be captured, so it can be used by the control logic of the program. The help text associated with each screen must be easily obtainable by an end user (e.g., by pressing a key). A related task is to restore a screen to its former state after the help session is completed. These are representative of the screen handling tasks needed for a user-friendly, interactive application system. Such tasks can be time consuming and cumbersome for a developer to implement with programming languages.

Here we survey the features of SCREEN MASTER, which is a highly versatile high-level screen handling tool currently available for use with MDBS. An exhaustive study of its facilities is far beyond the present scope. Nevertheless, it is useful to present briefly some of its highlights, for they are indicative of what an application developer should expect from a high-level screen handling tool.

As shown in Fig. 14.9, just as MDBS provides an interface between an application program and a database, SCREEN MASTER provides an interface between the application program and the console of an end user. Two languages are supported by SCREEN MASTER. There is a *screen description language* (SDL) and a *screen manipulation language* (SML). The roles of these languages are analogous to those of the DDL and DML.

An application developer uses the SDL to formally specify the structure and characteristics of all screens that are to be presented on a console to end users. This formal specification is submitted to an SDL Analyzer, which checks it for syntactic correctness and logical consistency. The SDL Analyzer also creates the screen dictionary, integrating it with an existing data dictionary. With SDL, the organization and characteristics of screens and the elements they contain are specified independently of all application programs and programming languages.

SML commands are invoked from an application program in the same way that DML commands are invoked. When an SML command is invoked, the *screen control system* (SCS) consults the screen dictionary and carries out the desired screen manipulation task. SCREEN MASTER provides approximately 50 high-level SML commands. These commands are used to select a desired screen or screen element (i.e., make it current), display–clear screens and screen elements, accept input through a screen, send output to a screen, display menu options and capture user responses, and so on. When an end user is entering data into a screen, the SCS automatically performs all data editing and integrity checking as defined in the SDL specification.

The SCS responds not only to SML commands within an application program,

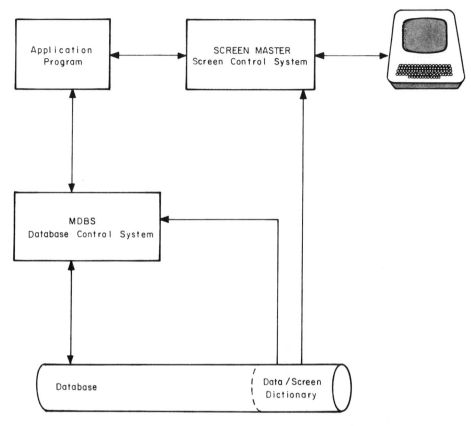

Fig. 14.9 The role SCREEN MASTER in an application system.

but also to a variety of control keys when they are pressed by an end user. By pressing an appropriate control key, an end user can control cursor movement, revise displayed data values, select a menu option, cause help messages to appear, cause the screen to be restored after a help session, and so on.

14.3 SCREEN ORGANIZATION AND CHARACTERISTICS

In SCREEN MASTER terminology, a *screen* is a rectangular image that can appear on a console. Each screen can contain windows and/or menus. Each *window* is a rectangular image that can contain titles, pictures, and/or frames for data entry and display. A *frame* is a *slot* that can accept data input from an end user or display data output from an application program. A *title* is a literal string used for description or prompting. A *picture* is a pattern of characters within a rectangular area. A *menu* is a rectangular image that can contain titles, pictures, and/or frames which are options that can be selected by an end user. When a frame appears in a menu, it displays data output but does not accept data input. Fig. 14.10 illustrates a screen having one window and one menu.

With the SDL, a frame is defined independently of the windows and menus in which we may want it to appear. When a frame is defined it is given a name and its characteristics are specified. Frame characteristics fall into four categories: type–size, background–foreground characteristics, input characteristics, and edit–integrity conditions. Permissible frame types are integer, real, money, unsigned, character, text, letter (i.e., single character values), date, and time. The size of the frame (i.e., number of positions occupied by a frame) is also stated. The background of a frame can be specified as any one of eight colors, as full or half intensity and as blinking or nonblinking. The foreground color of a frame can also be specified. Automatic underlining of the contents of a frame can be declared.

Any combination of eight optional input characteristics can be specified for a frame. These control the behavior of the screen control system as data are being entered into a frame by an end user. The data input can be declared to be invisible, meaning that the SCS does not echo the keys pressed by an end user to the console. A developer can declare that a bell is to sound whenever the cursor enters the frame. A prompt character can be specified for the frame. This character fills the frame until the end user enters a data value. An input default value can be defined for the frame; whenever a user does not enter data into this frame, the default value appears.

Left, right, or center justification can be declared for a frame, indicating to the SCS how cursor movement should function within the frame. A frame can be declared to be *completion required* which means that the SCS will not allow a user to exit the frame until it is entirely filled with data input. If desired, input to a frame can be prohibited by stating that input is not allowed. Finally, automatic advancing can be specified for a frame. This causes the SCS to automatically advance out of the frame as soon as it is filled with data.

The SDL supports nine optional editing and integrity checking conditions. First, a mask can be specified for a frame to indicate the type of processing SCS should perform for each position within the scope of the size of the frame. This processing includes automatic insertion of literal symbols in desired positions (e.g., appropriate insertion of hyphens in an employee identifier), conversion of the character entered in a position to upper (or lower) case, and integrity checking to guarantee that the symbol entered at a particular position is a digit (or alphabetic or alphanumeric).

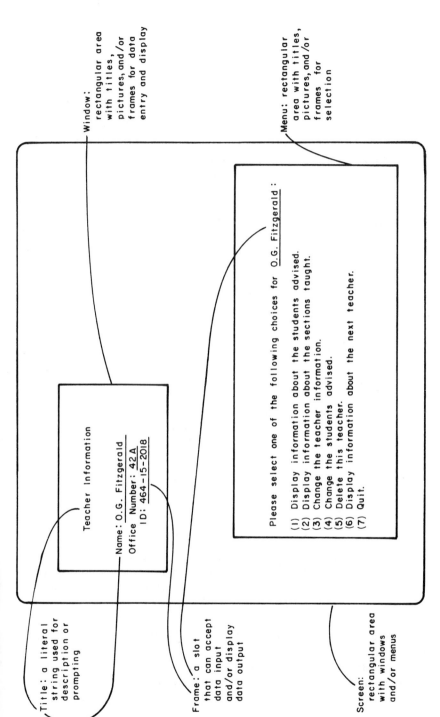

Fig. 14.10 A sample screen (with all frames underlined).

Window:
rectangular area
with titles,
pictures, and/or
frames for data
entry and display

Menu: rectangular
area with titles,
pictures, and/or
frames for
selection

Teacher Information

Name: O.G. Fitzgerald
Office Number: 42 A
ID: 464-15-2018

Please select one of the following choices for O.G. Fitzgerald :

(1) Display information about the students advised.
(2) Display information about the sections taught.
(3) Change the teacher information.
(4) Change the students advised.
(5) Delete this teacher.
(6) Display information about the next teacher.
(7) Quit.

Title: a literal
string used for
description or
prompting

Frame: a slot
that can accept
data input
and/or display
data output

Screen:
rectangular area
with windows
and/or menus

A second condition allows the developer to specify a fill character for a frame. If a user does not completely fill a frame, SCS automatically completes it with the fill character. Third, a format convention can be specified for money frames to indicate whether a U.S. or European format is to be used during automatic editing (e.g., 123,456.75 versus 123.456,75). Fourth a range of feasible values can be specified for a frame. Fifth, automatic case conversion (upper or lower) can be declared for all of the contents of a frame.

Sixth, the decimal point can be declared to be forced to a predetermined position in a numeric frame. Seventh, digits can be prohibited from a frame by so stating in the SDL source specification. Similarly, blanks and/or punctuation can also be declared to be disallowed within a frame.

The important point to emphasize is that all of the foregoing frame characteristics are declared only once for any particular frame. This information is held in the screen dictionary. All processing of a frame by the screen control system, automatically obeys all of the defined characteristics of that frame. That is, the processing is dictionary driven.

Like a frame, a picture is defined independently of the menus or windows in which it may appear. A picture is given a name and the locations of characters that constitute the picture are specified. The background and foreground colors of the picture are declared, as are its intensity and whether blinking is desired.

When defining a window in an SDL source specification, we give the window a name, indicate its rectangular dimensions, and state its background color and intensity. Beyond this, we can indicate which of the previously defined frames (or pictures) are to appear in the window and their positioning within the window. Titles can also be defined to exist within a window. As each title is specified, we indicate what the title (e.g., prompt message) says and where it is to be positioned in the window. Background–foreground characteristics for a title are declared just as they are for a frame.

A menu is defined in the same manner as a window, except that as a title, picture, or frame is assigned to a menu we can optionally indicate that it is a user option. Each such option within a menu is given a unique identifying number in the SDL source specification for that menu. During the processing of a menu, the screen control system allows the end user to position the cursor only on the options within the menu. Once an option is selected, the corresponding identifying number is passed to the application program where it is used in the control logic.

When a screen is defined in an SDL source specification, we give it a name and indicate its rectangular boundaries (it must fit on a console). Its background color and intensity are declared. All menus and/or windows that are to appear in the screen are indicated by name and their positions within the screen are stated. Furthermore, each window or menu appearing in the screen is mapped to a record type. For instance, a window with employee-oriented frames might be mapped to an EMPLOYEE record type. The window does not need to have a frame for every data item of the corresponding record type. Many windows or menus in various screens can be mapped to the same record type. When a screen is defined, we can optionally specify the content of a help message that describes the screen to an end user.

All of the above layouts and characteristics are declared only once and are held in the screen dictionary. Because all screen processing is dictionary driven, the application developer is relieved from all of the screen handling tasks mentioned in Section 14.2. Furthermore, the resultant application system is highly screen independent. We can alter the layout and characteristics of any frame, picture, title, menu, window, or screen at any time without needing to alter any existing application program. No program recompilation is necessary when we change colors, masks, frame positionings, titles (e.g., change English prompts to French prompts), and so on. The impact of all of this on developer productivity is obvious.

14.4   SCREEN PROCESSING

With the SCREEN MASTER system, end user interaction with screens is accomplished with screen control keys. These keys are configurable by the developer. They allow an end user to move the cursor within frames and between frames. They allow the modification of the contents of a frame during data entry. There is a key for making menu selections. Another key, when pressed, causes the help message of the current screen to be displayed. When pressed again, this key causes the SCS to restore the screen to its former state. During data entry an end user may inadvertantly attempt to violate the defined input characteristics of a frame. In such cases, descriptive entry status messages are given to the end user who can then rectify the error.

By using SML commands an application developer controls the sequence of screen (window or menu) presentation to an end user. Other SML commands control the transfer of data to and from a screen. For instance, there is a get current window (**gcw**) command which has a data block (or program record) as its argument. The variables of the data block are consistent in type, size, and sequence with the data items of the record type to which the current window is mapped. This command causes the cursor to enter the first frame of the window. When the end user has entered acceptable data for that frame, the cursor moves to the next frame. This continues until the user has finished entering all data for the window, at which point the data are transferred to corresponding host language variables of the data block. The program is then poised to perform an immediate **crs** or **putm.**

When SCREEN MASTER is used with MDBS, up to 90% of each resultant application program is typically composed of DML and SML commands. The remaining executable statements are for control logic and possibly computations. The DBCS and SCS perform the vast majority of processing (recall Fig. 14.9), in place of the application developer's own program code. This yields very compact application programs.

Application software developed with SCREEN MASTER is terminal independent as well as screen independent. This means that the same program can be used, without alteration or recompilation, for a wide range of terminal devices. The SDL and SML are both independent of terminal types.

As a final note, it must be restated that only the basics of SCREEN MASTER were discussed here. It has a number of more advanced facilities, many of which are quite subtle in nature, requiring careful study to fully appreciate their sizable impacts on developer productivity.

14.5 A REPORT DEFINITION LANGUAGE

The report definition language (RDL) is another aid that helps magnify the productivity of application system developers who build interactive systems using MDBS. A developer uses the RDL to formally specify the characteristics of a desired report and the prompting behavior of a program which generates that report. An RDL specification is input to the RDL Analyzer which checks the specification for consistency and syntactic correctness. If no errors are detected, the RDL Analyzer automatically generates a complete program which behaves in accordance with the RDL specifications. The resultant program contains the DML commands needed to generate the desired report. These are embedded within the control structures of a C host language. Optionally, the RDL Analyzer will generate a program that also contains SML commands.

The role of RDL in application system development and usage is illustrated in Fig. 14.11. RDL enables a person who knows nothing about DML, SML, and C to produce application programs written in C and containing all necessary DML (and SML) logic for extracting desired data from an MDBS database. The generated program handles all report formatting as specified with the RDL and can route the report to a printer (using preprinted forms, if desired), a console, or a disk file. The generated program will also prompt an end user for various information as indicated in the RDL specification. An end user's responses serve to initialize variables in the generated program at execution time, thereby allowing the end user to place conditions on the retrieval of data for the report and to control the appearance of the report.

An RDL specification can have up to seven distinct sections for specifying the behavior of the program that is to be generated:

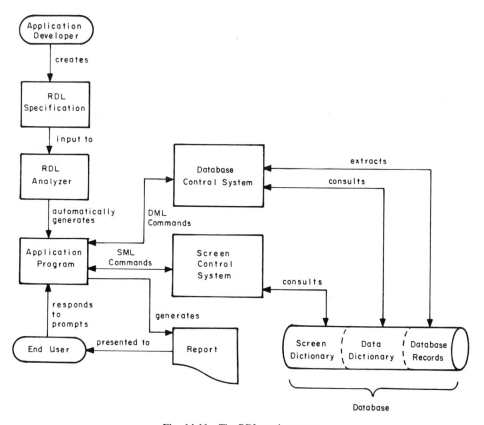

Fig. 14.11   The RDL environment.

(a)   Identification section.
(b)   Prompt section.
(c)   Output format section.
(d)   Function definition section.
(e)   Virtual item definition section.
(f)   Report details section.
(g)   Break section.

The sections must appear in this sequence. All specifications within a section are made in a free-form manner. The major characteristics of each section are summarized here.

The identification section is used to declare the name of the file that will hold the generated program. It is also used to indicate the name of the database which the generated program will utilize, a user id for that database, and that user's password.

A prompt variable is used to gather information from an end user. For each prompt variable declared in the RDL prompt section, the generated application program will prompt the end user to enter some data which will be used by the program to determine the ultimate appearance and content of the report being produced. For instance, the database name, user ID, and password might be treated as prompt variables. When specifying a prompt variable, the developer gives its name, type, size, and the prompt message that is to be presented on the console to an end user. Thus, prompt variables serve as parameters to the generated application program.

The output format section is used to specify output page depth and width, left and top margins, and the device to which the output report is to be routed. These can be either explicitly declared or they can be handled as prompt variables, enabling the end user of the generated program to determine these output traits.

A developer can optionally specify one or more functions that are to be used within the generated program. These are declared in the RDL function definition section. A function can have multiple input parameters. Within the definition of a function, local variables can be declared. These, together with global variables (e.g., prompt variables) and data items, can be used within assignment statements, if-then-else control structures, and test-case control structures inside the body of the function. Each function is specified so that it returns a single value.

Developer-defined functions, together with various built-in statistical functions (SUM, MAX, MIN, MEAN, COUNT), can be used to declare virtual items. This is accomplished in the virtual item definition section. Each data item is given a name, type, and size. In addition, a formula is specified, indicating how the value of the item is to be determined. The formula consists of a function (with data item parameters), plus an optional conditional clause involving data items. For example, FOR (YTDEARN<10000) SUM (YTDEARN) is a formula which says that the value of the virtual item will be the sum of all values of the YTDEARN data item (in the database) which are less than 10,000.

The report detail section defines the content of the report. In this section the developer indicates which data items (from the data dictionary), virtual items, prompt variables, and expressions involving any of the former three are to have their value(s) appear in the report. The physical position of each of these in the output report is specified. This section also has an optional **for** clause and a required **thru** clause like those that appear in a QRS statement. Furthermore, an optional **sort** clause can be specified to cause the report contents to be sorted on various criteria.

The break section allows a developer to specify page breaks and/or control breaks for the report. As in QRS, control breaks are stated in terms of data items. Headers and footers can be declared for control breaks. Page breaks are also stated in terms of data items; both page headers and page footers can be specified. Furthermore, an overall report header and report summary can be specified.

14.6   DATABASE RESTRUCTURING

Chapters 1, 5, 10, 11, and 13 have stressed the fact that there is no substitute for careful systems analysis and design during the initial development of an application system. The importance of building prototype systems, using relatively small volumes of data, and iterative prototype modification based on end-user feedback should not be overlooked. Failure to observe these considerations generally results in a patchwork system that is unnecessarily complicated to use and maintain, to say nothing of its relative inefficiency. However, even the prudent application developer finds that the nature of an application may occasionally change over time, necessitating changes in the application system. This is more often the case for certain kinds of tailor-made application systems, than it is for off-the-shelf application systems.

There are three types of extensions with which an application developer (i.e., maintainer) may need to deal. One of these involves the addition of new application programs, new query macros, new tabular end-user views, or new menu options without requiring any changes in the physical or logical organization of the existing database. These kinds of extensions are handled in a straightforward manner using the query system or data manipulation language. A second type of change necessitates physical restructuring of the database such as changing the page size of an area, the number of pages in an area, the number of areas, the actual positions of records in the database, and so forth. The third kind of extension involves alterations to the logical structure of a database. Logical restructuring encompasses the addition and deletion of data items, record types, and record type interrelationships.

Physical Restructuring

The motivation behind physical restructuring generally is to improve the efficiency of an application system. For instance, using the MDBS design modification utility (DMU) a developer can obtain statistics on the space utilization within each area. If DMU were to indicate that many calc overflows have occurred in a given area, then the developer may want to consider increasing the page size of the area or increasing the number of pages in the area. Physical changes such as these can be accomplished with a restructuring utility, such as the interactive *database restructuring system* (DBRS).

Even without the physical DBRS, a developer can perform physical restructuring. First, data existing in the database is dumped out to flat files which conform as nearly as possible to the existing DML program logic for loading data. The dumping process can be accomplished either with queries or DML programs. Next the source DDL specification is modified to reflect the new physical structure and a new database is initialized. The data on flat files is then reloaded. This usually requires versions of original load programs that have been modified to input data from files, rather than interactively.

Existing application programs are unaffected by physical restructuring of an MDBS database. This physical data independence exists because nearly all data manipulation commands are stated solely in terms of the logical structure of a database. The only exceptions are those relatively infrequently needed commands that explicitly reference a particular area (e.g., **dbclsa, dbopna**). If physical restructuring entails the reassignment of record types to areas, such commands (if they appear) should be carefully considered. Since these commands are sometimes used on the presumption that certain record types are assigned to certain areas, minor modification may be needed where such commands have been employed.

Logical Restructuring

While no DBMS guarantees complete logical data independence, it is fair to say that the degree of logical data independence attainable with MDBS is comparable to that of existing mainframe database management systems. The greatest insulation from changes in the logical structure of a database is achieved when a developer follows a discipline of using field-oriented DML commands (e.g., **pfc**), rather than record-oriented commands (e.g., **putc**). This protects against application program changes in cases where data items are added to or deleted from a logical structure. Of course, if there is little prospect of later needing to alter the fields of a record type, then there is no reason not to use record-oriented commands when dealing with the occurrences of that record type.

It should be clear that the addition of new record types or relationships to a logical structure in no way affects the functionality of existing application programs. It should also be clear that, regardless of the data model used, the deletion of a record type or relationship inevitably affects those application programs which relied on the existence of that record type or relationship. Program changes are needed in such cases. Application programs that do not reference the needed record type or relationship need no modification.

A separate issue from logical data independence is how to accomplish the desired changes in the logical structure of an existing database. There are two major approaches. One involves planning for change at the time that a database is designed. The other approach is to ignore the possibility of change until a change is forced upon us. We examine both approaches here.

Planning for change means that we build our schema in such a way that certain kinds of change are very easily and quickly accommodated. For instance, suppose we are uncertain as to whether a particular record type may eventually need to be system-owned. It would then be reasonable to declare a manual system-owned set for that record type in the initial design. No programs would utilize this set and, because it is manual, no storage cost is incurred by its existence. If it is later needed, then it already exists and is ready for use.

As another example, if we expect that we may need to add a data item(s) to a record type sometime in the future, then an extra data item(s) can be included in the record type when the schema is designed. If this is a string data item, then no appreciable storage cost is incurred until the data item is actually needed (if ever). When it is needed, the macro facility can be used to give it a new descriptive name for QRS or IDML processing. A variation of this technique is to define only one data item for a record type. This single data item is declared to be string in type with a large size (e.g., 200 bytes, with replication if desired).

For instance, rather than declaring five known data items with a combined size of up to 67 bytes, we might instead declare a one string data item whose maximum size exceeds 67 bytes (say, 155 bytes). Instead of storing a data value for each of five data items, we store a single string data value consisting of a value for each five kinds of data. As long as no additional kinds of data are required for this record type, the maximum length of any of its occurrences is about 67 bytes. This leaves the possibility of later accommodating other kinds of data within the record occurrences, up to a maximum of 88 additional bytes.

The advantage of this technique is that it allows new kinds of data to be easily added to a record type, without incurring any additional storage cost before the new data is actually added. Another (unrelated) advantage of this technique is that it leads to a relatively small data dictionary; this is important in environments that are severely restricted in terms of the main memory available. The main disadvantage is that an application programmer is responsible for parsing desired values out of a retrieved string data value.

Even though we may have planned for change, it may happen that we need to change the logical structure of an existing database. Many types of logical restructuring have an impact on the physical organization of a database. One way to accomplish a logical restructuring is to dump the database contents to flat files (e.g., via QRS), revise the DDL source specification, use it to initialize a new database, and reload the dumped data with modified versions of existing load programs. An alternative is to use a database restructuring facility, that allows incremental changes to an existing data dictionary and then performs all physical changes in the database that are implied by the schema changes. In the case of MDBS, the DBRS cited earlier handles both schema and database changes.

Such a facility can operate in one of two ways. It may automatically perform dumping and reloading of data to reconcile the database with its new schema or it may make the necessary physical changes in place. In theory, either method could be used by a DBMS implementor, regardless of the variety of logical structuring supported by the DBMS. In practice, making changes in place is a very difficult proposition for any type of DBMS that uses direct addressing or direct indexing. It is comparatively easy for a DBMS that uses indirect addressing or indexing, because all references to a record are in terms of a logical identifier (i.e., a logical database key) instead of a physical database key. The disadvantage of the indirect implementation is a relatively slower average access time.

14.7 ABNORMAL TERMINATION AND DATA INCONSISTENCY

It is an inescapable fact that abnormal termination will occur at some point(s) in the life of an application system. Abnormal termination is an uncontrollable or unexpected interruption in the execution of an application program. It poses two major questions for a serious application developer. First, what precautions can be taken to minimize the probability that an abnormal termination will leave the database in an inconsistent state? Second, if the database is left in an inconsistent state, how can it be restored to its most recent consistent state? These issues are of concern only for application programs that can modify the contents of a database.

We define a *transaction sequence* to be an interdependent sequence of database modifications which are interrelated in such a way that we want either all or none of the modifications to be reflected in the database. If only a portion of a transaction sequence enters the database, then the database is said to be *inconsistent*. A transaction involves one DML command. A transaction sequence can involve one or more DML commands. For instance, if a transaction sequence consists of a record creation followed by two set insertions, then the database is inconsistent if the transaction sequence is interrupted after a record is created and before the second insertion.

As a transaction sequence proceeds, the contents of some pages in the main memory buffer are altered. Eventually some of these changed pages may be flushed out of memory (i.e., written back into the database) in order to make room for other pages needed in processing the transaction sequence. When an abnormal termination occurs after one page has been flushed, but before all pages that a transaction sequence changes (or needs to change) have been flushed, then the database is inconsistent. At the very least, a DBMS should give us a warning if the database is inconsistent when we try to open the database following an abnormal termination. Attempting to further process an inconsistent database will only serve to compound the integrity problem. It should be clear that abnormal termination of a program that performs only retrieval should in no way affect database consistency.

There is a variety of causes for abnormal termination of an application program. They fall into two main categories. One category consists of media failures. For instance, a bad sector is encountered when the DBCS attempts to read or write a database page. Media failures typically involve the physical destruction of the data held on a medium. The second category involves system failures such as electrical power fluctuation, complete power loss, failure of the application software to take appropriate action in the event of a command status error, and so forth. These kinds of failures generally do not physically destroy data held in the database, but they can leave it inconsistent.

The same mechanisms that are used to recover from database inconsistency can also be used to recover from other types of breaches in data integrity. These include situations where the medium is lost, stolen, destroyed by fire, and so on. Also included are cases where a user enters erroneous transactions and the database needs to be *rolled back* to its state before the erroneous entries.

MDBS is available in two forms which illustrate the main alternatives for reducing the chance of database inconsistency and for recovery from an inconsistent, corrupt state. There is the standard form and the *recovery and transaction logging* (RTL) form. All previous descriptions of MDBS are applicable to both forms. Sections 14.8 and 14.9 examine how the RTL form differs from the standard form.

14.8   THE STANDARD FORM

As an aid in reducing the chance of database inconsistency, the standard form of MDBS provides a DML command called **dbsave.** This command has no arguments. Whenever **dbsave** is invoked, every page currently in main memory, whose contents have been altered since entering main memory, is flushed back out to the database. It may therefore be advisable to invoke **dbsave** immediately after the last DML command involved in a transaction sequence, particularly if the transaction sequence is a complicated one (i.e., consists of many DML commands).

In addition to **dbsave,** there is the **dbenv** command, which can be used to set the environment of a run unit. This command has a single variable argument whose value is input to **dbenv.** If the value is 3, then the DBCS will automatically invoke **dbsave** whenever there has been a change to a page in main memory. If the value is 2, then the DBCS performs *checksum* integrity checks on each page as it is transferred from auxiliary memory to main memory. A value of 1 suppresses certain error checking related to correctness of the DML logic of the run unit. For instance, it suppresses the check to see whether a record that is being connected in a set has already been connected. This has the effect of speeding up processing in a program whose DML logic is known to be correct.

The **dbsave** DML command provides no protection against media failures nor does it totally eliminate the possibility of database inconsistency. It does, however, allow us to substantially reduce the chance of inconsistency due to system failures by permitting us to control when pages are flushed out of main memory. For instance, suppose that an application program has a loop that prompts an end user for data, waits while the end user types in data, and then uses those data to alter the contents of the database. If we use **dbsave** at the bottom of the loop, then we can be sure that the database will be consistent while the end user is being prompted for the data of the next transaction sequence. If **dbsave** is not used, there is no such assurance of consistency.

If an application program terminates while the database is in an inconsistent state, subsequent attempts to open the database will yield a command status message indicating inconsistency. Recovery from such a situation depends on the existence of a *backup copy* of the database. This is an exact copy of the database as it existed in an earlier consistent state. Many transactions may have occurred since the last backup, because it is normally quite infeasible to backup the database after each transaction. The problem then is how to bring the backup copy up-to-date, so that it is identical to the last consistent state of the database before the inconsistency arose.

Very often, the data input for transactions will exist on paper after the transactions have been incorporated into a database. When the database becomes inconsistent, a copy of the backup copy is made and all transactions that had occurred since the backup are entered into the backup copy, just as they were previously entered into the original database. This can be a tedious, time-consuming process if many transactions are involved. It can also be a complicated process in those applications where the transactions must be re-entered in exactly the same order in which they were entered into the original database. For applications where transactions do not exist on paper (e.g., a transaction entered in the course of a telephone conversation), the recovery problems are even greater.

The inconveniences and problems just cited can be substantially alleviated by batching transactions to a file before they are incorporated into the database. This file then serves as input to a load or modification program. For instance, all of the transactions of a day might be batched by a non-DML program into a file, which is input to a DML load or update program at the end of the day. This technique has the advantage that the file(s) of batched transactions created since the last backup can be reinput to the load or modification program(s) to bring a backup copy of the database to the most-recent consistent state. It has the possible disadvantage that, while transactions are being batched, the database does not contain the very latest information. Another possible disadvantage is that this technique is not well-suited to those kinds of interactive data modification or loading in which the nature of each transaction depends on the present, entirely up-to-date contents of the database.

A variation of the foregoing technique, which overcomes its potential draw-backs, is to alter the database as each transaction occurs and also write the transaction to a file as soon as it has been incorporated into the database (e.g., just after a **dbsave**). This keeps the database up-to-date and still provides a file of transactions that can be used for recovery. It is advisable to structure the transaction file in such a way that the interactive load–modification program can be easily adapted to accept the file as input during recovery processing. This adaptation involves the suppression of most display messages (e.g., prompts) and the substitution of file input statements for console input statements. As we shall see in Section 14.9, this transaction file notion has been generalized, automated, and integrated into the DBCS of the RTL form of MDBS.

14.9   THE RTL FORM

The RTL form of MDBS has all of the facilities of the standard form. A database built, loaded, and maintained with the standard form can later be maintained with the RTL form. Any DML application program that executes with the standard DBCS will also execute with the RTL DBCS. However, these two database control systems are substantially different in terms of their internal implementations. Also the RTL DBCS is moderately larger in object code size than the standard DBCS. Whenever a DML command which can alter the database is executed the RTL form internally performs additional processing. This processing involves certain mechanisms which reduce the chance of database inconsistency in the event of abnormal termination and which prepare for recovery in case inconsistency does occur.

There are two major integrity mechanisms built into RTL version of the DBCS: transaction logging and page image posting. The RTL DML furnishes seven additional DML commands for utilizing these mechanisms: **trbgn, trcom, trabt, lgfile, lgmsg, lgflsh,** and **pifd.** Initially, we shall examine the transaction logging which is always performed by the DBCS and then the optional page image posting.

Transaction Logging

With transaction logging, every execution of a DML command that alters the database is automatically written to a separate file, called the *transaction log file*. The name of this file may have been specified when the database structure was defined. For instance,

DATABASE NAME IS DEPT
LOGFILE NAME IS "filename"

causes all transactions for the DEPT database to be logged to filename, where filename is the fully qualified name of a file under the host operating system. The **lgfile** command can be used in a program to override the log file specified in the DDL within the scope of that program. If used, **lgfile** must precede the **dbopn** command and the value of its argument must be a fully qualified file name. Another situation where **lgfile** is useful is in cases where the original DDL specification did not declare a log file.

As each execution of a DML command is logged, the DBCS automatically assigns a transaction number to it and stores enough information to reconstruct the effect of that particular execution of the command. This logged information is stored in a compressed form. Typically, the application system administrator begins with a fresh log file whenever a database backup is made. Old log files are generally retained off-line for archival and audit trail purposes.

At any moment the log file contains sufficient information to retrace (i.e., re-execute) all DML command executions that have taken place since the last backup. Accompanying the RTL form of MDBS, there is a special utility program called RCV that can use the log file to automatically reenact all processing that has occurred since the last backup, thereby bringing the backup copy up-to-date.

Very often the nature of an application demands that a sequence of DML commands be treated together as a transaction sequence, rather than as individual transactions. That is, either the entire transaction sequence should be committed to the database or none of it should enter the databse. An application programmer can indicate the beginning of a transaction sequence by invoking the **trbgn** command. The end of the transaction sequence is indicated by the transaction commit (**trcom**) command. These commands have no arguments. Logging continues as usual. However, there is a difference in the operation of RCV, which will not reenact any DML operation that occurred after a **trbgn** unless a matching **trcom** command has been logged. This means that if a program is interrupted in the midst of a transaction sequence, the RCV processor will restore the database up to the beginning of the interrupted transaction sequence. No trace of the partially completed transaction will appear in the database.

The RCV processor is an interactive utility that can be used to automatically apply all complete transactions existing on a log file to a backup copy of a database, restoring the database to its most-recent consistent state. An RCV user can optionally specify that only a certain range of transactions (i.e., transaction numbers) are to be used in restoring the database. This allows recovery from situations where erroneous (and complete) transactions were inadvertently entered into the database.

For an RCV user to determine which transaction numbers are to be used for recovery, RCV allows the user to scan the log file. This displays information about each DML command execution and its unique transaction number (as assigned by the DBCS). During this scan, any data values pertaining to encrypted data items will be displayed in an encrypted form only. To assist in understanding log file contents, the **lgmsg** command can be invoked at any juncture in an application program. This causes a message to appear in the log file. The programmer controls the content of the message by passing it as an argument of **lgmsg.** During recovery, RCV ignores all messages appearing in the transaction log file.

There is one last DML command related to transaction logging. When a DML transaction occurs it is not immediately written to the log file. Instead, it is placed in a small buffer in main memory. Whenever this log buffer is filled, the DBCS flushes its contents to the log file. If the developer desires to have its contents flushed more often (e.g., immediately after a particularly crucial DML transaction), then the **lgflsh** command is used as needed. This command has no arguments. It reduces the chance of losing DML transactions held in the log buffer due to an abnormal termination. Even if such DML transactions are lost, RCV can restore the database to a consistent state. However, the last couple of transaction sequences may have been lost because they were not recorded on the log file.

The transaction logging mechanism built into the RTL form of MDBS, together with the RCV processor, provides a comprehensive safety net that permits recovery from nearly all situations in which database integrity is compromised. The only exception is a case where both the database and the log file (or the database and the backup copy of the database) are simultaneously corrupted or destroyed. It is therefore prudent to have the log file (and the backup database copy) on a different medium than the database itself. It is also sensible to make new database backups (thus initiating new log files) and to make log file backups at reasonable intervals.

Beyond its value for recovery, the RTL transaction logging facilities are also useful in automatically maintaining an audit trail of transactions. The collection of log files generated since the inception of a database provides a complete trail of all transactions, showing the nature of each transaction and the sequence in which transactions occurred. Each logged transaction on a log file is uniquely identified by a transaction number. The identifier of the user who instigated a transaction is also logged. Also, messages (e.g., dates) can be inserted into the stream of logged transactions. RCV is used to examine transaction trails.

The RTL form of MDBS is also useful in application systems where it is important to maintain multiple duplicate copies of a database at remote sites. For instance, transactions may be entered into a primary database during the course of a day. Suppose that we need to have these transactions incorporated into many geographically remote secondary databases, before the start of the next business day. With the RTL form of MDBS, the transactions of a day are logged at the primary site. The daily primary log is passed to remote secondary sites over communication lines which can transfer text files. Each secondary site executes RCV, updating its current database with those transactions in the daily log received from the primary site.

Page Image Posting

The second RTL mechanism, page image posting, reduces the chance of database inconsistency due to nonmedia failures. It therefore reduces the likelihood of needing to recover from inconsistency (i.e., by using RCV). The posting mechanism uses a separate file to hold images of database pages. This page image file should not be confused with the transaction log file described earlier. The two are quite different. To activate the optional posting mechanism for a run unit, the page image file declaration **pifd** command is invoked prior to the **dbopn** command. The argument for **pifd** must have a fully qualified file name as its value. This file serves as the page image file used by the DBCS throughout the course of the execution of the run unit.

The DBCS will perform page image posting for a run unit only if the **pifd** command has been invoked. All transaction logging proceeds normally, as previously described. With the posting mechanism activated, the DBCS processes transaction sequences (i.e., series of DML transactions following a **trbgn**) in a special way. Within a transaction sequence, a page that has been altered since entering main memory is never flushed out to the database. Instead, when that page needs to be flushed, the DBCS writes the altered image of that page onto the page image file. The original version of the page, at the outset of the transaction sequence, remains untouched in the database itself.

This flushing of altered page images to the separate page image file occurs throughout the processing of all DML transactions in the transaction sequence. If a page that has been flushed to the page image file is once again needed in main memory for later processing in the transaction sequence, the DBCS brings in the altered page image existing in the page image file. It does not read in the original page version existing in the database.

At the end of a transaction sequence, the DBCS encounters a transaction commit (**trcom**) command. This causes the DBCS to transfer all page images on the page image file to the database, where they overwrite the corresponding original page images. After this transferral, the contents of the page image file are erased. In other words, the DBCS waits until the end of a transaction sequence before committing the effects of the transaction sequence to the database. This nearly eliminates the possibility of database inconsistency due to the interruption of a transaction sequence.

For instance, if a power failure occurs in the midst of a transaction sequence, the database is entirely consistent and current up to the start of the unfinished transaction sequence. The user merely restarts execution of the application program. The **dbopn** command causes the DBCS to clear the page image file contents. The user then restarts data entry for the interrupted transaction sequence.

To make the application system even more user-friendly, the developer can easily keep track of the last successfully committed transaction sequence. This is accomplished with a system-owned record type that has only one occurrence. The data item of this record type is of the string type. At any moment during the execution of a run unit, the record occurrence's data item value is descriptive of the last completed transaction sequence (e.g., a **putm** is invoked immediately following a **trcom**). Whenever the run unit is executed, the user is immediately presented with the description of the last committed transaction sequence (e.g., by means of a **getm**). This *warm restart* facility allows the user to easily know the transaction data with which processing should be restarted. Of course, there are several variations on this method for warm restarts.

There is one other DML command that can be used when posting is operative: **trabt**. This command causes the current transaction sequence to be aborted. Between the beginning of a transaction sequence and the committing of that transaction sequence, it may be desirable to abort the transaction sequence if certain conditions prevail. In such situations the **trabt** command can be invoked conditionally by the application program prior to **trcom**. This causes the page image file to be cleared. The database is still consistent and current up to the last **trbgn**. Furthermore, **trabt** is logged to the transaction log file, so that the aborted transaction sequence will be entirely ignored during any RCV recovery processing.

While the posting mechanism is very valuable in preventing inconsistencies due to system failures, it does not help in the prevention of media failures. However, transaction logging is available to recover from media failures that do occur. As an example of RTL usage within an application program, Fig. 14.12 illustrates how we can adapt the user load program of Section 8.5 to make use of various commands introduced in this section.

14.10 SUMMARY

In this chapter we have explored several miscellaneous development issues: end-user interfaces, database restructuring, and database inconsistency. As we saw in Chapter 2, all of these are important considerations for an application developer.

```
lgfile ("DCNSLOG");
pifd ("DCNSPIF");
dbopn(openrec);
altflag = 0;
trbgn();
do while ({display "Enter a user ID (or *):";
            input user.id;
            user.id ≠ "*"})
    if (altflag = 1) then
      {trcom();
       trbgn();
       altflag = 0;
       }
    {fmsk(SU, user.id);
     if (found) then
         getm(SU, user);
     else
         {display "Is this a new user (Y/N)?";
          if (not qyn ()) then continue;
          display "User name:";
          input user.name;
          perform find-site;
          altflag = 1;
          crs(USER, user);
          ims(SU);
          ims(WORK);
          }
     display "User ID:", user.id;
     display "     name:", user.name;
     display "Should this person be deleted (Y/N)?";
     if (qyn ()) then
         {som(SUBMIT, SU);
          if (found) then
              display "Can't delete—still linked to tasks";
          else
              {drm(SU);
               display "User deleted";
               altflag = 1;
               }
          }
     else
         {do while ({display "Any changes (Y/N)?";
                      qyn ()})
             {altflag = 1;
              display "Corrected user ID (or blank):";
              input temp;
              if (temp ≠ blank) then user.id = value-of (temp);
              display "          Name (or blank):";
              input temp;
```

Fig. 14.12 RTL command usages.

```
                    if (temp ≠ blank) then user.name = temp;
                    putm(SU, user);
                    display "User ID:", user.id;
                    display "       name:", user.name;
                    }
              smm(WORK, SU);
              geto(WORK, site);
              display "This user's present site is", site.name;
              display "Should this be changed (Y/N)?";
              if (qyn ( )) then
                        {altflag = 1;
                        rms(WORK);
                        perform find-site;
                        scm(SU);
                        ims(WORK);
                        }
              }
         }
    }
```

Fig. 14.12   *(Continued)*

While QRS, as described in Chapter 9, is readily usable by end users, it also supports tabular end-user views. Using the macro facility, a developer can define virtual tables (and fields) in terms of named relationships that exist among their fields. An end user can pose queries to extract data from any virtual table, using any of the usual QRS conditional clause features. At no time is the redundancy or processing inefficiency of actually storing data in tables (i.e., flat files) actually incurred.

Aside from end user interfaces for ad hoc interrogation of a database, we have also considered the creation of interactive application software for routine, repetitive end-user interaction with a database. An important aspect of this is accomplishing all of the needed screen handling tasks. A tool for automatically performing such tasks was briefly described. Called SCREEN MASTER, this tool supports a screen description language and screen manipulation language. These languages greatly simplify the definition and manipulation of user friendly interfaces. Moreover, they furnish a high degree of both screen independence and terminal independence. Another language for developing interactive software is the report definition language, which permits the automatic generation of interactive application programs.

The restructuring issue has two aspects: logical restructuring and physical restructuring. As a separate consideration from logical and physical data independence, there is also the question of how to accomplish logical or physical restructuring. With respect to logical restructuring, we saw that there are methods for reducing the need to restructure.

Database inconsistency was discussed from three angles: what is it, how can it be prevented, and how can we recover from inconsistent states. There are two forms of the MDBS DBCS: the standard form and the RTL form. Both provide safeguards for reducing the chance of inconsistency and database recovery can be accomplished with both. Many developers prefer to use the standard form. Others select the RTL form which performs automatic page image posting and transaction logging. This form also includes a utility that automates selective recovery from inconsistent states.

RELATED READINGS

C. W. Holsapple, SQL on the IBM PC, *PC Tech J.* **1,** No. 3 (1983).

Micro Data Base Systems Inc., "Query Retrieval System Reference Manual," Lafayette, Indiana, 1982.

Micro Data Base Systems Inc., "Recovery and Transaction Logging Reference Manual," Lafayette, Indiana, 1982.

Micro Data Base Systems Inc., "Screen Design Reference Manual," Lafayette, Indiana, 1982.

Micro Data Base Systems Inc., "Screen Manipulation Reference Manual," Lafayette, Indiana, 1982.

Micro Data Base Systems Inc., "Interactive Screen Definition Utility Reference Manual," Lafayette, Indiana, 1983.

Micro Data Base Systems Inc., "Report Definition Reference Manual," Lafayette, Indiana, 1983.

Micro Data Base Systems Inc., "Data Base Restructuring System Reference Manual," Lafayette, Indiana, 1984.

T. W. Olle, A tutorial on data modelling using entity types, attributes and relationships, *in* "Data Base Management Theory and Applications" (C. Holsapple and A. Whinston, eds.), Reidel, Dordrecht, Holland, 1982.

EXERCISES

1. Sketch out five different tabular views for the car rental schema of Chapter 13. These should be presented in a form suitable for end users. Characterize the potential end user of each view.
2. For each tabular view devised in Exercise 1, show how it is formally defined using QRS facilities.
3. For each tabular view in Exercise 1, state three queries for extracting data from that virtual table.

4. Show the normal QRS queries that correspond to the tabular-oriented queries of Exercise 3.

5. What are the advantages and disadvantages of using tabular views?

6. Why are virtual tables preferable to a system that generates actual tables (i.e., files) from which data is retrieved?

7. Are there certain kinds of QRS queries that an end user cannot ask for a virtual table which has been defined in terms of more than one relationship? How would you characterize these?

8. Explain how virtual fields defined for QRS behave like cells in an electronic spreadsheet.

9. What are the differences between frames and titles?

10. How do windows and menus differ from the standpoint of data entry? Do they differ from the standpoint of data output from a program to a console?

11. How are menus and windows related to screens?

12. Explain the significance of being able to process an entire window or menu with a single command. What are the implications for developer productivity?

13. Describe what is meant by terminal independence.

14. How would you perform all of the SCREEN MASTER editing and integrity checking, if you did not have this software tool? What would happen when you need to revise the characteristics of a frame, window, menu, or screen?

15. Discuss the analogy between the notions of data independence and screen independence.

16. Comment on the importance of careful systems analysis–design and application system prototyping as opposed to ad hoc, desultory application system development.

17. Explain how an extended-network schema can be designed so that a subsequent need for unforeseen data items does not necessitate schema restructuring. Why is this method inexpensive from a storage standpoint?

18. Describe how to maximize the data independence provided by MDBS application programs.

19. Suggest a series of queries for *dumping* data from the comprehensive schema of Fig. 14.1 into flat files which can then be used as input for loading data according to a different schema. Why do these flat files have redundant data?

20. What is the difference between a media failure and a system failure? Explain how each kind of failure can leave a database in an inconsistent state.

21. Why is a system failure in the midst of a transaction sequence troublesome? Explain how page image posting practically eliminates this problem.

22. What kinds of failures will the **dbsave** command protect against?

23. Describe the advantages of transaction batching.

24.   Would you expect the RTL form of MDBS to process updates more rapidly
       or more slowly than the standard form? Why?
25.   What is meant by transaction logging? Describe the kinds of protection
       furnished by transaction logging which are not handled by page-image
       posting.

PROJECT

Decide where the **dbsave** command should be inserted in your application
programs. Assume that the RTL form of MDBS is available. Determine which
programs should use page image posting and identify all transaction sequences
that exist in your programs.

Use QRS define tabular views pertinent to the application system. Have an end
user utilize QRS to produce reports from these virtual tables.

Chapter 15

MULTI-USER PROCESSING

The example presented in Chapter 13 illustrated both the use of database management techniques in programming and the process of designing an application system around a database. The methods followed were those presented in Chapters 5–12.

Many problems, including the case given in Chapter 13, have a layer of processing not yet considered in this presentation: the systems developed must be used simultaneously by many different individuals. For example, each rental and service office in the chain must have access to the computer system; it is highly likely that many users would require access to the computer at the same time. This, as we shall see, constitutes a major problem.

Modifications to the programming templates presented in Chapters 6–8 and 12–14 are required for these multi-user systems. This includes the introduction of another group of DML commands.

15.1 THE MULTI-USER ENVIRONMENT

One definition of a *multi-user system* is simply an application system that allows several users to access the database at the same time. In other words, several individuals are simultaneously running application programs (possibly the same program, in fact) and utilities (QRS, IDML) which use the same database.

In a computer system capable of supporting more than one simultaneous user, each run-unit is allocated a certain amount of memory. Such an allocation is often called a memory *partition*. Each partition is (normally) independent of all other partitions. Thus the processing performed by one user will in no way affect the processing of any other user.

In the database environment, there is a slight modification to this scheme. As before, each user is given a partition, independently of all other run-units; but a separate partition is reserved for the DBCS itself. This situation is depicted in Fig. 15.1. By allocating a separate partition for the DBCS, both the database control system and the user run-units have more "elbow room," that is, more available memory for processing. Each user accessing the common database shares both the DBCS and its data buffer partition with all other users. This is accomplished by implementing the DBCS using the concept of *re-entrant* pro-

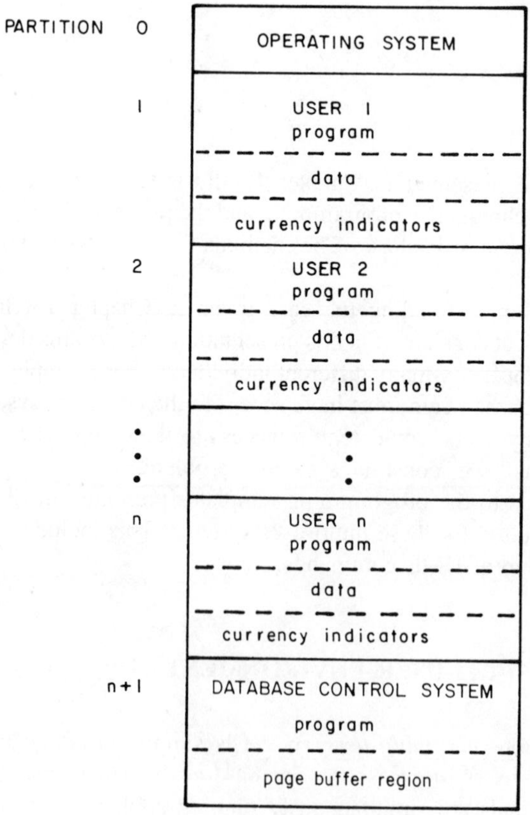

Fig. 15.1 Multi-user memory layout.

gramming, which means that different run-units can be accessing the same section of the DBCS program simultaneously.

In a well-designed application system, the user should not be aware of the fact that multi-user processing is occurring. In the case presented in Chapter 13, each salesperson would be updating contracts and the status of cars independently of other users. It would be a rare event that two users of the system would try to update the same record occurrence at the same time. When this happens, though, there can be trouble.

15.2 FUNDAMENTAL PROBLEMS OF MULTI-USER SYSTEMS

There are a number of inherent problems in a multi-user environment that are common to all multi-user applications (that is, which are not specific to database management). The most basic of these problems is how to handle the *concurrent update* situation.

Consider for a moment a simple inventory system where there are presently 100 boxes of item no. 23 in stock. Salesperson A has convinced a customer to purchase 75 boxes of item no. 23, contingent upon immediate delivery. Salesperson A sits down at a terminal, executes an application program, and is told that the current inventory level of item no. 23 is 100 boxes. However, in another office, salesperson B has just arranged a similar deal with another customer, this time for 60 boxes. When salesperson B executes the (same) application program, she is told that there are 100 boxes of item no. 23 in stock.

Salesperson A completes the deal and tells the application program that 75 boxes must be shipped immediately. Inventory is reduced to 25 boxes. Now B has made her sale too; what will the response of the computer be?

There are several possible responses. In many older systems, each application program accessed its own copy of the database; thus A's transaction would not have been recorded in B's copy. B's update would set the inventory value to 40 boxes. Then her version of the database would be written over the original, and presumably over A's version as well. This leads to the marvellous situation of starting with a stock of 100 units, selling 135 units, and having 40 units left in inventory.

Perhaps this situation could be avoided if A and B were not given their own copy of the database to update, but used the same version. Not necessarily. The standard method of programming the application program described above is given in Fig. 15.2. The appropriate item number is found and its inventory level retrieved. If the quantity needed is more than the current inventory level, then the *stock-out* message is displayed. Otherwise, the inventory size is shown to the

```
input need, item;
fmi(ITEM, SI, item);
gfm(INVTRY, SI, inv);
if (need > inv) then
    display "item must be backordered";
else
    {display "inventory is", inv, "units—is it a deal?";
    if (qyn ()) then
        {inv = inv − need;
        pfm(INVTRY, SI, inv);
        perform invoice-process;
        }
    }
```

Fig. 15.2   Updating inventory levels.

salesperson, and the program waits for a positive response. Once received, the inventory is updated in the usual way.

But this solution is just as bad as the previous one: A enters 75 boxes of item no. 23 and is told that the value of item INVTRY is 100 boxes. A turns to his customer for confirmation. Then B enters into her variables the values 60 boxes and item no. 23 and is told that the current value of data item INVTRY is 100 boxes. At this time, in both A's and B's programs their variables inv have the value 100. A now concludes the sale, A's inventory variable is reduced to 25, and the **pfm** sets the inventory value to 25 boxes. But now B concludes her sale. And B's inventory variable is *still* 100 boxes. Thus the reduction would compute 100 − 60 = 40, and the **pfm** would record the new inventory level as 40 boxes. This is of course identical to the above procedure.

How can this problem be solved? It is not feasible to attempt to change the values of variables in another user's partition when our own variables change value; apart from the technical difficulty of such an undertaking, it could make the second program behave erratically. At least conceptually, the update commands (such as **pfm**) could check both the old and new values of the item being updated; if the old value in the program variable does not match the database, an error indicator could be set, indicating that a possible concurrent update situation has occurred. This of course would have the effect of losing B's sale, since the desired inventory would not be in stock. The database, however, would remain consistent both in itself and with respect to the application.

There is another problem here—both B and her customer would have bad feelings toward the computer system. The system said there were 100 units of item no. 23, and then changed its mind. This can be unnerving, and has been known to generate much bad will.

One solution that many systems employ involves the concept of a *lock*. Generally speaking, a record occurrence can be locked (and then unlocked) by an application program. If an occurrence is locked, then no other program can access that information. In our example (Fig. 15.2), suppose that after the **fmi** command is executed, the inventory occurrence is locked. When A's program reaches this point, it will lock the occurrence. Then when B tries to find the same occurrence, an error indicator is set, saying that the desired occurrence is momentarily locked by another user. Note that this is determined before B's program can perform its **gfm;** thus B will not be told the inventory value until after A's transaction is completed and B would be informed (properly) that there is not enough inventory to cover her sale.

This is the more generally accepted solution. However, it too has its share of dangers. One is that A might need an hour to convince his customer to buy— they might even go to lunch. All this time the occurrence would be locked, that is, no other salesperson could access the information. The company could potentially lose many sales this way. It would also affect the re-order policy of the company.

One answer to this complaint is to train the users in system etiquette, so that A would understand the importance of quickly finishing the transaction. This could be backed up by inserting into the program the necessary tests that would deactivate the lock after a certain length of time, if no action has taken place in that time period. Giving the salesperson the knowledge that the lock will be removed in just a few minutes might increase his or her enthusiasm for making the sale.

There is a more insidious problem lurking here. Suppose that item no. 23 is never purchased alone, but always in combination with item no. 33. The current inventory levels of item nos. 23 and 33 are 100 and 120, respectively. Salesperson A's customer is interested in 75 boxes of no. 23, and needs 50 boxes of no. 33 to go along with it. Salesperson B's customer is actually interested in 60 boxes of no. 33, and need now only 25 boxes of no. 23 to go with them.

Note that in this case there is no longer the stock-out problem—there is sufficient inventory to satisfy both customers. Notice also that A's customer is primarily interested in item no. 23, while B's customer is most interested in item no. 33.

Figure 15.3 illustrates a program for handling primary and secondary requests. Following the pattern established above, the program first finds and locks the primary item. Then the inventory level of that item is checked and the user (the salesperson) is asked whether the customer wants to proceed. Once a positive response is obtained, the program repeats the processing for the secondary item.

Now A enters 75 units of item no. 23, and is told that there are 100 units in stock. While A is conferring with his customer, B comes along and enters 60 boxes of item no. 33. B is told that the stock level is 120 boxes. B now confers with her customer.

Note that A has found, and hence locked, the item no. 23 occurrence. B, on

```
/* primary */
input n1, i1;
fmi(ITEM, SI, i1);
lock;
gfm(INVTRY, SI, inv1);
if (n1 > inv1) then perform stock-out;
v = 1;
sum(SI, v);
display "Inventory is ", inv1, " units—proceed?"
if (not qyn ( )) then;
    {unlock all;
    return;
    }
/* secondary */
input n2, i2;
fmi(ITEM, SI, i2);
lock;
gfm(INVTRY, SI, inv2);
if (n2 > inv2) then perform stock-out;
display "inventory is ", inv2, " units—proceed?"
if (not qyn ( )) then;
    {unlock all;
    return;
    }
inv2 = inv2 - n2;
pfm(INVTRY, SI, inv2);
smu(SI, v);
inv1 = inv1 - n1;
pfm(INVTRY, SI, inv1);
unlock all;
```

Fig. 15.3 Processing combinations of items.

the other hand, has found, and hence locked, the no. 33 occurrence. Guess what happens next? A tries to find his customer's secondary item, no. 33, but is told that it is locked. At the same time, B is trying to access the no. 23 item, but is told that that occurrence is locked. A is waiting on B, and B is waiting on A. They will wait until one of their customers tires and calls the competition. This situation is referred to as a *deadlock,* or more poetically, a deadly embrace.

Deadlock is a big source of concern of multi-user systems. It need not be restricted to a pair of users (A and B in our example). It is easy to imagine situations where user A_1 is waiting for an occurrence locked by user A_2, who is waiting for an occurrence locked by user A_3, who is waiting for an occurrence locked by user A_4, and so forth, through user A_n, who is waiting for an occurrence locked by user A_1. There are two approaches to handling the deadlock problem: detection and prevention.

Deadlock detection involves trying to ascertain whether two or more run-units are in a state of deadlock. There are a number of methods of performing this test;

most are based on ideas of graph theory and matrix manipulations. Prevention tries to establish before the fact whether a particular action would lead to deadlock. The algorithms are similar. Both kinds of algorithms are relatively expensive in terms of system overhead. But this is not so much a problem for the design of application software as it is for the implementor of the DBMS.

From the point of view of the application program, the main problem is to react to the information that a deadlock may be occurring. In the example above, there are two possible behaviors that will break up the deadlock situation: A's program can unlock occurrence no. 23, or B's program can unlock occurrence no. 33. But we must remember that A and B are using the same program, (that is, two executing instances of the same set of instructions). How can the program be organized to release one lock, but keep the other? This is the primary problem of deadlock processing; we consider solutions.

There is one, rather trivial, approach to deadlock prevention that must be noted. To avoid the problems of concurrent update and deadlock, a user could request that no other user be allowed to execute at the same time that the first user's program is running. This is called *exclusive* processing. It solves the problems by converting (at least temporarily) the multi-user system into a single user system.

The database can be accessed exclusively by requesting such access when the database is opened. In the command **dbopn,** the third parameter can be specified as "EXCLUSIVE", instead of the usual "READ" or "MODIFY". "EXCLUSIVE" access permits modification, but locks out all other users while the program is executing. "EXCLUSIVE" access is only granted, however, if there are no other users currently using the database.

There is in this concept the potential for unethical behavior on the part of any one user. A user could request "EXCLUSIVE" access to the database; once granted, the user could "sit" on the database for long periods of time. During these periods, no other user could gain access to the database. This sort of behavior can only be controlled through administrative procedures and policies regarding nonproductive behavior.

The kind of locking mechanisms described in this section are examples of *active* locks, that is, locks which the application program must explicitly request. However, another kind of locking mechanism, the *passive* lock, can also be used in certain situations. Passive locking mechanisms for the database control system will be discussed first, and then the more potent active locks will be presented.

15.3 PASSIVE LOCKS

There are two major concepts underlying the philosophy of passive locks. We state that the database should not appear inconsistent to any user. This means that while a user is accessing and working with any occurrence, then that occurrence will not be changed by any other user. The second concept is that each user should be allowed to access (i.e., read) as much of the database as possible. This is because update operations often need to read many occurrences for every occurrence they update.

Passive locks are managed automatically by the DBCS. Whenever a run unit has in one of its currency indicators a nonnull dbk, then the record occurrence for that dbk is passively locked. This means that the record occurrence can be accessed (made current) by any other program, but that no other run-unit can change the values of the occurrence.

Having a passive lock on a record occurrence does *not* imply that our program may change that occurrence—it simply means that no other run-unit will change that occurrence.

For example, if programs A and B both have the same occurrence as a current member of a set, then both A and B can perform get and assign operations on that occurrence; but neither can modify the occurrence in any way. This applies equally to the situation where the occurrence is current for more than two programs. It is not necessary for run-units A and B to have the record occurrence in the same currency indicator. For example, A might have the x occurrence as current member of some set, while B might have x as the current owner of another set. Then neither may modify the values of x.

All currency indicators are checked in the determination of passive locks. This includes current owners and members of all sets, the cru, and all udi's. There is no way for a record occurrence to be in the currency indicators of a program and not be subject to passive locking.

Figure 15.4 shows the effect of passive locking on the various classes of commands, when the occurrence in question is passively locked by two or more programs.

The main problem yet to be resolved concerning passive locks is what action to take should a passive lock be detected when a DML command attempts to alter

Command Group	Effect of Lock
find	always permitted
assign	always permitted
get	always permitted
put	not permitted
build: create	always permitted
insert	always permitted
eliminate: delete	not permitted
rms, ros	permitted unless both owner and member occurrences are locked
rsm (rso)	permitted unless owner (member) is locked and member (owner) is not null
Boolean	always permitted

Fig. 15.4 Passive locking chart.

a record. One idea that comes to mind is to wait for a little bit and then try the command again; perhaps the other program will have finished with the locked occurrence, and it will no longer be current in that program. But testing after each usage of a DML command for an error indication of passive locks and then entering a delay loop within our program, would increase the size and overhead of our application program considerably. To the rescue comes:

mcc(p-record)   Retry each command var-2 times with a minimum delay of var-1 time units between tries.

Multi-user contention count (**mcc**) is used in a program to define how the program should handle the command retry and delay problem. The specified p-record must contain two integer quantities. The first, var-1, specifies the minimum number of time units that the DBCS should wait before retrying a command blocked by a lock. The time units involved are very much operating system dependent. The other variable, var-2, specifies the number of retries that the DBCS should perform before giving up and returning an error condition to the program.

The **mcc** command can be used repeatedly in a program to change the delay and retry parameters; the last invocation of **mcc** defines the current values of these. If both parameters are specified with a value of 0, then operating system dependent defaults are employed. The **mcc** may not be called before the database has been opened and **mcc** does not cause delays in our program—it only establishes the contention protocols to be used in the future.

When a DML command (e.g., **putm**) is issued, the DBCS checks for passive locks on that (member) record. If a lock exists, then the **mcc** protocols come into play; the DBCS waits for at least the specified time, and then attempts to perform the put operation again. This sequence is repeated until either the operation is performed or the given number of retries have been attempted without success. In this case, the put command is not performed and an error condition notifies the program of a passive lock conflict.

Logically, the next question is, what should the program do if the operation is not performed after the retries have been attempted? The best course of action would be for the program to release its passive locks on one or more record occurrences. In other words, the program must relinquish its currency indicators that contain the locked occurrences. To aid in this process is a set of new assignment commands, all designed to assign the null value to a particular indicator:

scn( )   Set the cru to null.
smn(set-name)   Assign to the current member indicator of the specified set the null value.
son(set-name)   Assign to the current owner indicator of the specified set the null value.
sun(variable)   Assign to the udi specified by the variable the null value.

These four commands can be used to effectively and efficiently remove a program's passive lock on an occurrence by eliminating it from the currency indicators of a program. There is yet another relevant DML command, one that works on a somewhat more global scale:

> **nci( )**   Assign the null value to all currency indicators (except for the owners of system-owned sets).

The null all currency indicators (**nci**) command restores the currency table to the state it has at the beginning of a program: only the system record is current. This is quite a drastic command in terms of its overall effect.

Once a currency indicator has been made null (or *zapped*), the program should be made to delay a few time units before the occurrence is reestablished as current. Usually this is easy to accomplish. The data values of the occurrence can be used in conjunction with one of the find commands to restore the indicator at a later time. Remember, all currency indicators, including udi's participate in the determination of passive locks.

Some general prescriptions can be made about program design with passive locking. One is to minimize the number of currency indicators that the program uses. When a record no longer needs to be current, then its indicator(s) should be nulled. A corollary is to avoid very long program sequences involving many sets, and hence, many currency indicators. In the multi-user environment it is much more preferable to have shorter sequences. Finally, try to restrict the use of report programs (i.e., those with read access) and the query system when data entry is being performed; such report programs have currency indicators, which produce passive locking as well.

15.4 PROGRAMMING USING PASSIVE LOCKING

Perhaps the most important decision to be made when writing multi-user programs concerns the contention count function: selecting values for the time delay and the number of retries and the processing that would ensue if the command is not completed. Although this problem cannot be fully resolved with any degree of generality, we can provide certain guidelines to be followed.

First, we must assume that the database is being accessed by a consistent set of programs. This means that the locking mechanisms of the programs have been coordinated in such a way that locking is performed in an equitable fashion. This can only be accomplished by strict design controls and procedures during the program construction phase. In particular, we assume for the moment that no run-unit will be using active locks.

A second, equally important consideration is that all of the users of the system have as their goal to maximize the *total* system throughput (i.e., the total amount of work accomplished). This will not happen without indoctrinating the users in the problems and benefits of multi-user systems. Each user must be convinced to temper his or her own data processing objectives for the good of the enterprise.

The third safeguard is control over report programs and query sessions while data entry is being carried out. Since record occurrences cannot be modified if they are passively locked, it is possible that run-units opened with "READ"-only status may strangle a data entry process. Administrative procedures must be established, and enforced, to minimize such situations.

Let us now examine a load program that employs passive locking. We will refer to the schema shown in Fig. 15.5 The employee information includes both each employee's current job, as well as past jobs held by that employee (in LIFO order). Two system-owned sets exist. These, plus the CURRENT set, are defined with automatic member insertion.

We shall consider the program that loads and updates employee information, including current and past jobs. We assume that occurrences of the record type JOB have been loaded by a separate program. The program in question will be constructed along the same lines as all those previously examined, but will incorporate some multi-user considerations.

Figure 15.6 shows the beginning of this program. There is no difference between this program and those previously considered (e.g., Fig. 8.8), since passive locking does not affect finding, retrieval, or creation. These operations can always be performed in a passive locking environment.

The next section of the program is the deletion section (Fig. 15.7). Here there is a chance for having an operation denied, since the given employee (the current member of SE) may also be current in the currency indicators of another run-unit, and hence, passively locked. Thus we specify a contention count through the call to **mcc**. We must also consider the possibility that the **drm** operation cannot be performed. If after the specified number of retries the error condition results, we will perform the procedure free-emp. This procedure (Fig. 15.8)

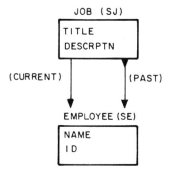

Fig. 15.5 Employee–job data structure.

```
do while ({display "Enter an employee ID (or *):";
            input emp.id;
            emp.id ≠ "*"})
   {fmsk(SE, emp.id);
    if (found) then
       getm(SE, emp);
    else
        {display "Is this a new employee (Y/N)?";
         if (not qyn ( )) then continue;
         display "Enter employee name:";
         input emp.name;
         perform find-job;
         crs(EMPLOYEE, emp);
         }
    display "employee name:", emp.name;
    display "          ID:", emp.id;
```

Fig. 15.6 Creation section.

```
display "Should this employee be deleted (Y/N)?";
if (qyn( )) then
   {cc.wait = value-1;
    cc.tries = value-2;
    mcc(cc);
    drm(SE);
    if(locked) then perform free-emp;
    }
```

Fig. 15.7 Deletion section.

```
free-emp /* clear currency indicators */
   {scn( );
    smn(SE);
    display "occurrence being accessed by another user -";
    display "change not made."
    }
```

Fig. 15.8 Releasing the employee occurrence.

assigns null to both the current member of SE and the cru. Then the primary program is repeated. Since this step involves an input operation from the user, this should constitute enough of a delay before the same employee occurrence is made current again by this run-unit. We hope that in that time span the other run-unit(s) accessing this record occurrence will be finished with it.

The same considerations apply to the update section (Fig. 15.9) of the employee load program. It is possible that a different set of contention count values are required for updating; thus **mcc** is called again here. If the **putm** cannot be performed, then free-emp is used to eliminate the passive lock on the occurrence from this run-unit.

The final section of this load program deals with updating the occurrences associated through the sets CURRENT (Fig. 15.10) and PAST (Fig. 15.11). For both removes and inserts, the only problem that may arise is that another run-unit may have the same combination of owner and member occurrences. After the specified contention period, we perform an **nci** to make all indicators null (Fig. 15.12); the same effect could have been accomplished through individual zapping commands.

It is necessary in Fig. 15.10 to consider the case of an employee being without a current job, even though one must always be specified during normal updating conditions. This is because, if the **ims** of that figure were to end in a locked state,

```
else
  {t = 0;
  do while ({display "Should these values be changed (Y/N)?";
             qyn ()})
      {cc.wait = value-3;
      cc.tries = value-4;
      mcc(cc);
      display "Enter correct name:";
      input temp;
      if (temp ≠ blank) emp.name = temp;
      display "                ID:";
      input temp;
      if (temp ≠ blank) emp.id = temp;
      putm(SE, emp);
      if (locked) then
          {t = 1;
          perform free-emp;
          break;
          }
      display "NAME:", emp.name;
      display "ID:", emp.id;
      }
  if (t = 1) continue;
```

Fig. 15.9   Update section.

```
smm(CURRENT, SE);
if (found) then
    gfo(TITLE, CURRENT, title);
else
    title = "none";
display "Current job is", title;
display "Any change (Y/N)?"
if (qyn ()) then
    {cc.wait = value-5;
    cc.tries = value-6;
    mcc(cc);
    if (found) then rms(CURRENT);
    if (locked) then
        {perform free-all;
        continue;
        }
    perform find-job;
    scm(SE);
    ims(CURRENT);
    if (locked) then
        {perform free-all;
        continue;
        }
    }
```

Fig. 15.10 Update the current job.

then the employee occurrence would have no current job, having already had the **rms** performed upon it.

In multi-user processing it is necessary to examine very closely the operating conditions that locking may potentially impose upon a program. In a single user environment, the employee would always be associated with a current job; the test after the **smm** would not be required.

15.5 ZAPPING STRATEGIES

It is clear that a currency indicator should be made null as soon as that indicator is no longer required for use by the program. A corollary to this statement is that after each iteration of a program loop, it is often wise to make null all of the currency indicators set (or potentially set) within the loop. In this way the number of nonnull indicators in our run-unit will be kept to a minimum.

Consider the linear structure depicted in Fig. 15.13. Suppose that we need to find a particular occurrence of E by first determining the proper A occurrence,

```
smm(PAST, SE);
if (found) then
    gfo(TITLE, PAST, title);
else
    title = "none";
display "Last job was", title;
display "Any change (Y/N)?"
if (qyn ()) then
        {if (found) then
            {ros(PAST);
            if (locked) then
                {perform free-all;
                continue;
                }
            }
        perform find-job;
        sco(CURRENT);
        ios(PAST);
        if (locked) then
            {perform free-all;
            continue;
            }
        }
    }
}
```

Fig. 15.11   Updating past jobs.

then the proper B occurrence, and so forth, using the sets SA, AB, BC, CD, and DE. If we assume that all of these sets are sorted, then a series of 5 **fmsk** and 4 **som** commands will locate the desired occurrence of E. These would also set 10 currency indicators (current owners and members of each set).

But consider the fact that we only wish to find the E occurrence. Thus after each currency indicator is used, we could zap that indicator. This is done in Fig. 15.14. After this sequence of code has been executed, the only nonnull currency indicator will be the current member of the set DE (and trivially the current owner of SA). This also will tend to minimize passive locking conflicts.

It may appear that we really have not lost anything by doing all of this, since

```
free-all /* restore all indicators to null state */
{nci( );
display "Change not accomplished—try again";
}
```

Fig. 15.12   Zapping all indicators.

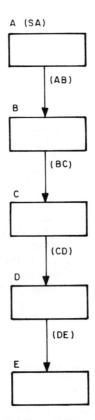

A (SA)

(AB)

B

(BC)

C

(CD)

D

(DE)

E

Fig. 15.13   Example linear structure.

we could use a series of **smo** commands to reestablish the members and owners
of these sets right back through the set AB. The difficulty here is the fact that
another run-unit may have altered one or more of the occurrences along this path.
This could have been either a change in data values, a removal and reinsertion
(changed owner for a member), or an outright deletion.

Perhaps the most insidious of these is the first, for it can lead to problems
reminiscent of the concurrent update described above. If one run-unit has retrieved information from an occurrence of A, and then released that occurrence,
another run-unit could modify the data values for that occurrence. If our program
returns to that occurrence, the values previously retrieved into *our* program
variables will no longer be consistent with those stored in the database. An
attempt to modify these values without examination could lead to the strange
behavior noted above of having 100 units, selling 135, and having 40 left.

Thus an occurrence should remain locked if it is to be modified. Further, we
should always perform a get on record occurrences that have been newly locked,
rather than trusting the prelock data values.

fmsk(SA, a);
som(AB, SA);
smn(SA);
fmsk(AB, b);
son(AB);
som(BC, AB);
smn(AB);
fmsk(BC, c);
son(BC);
som(CD, BC);
smn(BC);
fmsk(CD, d);
son(CD);
som(DE, CD);
smn(CD);
fmsk(DE, e);
son(DE);

Fig. 15.14 Minimal indicators.

There is another zapping strategy, namely the global zap. In this situation the run-unit detecting the lock will immediately perform an **nci** command. The effect is to release all of its passively locked occurrences, to ensure that a deadlock situation is not imminent. The idea is that the other run-unit(s) will then be free to perform their work.

There are two problems associated with this kind of strategy. One is that after we performed the **nci** command another run-unit could change one of the record occurrences assigned to our currency indicators. Thus when we attempt to restore those indicators, the occurrences may have different data values or the owner–member combinations may be very different. In either case, the restoration of the currency indicators may not be a simple process.

The second, but related, problem is that data values entered by the user will probably have been used to establish our currency indicators in the first place. Even if we have kept these entered values in our program variables, they may operate differently than they did the first time. For instance, an **fmsk** that worked before may not work now; or, the **som** may find a different first member than it did before. As noted above, it is a potentially dangerous practice to rely on data values obtained before locking.

15.6 ACTIVE LOCKING

Fortunately, many of the concepts discussed above with respect to passive locking also apply to active locking. The zapping commands, plus **mcc**, all perform the same functions. The zapping strategies also can be applied effectively. However, there are some differences.

if run-unit I has occurrence *x*	then run-unit II
passively locked	may passively lock *x,* that is, read from *x*
passively locked	may not actively lock *x*
actively locked	may not make *x* current in any indicator

Fig. 15.15   Locking precedence.

Most importantly, active locking is performed by the program under program control. This means that the program designer must plan for locking and antici-pate the repercussions of unsuccessful operations. The consistency and coopera-tion among programs is vital in this regard. Without standard coding conven-tions, plus the associated controls, the application programs will not perform any useful work—most of their efforts will be spent battling each other for access to record occurrences.

Having an active lock on a record occurrence means that our run-unit has exclusive access to that occurrence. In other words, no other run-unit can access that occurrence (i.e., make it current) as long as our run-unit has it actively locked. Our run-unit is free to access and modify the occurrence, secure in the knowledge that no other run-unit will tamper with it.

An occurrence can be actively locked only if it is not passively locked by another run-unit. Thus if we want to actively lock occurrence *x,* then *x* cannot be current in the currency indicators of any other run-unit. This includes current owners and members of all sets, the cru, and all udi's. The various cases are summarized in Fig. 15.15.

The importance of releasing locks cannot be over emphasized. Thus, for every active locking command, there is a corresponding unlocking, or freeing, com-mand. It is up to the application developer to ensure that occurrences are freed as quickly as possible; otherwise the effectiveness of the application system may be crippled.

15.7   LOCKING INDIVIDUAL OCCURRENCES

Before a record occurrence can be actively locked, it must first be passively locked. That is, it must be assigned to a currency indicator of our run-unit. In the processing for finding that particular occurrence, we will already have deter-mined if that occurrence is actively locked by another run-unit, for if it had been, we would not have been able to make it current.

The simplest command for locking a record occurrence is

mcp( )   Actively lock the record occurrence that is referenced by the cru.

The multi-user cru protect (**mcp**) command places an active lock upon the cru occurrence. The cru must be nonnull, that is, the occurrence to be actively locked must first be passively locked. The associated unlocking command is

    mcf( )   Free the active lock from the cru occurrence.

The multi-user cru free (**mcf**) command is one way to unlock a record occurrence that is actively locked. A second way is to modify the cru through the **scn** command or through any of the DML commands that alter the cru. Assigning a different record to the cru automatically will free any active lock on the previous cru occurrence and lock the newly assigned record.

Because of this fact, and the volatility of the cru, the usefulness of the **mcp** command is limited. We can only actively lock an occurrence after we have performed all of the desired assignment operations, since these all involve automatic finds and thus changes of the cru. In the program developed in Section 15.4, there is no benefit derived from active locking. For example, in the deletion section shown in Fig. 15.7, we might consider placing an active lock on the employee occurrence before performing the **drm;** this would give us the information of whether another run-unit is accessing that employee occurrence. But **drm** itself gives us that information.

The **mcp** command can be used effectively in a situation similar to that of Fig. 15.2, where only a single record type is involved. The difference between this situation and that of Fig. 15.7 is that the salesperson using the Fig. 15.2 program is in principle reserving units of inventory in anticipation of a sale. The active locking of the inventory occurrence has this effect. The revised program is shown in Fig. 15.16.

The **mcp** command cannot be used effectively in the processing outlined in Fig. 15.3, however. Here each salesperson is attempting to lock two record occurrences. A different mechanism must be employed in such situations. It is a quite common event that several record occurrences need to be actively locked. Since the number of active locks required is highly variable, the extention to the active locking mechanism must employ objects (currency indicators) whose number may vary. The obvious choices are the udi's,

    mau(variable)   Define active locks on record occurrences current in udi(1), udi(2), . . . , udi(variable).

The multi-user active udi's (**mau**) command is used to establish additional actively locked currency indicators. The value of the specified variable indicates how many of the udi's may be used for active locking. The **mau** command may be used repeatedly in a program to vary this number over time. Specifying a value of zero removes all udi's from actively locked status. The udi's (beyond the first 4) must first be allocated through the use of an **aui** command.

We now have the ability to specify up to 256 individual active occurrence

```
cc.wait = value-7;
cc.tries = value-8;
mcc(cc);
input need, item;
fmi(ITEM, SI, item);
if (locked) then
    display "This item is being modified by someone else";
else
    {mcp( );
    if (locked) then /* i.e., passively locked by another run-unit */
        display "This item is being accessed by someone else";
    else
        {gfm(INVTRY, SI, inv);
        if (need > inv) then
            display "Item must be backordered";
        else
            {display "inventory is", inv, "units. is it a deal?";
            if (qyn ()) then
                {inv = inv - need;
                pfm(INVTRY, SI, inv);
                mcf( );
                perform invoice-process;
                }
            else
                mcf( );
            }
        }
    }
}
```

Fig. 15.16   Using active locks on cru.

locks using the cru and the 255 udi's. As a rule of thumb, however, if we find ourselves requiring more than 10 actively locked occurrences simultaneously, there is a good chance that our application program is poorly designed.

An occurrence actively locked in a udi can be unlocked in two ways. One is to change the value of the udi, by one of the assignment commands (this would actively lock the occurrence being assigned) or by the zapping **sun** command. Another is to deallocate the udi as an active lock. If we have executed an **aui**(9) and an **mau**(9), and assign occurrence x to udi(9), then x is actively locked; a subsequent **mau**(8) will leave x in udi(9), but the active lock will be removed; x will of course still be passively locked.

Recall that the udi's do not participate in any commands other than assignment and boolean commands; in particular, the find commands have no effect on the udi's. Thus before an occurrence can be actively locked in a udi, it must be current in the cru or a set indicator. This implies that the occurrence must first be passively locked before it can be actively locked. This is of course consistent with the behavior of the **mcp** command.

Figure 15.17 illustrates a realization of Fig. 15.3 using the udi's as active locks. To aid the application program designer in anticipating and responding to potential deadlock situations, the DBCS will indicate, through its error reporting mechanism, if an operation was refused because of passive or active locking. Note also that the record occurrence is actively locked before confirmation by the user, so that the user is guaranteed exclusive use of that occurrence.

```
      {cc.wait − value-9;
       cc.tries = value-10;
       mcc(cc);
       v = 1;
       mau(v);
/* primary */
       input n1, i1;
       fmi(ITEM, SI, i1);
       if (active-lock) then
           {display "Someone else is modifying this occurrence";
            perform zap-all;
            return;
            }
       gfm(INVTRY, SI, inv1);                    /* perform get before active locking */
       if (n1 > inv1) then perform stock-out;
       suc(v);                                   /* actively lock item 1 */
       if (passive-lock) then
           {display "Someone else is accessing this occurrence";
            perform zap-all;                     /* release your indicators to avoid deadlock */
            return;
            }
       display "Inventory is", inv1, "units—proceed?";
       if (not qyn ()) then
           {perform zap-all;
            return;
            }
/* secondary */
       input n2, i2;
       fmi(ITEM, SI, i2);
       if (active-lock) then
           {display "Someone is modifying the occurrence";
            perform zap-all;
            return;
            }
       gfm(INVTRY, SI, inv2);
       if (n2 > inv2) then perform stock-out;
       mcp();                                    /* actively lock cru */
       if (passive-lock) then
           {display "Someone else is accessing this occurrence";
            perform zap-all;
```

Fig. 15.17   Active locking using udi's.

```
        return;
        }
    display "Inventory is", inv2, "units—proceed";
    if (not qyn ()) then
        {perform zap-all;
        return;
        }
    inv2 = inv2 − n2;
    pfm(INVTRY, SI, inv2);
    mcf();                                    /* unlock item 2 */
    smu(SI, v);
    inv1 = inv1 − n1;
    pfm(INVTRY, SI, inv1);
    perform zap-all;                          /* complete unlocking */
    return;
    }
zap-all      /* null all indicators, remove active udi locking */
    {nci();
    v = 0;
    mau(v);
    return;
    }
```

Fig. 15.17   *(Continued)*

One additional aspect of active udi locking must be pointed out. The **mau** command always begins actively locking udi occurrences starting with udi(1). The problem is that the boolean commands use udi(1) and udi(2) as input parameters. Generally, it is not necessary for those occurrences to be actively locked during a boolean operation. Thus it is advisable to perform a **mau**(0) before a boolean command sequence is to begin. This will eliminate delays caused by the active locking mechanism.

15.8   ACTIVE LOCKING BEYOND THE OCCURRENCE LEVEL

The active locking commands presented above should provide the application developer with a set of tools sufficient for most multi-user applications. The exclusive access mode described in Section 15.2 allows the database administrator access without interruption from other users. Mechanisms also exist for intermediate locking, that is, the active locking of selected groups of occurrences, independent of the status of the currency indicators.

One of these mechanisms is used to actively lock all occurrences of a specified record type. The command is

    mrtp(record-name)   Actively lock the specified record type.

The multi-user record type protect (**mrtp**) command is logically equivalent to locking a data file in a file management context. No other run-unit may access, much less modify, any occurrences of that record type. This includes the creation of new occurrences of that record type. The **mrtp** will not succeed if another run-unit has a passive lock on any occurrence of that record type. The inverse DML command is

    mrtf(record-name)   Free the record-type lock.

The multi-user record type free (**mrtf**) command eliminates the active lock restriction on occurrences of the specified record type. It does not influence any active occurrence locks specified through the use of **mcp** or **mau** or any passive locks.

    The **mrtp** command can have a profound effect on the overall processing performed by the system. It should be used only in those situations where all (or many) of the occurrences of a record type need be considered simultaneously during processing. One situation where this kind of processing could prove useful is the evaluation of all occurrences of a calced record type. Another situation would involve the programming simplification of using **mrtp** rather than **mau**(255) and the associated loops.

    A third case is presented in Fig. 15.18. Here we see a simple transaction oriented accounting schema. Each transaction is split into one or more subtransactions, each of which is debited and credited to accounts. During the account reconcilliation process or the production of financial statements, it may prove disasterous if another run-unit were to add new subtransactions. Thus these

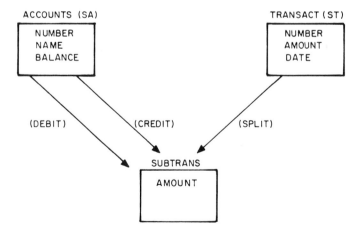

Fig. 15.18   Example of mrtp usage.

programs would include a command of the form **mrtp**(SUBTRANS); all occurrences of the record type SUBTRANS would be actively locked, that is, inaccessible to other run-units.

The other mechanism provided for actively locking many occurrences has a somewhat different effect:

msp(set-name)   Actively lock all set occurrences of the specified set relationship

The multi-user set protect (**msp**) command preserves the integrity of the specified set. The set occurrences (i.e., owner-member relationships and orderings) are actively locked. If a record occurrence is capable of participating in a set that is locked, then another run-unit may not perform a delete, remove, or insert with respect to that set and record. This includes any AUTO insertions performed by the create commands. The data item values of the record occurrence may be changed if they do not alter the set ordering, that is, if they are not sort key values of the locked set.

The **msp** command will not succeed if a locking conflict would occur. This includes both passive and active locks. Thus if another run-unit has a passive or active lock on a record occurrence that is capable of participating in a set, then that set may not be locked using **msp**. In particular, both the owner and member currency indicators for that set must be null in every other run-unit for the **msp** command to be successful; the obvious exceptions are the current owners of the system-owned sets.

The corresponding unlocking command is

msf(set-name)   Free the active lock from the specified set relationship.

The multi-user set free (**msf**) command eliminates the active locks on the set occurrences of the specified set. It does not influence any other active or passive locks that might otherwise be in effect.

As an example of the kind of processing that the **msp** command would be useful for, recall from Chapter 12 (Figs. 12.9 and 12.11) the problem of finding the highest numbered course taken by a student within each department. The solution to this problem (Fig. 12.12) incorporated the **sme** and **soe** commands. For this kind of processing, which involved several passes through the record occurrences within the set TAKE, it is imperative that the set occurrences do not change; otherwise, incorrect processing can occur. Thus, in a multi-user environment, this program could effectively make use of **msp**.

Note that the values of the owner and member occurrences can be altered, if the only locking mechanism in effect is **msp.** The only exceptions here are sort key data items for the locked set. Thus, **mrtp** preserves both the data and relationships of the associated record occurrences, while **msp** preserves the relationships among record occurrences only.

In practice, it may be difficult for either **mrtp** or **msp** to be performed successfully. Both have stringent requirements—no record occurrence that would be locked by either one may be passively or actively locked by another run unit. In a system with a high degree of utilization, this may be difficult to accomplish in the absence of administrative controls.

15.9   SUMMARY

Multi-user systems introduce a number of difficulties that both the DBCS and the application developer must address. The problem of concurrent update and deadlock prevention are issues confronted within the DBCS. Deadlock potential and the steps taken when operations are not successful are in the realm of the application developer.

Passive locking provides one solution to the concurrent update problem. Any record occurrence that occurs in any currency indicator of any run-unit is passively locked. This means that the occurrence may not be modified in any way by any other run-unit. The **mcc** command is used to specify the number and frequency of retries of DML commands. The zapping commands **scn, smn, son, sun,** and **nci** are used to set indicators to null providing a way out of possible deadlock situations among the run-units.

Active locking of record occurrences implies exclusive access (both for reading and modifying) of those occurrences. The **mcp** and **mau** commands are used to actively lock the cru and udi indicators, respectively. The **mcf** command frees the cru lock, as does changing the cru in any way; freeing the udi's is accomplished through successive **mau** commands with different parameter values.

Groups of record occurrences can be locked (and freed) through the use of **mrtp (mrtf)** and **msp (msf)**. These operate independently of the currency indicator oriented locking mechanisms.

Perhaps the most important aspect of designing multi-user application systems is the consistent use of locking mechanisms. The various programs must be developed with sufficient controls so that all possible locking combinations are anticipated. Further, administrative controls are necessary to prevent users from abusing the locking mechanism.

One issue that has not been addressed is the potential for redesigning the data structure to facilitate multi-user program design. This area as yet is not well understood. One typical technique that can be used is the girdle design. Consider the data structure of Fig. 15.19. Suppose the context of these records is such that record types A, B, C, and D are relatively independent, but E, F, G, and H would always be locked at the same time (i.e., two run-units could not be accessing these occurrences simultaneously). One solution is to modify the structure as shown in Fig. 15.20. The record type GIRDLE (the choice of the name

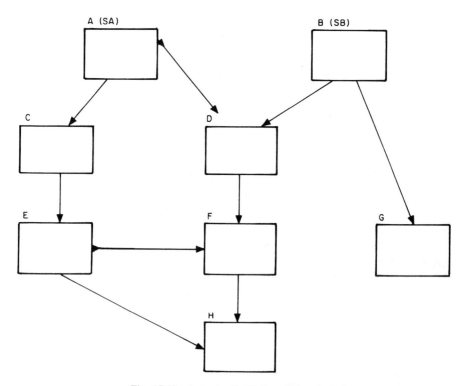

Fig. 15.19   Accessing E, F, G, and H exclusively.

should by now be obvious) is a member of a multiple owner, 1:1 set and owner of a multiple member, 1:N set. The application program could then simply attempt to execute an **mrtp**(GIRDLE) command. If successful, then that run-unit will have exclusive access to the lower record types. This simple example should indicate some of the potential benefits of considering schema design refinements when working in a multi-user environment.

RELATED READINGS

Micro Data Base Systems Inc., "Application Programming Reference Manual," Lafayette, Indiana, 1981.

T. W. Olle, "The CODASYL Approach to Data Base Management," Wiley, New York, 1978.

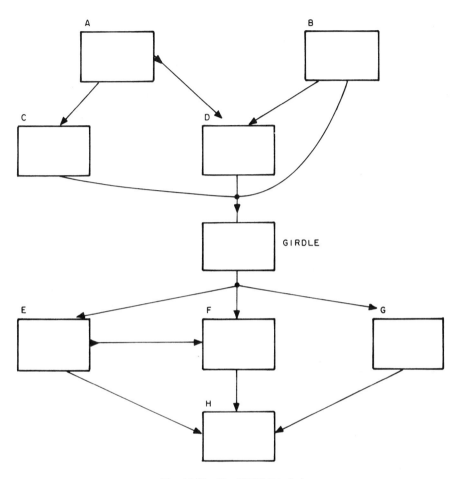

Fig. 15.20 The GIRDLE technique.

EXERCISES

1. What is deadlock? Is there any other way to prevent deadlock aside from locking techniques? If so, explain your method and show that it is feasible.
2. What are the differences between passive locking and active locking concerning:
   (a) how the locks are set,
   (b) under what situations should locks be set,

(c)   the effect of locks,

(d)   the unlocking commands?

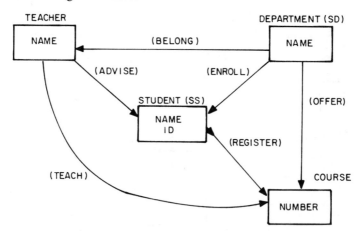

3.   Multi-user processing is desired for a database having the schema depicted above. Assuming that we have loaded the information into the database, outline the programs needed to meet the following requirements:

(a)   a student changes from course A to course B;

(b)   a new teacher is employed by the computer science department and will teach course 420;

(c)   a scheduled course 403 offered by the computer science department is cancelled;

(d)   course 403 is offered by the mathematics department, instead of the computer science department;

(e)   a student graduates;

(f)   a student switches from the department of geology to the mathematics department.

4.   Using the database for the schema of Exercise 3, suppose we want to list all courses offered by the department in which a particular student is enrolled. Write a program suitable for multi-user processing.

5.   Write the programs for Exercise 3, assuming a single-user processing mode. Compare the complexities of the programs under the two different processing modes.

PROJECT

If multi-user processing is reasonable for your application, revise your application programs to create a multi-user application system.

Appendix A

FILE MANAGEMENT SUMMARY

A. BASIC TERMINOLOGY

(1) **A record type** is a group of one or more types of data, where each type of data is called a *field*. A customer record type consists of fields such as name, address, phone, and so on.

(2) **A logical record** is an occurrence of a record type. A logical record of a customer record type consists of data about a specific customer; it consists of a data value for each of the fields of the record type. A logical record is sometimes simply called a record or a record occurrence.

(3) **A file** is a collection of logical records of some record type. Customer records constitute a file of customer data. A file is typically stored on some medium external to the central memory of a computer, such as punched cards, magnetic tape, floppy diskette, or hard disk. Logically, a file may be thought of as a table of data in which there is a column for each field and a row for each record in the file.

(4) **A master file** contains data about the current status of each of a group of persons (e.g., customers) or objects (e.g., products). Each record in a master file is subject to updating. A master file is typically used to periodically generate reports (e.g., invoices, financial statements).

(5) **A transaction file** is a file whose records contain data about how to update a master file. Updates may involve creating new master file records, modifying master file records, or deleting records from a master file.

(6)   **A header-detail file** contains records of two related, but different, record types (the header and the detail). Each occurrence of a header record in the file contains a number indicating how many detail records will follow it in the file. These detail records are followed by another header record and its details, and so on. Each header record must hold the number of its details because the number of details for different header records varies. One department might have 20 employees, while another department header is followed by 50 employee records. Header-detail files differ from flat files, as defined in (3). Here, we shall focus on flat files.

(7)   **Structure versus content.** The logical structure of a file is specified in terms of a record type which is specified in terms of its fields. The file itself is composed of records, each of which is composed of a data value for each of the fields of the record type.

(8)   **A key** is a field or group of fields. A key is *unique* if its value is different for every record in the file. A value of a unique key therefore uniquely identifies a particular record in the file. A key can be used to control the sequencing of records in a file. Access to a particular record in a file can be based on the key value of that record. A key can also be used as a basis for correctly applying transaction file records to master file records; the master file key field(s) is also a field in the transaction file, so that we know which master record to update with a given transaction record.

(9)   **A block** (also called a physical record) is a group of one or more logical records that is transferred as a whole between central and auxiliary memory.

B.   FILE PROCESSING VERSUS FILE ORGANIZATION

(1)   **File processing** refers to the *order* in which the record of a file is processed. There are two classes of file processing: sequential and random. *Sequential processing* means that the next record to be processed (i.e., accessed) is the physically next record on the storage medium. With sequential processing, the 100th record stored on the storage medium cannot be accessed until the 99 records that physically precede it in the file have been accessed. *Random processing* (sometimes called direct processing) allows a record to be accessed without having accessed the records that physically precede it. The 100th record can be directly accessed, without having previously processed the 99 records that physically precede it. Random processing is not possible if a file is stored on tape, but is possible if it is stored on disk.

(2)   **File organization** refers to the relationship between the key values of records and the relative physical arrangement of those records on the storage

medium. There are two classes of file organization: sequential and random. When a file is *sequentially organized,* there exists a numeric (or alphanumeric) sequence of key values for physically adjacent records. The key value of any record is always higher (or always lower) than the key value of the record that physically precedes it. When a file is *randomly organized* (sometimes called direct organization), records are physically positioned without regard for their relative key values. The key value of any record may be higher or lower than the key value of the record that physically precedes it.

(3) **Four cases.** It is important to understand that file organization and file processing are fundamentally different concepts. For instance, knowing the organization of a file implies nothing about how it can be processed. The two different kinds of organization and the two different kinds of processing give rise to the following four cases:

(a) sequential processing of a sequentially organized file,
(b) sequential processing of a randomly organized file,
(c) random processing of a sequentially organized file,
(d) random processing of a randomly organized file.

(4) **Sequential processing–sequential organization.** The classic example of this case involves a master file that is sequentially organized on tape and a transaction file that is sequentially organized (with the same key as the master) on tape. Due to the physical characteristics of tape, these files cannot be processed other than sequentially. An update program iteratively reads the next transaction record. For each transaction the program checks to see whether the most recently read master record has the same key value as the transaction record. If so, the transaction is applied to the master record and the process is repeated with the next transaction record that is read. Otherwise, the current master record is written to a new master file and the next old master record is read. Old master records are read (and written to the new master file) until the one whose key value matches the present transaction record is found or until a master record is read whose key value exceeds the key value of the present transaction record. In the latter case, the transaction is erroneous (there is no master record corresponding to the transaction record); an error message is output and processing continues with the next transaction record.

(5) **Sequential processing/random organization.** An example of this case occurs where the master file records can be directly accessed (e.g., the master file is on disk) during update processing. Here, there is no reason to have transaction records sorted in any particular order. In other words, the transaction file has a random organization, its records being added to the transaction file in the random sequence in which they occur. At the end of a period (e.g., a day), the randomly organized transactions are processed sequentially. As each transac-

tion record is sequentially accessed, the corresponding master record is directly accessed, updated, and rewritten to the master file.

(6) **Random processing–sequential organizations.** In this case, records are sequentially organized on disk. These records can be processed sequentially or randomly (on the basis of a key value). This direct access to records in a sequentially organized file is accomplished by means of an index. A software system that supports this case is called an *indexed sequential access method* (ISAM) file handler. Upon indicating the key value of a desired record, the file handler looks in the index to find where the record is located. Knowing this location, the ISAM software can retrieve the desired record.

ISAM systems typically use more than one level of indexing, to rapidly narrow the search for a particular record. Figure A.1 illustrates the ISAM principle with a two-level index. A sequentially organized file is shown on the right and the indices are shown on the left with the arrows indicating pointers (i.e.,

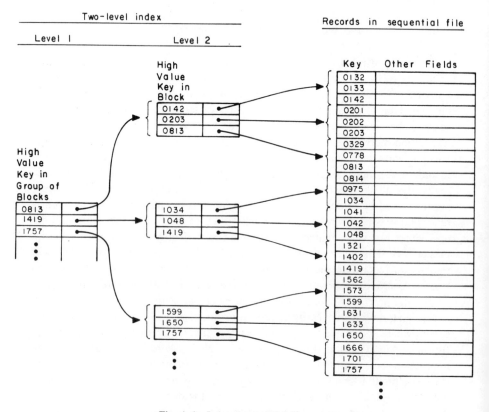

Fig. A.1 Indexed-sequential file system.

disk location to which an arrow points). If the record with a key value of 1042 is desired, the ISAM file handler looks in the Level 1 index to find out what part of the Level 2 index to examine. Since the first key value in the Level 1 index to exceed 1042 is 1419, the system looks only at the portion of the Level 2 index pointed to by 1419. Looking at this portion, the system determines that 1048 is the first key value in the Level 2 index to exceed 1042. The block indicated by 1048 is transferred into main memory, where the block is searched for the record with a key value of 1042.

An ISAM system must be able to accommodate the insertion of new records into the file. Sequentiality of the main file must be preserved. A common method for handling this is to reserve space in each record to hold a pointer to an overflow area of storage. Instead of inserting a new record into the main file, it is stored in an overflow area. The record that normally would precede it in the main file contains a pointer to the overflow record. In Fig. A.2, we can see that a pointer in the 1042 record allows the system to access the 1043 overflow record.

Similarly, an overflow record can have a pointer to other overflow records, for instance, when the 1045 record is stored in the overflow area and it is pointed to by the 1043 record. When the 1045 record is desired, the ISAM file handler uses the indices to retrieve the 1048 block of records. It finds that 1045 is not in this block and follows the pointer to bring in record 1043. Upon seeing that this is not the desired record, the pointer is used to bring in the 1045 record. As the number of overflow records grows, performance degrades. This is corrected by occasional file reorganization that merges overflow records into the main file and rebuilds the indices.

The foregoing description conveys the basic notions of ISAM. It does not present all details of an ISAM system and does not discuss indexing and overflow variations.

(7) **Random processing/random organization.** In this case, records are randomly organized and can be randomly processed. One of the most common methods for accomplishing this is to use an address calculation (i.e., hashing) technique. In this method, the key value of a new record is input to an algorithm that calculates an address for a block (often called a *bucket*) where the record will

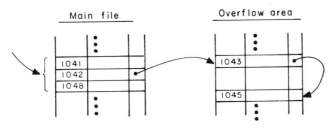

Fig. A.2 Handling ISAM overflow.

be stored. This hashing algorithm has the effect of scattering records randomly throughout the file. A record in the file is not directly accessed through an index, but is directly accessed via the hashing algorithm. Just as the algorithm is used to determine where to store the record, it can be used to find the record by calculating the address of the bucket in which it is stored.

Inherent in the nature of hashing algorithms is the occurrence of synonyms. When two key values hash to the same bucket they are called synonyms. This gives rise to the problem of bucket overflow. When a bucket is full and a new record is hashed to that bucket, some overflow technique must be employed to determine where to store the record and to allow that record to be accessed. Just as there are many possible hashing algorithms, there are numerous overflow handling techniques. Three are briefly described here.

One involves using buckets in an overflow area that is separate from the main file. When a main file bucket overflows, its overflow records are stored in an overflow bucket and a pointer to this overflow bucket is stored in the main bucket. If this overflow bucket overflows, it will contain a pointer to another overflow bucket, and so on. When a record having a specified key value is desired, the key value is input to the hash algorithm. The bucket with the resultant address is read into main memory. If the desired record is not found in this bucket, then the overflow bucket pointed to by the main bucket is read into memory, and so forth until the desired record is found.

Another overflow technique relies on having overflow buckets periodically distributed among the main file buckets. These overflow buckets are reserved exclusively for overflow records. When a main bucket overflows, the overflow records are stored in the first overflow bucket that follows it. When this overflow bucket overflows, its overflow is stored in the next overflow bucket having sufficient space, and so on. During retrieval, the main bucket indicated by the hash address is examined first, then the overflow bucket that follows it, and so forth, until the desired record is found.

A third overflow technique is one which does not reserve any buckets exclusively for overflow. When a bucket overflows, the overflow record is placed in the next bucket that has sufficient space. During retrieval, the bucket with the hash address is examined first, then the next bucket, and so forth, until the record is found.

C.   MULTIKEY FILE SYSTEMS

(1)   **Overview.** In each of the foregoing four cases [(4)–(7)] there was a single key (composed of one or more fields) per file. To access records on the basis of any fields other than the key, an exhaustive search of the entire file is

necessary. To overcome this limitation, multikey file systems were devised. In such a system there is one primary key and one or more secondary keys.

(2)   **A primary key** is a key that is used as the basis for the organization of a file and which typically can be used for directly accessing records in the file.

(3)   **A secondary key** consists of one or more fields. The values of a secondary key within a file typically are not unique. File organization does not depend on a secondary key. A record within the file can be randomly accessed on the basis of a secondary key value. This direct access can be accomplished through secondary key linked lists or secondary key indices. The latter case, often referred to as an inverted file (or inverted list) system, is examined here.

(4)   **An inverted file system** consists of a main data file, which may be an ISAM file, a hashed file, or it may have no primary key. Also involved in the system is a secondary key index for each of the secondary keys of the file. If each field of the file is a secondary key, then the file is said to be fully inverted. Otherwise, it is partially inverted.

(5)   **A secondary key index,** conceptually, has the form shown in Fig. A.3. There is one entry (i.e., row) in the index for each record occurrence in the file. The index is sequentially organized on the basis of the secondary key.

There are two kinds of secondary key indexing: direct and indirect. In the direct case, each index entry consists of a key value and a pointer to (i.e., the address of) a record having that key value. To access all records having a particular secondary key value, the system software finds that key value in the index and accesses records at the locations indicated by the index. In the case of indirect indexing, the location of a record does not appear in the index. Instead, there is an indicator of how to retrieve the record. Often, this indicator is the primary key of the record, thereby allowing indirect random access.

Physically, a secondary key index may have multiple levels and it may be packed to avoid repetition of a key value for every record having that key value.

(6)   **Direct versus indirect indexing.** The major advantage of direct indexing over indirect indexing is that it allows faster access. That is, random access

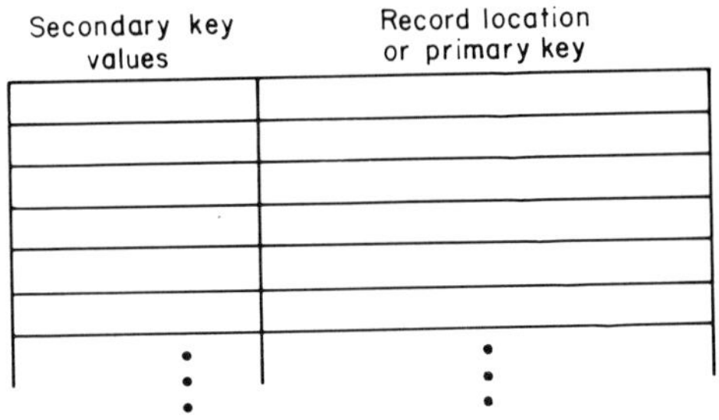

Fig. A.3   A secondary key index.

does not involve an extra (indirect) step, such as using the primary key of a record in order to access the record. In another respect, indirect indexing has the advantage of insulating secondary key indices from the effects of file reorganization. Reorganization changes record locations, but does not affect primary keys. In both cases, the insertion (or deletion) of a new record into the file causes alterations to all secondary key indices.

(7) **Intersecting secondary key indices.** Suppose an employee file has two secondary keys: department number and job code. To find all employees in department 299 with a job code of 34, the file system uses the indices to obtain the locations of all records for department 299 and the locations of all records with a job code of 34. The intersection of these two groups yields the locations of all records satisfying the desired criteria. In other words, locations of desired records can be determined before a single record is accessed.

Appendix B

THE CODASYL-NETWORK SPECIFICATIONS

A. THE CONFERENCE ON DATA SYSTEMS LANGUAGES (CODASYL)

CODASYL is a group of committees, each of which develops the specification of a particular language or facility. One of the best known CODASYL committees is the COBOL Programming Language Committee which developed the COBOL programming language in the late 1950s. With a few exceptions, each of the committees publishes a Journal of Development which presents the evolving specifications of its particular language or facility. Committee membership is open and typically consists of persons from government, industry, and academia.

Of particular interest here are the CODASYL Data Base Task Group (DBTG), the Data Description Language Committee (DDLC), and the Data Base Language Task Group (DBLTG). The DBTG, a subgroup of the Programming Language Committee, came into existence in 1967 as a continuation of the List Processing Task Force formed a year and a half earlier to try to find ways to extend the data-handling capabilities of COBOL beyond the limitations of file management. The DBTG study and debate on this topic led to the DBTG Report of 1971 which presented DDL and DML specifications for what is known as the CODASYL-network approach to database management. The CODASYL notion of a set (i.e., a 1:N set) was borrowed from the earlier work of Dr. Charles

Bachman who used this type of construct in his development of Integrated Data Store (IDS) in the early and mid 1960s.

With the publication of its 1971 report, the DBTG was disbanded. At the same time a new CODASYL committee, the DDLC, was formed to be responsible for the maintenance/evolution of the 1971 DDL specifications. The 1978 DDLC Journal of Development presents a number of refinements and modifications to original 1971 DDL specifications. This committee is also working on relational architecture proposals. Also a new subgroup (the DBLTG) within the COBOL Committee was formed to adapt the DML of the DBTG Report to COBOL, so that it could be included in the CODASYL COBOL JOD as an integral part of the COBOL language. This group's work is reflected in the 1976 CODASYL COBOL JOD. Yet another related CODASYL committee is the FORTRAN Data Manipulation Language Committee.

In the 1970s many implementations of the CODASYL-network approach appeared. The most notable mainframe implementations include the Honeywell IDS II, the univac DMS 1100, and the Cullinet IDMS. In the late 1970s and 1980s, CODASYL-network implementations began to appear on minicomputers, including Prime's DBMS, Data General's DG/DBMS, and Digital Equipment's VAX-11 DBMS. Although there is some variation among these systems, they all follow the major elements of the CODASYL specifications. Here, we outline the major aspects of the CODASYL specifications that are embodied in existing systems.

B.   DATA STRUCTURING

(1)   A CODASYL-network schema is constructed from data items, record types, and sets. The CODASYL specifications do not allow 1:1 or N:M sets. A 1:N set with multiple member record types is allowed, but sets with multiple owner record types are prohibited. The 1:N sets can be used in any noncyclic configuration; this restriction was relaxed in the 1978 DDLC JOD. However, the CODASYL DML is not well suited for processing such structures, and the existing CODASYL implementations generally do not permit them.

(2)   Record types can be assigned to one or more areas (though some implementations do not support this), and an area can have multiple record types assigned to it. The records of a record type can be declared to be stored by address calculation (calc), by clustering member records with their owner record (via a set), by directly stating an address (e.g., page number) for where the record is to be stored as the DML command for creating that record is invoked, or by allowing the system to determine where records will be stored.

(3)   The CODASYL specifications describe two ways by which 1:N sets can

be implemented: chaining and pointer arrays. Most implementations allow chaining only.

(4) A set can have a member order. The permissible orders are FIFO, LIFO, NEXT, PRIOR, IMMATERIAL, and SORTED (with a sort key). Though it is not often implemented, there is an optional clause in the CODASYL DDL specifications that results in an index. The index is named and can be assigned to a fast storage device. The index is based on the sort key and is intended to expedite the process of determining where to insert a record in a set occurrence.

(5) A *search key* can be specified for a record type. It consists of one or more of the data items of that record type. A secondary key index is constructed and maintained based on a search key. This index expedites the process of finding a particular record occurrence based on its search key value. Note that, physically speaking, a CODASYL search key is equivalent to an extended-network sort key for a sorted SYSTEM-owned set.

(6) Automatic and manual member record insertion into set occurrences is supported. Fixed (called *mandatory*) retention is supported.

(7) There is considerable variation among the ways in which CODASYL implementations address the issue of data security.

C. DATA MANIPULATION

(1) A subschema must be defined for each application program. It is stated in terms of a subschema data definition language and analyzed by a subschema DDL Analyzer. Subschema DDLs are host language dependent. A subschema is a connected subset of the schema and it defines the nature of the user working area (UWA) of a program. The UWA is the space in main memory reserved for holding one occurrence of each subschema record type. All data transfer between the database and the program occurs through the UWA. Thus, the UWA plays a role analogous to that of data blocks (or program records), though it is somewhat less flexible.

(2) When a DML command is invoked, a command status is returned by the DBCS. In many implementations it is returned in a global variable specifically allocated for this purpose, and the DML commands themselves are not invoked as normal subroutines. Instead, they appear to be built-in components of the host language. This is accomplished by a preprocessor that converts these DML statements into normal subroutine invocations prior to compilation.

(3) The CODASYL specifications allow four kinds of currency indicators: current of run-unit, current of set, current of record type, and current of area. The current of run-unit behaves in the same way that it does under the extended-network approach. The current of set is the most recently found occurrence of the

owner or member record type of the set. It is up to the application programmer to keep track of whether the current of a set is an owner occurrence or member record occurrence. There is no notion of a current owner and current member for each set. This lack of refinement tends to make programming somewhat more cumbersome and it precludes a straightforward method of manipulating N:M sets and recursive sets, even if they were allowed in a CODASYL-network schema. The most recently found occurrence of a record type is the current of record type. Similarly, the most recently found record in an area is the current of that area. The latter two kinds of currency indicators could be thought of as a very limited substitute for user-defined indicators, which do not exist in most CODASYL implementations.

(4)   The CODASYL-network DML differs from the extended-network DML in several major respects, beyond the differences in currency indicators and data transfer mechanisms. The CODASYL DML has many fewer commands. This is partially due to the comparatively limited structuring permitted by the CODASYL-network approach. It is also caused by the CODASYL DML syntax which opts for relatively few commands each of which is relatively complex (having more arguments), rather than a larger number of simpler commands having few arguments.

(5)   The CODASYL DML supports a variety of commands for finding a desired record. A record can be found based on its calc key value, its logical position in a set occurrence as implied by the order of the set, or its physical position in the database. Once a record is found, it becomes the current of its area, the current of its record type, the current of run-unit, and the current of set for *every* set in which it participates. Thus CODASYL-network find commands have very drastic effects compared to extended-network DML commands. In many cases this results in relatively awkward programming, because of a necessity to backtrack and re-find records that had been found just moments earlier. To assist in backtracking the CODASYL DML has a find command that resets the current of run-unit based on some other currency indicator (e.g., current of record type or current of set). Also, some implementations of the CODASYL-network approach provide the programmer with options of suppressing the modification of various currency indicators when a record is being found.

(6)   Another major difference between the CODASYL-network and extended-network DMLs is that CODASYL does not allow data to be retrieved from a record unless it is the current of run-unit. Thus there is a single, narrow "window" for retrieval.

(7)   Not only is retrieval relatively inconvenient, but the same problem is encountered for data modification. A record can be modified *only* if it is the current of run-unit.

(8)   The command to delete a record also deals only with the current of run-unit. If the current of run-unit owns no other records then it is deleted. If it does

own other records it will not be deleted unless a special option is specified. This option causes all decendents (members, members of members, etc.) to be deleted.

(9)   Commands to connect and disconnect a member record to and from an owner operate on the current of run-unit. In the case of connection it is connected to the current of an indicated set(s).

(10)   The command to create a record is straightforward.

(11)   The CODASYL DML has no commands comparable to the extended-network Boolean commands.

(12)   The CODASYL specifications support area locking in multiuser situations. An area can be opened in an exclusive use mode, a protected mode, or an unrestricted mode. Exclusive read/write mode means no other run-unit can read/write in that area (i.e., like an active lock at the area level). Protected mode and unrestricted mode are variations of passive locking at the area level.

The CODASYL specifications make no provision for active or passive locking of sets, record types, or individual records. However, there is a KEEP command which causes the record which is the current of run-unit to be monitored by the DBCS (until released by the FREE command). This monitoring does not prohibit other run-units from changing the record, but does alert the run-unit (that requested monitoring) if the record has been changed since KEEP was invoked. Some CODASYL implementors provide easier, less error-prone facilities such as active locking for individual records. The manner in which potential for deadlock is handled (or not handled) is implementation-specific.

(13)   The DBTG Report of 1971 recognized the value of a query language but did not specify such a language for use with CODASYL-networks. A sizeable number of CODASYL implementors have designed their own query systems. These vary widely in terms of syntax, ease of use, expressive power, and flexibility.

Appendix C

RELATIONAL NOTES

A. BASIC TERMINOLOGY AND RULES

(1) A relation is a record type.
An attribute is a data item.
A tuple is a record (i.e., a record occurrence).
Here we use the familiar terms record type, data item and record.

(2) Prime key.
Every record type *must* have a prime key consisting of one or more data items.

The prime key value of a record *uniquely* identifies that record.

(3) Functional dependence.
Let A be an aggregate of data items.
Let B be an aggregate of data items.
A is functionally dependent on B if we can write

where there are no duplicate occurrences of B.

This is comparable to saying "A owns B" in a one-to-many relationship.

(4) First normal form (1NF).

A record type is in first normal form if it contains no repeating data items.

The record type must have a prime key.

(5)   Second normal form (2NF).

Let B be the data items in the prime key of a record type.

Let A be the data items not in the prime key of a record type.

Let B′ be any *proper* subset of B.

Let a_j be any data item in A.

A record type is in second normal form if

(a) it is in 1NF,

(b) we can write

with no duplicate occurrences of B, and

(c) for each a_j we *cannot* write

for any B′, without having duplicate B′ occurrences.

This third condition says that a nonkey data item is not functionally dependent on any proper subset of the prime key. If the prime key consists of a single data item, there is no need to check this third condition (because there is no proper subset of B).

(6)   Third normal form (3NF).

Let a_i and a_j be any data items that are not in the prime key of a record type.

A record type is in third normal form if

(a) it is in 2NF, and

(b) we *cannot* write

for any a_i and a_j without having duplicate a_i occurrences.

(7)   Boyce–Codd normal form (BCNF).

Let b_k be any data item in the primary key B.

A record type is in BCNF if

(a) it is in 3NF, and

(b) for every b_k we can write

only if C = B

Note that if the prime key has only one data item, then BCNF is the same as 3NF.

(8)   Fourth normal form (4NF).

Let b_i, b_j, and b_k be any data items in the primary key B.

A record type is in fourth normal form if

(a) it is in BCNF, and

(b) for any b_i, b_j, b_k we cannot write

Of course, if the prime key has only one data item, then 4NF is the same as 3NF.

(9)   Other normal forms.

Researchers have invented other normal forms in the effort to further reduce the processing anomalies that can arise in processing relational databases.†

B.   DESIGN

(1)   No named relationships are permitted between record types in a relational schema.

(2)   All relationships are represented by redundant use of data items.

(3)   A schema is in a particular normal form if all of its record types are in that normal form.

(4)   The 4NF is a special kind of BCNF, which is a special kind of 3NF, which is a special kind of 2NF, which is a special kind of 1NF.

(5)   Relational theorists generally consider 1NF and 2NF to be quite undesirable because of the creation, modification, and retrieval anomalies (e.g., inconsistent data, spurious reports) that result for such schemas.

---

†For descriptions of these see: C. J. Date, "An Introduction to Database Systems," Addison-Wesley, Reading, Massachusetts, 1981; R. Fagin, A normal form for relational databases that is based on domains and keys, *Trans. Database Systems* **6**, No. 3, 1981.

(6) The 3NF solves many of these anomalies, the BCNF solves more, and 4NF solves most anomalies. Note that a 3NF schema having prime keys of one data item apiece is also in BCNF and 4NF.

(7) A schema in a given normal form is converted into a schema of a higher normal form by breaking its record types into more record types (each of the higher normal form).

(8) One approach to arriving at a 4NF design for a given application is to begin with record types in a lower normal form. These are then converted into more record types of a higher normal form, and so forth, until 4NF is reached.

(9) A second approach involves the identification of all unique identifiers and all functional dependencies. These are then used to construct 4NF record types.

(10) An easier design approach is to follow the seven-step design procedure and convert the resulting CODASYL-network schema to its relational counterpart. No design refinements should be used prior to conversion. Also comments about nearly one-to-one and nearly one-to-many relationships can be ignored. The conversion itself is accomplished by copying the prime key of unowned record types into all of their member record types (perhaps making it part of the prime key of the member record type) and eliminating the set between owner and member. For instance,

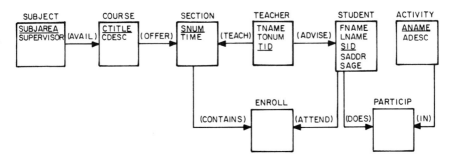

becomes

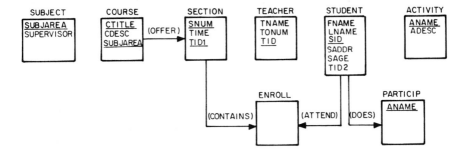

by eliminating the sets owned by unowned record types. Since the prime key of an owner (e.g., SUBJAREA) becomes part of the new prime key of the member (e.g., CTITLE SUBJAREA), there is no loss of information other than the loss of the semantics (e.g., AVAIL) of the relationship. It is possible for courses in different subject areas to have the same title. Note that since SID is globally a unique identifier for STUDENT occurrences, TID2 is not included as part of the STUDENT prime key. Continuing the process yields

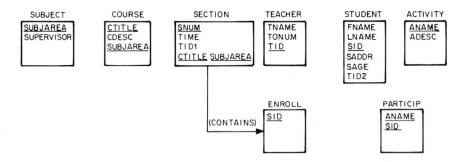

by the elimination of still more named relationships. A final step yields the 4NF schema

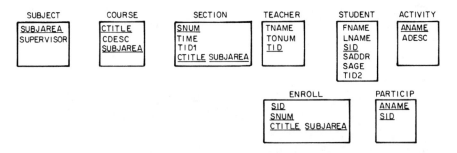

(11)   It should be clear that this design process is reversible, provided one can add the semantics for sets that replace the repeated data items. In other words, one can begin with a 4NF schema and easily devise the corresponding CODA-SYL-network (or extended-network) schema.

(12)   The price to be paid for preventing common anomalies is a cluttered schema and quite drastic increases in storage overhead (if the relational system is implemented to actually store repeated data item values, rather than using pointers).

(13)   It is instructive to examine the corresponding relational, CODASYL-network and extended-network schemas from the standpoints of semantic clarity, conciseness, and elegance. The corresponding extended-network schema is

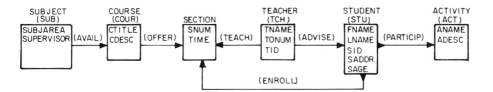

(14)   Observe that 4NF schemas *nearly* always have one-to-many relationships between record types with duplicate data items. For instance, we can be
reasonably certain that

implies a one-to-many relationship between R_1 and R_2 in which R_1 is the owner
(because its prime key is a part of the prime key of R_2). However, there are
exceptions. The following 4NF structure represents a possibly one-to-one or
many-to-many relationship between record types.

In the latter case this corresponds to the CODASYL-network schema

When considering a relational DBMS, it is important to understand if and how
that DBMS guarantees the integrity of one-to-one and one-to-many relationships
while accommodating many-to-many relationships.

(15)   Just as a set indicates a logical relationship and implies an access path in
some database management approaches, duplicate data items indicate a logical
relationship and imply an access path in the relational approach.

(16)   Caution must be exercised in cases where multiple semantically different relationships exist between a pair of record types. In extended-network
schemas the different semantics are obvious from the relationship names. For
instance

indicates that a country contains many cities and has many state capitals. In a comparable relational schema, names of the redundant data items should be selected to reflect the nature of the relationship in which they are involved. For example,

(17) Every record type in a relational schema *must* have a prime key. Frequently there are data items that can naturally serve as prime keys. Sometimes, however, the designer must contrive new data items to serve as prime keys. For instance, in the schema

the PASTJOB record type quite reasonably does not have a data item to uniquely identify its occurrences. Before converting it to the relational counterpart, we need to invent a unique identifier for pastjob. Call it PJID. The resultant 4NF schema is

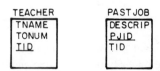

(18) Relational theory does not allow the designer to specify an ordering for the records that are logically associated with some other record by virtue of their matching data values for duplicate data items. In effect, this is comparable to requiring every ordering in an MDBS schema to be IMMATERIAL. When a group of records related to some other record is retrieved, many relational systems allow the records to be sorted into a desired order at retrieval time. This extra sorting operation does, of course, slow down the retrieval response times.

FIFO, LIFO, NEXT, and PRIOR logical orderings are not supported in relational systems.

(19)   Relational schemas do not support any counterpart to a relationship with multiple owner or multiple member record types.

(20)   When record types in a relational schema are specified, the designer is unable to control the location mode of their record occurrences. Clustering of logically related records and calcing are generally not supported.

(21)   In general, current relational implementations have no counterpart to fixed retention integrity conditions.

(22)   Relational systems do not support partial relationships. This means that in the following schema, there can be no occurrence of R_2 that is not logically associated with an occurrence of R_1.

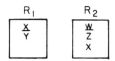

Shallow-network and hierarchical systems also suffer from this restriction. This restriction is comparable to requiring all 1:N sets in an extended-network schema to have automatic membership, with manual membership being prohibited. Such a limitation is highly undesirable for modeling real world relationships, which are very often partial in nature.

C.   DATA MANIPULATION

(1)   There are two major approaches to manipulation of data organized according to a relational schema: relational algebra and relational calculus.

(2)   Relational algebra is a relatively low-level, procedural language and relational calculus is a relatively high-level, nonprocedural language.

(3)   Relational algebra operators operate on record types to produce flat files. Because a flat file can be schematically described by a record type, algebraic operators can operate on derived record types as well as those that are permanently part of a relational schema.

(4)   The major algebraic operators include select, project, join, and divide.

(5)   The select operator produces a file of all occurrences of a single record type which have data values satisfying specified criteria. This is akin to the usual file management operation of extracting desired records from a file.

(6)   The project operator produces a file of all occurrences of a single record type, except that the data values for some data items are excluded from the new

file. This is akin to the usual file management operation of reading the records in a file with the exception of certain fields.

(7)   The join operator (i.e., the natural join) merges the occurrences of two records together, based on matching values of redundant data items. The result is a file composed of records formed by joining together related occurrences of the two original record types. This is akin to the usual file management operation of merging two files together on the basis of a field(s) that exists for both.

(8)   The divide operator *divides* the occurrences of one record type, called the dividend, by the records in a file (or of a record type) called the divisor. Usually the dividend has two data items (A, B) and the divisor has one data item (B). The data item of the divisor must exist in the dividend. The result of the divide operation is a file called the quotient. The quotient has a field (A) for each dividend data item that is not also in the divisor. Occurrences of the quotient consist of each value (of A) that is repeated in the dividend for *every* occurrence in the divisor (i.e., that is coupled, in the occurrences of the dividend, with every value of B that exists in the divisor).

(9)   Relational algebra is valuable from a research standpoint in facilitating the development of relational theory. However, the development and maintenance of algebraic procedures for nontrivial (i.e., realistic) applications is relatively difficult.

(10)   The relational calculus is a higher level language than relational algebra.

(11)   The original relational calculus proposals involved a form of relational calculus that is mathematically oriented, involving the usage of existential and universal quantifiers. It closely resembles predicate calculus.

(12)   In order to provide a more developer-friendly form of relational calculus, Structured Query Language (SQL) was devised. SQL must be considered as the major relational language for users. Relational systems, or systems claiming to be relational, can be judged with respect to how close they come to providing the features of SQL.

(13)   SQL is comparable to QRS in terms of its nonprocedurality and retrieval power.

(14)   Just as the user of QRS must understand an extended-network schema, the user of SQL must understand a relational schema.

(15)   SQL queries are stated in terms of a relational schema.

(16)   The structure of an SQL query is in some respects quite similar to the structure of a QRS query. Where QRS uses

LIST data-item-1,data-item-2, . . . ,

SQL uses

SELECT data-item-1,data-item-2, ...

Where QRS uses a conditional clause of the form

FOR condition-1,condition-2, . . . ,

SQL uses

WHERE condition-1,condition-2, ...

Where QRS uses a break clause of the form

BY data-item-*a*,data-item-*b*, . . . ,

SQL uses

GROUP BY data-item-*a*,data-item-*b*, ...

(17) A major difference between SQL and QRS is the manner in which the relationships between the data items of a query are expressed. This is to be expected since QRS utilizes schemas in which a relationship name represents a relationship, whereas SQL uses schemas in which redundant data items are used to represent a relationship. The SQL counterpart of the QRS relationship clause (i.e., the THRU clause) is twofold. First, there is a FROM clause that shows which record types' occurrences must be accessed during SQL processing. Second, the SQL WHERE clause may need to contain conditions which specify that a data item in one record type is to be matched with a data item of another record type. Thus an SQL conditional clause contains conditions on data values (as with QRS) and conditions on relationships that are to be used in processing the query.

(18) Both QRS and SQL support nested queries within a conditional clause. Examples are shown below.

(19) For QRS, occurrences in the output file are ordered on the basis of the DDL specified ordering for relationships which are used (e.g., FIFO, LIFO, SORTED, etc.). Alternatively, QRS will sort the occurrences at retrieval time, if environment option 14 is turned on. SQL is also able to sort occurrences at retrieval time, if the user so specifies within a query. SQL does not support FIFO, LIFO, NEXT, or PRIOR orderings.

(20) The SQL examples shown here are for the relational schema previously derived in Section B.10. For each SQL query, the corresponding QRS query is shown. QRS examples are for the equivalent MDBS schema shown in Section B.13.

      (a) List the name, age, and identification number of students, in sorted order.

QRS

LIST LNAME,FNAME,SAGE,SID THRU STU

SQL

SELECT LNAME,FNAME,SAGE,SID FROM STUDENT ORDER BY LNAME,FNAME

If the extended-network schema had another system-owned relationship with a different ordering, such as FSTU with FIFO ordering, then

LIST LNAME,FNAME,SAGE,SID THRU FSTU

produces a table of student information in a FIFO order.

(b)   List name and identification number for students under 18 years of age.

QRS

LIST LNAME,FNAME,SID FOR SAGE < 18 THRU STU

SQL

SELECT LNAME,FNAME,SID FROM STUDENT WHERE SAGE < 18

(c)   For every teacher, list the students (name and identification number) advised by that teacher.

QRS

LIST TNAME,LNAME,FNAME,SID THRU TCH,ADVISE

SQL

SELECT TNAME,LNAME,FNAME,SID FROM TEACHER,STUDENT
WHERE TEACHER.TID=STUDENT.TID2

(d)   List the students advised by "O.G.FITZGERALD".

QRS

LIST LNAME,FNAME,SID FOR TNAME="O.G.FITZGERALD"
THRU TCH,ADVISE

SQL

SELECT LNAME,FNAME,SID FROM STUDENT WHERE
TNAME='O.G.FITZGERALD' AND TEACHER.TID=STUDENT.TID2

(e)   List the students taught by "O.G.FITZGERALD" and for each of these students indicate the section number(s) and course title(s) in which this teaching occurs.

QRS

LIST LNAME,FNAME,CTITLE,SNUM FOR
TNAME="O.G. FITZGERALD" THRU TCH,TEACH,>OFFER,>ENROLL

SQL

SELECT LNAME,FNAME,CTITLE,SNUM FROM STUDENT,ENROLL
WHERE TNAME='O.G.FITZGERALD' AND TEACHER.TID=

SECTION.TID1 AND SECTION.(SNUM,CTITLE,SUBJAREA)=
ENROLL.(SNUM,CTITLE,SUBJAREA) AND ENROLL.SID=STUDENT.SID

(f) List the students, and the advisor for each, who participate in the "CHESS" activity.

QRS

LIST LNAME,FNAME,TNAME FOR ANAME="CHESS"
THRU ACT,>PARTICIP, > ADVISE

SQL

SELECT LNAME,FNAME,TNAME FROM STUDENT,TEACHER
WHERE ANAME='CHESS' AND PARTICIP.SID=STUDENT.SID
AND STUDENT.TID2=TEACHER.TID

(g) For every subject, list its supervisor and the titles and descriptions of its courses; for each such course also list its section numbers and times; for each such section list the teacher's name.

QRS

LIST SUBJAREA,SUPERVISOR,CTITLE,CDESC,SNUM,TIME,TNAME
THRU SUB,AVAIL,OFFER,>TEACH

SQL

SELECT SUBJAREA,SUPERVISOR,CTITLE,CDESC,SNUM,TIME,TNAME
FROM SUBJECT,COURSE,SECTION,TEACHER WHERE
SUBJECT.SUBJAREA=COURSE.SUBJAREA AND
COURSE.CTITLE=SECTION.CTITLE AND SECTION.TID1=TEACHER.TID

(h) List all teachers in offices 18, 19, 28, 29, 43.

QRS

LIST TNAME FOR TONUM IN [18,19,28,29,43] THRU TCH

SQL

SELECT TNAME FROM TEACHER WHERE TONUM IS IN (18,19,28,29,43)

(i) List all teachers who do not teach a "MATH" course.

QRS

LIST TNAME FOR SNUM NOT IN {SELECT SNUM FOR
SUBJAREA="MATH" THRU SUB,AVAIL,OFFER} THRU TCH,TEACH

SQL

SELECT TNAME FROM TEACHER WHERE SNUM IS NOT IN

(SELECT SNUM FROM SECTION WHERE SUBJAREA='MATH')
AND TEACHER.TID=SECTION.TID1

(j)   List the teachers who teach students advised by ''O.G.FITZGERALD''.

QRS

LIST TNAME,TID FOR SID IN {SELECT SID FOR
TNAME=''O.G.FITZGERALD'' THRU TCH,ADVISE}
THRU STU,ENROLL,>TEACH

SQL

SELECT TNAME,TID FROM TEACHER WHERE SID IS IN
(SELECT SID FROM STUDENT WHERE TNAME='O.G.FITZGERALD'
AND TEACHER.TID=STUDENT.TID2) AND TEACHER.TID=
SECTION.TID1 AND SECTION. (SNUM,CTITLE,SUBJAREA)=
ENROLL. (SNUM,CTITLE,SUBJAREA) AND ENROLL.SID=STUDENT.SID

(k)   Determine the total number of students advised by ''O.G.FITZGER-
ALD''; also determine the sum of their ages, their average age, the maximum
age, and the minimum age.

QRS

STAT SAGE FOR TNAME=''O.G.FITZGERALD'' THRU TCH,ADVISE

SQL

SELECT COUNT(SAGE),SUM(SAGE),AVE(SAGE),MAX(SAGE),
MIN(SAGE) FROM STUDENT WHERE TNAME='O.G.FITZGERALD'
AND STUDENT.TID2=TEACHER.TID

Note that the QRS query also determines the variance and standard
deviation.

(l)   List the students having addresses in ''CHICAGO''.

QRS

LIST LNAME,FNAME FOR SADDR=''*CHICAGO*'' THRU STU

SQL

SELECT LNAME,FNAME FROM STUDENT FOR SADDR=''%CHICAGO%''

D.   IMPLEMENTATION CONSIDERATIONS

(1)   The relational approach is strictly a logical view. Implementation techniques are not involved in this view.

(2)   A common implementation technique is to build an SQL-like language

on top of an inverted file system. The Knowledge Manager system is a micro-based example of this approach.

(3) To partially avoid the redundancy problems of inverted files, a few implementations use pointers (e.g., chaining, pointer arrays) between files. The application developer needs to specify these physical linkages at design time. At retrieval time, the logical view of repetitious fields must be observed.

E. MYTHS

Against the backdrop of the foregoing technical synopsis of relational traits, we close with a few observations on the body of relational lore that have appeared over the last few years. In the micro world, there are several myths about the relational approach that have become particularly prevalent by being repeatedly echoed. Of course, continued repetition will not transform these cliches into facts. There is, however, the danger that neophytes will mistake them for facts and base important decisions on them.

The intent here is by no means to denigrate the relational approach. It has been an interesting and stimulating contribution to the DBMS field. Though relatively few† truly relational implementations currently exist for micros, it is nevertheless an important factor in the DBMS field. The intent here is to put some of the oft-repeated claims about the relational approach into proper perspective.

(1) "The relational approach is a recent advance in database management."

The relational approach was introduced more than a dozen years ago, a year before the publication of the CODASYL DBTG Report. Both of these approaches have their roots in the 1960s and both are ancient developments in the history of DBMS. In contrast, the new extended-network approach is a very recent advance.

(2) "A relational DBMS is easier to use than other kinds of DBMSs: it is more natural. It offers the simplest possible way to represent data."

To a person whose DP experience has revolved around file management, the relational approach presents an attractive alternative. It is consistent with the old familiar file processing view, but at the same time it offers the conveniences of unconcern about physical details of file handling and a high level language for file manipulation. It is also understandable that a relational DBMS could be regarded as being more convenient than those hierarchical and shallow-network

---

†Exceptions include R:base 4000 (though it supports only the low-level, procedural relational algebra) and the Knowledge Manager which supports the higher level, nonprocedural SQL.

DBMSs which cause a developer to be excessively concerned with physical details.

At first glance, the relational approach appears to be easy. What could be simpler to understand than a table of data? The example relational schemas shown in database management textbooks and articles seem simple enough, typically showing three tables and occasionally as many as five tables (i.e., five record types). However, as one progresses beyond these toy schemas, to the intricacies of real-life applications, the apparent simplicity quickly vanishes and the tabular view becomes simplistic rather than simple.

The world is not composed of disjoint flat files, but of entities (or concepts) which are related to each other in various ways. For descriptive convenience, these relationships are typically given semantically meaningful names. The simplest way to represent the world is with a descriptive technique that closely mirrors the nature of the world. The ease with which an application system can be developed depends heavily on the descriptive power and flexibility of the representation technique employed; the more primitive the representation technique, the greater the difficulty in capturing the intricacies of an application and the greater the burden on the application developer. Four-word sentences may be fine for expressing simple thoughts, but they are not at all well-suited for expressing nontrivial ideas.

Perhaps the greatest single weakness of the relational model is the absence of a natural way for representing relationships. In view of this, the name ''relational'' is quite ironic. Anything other than field redundancy is expressly prohibited. Not only does this file view result in cumbersome schemas, it is at the root of implementation problems dealing with performance and data integrity. As an exercise, convert the extended-network schema for the vehicle leasing application (presented in Chapter 13) to a 4NF relational schema. The relational schema for this modest application does not begin to approach the conceptual elegance, conciseness, and semantic clarity of the extended-network schema.

For simple application problems, a well-implemented relational DBMS is simple to use (as are some other DBMSs and some file management systems). For complex applications, it is very difficult to seriously claim that the relational approach is natural or simple, or that the relationships implicit in its disjoint record type schemas are easy to understand and utilize. In no way can its schemas be considered to be simpler than extended-network schemas.

(3)   ''The relational approach is the only one that avoids record-at-a-time data manipulation.''

As we have seen in an earlier discussion of Boolean DML commands and the QRS language, this is simply not true.

(4)   ''The relational approach is the only one that offers a nonnavigational method of data retrieval.''

The concept of nonnavigational retrieval, as embodied in the SQL SELECT command, is very valuable. The SELECT command is easy to use, provided data from more than one table is not needed. As we have seen in the earlier description of QRS, it also supports nonnavigational retrieval (which can be disguised to be like the SELECT command, if desired). For either language, when fields from more than one record type are involved, the query must indicate which relationships are to be used. As we have seen, QRS allows these relationships to be stated very simply, compared to what is required in SQL.

(5) "Relational data manipulation is the only kind where a user need not be concerned with physical details such as pointers, indices, and so forth."

As shown in Chapters 6–8 and 12–15, knowledge of these kinds of physical details is irrelevant for both DML and QRS processing.

(6) "A programming staff can learn the relational approach easier than any other approach."

There have been no substantive studies to support such a conjecture. The rapidity of learning is heavily dependent on the background of the learner and the quality of the educational effort. It is the authors' experience that the extended-network approach is extremely easy to teach and can be quickly grasped by students who have had no prior database management exposure. Of course, a more important issue (to the professional developer) than ease of learning is whether a system is easy to live with once it has been learned.

(7) "The relational approach provides more data independence than any other approach."

This is incorrect. For instance, if a QRS query is affected by a schematic change, then the corresponding relational schema change will cause a change in the corresponding SQL query.

(8) "It is easier to alter a relational schema than any other kind of schema."

The ease of schema alteration is primarily a function of how a DBMS was implemented and the nature of restructuring facilities incorporated into the DBMS software. If a "DBMS" has been implemented with one record type per file and relying solely on data value redundancy to handle interrecord relationships, then restructuring amounts to nothing more than copying a file. In more sophisticated implementations where relationships are not handled by redundancy, there are two choices for an implementor: indirect addressing or direct addressing. The former makes restructuring relatively easy for an implementor and relatively fast in operation. The latter makes restructuring more difficult to implement and relatively slower in operation. However, there is a very important tradeoff: the indirect technique results in slower data access speeds than the direct technique. Since data access is normally a more frequent and time-sensitive activity than schema restructuring, the direct technique is often preferred by DBMS implementors. These rules of thumb are valid regardless of the logical view(s) furnished by a DBMS.

(9) "Development of an application system can be accomplished faster using a relational DBMS than it is with other kinds of DBMSs."

With a relational DBMS (as with many file management systems), one can define a file quickly, immediately begin putting data into it, and then retrieve data from it. This may be fine for trivial applications, involving a file or two. But ad hoc file creation is hardly a suitable method for developing nontrivial, high quality application systems where there is an interest in data integrity, high performance, user-friendliness, and so on. There is no substitute for careful systems analysis and design, regardless of the DBMS approach employed. Without it, files proliferate, performance is suboptimal, integrity is difficult (at best) to maintain, and a patchwork system results.

(10) "The relational approach will make up for the shortage of skilled DP personnel."

It certainly has not done so in the past dozen years, and there is little reason to suspect a sudden change. Development of professional quality software requires planning and skill. It is unrealistic to expect an unskilled person to produce application software comparable to (or as rapidly as) what a skilled person can produce.

(11) "Today there is no choice. Either you go relational or nothing."

This preposterous, yet oft-repeated, contention may be effective marketing hype for naive market segments, or it may reveal a superficial appreciation of the database management field and the nature of application development. It certainly suggests an ignorance of recent advances in the DBMS field and it ignores the thousands of nonrelational DBMS installations in use today. The relational approach has some strengths and some weaknesses relative to the other old-time DBMS approaches, such as CODASYL-networks. It is in no sense superior to these other approaches in all features and under all application circumstances.

Appendix D

REPRESENTATIVE HIERARCHICAL, SHALLOW-NETWORK, AND INVERTED LIST SYSTEMS

Highlights of prominent hierarchical, shallow-network, and inverted list systems are examined here. The hierarchical representative is DL/1, one of the oldest and most widely used DBMSs on IBM mainframes. The shallow-network example is TOTAL, another old and widely used DBMS which is particularly notable because of its availability on numerous minis and mainframes. ADABAS, a system available for IBM mainframes, is the inverted list example. The intent here is not to give an exhaustive discourse on any of these systems, but rather to provide an acquaintance with their major features.

A. DL/1

DL/1 is a product of IBM. Another IBM product, IMS, consists of DL/1 data management facilities plus other facilities for communications management. Other hierarchical systems include Intel's SYSTEM 2000 Mathematica's RAMIS II, and Information Builder's FOCUS. The latter two have versions available for certain 16-bit microcomputers that have very large (500–1000k) main memory resources.

(1) Data structuring.

(a) **Basic terminology.** In DL/1 terminology, a record type is called a *segment type* and a record is called a *segment.* A 1:N relationship is represented by what is called a *parent/child relationship;* this is like a 1:N set, except that it is unnamed, being identified by its parent segment type (i.e., owner) and child segment type (i.e., member). Two child segments with the same parent segment are called *twins.* A segment type having no parent is called a root. In DL/1 terminology, a *database record* consists of a root segment plus all of its descendent segments (i.e., its immediate child segments, their child segments, etc.).

A *sequence field* is a field whose values determine the access order to segments within a group of twins. In the case of a root segment type, a sequence field governs the order of access to root segments. A root segment type must have a sequence field. A *search field* is a field for which a secondary key index is maintained.

(b) **A physical database** has a hierarchic logical structure formed of segment types and parent/child relationships. There is one root segment type per physical database. Many physical databases may be needed to handle the data of a single application. A DDL is used to specify each physical database in terms of its fields, segment types, keys, and parent–child relationships.

(c) **Logical parent–child relationships** in DL/1 were invented to allow a segment type to be a child of up to two parent segment types, thereby giving DL/1 some limited networking capabilities. This feature was not included in the original system, but did appear in the early 1970s. The second parent segment type for a child segment type can be in a different (or the same) physical database. It is called the *logical parent,* while the other parent is called the *physical parent.* A logical parent–child relationship is declared in the physical database descriptions for the two segment types involved. The developer can choose from among several chaining options to declare how this relationship is to be implemented.

(d) **Mapping the segments of a physical database to storage.** When a physical database is declared, the developer can choose one or four options to specify how segments within a database record are to be arranged on disk and how physical parent–child relationships are to be physically implemented. The four methods are HSAM, HISAM, HDAM, and HIDAM (there are also other options of lesser importance). One of these must be chosen for each physical database.

HSAM is the *hierarchic sequential access method.* Segments within a database record are related by physical adjacency. The database records themselves are sequentially organized (based on the sequence field of the root) and sequentially processed. Insertion and deletion of database records or of segments within a database record are not allowed.

HISAM is the *hierarchic indexed sequential access method*. Under this type of arrangement, segments within a database record are also related by physical adjacency. These database records are treated in ISAM fashion, with an index being maintained based on the sequence field of the root segment type. Overflow due to insertions is handled by means of pointers to the overflow. Segments can be deleted, but the freed space is seldom reuseable.

HDAM is the *hierarchic direct access method*. Segments within a database record are related by chaining. Several chaining options are available. The default is to use first and next pointer chains for each physical parent–child relationship. Last, prior, and parent pointers can also be requested. As an alternative to this typical kind of chaining, a hierarchical chain could be specified. Such a chain involves a depth-first traversal of segments within a database record. A hierarchical chain can be either one-way (i.e., a prior record in the hierarchical sequence cannot be found) or two-way. HDAM allows direct access to any database record by hashing to its root segment based on the sequence field value of that root segment. Once a segment is stored it is never moved. Space from deleted segments is reuseable.

HIDAM is the *hierarchic indexed direct access method*. As with HIDAM, segments within a database record are related by chaining. Direct access to a database record is accomplished through an index to its root segment based on the sequence field of the root. Once a segment is stored it is never moved and space of deleted segments is reuseable.

(2)   Data manipulation.

(a)   **Program specification block.** Each application program must have one *program specification block* (PSB) defined for it. A PSB specifies the subhierarchies that can be accessed by a program. Each subhierarchy is called a program communication block (PCB). A PCB has as its root either the root segment type of a physical database or a segment type for which a search field has been defined. The remainder of the PCB can contain any segment type previously defined as a physical or logical child of the PCB root. If such a segment type(s) is included in the PCB, any of its physical or logical children can be included, and so forth, as long as the PCB remains hierarchical. Each DML command in an application program must explicitly specify the PCB on which it is going to operate.

(b)   **A segment search argument** (SSA) is a named variable or group of variables in the host language program. The value of the variable(s) is a segment type name or a relational expression involving fields. One or more SSAs are often used as DML command arguments. In effect, a sequence of

SSAs can be used to specify a path in a PCB by identifying a sequence of segments.

(c) **Get commands.** A DL/1 *get* command both finds a segment and extracts its data values from the database, depositing them in the input–output area specified in the argument list of the command. An input–output area is a named group of program variables (comparable to a data block or program record). The get unique (GU) command gets a segment satisfying a path of SSAs and makes that segment the *established parent*. This is somewhat akin to making it the *current owner* of all relationships in the PCB for which its segment type is the parent.

The get next (GN) command can be used to get the next segment in the hierarchical sequence or get the next segment in hierarchical sequence satisfying a collection of SSAs. Here, "next" means the next segment after the most recently found segment. The segment that GN gets becomes the new established parent.

The get next under parent (GNP) command can be used to get the next segment in hierarchical sequence under the established parent, get the next segment of a specified segment type in hierarchical sequence under the established parent, or get the next segment which is in hierarchical sequence under the established parent and which satisfies the specified SSAs.

Any of the foregoing get commands can be invoked with a "hold" option. This option must be used if the program intends to modify a record that has been obtained with a get command.

(d) **Modification commands.** There is an "insert" command which creates a new segment within a physical database record. It can use SSAs to specify a path from the root to the level in the hierarchy at which it will be inserted. The sequence field value of the new segment determines its position relative to its twins.

To change the values of an existing segment, that segment must first be found with a get command using the hold option. This brings an image of the segment into a specified input–output area. The values in this image are changed using normal program assignment commands. Now the DL/1 "replace" command can be invoked to replace the segment in the database with this new image. Values of sequence fields cannot be changed without deleting and recreating a segment.

The DL/1 "delete" command has a drastic effect. Not only does it delete a segment which has been found with a get–hold command, it also deletes all physical dependents of that segment. That is, it deletes all of the physical children of a segment, all of their physical children, and so forth, regardless of whether the segment types of these children have been included in the PSB of the program.

B. TOTAL

TOTAL is a product of CINCOM, an independent software vendor. The other notable shallow-network DBMS is the Hewlett-Packard IMAGE. CINCOM has announced a version of TOTAL that would give it more CODASYL-like capabilities.

(1) Data structuring.

(a) **Basic terminology.** In TOTAL terminology there are two kinds of record types: *master* and *detail*. The differences between these two are described below. A *data set* consists of all occurrences of a record type. It is unrelated to the notions of 1:1, 1:N, and N:M sets. The record occurrences of a master record type constitute a master data set. The occurrences of a detail record type constitute a detail data set. Variable length records are not supported. A *linkage path* represents a 1:N relationship between a master record type and a detail record type. The master serves as owner of this relationship and the detail plays the role of member.

(b) **Master record type.** One of the fields of a master record type must be designated as its *control key*. Each record in a master data set has a unique control key value. There is only one way to access an occurrence of a master record type: its control key value must be specified in a DML command. An address calculation (hashing) algorithm is used to store and access each master record occurrence, based on its control key value (see Appendix A). To allow synonyms to be handled by a chain of pointers, the schema designer must define a field in the master record type to accommodate synonym pointers. A master record type can be the owner of many detail record types by means of linkage paths.

(c) **Detail record type.** For each linkage path, the master control key is repeated as a field in the detail record type. A detail record type must be the member in at least one linkage path and can be the member in many linkage paths. A detail record can be accessed through any of the linkage paths of which it is the member. This is the only way to access a detail record.

(d) **Linkage path.** A record type is either master or detail; it cannot be both. It cannot be the owner in one linkage path and the member in another. To establish the existence of a linkage path, the schema designer must explicitly repeat the master control key in the detail record type, declare two fields in the master record type to hold (first and last) pointers, and declare two fields in the detail record type to hold (prior and next) pointers. A linkage path is implemented in the same way as a CODASYL set that uses chaining, except that detail records do not contain owner pointers. To access the master record that owns a given detail record, the DBCS uses the control key value of the detail record to hash to (i.e., calculate the address of) the related master record.

(e)   **Other considerations.** The data set for each record type resides in its own file. Thus there is no possibility of record clustering. The physical placement of master records is the result of hashing. The physical placement of detail records within a file is determined by the DBCS. Security is provided only at the record type level.

(2)   Data manipulation.

(a)   **Commands for master records.** Generally, a DML command that operates on master records has seven parameters that must be specified. Master records are accessed with a "read" command which both finds and extracts the record. This access is accomplished on the basis of the control key value of the record. Records in a randomly organized master data set can also be sequentially accessed.

Master records are created with an **addm** command and **writm** is used to change the data values of an existing record. A master record can be deleted only if there are no detail records related to it.

(b)   **Commands for detail records.** DML commands that operate on detail records generally have nine parameters. The "read" command for a detail record can be used to find and extract a detail record (or next detail record). One of the parameters must be the value of the control key for the master record that "owns" the desired detail record. The randomly organized records in a detail data set can also be accessed sequentially.

For detail record creation, there are variations of the **addv** command which allow the newly created record to be inserted into a linkage path on a FIFO, PRIOR, or NEXT basis. Different data modification commands must be used, depending on whether a control key field or noncontrol key field is being altered. The **addv** command is also a DML command that will delete the most recently read detail record.

C.   ADABAS

ADABAS is a product of Software AG. Other examples of inverted file systems include Model 204 of Computer Corporation of America and DATACOM/DB of Applied Data Research. All three are available on IBM mainframes. ADABAS-M is a version of ADABAS for Digital Equipment minicomputers.

(1)   Data structuring.

(a)   **Inverted files.** The records of each record type are stored in a file, apart from records of other record types. A file can be inverted on any field or fields that exist in its record type. That is, multiple secondary key indices can exist for a file (see Appendix A). The indices themselves are multi-level in nature.

(b) **Internal sequence number.** When a record is created, ADABAS assigns an *internal sequence number* (ISN) to it. Each record within a file has a unique, never-changing ISN. ADABAS maintains a table that associates the ISN of each record with its physical location. All secondary key indices are based on ISNs, rather than physical locations or primary key values (there are no primary keys in ADABAS files). Thus ADABAS has the advantages (and disadvantages) of indirect indexing.

(c) **Coupling.** ADABAS goes beyond usual inverted file systems by supporting *coupling*. Any two files can be coupled on the basis of redundant fields. A coupling is accomplished by means of a pair of indices that associate related records in the two files. For each coupled field value in one file, one of the indices has ISNs of records in the other file having the same field value. The converse is true for the other index. Thus coupling may be regarded as a way for representing a many-to-many relationship between two record types. No more than one coupling can exist between any two files.

(d) **Other considerations.** One-to-one and one-to-many relationships between record types are not supported. Data compression and thus variable length records are supported. The placement of a record in a file is determined by ADABAS; record clustering is not supported. The schema designer can specify a padding factor for records in anticipation of future record expansions. Note that, from an access standpoint, the ADABAS usage of multi-level secondary key indices is physically very similar to the role of system-owned sets in MDBS.

(2) Data manipulation.

A find command returns a list of ISNs of the found records. Thus a find command finds records by using indices rather than by accessing records. There is a conditional find command which allows records whose secondary key(s) satisfy specified conditions to be found. Another kind of find command returns a list of the ISNs in one file that are coupled to a specified record in another file. Once an ISN has been found, all or part of the data in the record of that ISN can be retrieved. Commands also exist to create a record in a file, change the data values of the record, and delete a record. During data modification ADABAS does not guarantee the integrity of one-to-one or one-to-many relationships; that must be handled by the application programmer.

Appendix E[†]

MDBS DDL Syntax

Notation:

_____ An underlined expression must appear.

[ ] Zero or one of the alternatives within the brackets must be used.

{ } Exactly one of the alternatives within the braces must appear.

{ }* One or more of the alternatives within the braces must appear.

Definitions:

<access-clause>:

$$\left\{ \begin{array}{l} [\underline{\text{READ}} \text{ ACCESS IS } \underline{\text{aclist-1}}] \; [\underline{\text{WRITE}} \text{ ACCESS IS } \underline{\text{aclist-2}}] \\ \underline{\text{ACCESS}} \text{ IS } \underline{\text{aclist-3}} \end{array} \right\}$$

<CALC-key-clause>:

$$\left\{ \begin{array}{l} \text{CALC } \underline{\text{KEY}} \\ \text{CALC } \underline{\text{KEYS}} \end{array} \right\} \left[\begin{array}{l} \text{IS} \\ \text{ARE} \end{array} \right] (\{\text{id-3},\}^*) \left[\begin{array}{l} \underline{\text{NODUP}} \text{ ALLOWED} \\ \underline{\text{DUPLICATES}} \text{ ARE [NOT] } \underline{\text{ALLOWED}} \end{array} \right.$$

<sort-clause>:

[†]Extracted from the MDBS III DDL Manual, Appendix B, MDBS, Inc., Lafayette, Indiana.

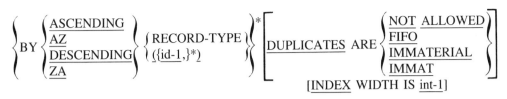

<comment>:
  /* comments */
Ordering of DDL Sections:
  Identification section
  User section
  Area section (optional)
  Record sections
    Data item sections for each record section
  Set sections
    Owner section for each set section
    Member section for each set section
  End section
DDL Sections:

(1) Identification section

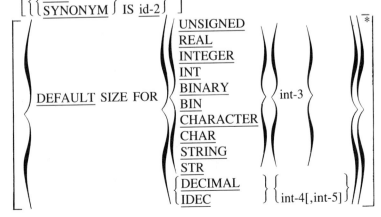

$\begin{Bmatrix} \text{DATABASE} \\ \underline{\text{DB}} \end{Bmatrix}$ NAME IS id-1
[FILE NAME IS "file-1"]
[SIZE IS int-1 PAGES]
$\left[\underline{\text{PAGE}} \text{ SIZE IS int-2} \begin{bmatrix} \text{BYTES} \\ \text{WORDS} \end{bmatrix} \right]$
$\left[\begin{Bmatrix} \underline{\text{LOG}} \text{ FILE} \\ \text{LOGFILE} \end{Bmatrix} \text{ NAME IS "file-2"} \right]$
[TITLE IS "string-1"]
$\left[\begin{Bmatrix} \begin{Bmatrix} \text{SYN} \\ \text{SYNONYM} \end{Bmatrix} \text{ IS id-2} \end{Bmatrix}^* \right]$

(2) User section
$$\underline{\text{USER}} \text{ IS} \left\{ \begin{array}{l} \underline{\text{usr}} \\ \text{``usr''} \end{array} \right\} \left[ \begin{array}{l} \text{WITH} \\ , \end{array} \right] \left\{ \begin{array}{l} \underline{\text{pass}} \\ \text{``}\underline{\text{pass}}\text{''} \end{array} \right\}$$
[<access-clause>]

(3) Area section (zero, one, or more per schema)
$$\underline{\text{AREA}} \text{ NAME IS } \underline{\text{id-1}}$$
[FILE NAME IS "file-1"]
[SIZE IS int-1 PAGES]
$$\left[\underline{\text{PAGE}} \text{ SIZE IS } \underline{\text{int-2}} \left[\begin{array}{l} \text{BYTES} \\ \text{WORDS} \end{array} \right] \right]$$
[POINTERS ARE [NOT] ALLOWED]
[<access-clause>]
[TITLE IS "string-1"]
$$\left[\left\{ \left\{ \begin{array}{l} \underline{\text{SYN}} \\ \underline{\text{SYNONYM}} \end{array} \right\} \text{ IS } \underline{\text{id-2}} \right\}^{*} \right]$$

(4) Record section (one or more per schema)
$$\underline{\text{RECORD}} \text{ NAME IS } \underline{\text{id-1}}$$
$$\left[\left\{ \begin{array}{l} \underline{\text{WITHIN}} \\ \underline{\text{IN}} \end{array} \right\} \left\{ \begin{array}{l} \left\{ \begin{array}{l} \underline{\text{ANY AREA}} \\ (\{\underline{\text{ar-1}},\}^{*}) \end{array} \right\} [<\text{CALC-key-clause}>] \\ \text{AREA OF} \quad \left\{ \begin{array}{l} \underline{\text{OWNER}} \\ \underline{\text{MEMBER}} \end{array} \right\} \text{ OF } \underline{\text{id-2}} \end{array} \right\} \right]$$
[<access-clause>]
[TITLE IS "string-1"]
$$\left[\left\{ \left\{ \begin{array}{l} \underline{\text{SYNONYM}} \\ \underline{\text{SYN}} \end{array} \right\} \text{ IS } \underline{\text{id-5}} \right\}^{*} \right]$$

(5) Item section (zero, one, or more per record type)

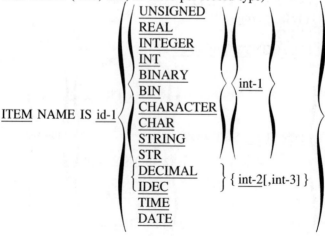

[OCCURS int-4 TIMES]
[IS ENCRYPTED]
[<access-clause>]
[TITLE IS "string-1"]
$$\left[\text{RANGE IS} \begin{Bmatrix} \text{lbound} \\ \text{LOWEST} \end{Bmatrix} \text{TO} \begin{Bmatrix} \text{ubound} \\ \text{HIGHEST} \end{Bmatrix} \right]$$
$$\left[\left\{ \begin{Bmatrix} \text{SYNONYM} \\ \text{SYN} \end{Bmatrix} \text{IS id-2} \right\}^* \right]$$

(6) Set section (zero, one, or more per schema)
SET NAME IS id-1
$$\left[\text{TYPE IS} \begin{Bmatrix} 1:N \\ N:M \\ M:N \\ 1:1 \\ N:1 \end{Bmatrix} \right]$$
$$\left[\text{RETENTION IS} \begin{Bmatrix} \text{FIXED} \\ \text{OPTIONAL} \end{Bmatrix} \right]$$
[<access-clause>]
[TITLE IS "string-1"]
$$\left[\left\{ \begin{Bmatrix} \text{SYNONYM} \\ \text{SYN} \end{Bmatrix} \text{IS id-2} \right\}^* \right]$$

(7) Owner section (one per set)
$$\begin{Bmatrix} \text{OWNER IS rt-1} \\ \text{OWNERS ARE (\{rt-2,\}*)} \end{Bmatrix}$$
$$\left[\text{INSERTION IS} \begin{Bmatrix} \text{AUTO} \\ \text{MANUAL} \end{Bmatrix} \right]$$
$$\left[\text{ORDER IS} \begin{Bmatrix} \text{FIFO} \\ \text{LIFO} \\ \text{NEXT} \\ \text{PRIOR} \\ \text{IMMATERIAL} \\ \text{IMMAT} \\ \text{SORTED <sort-clause>} \end{Bmatrix} \right]$$

(8) Member section (one per set)
$$\begin{Bmatrix} \text{MEMBER IS rt-1} \\ \text{MEMBERS ARE (\{rt-2,\}*)} \end{Bmatrix}$$
$$\left[\text{INSERTION IS} \begin{Bmatrix} \text{AUTO} \\ \text{MANUAL} \end{Bmatrix} \right]$$

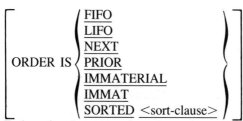

(9)   End section (one per schema)
      <u>END</u> [.]

Appendix F

PSEUDO-LANGUAGE DEFINITION

The examples of program structures in this text all appear in a procedural pseudo-language. We chose not to use any particular programming language (e.g., COBOL or BASIC) since we did not wish to prejudice the reader against any other particular languages. The features of this pseudo-language are not different from those found in most computer languages; most of these features will readily translate into the common languages.

There is no need in this pseudo-language for a detailed data section. There are three basic types of variable: integer (of unspecified length), real (of unspecified precision, also known as floating point), and character (the maximum length must be specified). A typical declaration would be

```
integer    x, y, z;
real       a, b;
char       s[30], t[5];
```

The character variable s is actually an array of 30 single characters; numerical arrays can be similarly defined.

One higher level data structure is allowed: the p-record (i.e., program record) is a collection of one or more variables, not necessarily of the same type, which can be referenced by a single name. A p-record called prec, consisting of the integer variable d and the character array e, would be declared:

```
p-record prec { integer d;
                char e[12]}
```

The order in which the variables are listed within the p-record is important for the processing of the p-record information.

Finally, to simplify the writing (and reading) of pseudo-language programs, the define declaration defines certain variables to contain constant character information. The declaration reads

$$\text{define } \{ST = \text{``This is a string''};$$
$$XYZ = \text{``xZy''};$$
$$HAS = \text{``HAS''}\}$$

These variables are notationally represented as capital letters, not in boldface; this distinguishes them from ordinary program variables and p-records. Their common use is the specification of database set, record type, and data item names.

Pseudo-language programs (and subprograms) usually begin with a series of declarations of the variables, p-records, and defines used in that program. Both function subprograms and subroutine subprograms are allowed within the pseudo-language. Functions are used within numeric and logical expressions, while subroutines are invoked through the "perform" statement.

The basic program structure in the pseudo-language is the block. A block is denoted by braces, i.e., { and }. The block construct has already been used in the p-record and define declarations.

A program consists of a block. A block consists of a left brace ({), followed by one or more program-units, followed by a right brace (}). A program-unit is either a program statement or it is another block.

In symbols, the basic program structure is

$$\{ \text{program-unit(s)}$$
$$\}$$

where a program-unit is either another block or a statement.

There are only a few program statements in our pseudo-language. The primary statements are identical to those in most programming languages. Statements include:

assignment: typical right to left assignment statement, followed by a semicolon. An example is "t = a − 3;". All of the typical rules of assignment statements apply.

if: The if statement has two forms:

        if (condition) then program-unit

    and

        if (condition) then
            program-unit
        else
            program-unit

As noted above, a program-unit is either a statement or it is a block. If

| | the condition is evaluated to be true, the program-unit associated with the *then* clause is executed. If the optional *else* clause is present, its associated program-unit is executed if the condition is not true (false). Control then passes to the next statement in the program. |
| do while: | This is the basic iteration statement. The form is: |

    do while (condition)
       program-unit

As long as the stated condition is true, the program-unit is executed. Once the condition becomes false, control passes to the next program statement. The condition is evaluated before the program-unit is executed.

(In both the last two statements, the condition could be a simple or complex logical expression, or it could be a local procedure: a block whose last statement is simply a logical expression.)

| continue: | This statement, when used, must appear within a loop. It causes the rest of the statement in the program-unit of the loop to be skipped, and the condition of the loop to be evaluated. |
| break: | This statement, when used, also must appear within a loop. This statement forces the immediate termination of the loop, that is, control immediately passes to the next program statement following the loop. |

(These last two statements only apply to the most recent, i.e., the innermost loop when nested loops are present.)

perform:	Perform the named subroutine.
return (value):	Used within a function subprogram, this statement specifies the value returned by the function.
display:	This is the basic output statement. Variables and quoted strings can be displayed.
input:	This is the basic input statement. Variables are assigned values by the user.
dms:	This refers to all of the various data manipulation commands callable from the program. These are described within the text.

Appendix G

VARIOUS HOST LANGUAGE EXAMPLES

In this appendix we present four versions of a program, each using a different programming language. The program selected is the user-load program of the Distributed Computer Network System, as developed in pseudo-language in Section 8.5. The DDL specifications are given in Fig. 8.4. Refer to Chapter 8 for details of the application and the specific program flow.

The four languages selected are C' (a trademark of MDBS, Inc.), COBOL-80 (a trademark of Microsoft, Inc.), FORTRAN-80 (another trademark of Microsoft, Inc.), and PC-BASIC (a trademark of IBM). These are, of course, not the only host languages that can be used with the MDBS DML. Other host languages supported include KnowledgeMan (MDBS, Inc. trademark) and numerous versions of BASIC, Pascal, COBOL, PL/1,C and assembler.

The chosen languages are representative, in the sense that they each show different techniques of DML programming and the different data and command forms required by different languages. Although each sample program is described independently of the others, it might prove useful to examine all of the programs, to fully appreciate the development of the programs.

Each program is presented in a similar manner. The discussions of the programs focus on two main issues: the database management constructs used in the programs and the programming language constructs used to implement the pseudo-language.

The four programs are not being presented as perfect examples of programming style; they are not necessarily the best implementations of the original pseudo-language program. However, they all do work, that is, they have been run and tested. It is important to develop a programming style of one's own and use it consistently.

G.1 THE C' LANGUAGE

C' is closest to the pseudo-language in terms of structure and data definition (see Fig. G.1). Thus it is not surprising that the C' version of the program is quite similar to the original pseudo-language version, C' runs under the CP/M (a trademark of Digital Research, Inc.) operating system.

```
#include <stdio.h>

#define FOUND !

struct { char sname[31];} site;

struct { char id[4];
         char uname[21]; } user;

struct { char ouser[17];
         char pass[13];
         char mode[5];
         char file[14]; } openrec;

int err;
char temp[21];

main()

{

/*   Open the data base    */

    strcpy (openrec.ouser,"DOUG");
    strcpy (openrec.pass,"CUTE");
    strcpy (openrec.mode,"M");
    strcpy (openrec.file,"B:DCNS.DB");

    if ( err = dbopn (&openrec) )
    {  printf("\n\n*** Error %d encountered during open***\n",err);
       exit(1);
       }

/*   beginning of user load program    */

    while ( get_user_id() )
    {  if ( FOUND fmsk("SU",user.id) )
          getm("SU",&user);
```

Fig. G.1 The C' language.

```
            else
            {  printf("\n  Is this a new user (Y/N)? ");
               if ( ! qyn() ) continue;
               printf("\n\nUser name: ");
               _gets(user.uname, 21);
               find_site();
               crs("USER",&user);
               ims("SU");
               ims("WORK");
               }
      printf("\nUser ID: %4.4s\n      Name: %s",user.id,user.uname);
      printf("\n\n  Should this person be deleted (Y/N)? ");
      if ( qyn() )
         if ( FOUND som("SUBMIT,SU") )
            printf("\nCan't delete - still linked to tasks");
         else
         {  drm("SU");
            printf("\nUser deleted");
            }
      else
      {  while ( printf("\n  Any changes (Y/N)? "), qyn() )
         {  printf("\n\nCorrected user ID (or blank): ");
            _gets(temp,5);
            if ( *temp )
            {  setmem (user.id,4,' ');
               movmem (temp,user.id,strlen(temp));
               }
            printf("\n                    Name (or blank): ");
            _gets(temp,21);
            if ( *temp ) strcpy (user.uname,temp);
            putm("SU",&user);
            printf("\nUser ID: %4.4s\n      Name: %s\n",user.id,user.uname)
            }
         smm("WORK,SU");
         geto("WORK",&site);
         printf("\n\nThis user's present site is %s",site.sname);
         printf("\n  Should this be changed (Y/N)? ");
         if ( qyn() )
         {  rms("WORK");
            find_site();
            scm("SU");
            ims("WORK");
            }
         }
      }

dbcls();
exit(0);
}
      find_site()

      /*   Determine a current owner for the set WORK   */

      {  while ( get_site_name() )
         {  printf("\nChoose one of the following sites:\n\n");
```

Fig. G.1   *(Continued)*

```
        for (err=ffm("SS") ; FOUND err ; err=fnm("SS") )
        {  getm("SS",&site);
           printf("        %s\n",site.sname);
           }
        }

    som("WORK,SS");
    }

get_user_id()

/*   Return false if * is entered    */

{  printf("\n\nEnter a user ID (or *): ");
   _gets(temp,5);
   setmem (user.id,4,' ');
   movmem (temp,user.id,strlen(temp));
   return ( *user.id != '*' );
   }

get_site_name()

/*   Return true if entered name is not found   */

{  printf("\nEnter site name: ");
   _gets(site.sname,31);
   return( /* ! FOUND */ fmsk("SS",site.sname) );
   }

qyn()

/*   Return true if Y or y is entered   */

{  return ( toupper(getchar()) == 'Y' );
   }
```

Fig. G.1   (*Continued*)

The symbolic constant FOUND is defined to be the same as the "not" operator "!". This makes if statements easier to read, since the find commands return a value of 0 (false) if the occurrence is found, and 255 (true) if the occurrence is not found. Thus the expression "FOUND **fmsk**" is true if **fmsk** returns a 0 and false, otherwise.

Structures are defined for the site record type, the user record type, and the **dbopn** command. In C', it is necessary to handle string and character (char) data types differently. In the DDL, the site name and user name are defined to be strings; thus in the C' program the corresponding character arrays must be set to be one character larger than the corresponding DDL declaration. The user id data item is declared in the DDL as "char 4"; in the C' program, id is also set to be "char [4]". For the openrec structure, all of its elements are strings.

When DML commands are invoked in C', each argument must be a pointer. Thus, if structures or numeric variables are being passed as arguments, the &

operator must be used; of course, character strings (arrays) are already in pointer form. Thus in the **dbopn** call, the address of the openrec structure is explicitly passed, while in the first **fmsk** call, the reference user.id is a pointer to an array of 4 characters.

The *local procedures* of the pseudo-languages can be implemented as separate C' functions, for example, get__user__id. This returns a true value as long as "*" is not entered. The qyn function uses the library function toupper to permit lower case y to be acceptable.

The find__site procedure is a fairly straightforward implementation. It calls get__site__name, which returns a true value if the entered name is not found: Thus in that routine the expression.

!FOUND fmsk

can be used. However, since FOUND is just !, and since "!!" cancels itself out, the simplest expression is just to return the value by **fmsk.** "! FOUND" is shown as a comment, just to indicate the actual nature of the processing involved.

In the find__site routine itself, notice how the for loop is constructed. The **ffm** and **fnm** define the iteration and thus are properly written within the for statement.

The update section uses the comma operator within the while statement to define the local procedure. The rest of this section would be straightforward, if it were not for the fact that that the user id is defined in the DDL to be of type char, rather than string. A value is read into the string variable temp; if the first character (*temp) is not zero (is not the string terminator), then it must contain a new user id value. The old value of user.id is cleared by using the library function *setmem* to move four blank characters into user.id. Then the *movmem* function copies the value of temp into user.id. The number of characters copied is determined by the length of temp, computed for us by the library function *strlen*. The same gyrations are performed in the routine get__user__id.

The purpose of all of these convolutions is to ensure that the value of the character array user.id does not contain a string terminator. When char declarations are made in the DDL, they represent true, complete arrays of characters and never strings. But since user.id is not a string, in the *printf* statements that display user.id the specification %s is not sufficient—user.id has no string terminator. The proper specification is that shown, %4.4s.

The moral of this exercise might be to avoid the use of char declarations in the DDL, since they complicate the writing of the C' application programs.

G.2   COBOL-80

COBOL-80, which runs under the CP/M operating system, has many useful features. This program (see Fig. G.2) uses only the standard elements of

```
       IDENTIFICATION DIVISION.
       PROGRAM-ID.  USERLOAD
       ENVIRONMENT DIVISION.
       *
       DATA DIVISION.
       WORKING-STORAGE SECTION.
       *
       77  ERR          PIC 999 COMP.
           88  FOUND        VALUE 0.
       77  DMS-BUF      PIC X(4000).
       77  BUF-LEN      PIC 99999 COMP, VALUE 4000.
       *
       *   STRING DEFINITIONS
       *
       77  SU           PIC X(3), VALUE "SU.".
       77  USER-REC     PIC X(5), VALUE "USER.".
       77  SUBMIT-SU    PIC X(10), VALUE "SUBMIT,SU.".
       77  WORK-SU      PIC X(8), VALUE "WORK,SU.".
       77  SS           PIC X(3), VALUE "SS.".
       77  WORK         PIC X(5), VALUE "WORK.".
       77  WORK-SS      PIC X(8), VALUE "WORK,SS.".
       *
       77  TEMP         PIC X(20).
       77  YY           PIC X.
           88  QYN          VALUE "Y", "y".
       77  E-OUT        PIC ZZ9.
       *
       *   P-RECORD DEFINITIONS
       *
       01  SITE         PIC X(30).
       01  USER.
           05  ID       PIC X(4).
           05  NAME     PIC X(20).
       01  OPENREC.
           05  OUSER    PIC X(16), VALUE "DOUG".
           05  OPASS    PIC X(12), VALUE "CUTE".
           05  OMODE    PIC X(4), VALUE "M".
           05  OFILE    PIC X(14), VALUE "B:DCNS.DB".
       *
       *
       PROCEDURE DIVISION.
       *
       OPEN-THE-DATA-BASE.
           CALL "VARCS" USING ERR.
           CALL "SETPBF" USING DMS-BUF, BUF-LEN.
           IF NOT FOUND GO TO DMS-ERR.
           CALL "DBOPN" USING OPENREC.
           IF NOT FOUND GO TO DMS-ERR.
       *
       *   BEGINNING OF USER LOAD PROGRAM
       *
       DO-USER
           DISPLAY " ".
           DISPLAY (24, 1) "Enter a user ID (or *): ".
           ACCEPT ID.
           IF ID="*" GO TO USER-EXIT.
```

Fig. G.2   COBOL-80.

```
*
      CALL "FMSK" USING SU, ID.
      IF FOUND
          CALL "GETM" USING SU, USER
      ELSE
          DISPLAY (24, 1) "  Is this a new user (Y/N)? "
          ACCEPT YY
          IF NOT QYN GO TO DO-USER
          ELSE
              DISPLAY (24, 1) "User Name: "
              ACCEPT NAME
              PERFORM FIND-SITE
              CALL "CRS" USING USER-REC, USER
              CALL "IMS" USING SU
              CALL "IMS" USING WORK.
*
      DISPLAY " ".
      DISPLAY "User ID: ", ID.
      DISPLAY "     Name: ", NAME.
      DISPLAY (24, 1) "  Should this person be deleted (Y/N)? ".
      ACCEPT YY.
      IF QYN
          CALL "SOM" USING SUBMIT-SU
          IF FOUND
              DISPLAY "Can't delete - still linked to tasks"
          ELSE
              CALL "DRM" USING SU
              DISPLAY "User deleted"
      ELSE
          PERFORM UPDATE-USER THRU UU-EXIT
          CALL "SMM" USING WORK-SU
          CALL "GETO" USING WORK, SITE
          DISPLAY "Present site is ", SITE
          DISPLAY (24, 1) "  Should this be changed (Y/N)? "
          ACCEPT YY
          IF QYN
              CALL "RMS" USING WORK
              PERFORM FIND-SITE
              CALL "SCM" USING SU
              CALL "IMS" USING WORK.
*
    GO TO DO-USER.
*
 USER-EXIT.
      CALL "DBCLS".
      STOP RUN.
*
*    DETERMINE A CURRENT OWNER FOR THE SET WORK
*
 FIND-SITE.
      DISPLAY (24, 1) "Enter site name: ".
      ACCEPT SITE.
      CALL "FMSK" USING SS, SITE.
      IF NOT FOUND
```

Fig. G.2   *(Continued)*

```
            DISPLAY "Choose one of the following sites:"
            DISPLAY " "
            CALL "FFM" USING SS
            PERFORM SITE-MENU UNTIL NOT FOUND
            DISPLAY " "
            GO TO FIND-SITE
        ELSE
            CALL "SOM" USING WORK-SS.
*
 SITE-MENU.
        CALL "GETM" USING SS, SITE.
        DISPLAY "        ", SITE.
        CALL "FNM" USING SS.
*
*   UPDATE USER INFORMATION
*
 UPDATE-USER.
        DISPLAY (24, 1) "  Any changes (Y/N)? ",
        ACCEPT YY.
        IF NOT QYN GO TO UU-EXIT.
        DISPLAY (24, 1) "Corrected user ID (or blank): ".
        ACCEPT TEMP.
        IF TEMP NOT = SPACES MOVE TEMP TO ID.
        DISPLAY (24, 1) "                Name (or blank): ".
        ACCEPT TEMP.
        IF TEMP NOT = SPACES MOVE TEMP TO NAME.
        CALL "PUTM" USING SU, USER.
        DISPLAY " ".
        DISPLAY "User ID: ", ID.
        DISPLAY "    Name: ", NAME.
        GO TO UPDATE-USER.
 UU-EXIT.
        EXIT.
*
*   START-UP ERRORS
*
 DMS-ERR.
        MOVE ERR TO E-OUT.
        DISPLAY "Error ", E-OUT, " encountered".
        STOP RUN.
```

Fig. G.2   *(Continued)*

COBOL; in particular, it ignores the screen-handling capability of COBOL-80, in order to keep the DML processing in focus. It would be a fairly simple task to upgrade this program into something more elegant in terms of input–output.

This program begins with a minimal IDENTIFICATION division, and the ENVIRONMENT division is null. So much for documentation. The WORK-ING–STORAGE section contains all of the internal data declarations for the program. The variable ERR is used to report the status of the various DML commands. The level 88 declaration of FOUND allows the IF statements to be rendered in exactly the manner of the pseudo-language: ''IF FOUND''. The

ERR variable attains its special status in the first paragraph of the PROCEDURE division. The command **varcs** is used to specify that ERR will automatically be set after each DML command execution. Thus ERR need not be specified with each command invocation.

In COBOL-80 it is necessary to explicitly allocate storage for the MDBS page buffers and data dictionary. DMS-BUF is used in this program for that purpose; BUF-LEN defines the size of the buffer region. In the first paragraph of the PROCEDURE division, the **setpbf** command uses these two variables as arguments to establish the requisite communications area. The test following this command establishes that enough memory has been found (i.e., allocated for DBCS processing).

A series of string definitions appears next. These define all of the regular arguments of DML commands to be used in this program. Notice that each string must be terminated with a period (.). Furthermore, the declared length of the string must include the period.

The variable YY is used in yes/no situations. The level 88 definition of QYN allows the substitution of "IF QYN" for IF YY="Y" or YY="y". The p-record definitions are straightforward.

The DO-USER paragraph begins the actual processing. "DISPLAY (24, 1)" is used to continue the scrolled nature of the screen-processing, but to suppress the automatic carriage return and line feed that a simple DISPLAY generates.

GO TO statements are used to simulate the "while" and "continue" statements of the pseudo-language. The rest of this paragraph is a quite literal translation of the pseudo-language version, with the exception of the removal of the update section to the paragraphs UPDATE-USER and UU-EXIT. These are separated from the DO-USER paragraph in order to simplify the nested loop structure.

The FIND-SITE paragraph is also rather straightforward. The only point of interest might be the PERFORM statement, but the intent here is obvious from the context.

With the possible exception of the string definitions, COBOL-80 is a fairly nice language for writing MDBS application programs. Although not demonstrated here, numeric variables are only a bit more cumbersome to process, since allowance must be made for both display and computational forms. But, of course, this is not news to COBOL programmers.

G.3   IBM PERSONAL COMPUTER BASIC

This language differs from the others chosen in this appendix in that the IBM Personal Computer BASIC (PC-BASIC) is an interpreted, rather than a compiled, language. PC-BASIC (see Fig. G.3), which runs under the PC-DOS (a

```
1000 PRINT
1010 PRINT "        User Load Program - please wait for DMS loading"
1020 PRINT
1030 '
1040 '    set memory limit for basic, to allow room for the dms -
1050 '    note that this command really must be the very first!
1060 '
1070 CLEAR ,54000!
1080 '
1090 '    set default types for variables
1100 '
1110 DEFINT D,V,M,N
1120 DEFSTR C,O,Q,U,I,S,T
1130 '
1140 '    define qyn - FNA(QYN) is true if a "Y" is entered
1150 '
1160 DEF FNA(QYN) = (QYN = "Y") OR (QYN = "y")
1170 '
1180 '    set up data base routines
1190 '
1200 MEMSIZ=128
1210 DMSSIZ=48
1220 DMSSEG=(MEMSIZ-DMSSIZ)/16*1024
1230 DEF SEG=DMSSEG
1240 BLOAD "b:dms.cim",0
1250 BDMSSIZ=DMSSIZ*1024-1
1260 DHIGH=INT(BDMSSIZ/256)
1270 POKE 7,DHIGH:POKE 6,BDMSSIZ-DHIGH*256
1280 DMS=8 : DMSD=DMS+8
1290 VARCS=DMSD+8 : VARCMD=VARCS+8
1300 '
1310 ON ERROR GOTO 2500
1320 '
1330 '    initial calls - NOTFOUND is false if "found" is true
1340 '
1350 CALL VARCS(NOTFOUND)
1360 CALL VARCMD(CMD)
1370 '
1380 '    block for dbopn
1390 '
1400 CMD="define,openrec"
1410 M=4
1420 CALL DMSD(OUSER,OPASS,OMODE,OFILE,M)
1430 IF NOTFOUND THEN 2520
1440 '
1450 '    open the data base
1460 '
1470 OUSER="DOUG"
1480 OPASS="CUTE"
1490 OMODE="M"
1500 OFILE="A:DCNS.DB"
1510 CMD="dbopn,openrec" : CALL DMS
1520 IF NOTFOUND THEN 2520
1530 '
1540 '    blocks
1550 '
```

Fig. G.3 PC-BASIC.

```
1560 CMD="define,site"
1570 M=1
1580 CALL DMSD(SITE,M)
1590 IF NOTFOUND THEN 2520
1600 '
1610 CMD="define,user"
1620 M=2
1630 CALL DMSD(ID,UNAME,M)
1640 IF NOTFOUND THEN 2520
1650 '
1660 CMD="define,id"
1670 M=1
1680 CALL DMSD(ID,M)
1690 IF NOTFOUND THEN 2520
1700 '
1710 '    beginning of user load program
1720 '
1730 PRINT : PRINT : LINE INPUT "Enter a user ID (or *): ";ID
1740 IF ID="*" THEN 2260
1750 CMD="fmsk,su,id" : CALL DMS
1760 IF NOTFOUND THEN 1820
1770     ID=SPACE$(4)
1780     UNAME=SPACE$(20)
1790     CMD="getm,su,user" : CALL DMS
1800     GOTO 1900
1810 'otherwise
1820     LINE INPUT "  Is this a new user (Y/N)? ";QYN
1830     IF NOT FNA(QYN) THEN 1730
1840     PRINT : LINE INPUT "User Name: "; UNAME
1850     GOSUB 2330
1860     CMD="crs,user,user" : CALL DMS
1870     CMD="ims,su" : CALL DMS
1880     CMD="ims,work" : CALL DMS
1890 '
1900 PRINT : PRINT "User ID: ";ID
1910 PRINT "     Name: ";UNAME
1920 PRINT : LINE INPUT "  Should this person be deleted (Y/N)? ";QYN
1930 IF NOT FNA(QYN) THEN 2030
1940     CMD="som,submit,su" : CALL DMS
1950     IF NOTFOUND THEN 1990
1960       PRINT "Can't delete - still linked to tasks"
1970       GOTO 1730
1980     'otherwise
1990       CMD="drm,su" : CALL DMS
2000       PRINT "User deleted"
2010       GOTO 1730
2020 'otherwise
2030     LINE INPUT "  Any changes (Y/N)? ";QYN
2040     IF NOT FNA(QYN) THEN 2140
2050       PRINT : LINE INPUT "Corrected user ID (or blank): ";TEMP
2060       IF LEN(TEMP) THEN ID = TEMP
2070       LINE INPUT "            Name (or blank): ";TEMP
2080       IF LEN(TEMP) THEN UNAME = TEMP
2090       CMD="putm,su,user" : CALL DMS
2100       PRINT : PRINT "User ID: ";ID
2110       PRINT :    Name: ";UNAME : PRINT
```

Fig. G.3 (*Continued*)

```
2120     GOTO 2030
2130 '
2140     CMD="smm,work,su" : CALL DMS
2150     SITE=SPACE$(30)
2160     CMD="geto,work,site" : CALL DMS
2170     PRINT : PRINT "This user's present site is ";SITE
2180     LINE INPUT "  Should this be changed (Y/N)? ";QYN
2190     IF NOT FNA(QYN) THEN 1730
2200       CMD="rms,work" : CALL DMS
2210       GOSUB 2330
2220       CMD="scm,su" : CALL DMS
2230       CMD="ims,work" : CALL DMS
2240       GOTO 1730
2250 '
2260 CMD="dbcls" : CALL DMS
2270 IF NOTFOUND THEN 2520
2280 END
2290 '
2300 '
2310 '    find-site subroutine
2320 '
2330 PRINT : LINE INPUT "Enter site name: ";SITE
2340 CMD="fmsk,ss,site" : CALL DMS
2350 IF NOTFOUND THEN 2390
2360   CMD="som,work,ss" : CALL DMS
2370   RETURN
2380 'otherwise
2390   PRINT : PRINT "Choose one of the following sites:" : PRINT
2400   CMD="ffm,ss" : CALL DMS
2410   SITE=SPACE$(30)
2420   IF NOTFOUND THEN 2330
2430     CMD="getm,ss,site" : CALL DMS
2440     PRINT TAB(6);SITE
2450     CMD="fnm,ss" : CALL DMS
2460     GOTO 2420
2470 '
2480 '    error processing
2490 '
2500 PRINT "Basic error #";ERR;" in line ";ERL
2510 '
2520 PRINT "DMS error is ";NOTFOUND;" in command ";CMD
2530 GOTO 2260
```

Fig. G.3   (*Continued*)

product of IBM) operating system, is similar to most interpretive BASICs in its
syntax and processing capabilities. Interpretive languages create some interesting
problems and some interesting opportunities for application developers.

One problem is that the DBCS routines must be loaded from the disk into
memory. Thus in line 1070 the CLEAR statement is used to set a memory limit
for PC-BASIC; the rest of the machine is then available for the DBCS. The
CLEAR statement also has the effect of zapping all definitions and assignments.
Therefore it is important to position the CLEAR statement before any important

processing is performed. In our program, the CLEAR is preceded only by a few PRINTs.

The DML commands are processed as strings; the status and entry points must be integer variables. To simplify both the entry and reading of the program, the DEFINT and DEFSTR commands are used. The DEFINT at 1110 says that variables beginning with the letters D, V, M, and N are automatically of type integer. Thus in the program the variable NOTFOUND, for example, is an integer variable. This saves us from having to write NOTFOUND% each time we need to use the variable. Similarly the DEFSTR command at 1120 provides implicit string definitions. The variable SITE is then interpreted as a string, and we are saved from having to write SITE$ each time.

It is not necessary to use DEFINT and/or DEFSTR. It is used here mainly for the convenience of not having to explicitly specify % and $ each time variables are used. It also tends to enhance the consistency and readability of the program.

At 1160, the statement function FNA is defined. This is the method of implementing the qyn function of the pseudo-language. The expression FNA(QYN) is true if the (string) variable QYN contains some kind of ''Y''.

The code from statements 1200 to 1290 is necessary for the proper loading of the DBCS routines. Generally speaking, these can be copied directly into other application programs. The statement at 1200 says that the memory configuration of the machine is 128K; we must modify this to match our own system. The statement at 1240 says that the DBCS routines live in the file ''dms.cim'' on drive b:; this, of course, might need to be changed. If we choose not to use the DEFINT command, then we must note that the variables DMS, DMSD, VARCS, and VARCMD must be integer variables.

At 1310 a safety feature is included. In the fairly likely event that an interpretive processing error occurs (e.g., division by zero), then processing will immediately be switched to line 2500. This error trap points out the value of the PC-BASIC variables ERR and ERL, and then performs a **dbcls** (at 2260). The idea is to protect the database by closing it in the event of a processing error.

The **varcs** command (1350) is used to define the variable NOTFOUND as the command status variable. All DBCS routines will set the value of NOTFOUND; in particular, the find commands will make NOTFOUND equal to 0 if the occurrence is found, and 255 if the occurrence is not found. Since 0 is the PC-BASIC value for false, the naming of NOTFOUND is consistent: NOTFOUND is true if its value is 255, that is, the occurrence was not found.

The **varcmd** command (1360) tells the DBCS that the (string) variable CMD will be used to hold the command string for all DML calls. The processing of CMD is shown in the very next section (1400 through 1430), where the openrec data block is defined. The variable CMD is set to the necessary command string, and then the entry point DMSD is called to establish the variables that will participate in the openrec data block. CMD will be used throughout the remainder of the program for communicating with the DBCS.

Since BASIC does not contain any program record types of data structures, the DBCS must provide the mechanism for defining such program records. The **define** command is used for this purpose; **define** indicates to the DBCS the existence of a named group of BASIC variables which may act together as a program record. Furthermore, it is required that such blocks of variables defined by **define** be the only objects that appear as data arguments in the DML commands. Thus even if only a single variable is to be referenced, it must be defined in a block of its own.

There are two additional commands for managing blocks of variables. The **extend** command permits a redefinition of a block, by appending more variables to the end of the block. And the **undef** command is used to *undefine* a block, that is, to drop a block definition. This function is quite useful, since block definitions do consume space that could otherwise be used for paging.

The actual forms of these commands and the positioning of their arguments are language dependent. In PC-BASIC, the **define** command has the form

```
CMD = "define,blockname"
M = m      [the number of variables]
CALL DMSD(var 1, . . . ,var m,M)
```

As noted above, DMSD and M must be integer variables.

The only data block that may be declared before **dbopn** is called is the one that **dbopn** uses. This is because **dbopn** issues an *undef* command automatically, that is, it undefines all data blocks. Thus the next section of this program opens the database. In 1510 the CMD variable is used to establish the command and arguments to be processed; DMS is called without arguments.

Blocks for the site and user record types are defined next. Then, a block is defined solely for the (string) variable ID. This is necessary for the processing of the **fmsk** command in line 1750.

Finally, the actual processing of USER records can begin (at 1730). Because of the limited nature of the IF statement of the PC-BASIC, GOTOs are used to simulate the if-else constructs of the pseudo-language. For readability, however, indentation is maintained in this program; furthermore, comments are included to denote the start of what would normally be the ''else'' sections.

There is something of an anomaly in the manner in which strings are maintained in PC-BASIC. As a result, before data are retrieved from the database, the strings must be initialized to their full length (as declared in the DDL specification). Thus before the **getm** command in 1790 can be executed, the two string variables ID and UNAME must be initialized to 4 and 20 spaces, respectively. The library function SPACE$ is perhaps the simplest way to accomplish this.

It is important to remember this fact when using interpretive languages. It is only a problem when a retrieval operation is being performed. Other examples of this processing occur at 2150 and 2410. The latter case occurs before the menu-producing loop of the find-site routine. SITE is initialized outside of the loop, since nothing in the loop would change its size from the full 30 characters.

The "while" and "continue" statements of the pseudo-language are implemented here with GOTO statements. Otherwise, the processing mirrors that of the pseudo-language in a fairly obvious manner.

In the update section (2030 to 2120), the two IF statements at 2060 and 2080 deserve comment. If the length of the (string) variable TEMP is zero, then only a carriage return was entered. But zero is the value PC-BASIC uses for "false"; so if the value of LEN(TEMP) is zero, then the assignments of TEMP to ID and UNAME, respectively, would not be performed.

The find-site routine is implemented as a subroutine in lines 2330 through 2460 and is called from lines 1850 and 2210. There is little else to comment on in regard to this routine.

G.4 FORTRAN-80

It turns out that the FORTRAN-80 implementation of the user-load program is, perhaps surprisingly, not too structurally difficult to follow. For the most part, the translation from the pseudo-language program to FORTRAN-80 is direct. FORTRAN-80 runs under the CP/M operating system.

One aspect of the FORTRAN-80 interface with the DBCS is the fact that each DBCS routine returns an integer value, indicating the status of the DML command. FORTRANs typing mechanism, however, assumes that a function named **FMSK,** for example, is returning a real value. Thus one must establish within all programs and subprograms that the DML commands (i.e., DBCS routines) return integer values. This can be done in one of two ways. The first is to explicitly declare the DBCS routines used in INTEGER statements. The second is to use the declaration "IMPLICIT INTEGER (A–Z)", and explicitly declare those variables that are not integers.

In our main program (see Fig. G.4), we use the latter technique. All variables are assumed to be integer variables, except for those explicitly mentioned in the other declaration statements. In the subroutine FNDSIT, the DML commands used are explicitly declared to be of type integer.

Data items defined to be char or string in the DDL are mapped into LOGICAL arrays in FORTRAN-80. The array DMSBUF is used as the primary communications area between the program and the DBCS; this memory region is used for page buffers and the data dictionary. It appears as the argument of the SETPBF command which establishes the area for the DBCS.

It is vital in FORTRAN-80 to terminate all command strings with a period (.). Thus the definition of the openrec data block includes the string "openrec.".

```
      PROGRAM UL
C
C
      IMPLICIT INTEGER (A-Z)
      LOGICAL SITE(30), ID(4), NAME(20), TEMP(20), QYN
      LOGICAL OUSER(16),OPASS(12),OMODE(4),OFILE(14)
      LOGICAL DMSBUF(4000),ASTRSK,BLANK
C
      DATA OUSER/1HD,1HO,1HU,1HG/,
     *     OPASS/1HC,1HU,1HT,1HE/,
     *     OMODE/1HM,3*1H /,
     *     OFILE/1HB,1H:,1HD,1HC,1HN,1HS,1H.,1HD,1HB,5*1H /
      DATA ASTRSK,BLANK/1H*,1H /
C
C   open the data base
C
      ERR = SETPBF(DMSBUF,4000)
      IF (ERR.NE.0) GO TO 9900
C
      ERR = DEFINE( 'openrec.',4,OUSER,OPASS,OMODE,OFILE)
      IF (ERR.NE.0) GO TO 9900
C
      ERR = DBOPN('openrec.')
      IF (ERR.NE.0) GO TO 9900
C
C   blocks
C
      ERR = DEFINE('site.',1,SITE)
      IF (ERR.NE.0) GO TO 9900
C
      ERR = DEFINE('user.',2,ID,NAME)
      IF (ERR.NE.0) GO TO 9900
C
      ERR = DEFINE('uid.',1,ID)
      IF (ERR.NE.0) GO TO 9900
C
      ERR = ALTEOS(0)
C
C   beginning of user load program
C
  100 WRITE(1,1)
    1 FORMAT(/' Enter a user ID (or *): ')
      READ(1,2) ID
    2 FORMAT(20A1)
      IF (ID(1).EQ.ASTRSK) GO TO 180
      IF ( FMSK('su,uid.') ) 120,110,9900
  110    ERR = GETM('su,user.')
         GO TO 130
C   otherwise
  120    WRITE(1,3)
    3    FORMAT('    Is this a new user (Y/N)? ')
         IF (.NOT. QYN(0)) GO TO 100
         WRITE(1,4)
    4 FORMAT(' User name:
         READ (1,2) NAME
```

Fig. G.4 FORTRAN-80.

```
            CALL FNDSIT(SITE)
            ERR = CRS('user,user.')
            ERR = IMS('su.')
            ERR = IMS('work.')
       130 WRITE(1,5) ID,NAME
         5 FORMAT(' User ID: ',4A1/'        Name: ',20A1/'
        *'   Should this person be deleted (Y/N)? ')
            IF (.NOT. QYN(0)) GO TO 160
               IF ( SOM('submit,su.') ) 150,140,9900
       140     WRITE(1,6)
         6     FORMAT(' Cannot delete - still linked to tasks')
               GO TO 100
C      otherwise
       150     ERR = DRM('su.')
               WRITE(1,7)
         7     FORMAT(' User deleted')
               GO TO 100
C    otherwise
       160   WRITE(1,8)
         8   FORMAT('    Any changes (Y/N)? ')
             IF (.NOT. QYN(0)) GO TO 170
               WRITE(1,9)
         9     FORMAT(' Corrected user ID (or blank): ')
               READ(1,2)TEMP
               IF (TEMP(1).NE.BLANK) CALL COPY(TEMP,ID,4)
               WRITE(1,10)
        10     FORMAT('                Name (or blank): ')
               READ(1,2) TEMP
               IF (TEMP(1).NE.BLANK) CALL COPY(TEMP,NAME,20)
               ERR = PUTM('su,user.')
               WRITE(1,11)ID,NAME
        11     FORMAT(' User ID: ',4A1/'        Name: ',20A1/)
               GO TO 160
C
       170   ERR = SMM('work,su.')
             ERR = GETO('work,site.')
             WRITE(1,12)SITE
        12 FORMAT(' The present site is ',30A1/
        *   '    Should this be changed (Y/N)? ')
             IF (.NOT. QYN(0)) GO TO 100
               ERR = RMS('work.')
               CALL FINDSIT(SITE)
               ERR = SCM('su.')
               ERR = IMS('work.')
               GO TO 100
C
       180 ERR = DBCLS(0)
           STOP
C
C   error processing
C
      9900 WRITE(1,13)ERR
        13 FORMAT(' Error ',I3,' encountered')
           GO TO 180
C
           END
```

Fig. G.4   *(Continued)*

```
      SUBROUTINE FNDSIT(SITE)
C
C   determine a current owner for the set work
C
      LOGICAL SITE(30)
      INTEGER FMSK, SOM, FFM, GETM, FNM
C
  100 WRITE(1,1)
    1 FORMAT(/' Enter site name: ')
      READ(1,2)SITE
    2 FORMAT(30A1)
      IF ( FMSK('ss,site.').LT.0) GO TO 110
        ERR = SOM('work,ss.')
        RETURN
C   otherwise
  110   WRITE(1,3)
    3   FORMAT(/' Choose one of the following sites:'/)
        ERR = FFM('ss.')
  120     IF (ERR.LT.0) GO TO 100
          ERR = GETM('ss,site.')
          WRITE(1,4) SITE
    4     FORMAT(7X,30A1)
          ERR = FNM('ss.')
          GO TO 120
C
      END



C
C
      LOGICAL FUNCTION QYN(K)
C
C   return true if Y or y is entered
C
      LOGICAL A, BIGY, LOWY
      DATA BIGY, LOWY /1HY,1Hy/
C
      READ(1,1) A
    1 FORMAT(A1)
      QYN = (A.EQ.BIGY) .OR. (A.EQ.LOWY)
      RETURN
      END



C
C
      SUBROUTINE COPY(FROM,TO,N)
C
C   copy N characters from FROM to TO
C
      LOGICAL FROM(N), TO(N)
C
      DO 10 I=1,N
   10   TO(I)=FROM(I)
      RETURN
      END
```

Fig. G.4 *(Continued)*

One common source of errors in DML programs when using FORTRAN as a host language is leaving out the periods in strings.

The **define** command allows the four specified variables to be processed as a unit for opening the data base (see the previous section for the details of **define**). The **dbopn** command occurs next. It is necessary to open the data base before any other data blocks are defined, since **dbopn** automatically performs an **undef,** that is, it automatically undefines all data blocks.

The definition of data blocks corresponding to the site and user record types appear next. A separate data block is defined for the ID variable. This is required for the processing of the **fmsk** command that occurs after statement number 100.

The **alteos** command changes the end-of-set value from 255 to -1. This is of immediate interest in FORTRAN programs, since it allows arithmetic (3-branch) IF statements to be employed in a very natural manner. Thus the IF statement following statement number 100 branches to 120 if the occurrence is not found; to 110 if the occurrence is found; and to 9900 if any error is detected.

The load program proper begins at statement number 100. GOTO statements are used to implement the while, continue, and if-else statements of the pseudo-language. However, for readability, indentation is maintained; furthermore, comments are included to indicate the *else* processing.

QYN is defined as a logical function which returns a true or false value depending on whether some sort of "Y" is entered. Otherwise the program follows the pseudo-language version fairly closely.

In the update section, beginning at statement number 160, a subroutine COPY is used to copy the value of TEMP to ID and NAME, respectively. A better solution would put the READ and IF statements into the subroutine; here the choice was made to preserve the correspondence between the present version and the original.

The FNDSIT subroutine is a straightforward rendition of the original as well. The SITE variable is passed as an argument, so that the site data block refers to the proper value. An alternative to this would be to place the SITE array into a common block.

Appendix H

DML Command Index

The following is a list of each DML command in alphabetical order, accompanied by its definition and the section number in which the command is discussed.

Command	Description	Section
alteos( )	Change eos to -1	G.4
amm(set-1, set-2, set-3)	Intersection	12.5
amo(set-1, set-2, set-3)	Intersection	12.5
aom(set-1, set-2, set-3)	Intersection	12.5
aoo(set-1, set-2, set-3)	Intersection	12.5
aui(number)	Allocate user indicators	12.4
ccu(number)	Compare cru and a udi	12.4
cra(rec, area, p-record)	Create in an area	12.2
crs(rec, p-record)	Create	7.2
dbcls( )	Database close	7.6
dbclsa(area)	Area close	12.2
dbenv(p-record)	Environment	14.8
dbopn(p-record)	Database open	7.6
dbopna(p-record)	Area open	12.2
dbsave( )	Save modified records	14.8
dbstat(p-record)	Statistics	11.7
define(. . .)	Define p-records (lang. dependent)	G.3

(continued)

503

Command	Description	Section
drc( )	Delete cru	7.4
drm(set)	Delete member	7.4
dro(set)	Delete owner	7.4
extend(. . .)	Extend p-records (lang. dependent)	G.3
fdrk(rec, p-record)	Find duplicate record by calc key	12.2
ffm(set)	Find first member	6.3
ffo(set)	Find first owner	12.1
ffs(area)	Find first sequential	12.2
flm(set)	Find last member	6.3
flo(set)	Find last owner	12.1
fmi(item, set, p-record)	Find member by item	6.8
fmsk(set, p-record)	Find member by sort key	6.8
fnm(set)	Find next member	6.3
fnmi(item, set, p-record)	Find next member by item	6.8
fnmsk(set, p-record)	Find next member by sort key	6.8
fno(set)	Find next owner	12.1
fnoi(item, set, p-record)	Find next owner by item	12.1
fnosk(set, p-record)	Find next owner by sort key	12.1
fns(area)	Find next sequential	12.2
foi(item, set, p-record)	Find owner by item	12.1
fosk(set, p-record)	Find owner by sort key	12.1
fpm(set)	Find previous member	6.3
fpo(set)	Find previous owner	12.1
frk(rec, p-record)	Find record by calc key	12.2
getc(p-record)	Get from cru	7.1
getm(set, p-record)	Get from member	6.7
geto(set, p-record)	Get from owner	6.7
gfc(item, p-record)	Get item from cru	7.1
gfm(item, set, p-record)	Get item from member	6.7
gfo(item, set, p-record)	Get item from owner	6.7
gmc(set, p-record)	Get member count	12.1
goc(set, p-record)	Get owner count	12.1
gtc(p-record)	Get type of cru	12.2
gtm(set, p-record)	Get type of member	12.3
gto(set, p-record)	Get type of owner	12.3
ims(set)	Insert member	7.3
ios(set)	Insert owner	12.1
lgfile(p-record)	Set log file	14.9
lgflsh( )	Flush log buffer	14.9
lgmsg(p-record)	Write message to log file	14.9
mau(number)	Multiuser udi lock	15.7
mcc(p-record)	Contention Count	15.3
mcf( )	Free cru	15.7
mcp( )	Lock cru	15.7
mrtf(rec)	Free record type	15.8
mrtp(rec)	Lock record type	15.8
msf(set)	Free set	15.8
msp(set)	Lock set	15.8

Command	Description	Section
nci( )	Null all indicators	15.4
pfc(item, p-record)	Put item into cru	7.1
pfm(item, set, p-record)	Put item into member	6.9
pfo(item, set, p-record)	Put item into owner	6.9
pifd(p-record)	Page image file name	14.9
putc(p-record)	Put into cru	7.1
putm(set, p-record)	Put into member	6.9
puto(set, p-record)	Put into owner	6.9
rms(set)	Remove member from set	7.5
ros(set)	Remove owner from set	12.1
rsm(set)	Remove all set members	12.1
rso(set)	Remove all set owners	12.1
scm(set)	Assign cru = member	7.1
scn( )	Assign cru = null	15.3
sco(set)	Assign cru = owner	7.1
scu(number)	Assign cru = udi	12.4
setpbf(array, size)	Set communications area	G.2
smc(set)	Assign member = cru	7.1
sme(set)	Assign member = cru, exceptionally	12.1
smm(set-1, set-2)	Assign member = member	6.6
smn(set)	Assign member = null	15.3
smo(set-1, set-2)	Assign member = owner	6.6
smu(set, number)	Assign member = udi	12.4
soc(set)	Assign owner = cru	7.1
soe(set)	Assign owner = cru, exceptionally	12.1
som(set-1, set-2)	Assign owner = member	6.4
son(set)	Assign owner = null	15.3
soo(set-1, set-2)	Assign owner = owner	6.6
sou(set, number)	Assign owner = udi	12.4
suc(number)	Assign udi = cru	12.4
sum(set, number)	Assign udi = number	12.4
sun(number)	Assign udi = null	15.3
suo(set, number)	Assign udi = owner	12.4
suu(number-1, number-2)	Assign udi = udi	12.4
tct(p-record)	Test cru type	12.2
tmt(set, p-record)	Test member type	12.3
tot(set, p-record)	Test owner type	12.3
trabt( )	Transaction abort	14.9
trbgn( )	Transaction begin	14.9
trcom( )	Transaction commit	14.9
undef(p-record)	Un-define p-record	G.3
varcmd(variable)	Set command string	G.3
varcs(variable)	Set command status	G.3
xmm(set-1, set-2, set-3)	Difference	12.5
xmo(set-1, set-2, set-3)	Difference	12.5
xom(set-1, set-2, set-3)	Difference	12.5
xoo(set-1, set-2, set-3)	Difference	12.5

INDEX

Computer Science and Applied Mathematics
A SERIES OF MONOGRAPHS AND TEXTBOOKS

Editor
Werner Rheinboldt
University of Pittsburgh

HANS P. KÜNZI, H. G. TZSCHACH, AND C. A. ZEHNDER. Numerical Methods of Mathematical Optimization: With ALGOL and FORTRAN Programs, Corrected and Augmented Edition

AZRIEL ROSENFELD. Picture Processing by Computer

JAMES ORTEGA AND WERNER RHEINBOLDT. Iterative Solution of Nonlinear Equations in Several Variables

AZARIA PAZ. Introduction to Probabilistic Automata

DAVID YOUNG. Iterative Solution of Large Linear Systems

ANN YASUHARA. Recursive Function Theory and Logic

JAMES M. ORTEGA. Numerical Analysis: A Second Course

G. W. STEWART. Introduction to Matrix Computations

CHIN-LIANG CHANG AND RICHARD CHAR-TUNG LEE. Symbolic Logic and Mechanical Theorem Proving

C. C. GOTLIEB AND A. BORODIN. Social Issues in Computing

ERWIN ENGELER. Introduction to the Theory of Computation

F. W. J. OLVER. Asymptotics and Special Functions.

A. T. BERZTISS. Data Structures: Theory and Practice, Second Edition

N. CHRISTOPHIDES. Graph Theory: An Algorithmic Approach

SAKTI P. GHOSH. Data Base Organization for Data Management

DIONYSIOS C. TSICHRITZIS AND FREDERICK H. LOCHOVSKY. Data Base Management Systems

JAMES L. PETERSON. Computer Organization and Assembly Language Programming

WILLIAM F. AMES. Numerical Methods for Partial Differential Equations, Second Edition

ARNOLD O. ALLEN. Probability, Statistics, and Queueing Theory: With Computer Science Applications

ELLIOTT I. ORGANICK, ALEXANDRA I. FORSYTHE, AND ROBERT P. PLUMMER. Programming Language Structures

ALBERT NIJENHUIS AND HERBERT S. WILF. Combinatorial Algorithms, Second Edition

AZRIEL ROSENFELD. Picture Languages, Formal Models for Picture Recognition

ISAAC FRIED. Numerical Solution of Differential Equations

ABRAHAM BERMAN AND ROBERT J. PLEMMONS. Nonnegative Matrices in the Mathematical Sciences

BERNARD KOLMAN AND ROBERT E. BECK. Elementary Linear Programming with Applications

CLIVE L. DYM AND ELIZABETH S. IVEY. Principles of Mathematical Modeling

ERNEST L. HALL. Computer Image Processing and Recognition

ALLEN B. TUCKER, JR. Text Processing: Algorithms, Languages, and Applications